LION LAUNDRY

Door to Drawer Laundry Service | www.lionlaundry.com

Tired? Busy? Overwhelmed?

Sign up for Lion Laundry's weekly service! We pick your clothes up from your door and bring them back the next day professionally washed and folded!

- Next day delivery
- Professional washing and folding
- Optional Dry Cleaning
- Great prices

Contact us:

Otto@lionlaundry.com
Carlo@lionlaundry.com
(212) 760–4705

Visit our website or contact us to find out if Lion Laundry is serving your area

Lion Laundry, Ltd. ❖ New York, NY

It is never too early to start planning your career!

Visit the Center for Career Education at Columbia University to attend great workshops and events, meet with a counselor, receive job and internship postings and more!

Students preparing to network at **Media Networking Night**

+ Meet with a career counselor for walk- in hours from 2 - 4 p.m. during the semester or call us to make an appointment.

+ Register with ColumbiaTrak on our web site to gain access to full time listings, internships and part-time jobs on and off campus.

+ Gain first hand career experiences through our internship programs. Please visit our web site for more information.

+ Attend workshops and events tailored to your career interests.

"[The Center for Career Education's] resources encouraged the personal reflection that helped me plan out the academic, professional and extracurricular experience that I wanted during and after my college career."   James Mahon CC '07

For more information please contact us at:

**East Campus, Lower Level
116th Street between Morningside
and Amsterdam
(Enter through Wien Courtyard)**

**Phone: (212) 854-5609
www.careereducation.columbia.edu
careereducation@columbia.edu**

INSIDE NEW YORK
2008

An Inside *New York* *Guidebook*

www.insidenewyork.com
2960 Broadway MC 5727 • New York, NY • 10027
Phone: 212-854-2804 • Fax: 212-663-9398

Printed by: DiYA USA Corporation
219 Loon Court, Foster City, CA 94404

Inside New York is always open to suggestions for new content or criticisms of current content. If you have a favorite restaurant, bar, or neighborhood hang-out, or anything else you would like to see in the guide, send an email to info@insidenewyork.com.

Maps supplied by Steve Duncan copyright © Opus Publishing 2007. www.opuspublishing.com

If you are interested in purchasing advertising space in Inside New York, contact
Inside New York • 2960 Broadway MC 5727 • New York, NY 10027
212-854-2804 • adsales@insidenewyork.com

Manhattan Subway Map copyright © Metropolitan Transportation Authority. Used with permission.

For bulk sales, university sales, corporate sales, or customized editions, please call 212-854-2804 or email info@insidenewyork.com.

If your bookstore would like to carry Inside New York, please contact Bookworld Companies at 800-444-2524.

We wish to extend a special thank you to: Rebecca Rodriguez, Alex Yepes, Bernadette Maxwell, Al Spuler, Kavita Sharma, Liz Wang, Russell Malborough, The Center for Career Education staff, David Sideman, AEPi, our advertisers, Columbia University, CUTTA, the Columbia Bartending Agency, Jing Jiang, the Robbins family, the Cornblum family, Sharon and Bill Alexander, John C. Williams, Raphael Levy, Steve Duncan, Lester Freundlich, Jesse Atkins, Chet Atkins, Christina Katz, Seth Berliner, and the stellar staff of Inside New York 2008.

Publisher's Dedication: For Mom, a true New Yorker.

This is a publication of the Student Enterprises Division of Columbia University.

Inside New York

PUBLISHER	Brett Austin Robbins
EDITOR-IN-CHIEF	James R. Williams
DEPUTY EDITOR-IN-CHIEF	Jill Colvin
GRAPHIC DESIGNER	Matt Franks
LAYOUT EDITOR	Madeleine Lopeman
NEIGHBORHOODS EDITOR	Joanna Zuckerman Bernstein
DINING EDITOR	Noah Youngs
ASSOCIATE DINING EDITOR	Colin Felsman
NIGHTLIFE EDITOR	Laura Stoffel
CHIEF COPY EDITOR	Alex Sharp
ASSOCIATE EDITOR	Laura Anderson
STAFF EDITORS	Jessica Kingdon
	Joseph Meyers
	Frank Nestor
	Aga Sablinska
STAFF WRITERS	Laura Catella
	Jane Friedhoff
	Chris Kulawik
	Erin McMahon
	JD Stettin
ASSOCIATE DIRECTORS OF ADVERTISING SALES	Jessie DeLuca
	Mickey Tesfaye

CONTRIBUTING WRITERS

Becky Abrahms, Nathalie Alonso, Andrew Avorn, Lenora Babb, Wendy Biddlecombe, Veronica Colon, Melissa Dolin, Lauri Feldman, Erika Gehrie, Jonathon Grant, Adrian Haimovich, Maria Insalaco, Jessica Isokawa, Ashley James, Peter Justice, Liat Kalikow, Christina Katz, Ellen Kessel, Laura Kleinbaum, Shruti Kumar, Sally Lauckner, Josh Lugar, Kate McKinnon, Kibby McMahon, Peter Mende-Siedlecki, Lauren Minches, Daniel Mohrer, Michael Nadler, Andrew Ness, Jonathan Neuman, Samantha Racanelli, Chris Radcliffe, Arion Robbins, Barbara Robbins, Heather Sachs, Dmitry Shevelenko, Caitlin Shure, Yelena Shuster, Aliza Simons, Keith Smith, Evelyn Ting, Jordan Tucker, Alec Turnbull, Sara Vogel, Aleksey Zelenberg, Senem Zeytinoglu

CONTRIBUTING PHOTOGRAPHERS

Linda Carrion, Asiya Khaki, Samantha Lewis, Isabelle Mills-Tannenbaum, Daniella Zalcman

WELCOME TO NEW YORK

There are two big mistakes you can make when you first move to New York. The first is thinking that the city is going to change you. The second is thinking that it won't.

We've all seen the movies, read the books, heard the songs; we all come to the city with an idea of what it is and what it will do to us, or for us. But that's the problem with movies and books and songs. How many times have we watched a film, thought "Only in New York," then imagined ourselves in the same place? The mindset is romantic—who wouldn't want to be swept up in a city whose energy is more powerful and more life-altering than any other force we've yet encountered?

They're not lying when they say that here, anything is possible—but the city is not the force that will change your life. The city can't harden you, or romanticize you, or break your spirits, or lift them up; it can only give you the freedom to do it all yourself. New York is amazing, not because there's always something to do here, or because it never sleeps, but because it is yours.

This book is not here to teach you how to become a New Yorker; it's here to teach you how to make New York your own. You'll always be from Alabama, or Jersey, or Barcelona, no matter how many years you spend here. But starting now, New York is your home.

Flip to a random page, walk along a different street, and get Inside New York.

Brett Austin Robbins, PUBLISHER
James R. Williams, EDITOR-IN-CHIEF

215 W. 94th St. (Broadway & 94th)
New York, NY, US, 10025
Phone: (212) 866-6400 or (800) 834-2972
Fax: (212) 866-1357

DAYS HOTEL
Broadway
10% Discount to Columbia students,
faculty, families, and friends

CONTENTS

CITY LIFE

Getting Around	10
Getting Settled	14
Arts	16
Dining Out	18
Night Life	20
Shopping	22
Museums	24
Architecture	28
Media	32
LGBT	34
City Deals	38
Sports	42
Outside New York	44
Classes & Workshops	50
Hotels & Hostels	52
Useful Information	54
Annual Events	68

NEIGHBORHOODS

Downtown

Financial District	76
SoHo	86
Chinatown/Little Italy	96
Lower East Side	106
Greenwich Village	120
East Village	134
TriBeCa	148

Midtown

Chelsea	162
Gramercy/Murray Hill	178
Midtown West	192
Midotwn East	218

Uptown

The Upper West Side	234
The Upper East Side	250
Morningside Heights	264
Harlem	286
Washington Heights/Inwood	298

The Outer Boroughs

Brooklyn	306
Queens	326
The Bronx	336
Staten Island	344

NEIGHBORHOODS

Downtown

Financial District *(page 76)*

Wall Street brokers in suits and tourists flocking to Ground Zero populate the southern tip of Manhattan, where tall buildings funded by modern entrepreneurship contrast with the narrow, cobbled streets that remain from the colony of New Amsterdam.

Chinatown/Little Italy *(page 96)*

The pagoda-topped buildings and Asian supermarkets of Chinatown are gradually overpowering the red, green, and white pennants of the increasingly little Little Italy. For now, both neighborhoods offer cheap souvenirs, ethnic restaurants, and a taste of the far-off world.

TriBeCa *(page 148)*

Peaceful, upscale, and arty, this Triangle Below Canal is popular with the affluent and the family-oriented. Come for some of the best restaurants and highest costs of living in the city; as old buildings are rapidly converted to lofts, already exorbitant rents climb ever higher.

SoHo *(page 86)*

Hip and eternally crowded, the blocks South of Houston and North of Little Italy boast upscale designer boutiques and street vendors hawking their art and jewelry. Despite the gentrification that has driven out many artists, the area is still densely packed with galleries.

Lower East Side *(page 106)*

One in four Americans has an ancestor who lived in this neighborhood during its overpopulated heyday at the turn of the 20th century. Today, the Eastern European and Irish immigrants of those years have been replaced by Japanese and Bangladeshi immigrants, and gentrifying hipsters.

Greenwich Village/Meatpacking *(page 120)*

Home to the famous arch of Washington Square Park, the scattered dorms of NYU, the eternally sought-after Magnolia cupcakes, streets intersecting at haphazard angles, brownstones inhabited by celebrities, the accurately named Gay Street, and nauseatingly trendy clubs, this region has something for everyone—except meatpackers, of whom there are surprisingly few.

East Village *(page 134)*

The Lower East Side's bad boy little brother harbored Beatniks in the '50s and gave birth to punk music in the '80s; today, it's been newly reincarnated with fewer drugs and more yuppies. A defiant vibe is palpable on St. Mark's Place, however, and the long-established Eastern European community hasn't thrown in the towel yet.

Midtown

Chelsea *(page 162)*

Stereotyped as a gay enclave—mostly because it is—Chelsea is also home to the Flatiron building, the urban paradise that is Madison Square Park, and so many contemporary art galleries that the guides of New York Gallery Tours can show you eight of them in two hours.

Gramercy/Murray Hill *(page 178)*

Home to the famously exclusive Gramercy Park and some of the most beautiful residential architecture in the city, the area above Union Square has been an aristocratic haven for centuries.

Midtown West *(page 192)*

Times Square, where tourists clog the sidewalks with their agonizingly slow gaits, is also home to the best live theater in the country. Clinton, the section further west, has outgrown its Hell's Kitchen past with a recent influx of restaurants, clubs, and rising rents.

Midtown East *(page 218)*

Self-important suit-clad men and women with briefcases in tow rush through the canyon-like streets of Midtown East, which is slightly less jam-packed than its twin to the west. Bryant Park, Rockefeller Center, Grand Central Terminal, the United Nations building, and MoMA lend cultural diversity to the area.

Uptown

Upper West Side *(page 234)*

Nannies and strollers are ubiquitous between Riverside Drive and Central Park West, where super-liberals come to raise their families. The rich and famous move here to get away from the bustle of downtown while maintaining their much-needed proximity to cultural institutions like Lincoln Center and the American Museum of Natural History.

Upper East Side *(page 250)*

Manhattan's wealthiest and most politically conservative neighborhood lays claim to Museum Mile, the stretch of Fifth Avenue that contains nine museums and countless priceless masterpieces. Guarded no less vigilantly than the art are the goods in the many designer boutiques that line the avenues.

Morningside Heights *(page 264)*

This small neighborhood between the Upper West Side and Harlem is dominated by the beautiful Beaux-Arts campus of Columbia University, with businesses and nightlife that cater mostly to students.

Harlem *(page 286)*

Home to numerous African-American historical and cultural sights, Harlem continues to fight its undeserved ghetto reputation. One of the last places in Manhattan with affordable rent, the neighborhood is currently locked in a battle between those who want to preserve its traditional character and those who want to develop.

Washington Heights/Inwood *(page 298)*

Students and artists choose to live in the northernmost tip of Manhattan for the cheapest apartments on the island. The traditionally Dominican area is far from Midtown, geographically and atmospherically, with crime levels that have plummeted since the '80s.

The Outer Boroughs

Brooklyn *(page 306)*

After attracting all the artists who were too poor to afford skyrocketing Manhattan rents, trendy Brooklyn neighborhoods now boast more expensive housing than ever before. As the most populated borough, there's still great diversity in many of the neighborhoods.

Queens *(page 326)*

The largest borough is home to many sports stadiums, both of New York City's airports, and a vast number of immigrants—almost half of Queens' total population was born outside the U.S. Thanks to this fact, the borough is known for its huge array of ethnic restaurants, from Peruvian to Middle Eastern to Korean.

The Bronx *(page 336)*

The only non-island borough and the birthplace of hip-hop, the Bronx has seen its share of gang violence and struggles with high crime rates in certain neighborhoods to this day. Cultural attractions, however, like the Bronx Museum of the Arts, the New York Botanical Garden, and the Bronx Zoo draw crowds from all parts of the city and the world.

Staten Island *(page 344)*

New York's much-maligned little borough to the southwest is the most residential part of the city, with lawns, cars, and few cultural attractions. Accessible from Manhattan only by the free Staten Island Ferry, the former Dutch settlement is best known for being where the rest of New York once sent its garbage.

GETTING AROUND

New York's mass transit system is the most extensive and widely used in the country, connecting the boroughs and their neighbors through buses, subways, ferries, railroad lines, and even a cable car. While the grid may look overwhelming at first, once you become familiar with the ins and outs of the system you'll see why seven million riders each day make the MTA a crucial part of their routines.

THE METROCARD

The **Metrocard** is the golden ticket of public transportation, used for rides on the **subway, buses in New York, Long Island, and Westchester**, the **Staten Island Railway**, **PATH trains**, the **Roosevelt Island Cable Car**, and the **JFK AirTrain**. You can purchase one at the vending machines in subway stations or from any authorized vendor. All machines take credit and debit cards, but only some take cash.

The standard fare is $2, and you'll get a free ride for every $10 bought in one purchase—$20, for instance, will actually buy you a $24 Metrocard. If you plan on using your card a lot, consider buying an unlimited ride pass; 1-day cards, which last until 3am on the day purchased, are $7, week-long cards are $24, and 30-day cards are $76. Unlimited cards aren't quite as flexible as the pay-per-ride kind; you'll have to wait 18 minutes after any swipe before you can use them again, and they aren't accepted on express buses, PATH trains, or the JFK AirTrain.

Each Metrocard swipe also comes with a free transfer. Riders switching from the subway to a bus, a bus to the subway, or between different bus lines can re-swipe the same Metrocard used to pay the first fare at no additional cost, as long as it's within 2 hours of the first swipe.

PLANNING YOUR ROUTE

It's easy to find most subway stations in Manhattan: just identify the cross streets nearest your destination on a subway map, and find the station closest to them. In the outer boroughs, the map gets trickier. Your best resource to help navigate the system is **HopStop** (*hopstop.com*)—just type in two addresses and the website will tell you the best public transit route between them.

The biggest obstacle you'll face in your subway travels stems from the fact that the system is constantly under repair. Trains whose lines are under construction run irregular routes and often skip stops, especially at night and on the weekends. You'll most likely see posters tacked up in stations notifying you of changes, but not always. Ask a fellow rider or MTA employee for information, or go to *mta.info/nyct/subway* for construction updates and the latest schedule information.

SAFETY

Despite what your small-town relatives might tell you, public transportation in New York is actually quite safe, as long as you stay off the subway tracks. Of course, riders should exercise the same caution they would in any city: Keep an eye on belongings and don't travel alone late at night. Beggars and performers frequently work the subway cars, but are almost universally harmless and non-confrontational. If there ever is a situation where you feel uncomfortable, it's best to trust your instincts: alert an MTA employee, then take a cab home.

SUBWAYS

Despite being more than a century old, the New York subway system is still the best way to get around the city, 24-hours a day, 7 days a week. It's not as cushy as a cab ride, but it's often faster and always cheaper, and the extensive routes are more than adequate to get you where you need to go.

Specific train routes are designated by either a number, (1-7), or letter, (A-Z). Numbered and lettered routes are then grouped into color categories, based on which routes share lines. Most subway lines have two kinds of trains—those that run local, and those that run express. **Local trains**, whose stops are designated by black dots on the subway map, make every stop on a given line; **express trains**, with stops designated by white dots, only stop at major stations. Passengers can switch between local and express trains at any express stop. Keep in mind that different trains on the same colored line often branch into different directions, especially as they approach the outer boroughs.

In Manhattan, train direction is referred to as either uptown or downtown; in the boroughs, it's designated by the train's final destination. Some of the smaller stations have separate entrances depending on direction; you'll lose your fare if you go back above ground to change direction, so double-check before you swipe in.

BUSES

Although usually less convenient to use than underground transport, buses are a great way to travel routes that subways aren't able to cover, and are also the only fully handicapped-accessible form of public transport in the city. The most frequently used are the cross-town buses that travel east and west across Manhattan's major two-way streets; they're especially helpful uptown, where there's no other way to get between the East and West Sides easily. Other than that, New Yorkers generally use buses much less frequently than subways. If you intend to ride a bus, don't count on strangers to give you directions—look up maps and route info before you leave at *mta.info/nyct/maps*.

Buses run frequently between 7am-10pm and intermittently after that, with late night buses sometimes coming only once an hour. Fare is payable with a Metrocard swipe or exact change only. Express buses, which travel from the boroughs and throughout Manhattan with minimal stops, are fast, but cost $5 a ride; they are marked with an upper case X in the route number.

FERRIES AND CABLE CARS

The free 30-minute ride on the **Staten Island Ferry**, between South Ferry Station in Manhattan and St. George Terminal in Staten Island, is the only way to get between the two islands without a car. All other ferry services, including those between other boroughs, are privately run; go to *nyc.gov* for a full listing.

The **Roosevelt Island Tramway**, perhaps the most unconventional public transport in the city, runs between East 60th Street and Roosevelt Island. Entrance is payable with a Metrocard Swipe.

TAXIS

Quintessentially New York, the **yellow taxi** is the easiest—not to mention most expensive—

way to get from point A to point B. Rates are standardized: there's a $2.50 base charge, plus $0.40 for every 1/5 mile or 60 seconds of stop-time. Surcharges for weekday rides between 4-8pm ($1) and nighttime rides between 8pm-6am ($0.50) also apply. Passengers have to cover any tolls, and tipping 10-20% is customary.

On-duty drivers can't legally refuse service to any paying customer, no matter the destination, and riders who want to determine the route are allowed to do so. Passengers are also entitled to a smoke- and incense-free environment, a quiet ride without music or cell phone conversation, and air conditioning if requested.

Yellow cabs are rare in the outer boroughs. If you see one, nab it—if not, take the subway, or ask the locals for the number of a **car service** that serves the area.

COMMUTER TRAINS

The tri-state area's network of commuter railways provide a cheap, fast way of getting into or out of the city that almost completely eliminates the possibility of traffic-induced road rage.

The Long Island Rail Road (LIRR) stretches from Pennsylvania Station in Manhattan to the tips of each fork of Long Island, carrying well over 200,000 passengers a day. Fares vary based on distance traveled. Tickets purchased on board are subject to a $3 penalty, so buy at the station. Also, be sure to show up at least five minutes before your train's scheduled departure, since they sometimes depart a little early. For a full list of fares and a schedule, check *lirr.org*.

Port Authority Trans-Hudson (PATH) trains provide access to Hoboken, Jersey City, Harrison, and Newark for a mere $1.50 each way. The main access point in New York is the Manhattan Mall Station (*33rd Street at Sixth Avenue*). For schedules and more information, visit *panynj.gov*.

As the name suggests, **Metro North** provides rail service north of New York City, as far as New Haven, CT. The railroad has two branches—one east of the Hudson that goes to New York and Connecticut, and one west of the Hudson that goes to New Jersey. The Manhattan terminus of the Eastern branch is Grand Central, while the Western branch ends at Penn Station. The price of a ticket depends on your final stop, but generally runs $6-8. For more info, visit *mta.info*.

NJ Transit connects New York City with most towns and cities in the state of New Jersey through a fleet of buses, based out of Port Authority, and trains, which leave from Penn Station. It's also the cheapest and easiest way to get between New York and Philadelphia. Go to *njtransit.com* for schedules, maps, and fare prices.

Amtrak, America's national rail company, makes its New York home in Penn Station; go there to get anywhere in America or Canada by rail. Visit *amtrak. com* for fares and schedules, and to buy tickets.

NATIONAL BUS LINES

The **Port Authority Bus Terminal** (*Eighth Avenue at 42nd*) is the New York City hub of nearly every national bus line, including **Greyhound** (*greyhound. com*); you can get anywhere in America or Canada by bus from there.

For the cheapest ride between New York and Boston, consider taking a so-called **Chinatown Bus**. **Lucky Star** (*luckystarbus.com*) and **Fung Wah** (*fungwahbus.com*) are the main competitors. Rides cost $15 each way, and leave every hour from—where else?—Chinatown.

CARS

Owning a car in New York is not only completely unnecessary—it's completely impractical, too. Between parking garage rates, alternate side of the street parking rules, traffic jams, and tolls, it hardly seems worth it. A good alternative is **ZipCar** (*zipcar.com*), which lets you rent cars, which have permanent parking spots in city garages, for about $10/hour or $70/day.

AIRPORTS

When you have to get out of the tri-state area, the first step is getting yourself to one of the three major airports that serve New York.

LaGuardia
By Taxi:

Taxis to and from LaGuardia charge metered fare and cost anywhere from $20-35, plus tip and toll, depending on your destination. Taxis are available outside all terminals.

By Bus:

LaGuardia Airport is not connected to the subway system, but is serviced by a number of public and private bus lines. For the cheapest fare, use your Metrocard on the **M60 bus** that starts at 106th and Broadway, travels east across 125th Street and Queens, and ends up at the airport. Those starting their journey in Queens can take the **Q33, Q47,** or **Q48** buses. The **New York Airport Service Express** private coach line (*nyairportservice.com*) offers service to and from Grand Central, Port Authority, and Penn Station every 15-60 minutes for $10-12.

John F. Kennedy Airport
By Subway/Train:

The above-ground **AirTrain** connects the subway with JFK; take the A to Howard Beach or the E/J/Z/LIRR to Jamaica Station for an easy transfer. It'll cost $5 on your Metrocard, but if you travel frequently you might want to buy an AirTrain 30-Day unlimited pass ($40) or 10-Trip pass ($25, expires in 6 months). The trip from Manhattan takes 1½-2 hours.

By Taxi:

Taxis run from JFK to and from any destination in Manhattan for a flat $45 dollar fare, plus tolls and tip; drivers can't charge extra for luggage or additional passengers. Taxis to and from JFK in the outer boroughs run at the metered fare.

By Bus:

The **Q10** and **Q3** run local service to Queens, while the **B15** runs to Brooklyn. The **New York Airport Service Express** (*see LGA*) to or from Penn Station departs every 20-30 minutes and costs $15.

Newark
By Subway/Train:

The Newark Air Train offers service from the airport to NJ Transit and Amtrak trains, which will deliver you straight to Penn Station anytime between 5am and 2am. The 20-minute ride costs about $12.

By Taxi:

Metered fairs from the airport to any Manhattan location will run you about $40-55, plus tolls and additional luggage handling fees of $1/piece. Cabs are available outside every terminal.

By Bus:

The **Newark Liberty Airport Express** (*olympiabus.com*) runs every 15-30 minutes between the airport, Grand Central, Port Authortity, and Penn Station, and is available from 4am-1am. One-way fares cost $13; round-trip tickets are $22.

Finding an apartment in New York City is a dramatic rite of passage, like your first kiss or passing your driver's test—and just as nerve-wracking. If money is no obstacle, landing an apartment will take less time than you think. If you're on a tight budget, be prepared to spend some time finding a place that's both affordable and inhabitable. Expect to be horrified by much of what you see, and learn to adjust your expectations. New York living, recently estimated to cost 40% more than much of the country, has rules all of its own. Landing an apartment is a game: Here are some strategies for how to play and win.

FINDING AN APARTMENT

Timing. The real estate market in New York is constantly evolving: The number of apartments available depends on the time of year, the economy, and maybe even the recent winning records of local sports teams. Start looking for a place a few months before you hope to move, and keep in mind that you'll have to act quickly once you find an apartment you like. While your inclination might be to think over the decision for a day or two, don't—the apartment will be offered to, and likely snatched up by, another buyer.

Price Range. The first step in narrowing down your apartment hunt is to set a price range. In SoHo, the average monthly rental for a studio with a doorman in 2007 was nearly $3,000—for a *studio*. Young people are almost priced out of Brooklyn already, and increasingly look to farther-flung locales like Long Island City, Queens, or Jersey City, although the metropolitan area is fairly pricey no matter where you go. There are also a number of expenses to take into account beyond the monthly rent: utilities can be $50-$100 per month, and cable and internet can add another $60 or so.

Roommates. The hands-down easiest way to save money on housing is to shack up with roommates. People constantly move to New York, and there are a number of websites to help itinerants find someone to live with. Just remember—it's a big internet, and there a lot of sketchy people out there. Be sure to trust your instinct if a potential roommate makes you uncomfortable.

Picking a neighborhood. Everyone wants to live in the new hip neighborhood—also known as the best thing that ever happened to Brooklyn—but there's a lot to keep in mind when picking a future home: proximity to a subway line, noise level, and the convenience of your commute to work or school are all important considerations. Also be sure to ask around about how safe an area is at different times of the day or year.

Identify your priorities. After choosing neighborhoods you'd like to live in, draw up a list of make-or-break amenities and features. Think about square footage, lighting, walk-ups versus elevators, hardwood floors, laundry facilities on site, the building's pet policy, doormen—not to mention the immortal co-op vs. rental vs. buying dilemma. Flexibility is crucial, so be prepared to sacrifice some of the things you thought were essential.

Brokers. Deciding whether or not to use a broker—a person who has a comprehensive sense of the housing market and access to apartments that aren't available to the general public—is one of the biggest decisions you'll have to make. For a fee, a broker will streamline and expedite your search, finding apartments and setting up appointments for you to see them. Typically the fee is one month's rent or 12-15% of the apartment's annual rent, and you only pay after you've committed on paper. It's possible to find an apartment without a broker, though it will take legwork and a willingness to become well-acquainted with the Craigslist refresh button. Strictly-online listings are notoriously hit-or-miss, and some listings direct you to a broker rather than an apartment. There are also listings in the real estate sections of publications like the **The New York Times** (*nyt.com*) and **Village Voice** (*villagevoice.com*).

Visiting apartments. With or without a broker, you'll need to see potential apartments in person. While you're there, check out the neighborhood, try to make a good impression on the landlord, see if you can catch a glimpse of the other tenants, and look for signs of poorly-maintained infrastructure that could bode badly for your chances of getting that broken toilet fixed down the line.

Drawing up a lease. Be prepared not only to commit, but also to plunk down large sums of money as soon as you find your apartment. A broker can also come in handy here, as can a lawer retained expressly for these negotiations. Typically, landlords expect you to make 30-40 times your monthly rent—meaning many young people require their parents to serve as guarantors of financial stability in lieu of the requisite money flow. You or your guarantor will need to provide proof of income, in the form of employer letters, tax forms, or bank statements. Check with the **New York State Tenant's Rights Guide** for definitions of real estate jargon, legal clarifications, and real estate advice.

Once you've found a place, paid first and last month's rent, gotten your friends to lug your boxes up four flights of stairs, and finally settled in, congratulate yourself—there's no place like home in New York.

FINDING A JOB

Contrary to popular belief, finding a job in New York isn't completely determined by who you know—although knowing people doesn't hurt. Working any connections you may have is a good first step. Ultimately, though, it's about putting in time and doing a lot of gruntwork. Newspaper classified sections have largely been eclipsed by online listings in recent years. **Craiglist** is constantly updated, covers a variety of fields, and offers everything from one-time gigs to permanent employment opportunities. As with everything on craigslist, though, beware of scams. **Monster.com** is another good option, and one with a more established reputation. Both Monster and **Careerbuilder.com** allow you to upload your resumé, and you can sign up to receive email alerts about jobs that fit your profile.

Another option is to use an employment agency; New York has countless such businesses which can help place you with a job, especially if you're looking for business, finance, or legal work. Try the New York section of **Headhuntersdirectory.com** for a list of options. Finally, colleges almost always offer students and alumni online listings and in-person career center aid—and the all-important help with constructing the perfect resumé and cover letter.

ARTS

*It's no secret that New York City is an artistic and cultural mecca. The ever-changing scene, as chronicled in publications like **Time Out** (timeoutny.com), **The New York Times** (nyt.com), and **New York Magazine** (nymag.com), is rife with institutions and special events. When the artsy mood strikes, get out there and find something: From theaters and concerts to galleries and readings, the city will not disappoint.*

MUSEUMS & GALLERIES

New York has over 80 museums to wander, ranging from the kinky-on-purpose **Museum of Sex** (museumofsex.com) to the dino-infested **Museum of Natural History** (amnh.org), and everything in between. New Yorkers and tourists alike flock most often to the mighty four—the **Met** (metmuseum.org), the **Whitney** (whitney.org), the **MoMA** (moma.org), and the **Guggenheim** (guggenheim.org)—but don't limit yourself to just the big names. For more info on these and many more options, see our Museum Guide on pages 24-27.

More unique to New York is the proliferation of small galleries that specialize in contemporary art and sales. Chelsea and SoHo, as well as Williamsburg in Brooklyn, are particularly flush with smaller art spaces. Galleries can be hard to find—sometimes on purpose—so go to *thenewyorkartworld.com* for guidance. Openings are a great way to check out emerging artists and score a few free drinks; contrary to popular myth, many are open to all.

THEATER

There's a reason Broadway is synonymous with theatrical success—not to mention world-class flops. New York is one of the best places in the world to catch a show, and would be even if Times Square hadn't gone through the mid-90s overhaul that wiped out most evidence of its former life as a red-light district. For listings of the big-name shows or to see what the critics have to say, go to playbill.com, *theatermania.com*, and *broadway.com*.

Broadway shows are known for being expensive,

but there are a few ways to save money. The **TKTS booths** (tdf.org/tkts) in Times Square and the South Street Seaport offer half-priced tickets for same-day shows. Or, if there's a specific production you'd like to see, check out the **rush policy**; each theater has different procedures, with most rush tickets costing around $25. For a listing of policies, check out *talkinbroadway.com/boards*.

For less mainstream acts, try off-Broadway shows, which seat anywhere from 100-500, or off-off Broadway, where crowds are smaller still. Go to *offbroadwayonline.com* for help navigating the choices, which are plentiful, and usually include productions that are more experimental and edgier than the offerings on Broadway. As with the larger theaters, off-Broadway is hit or miss; check out reviews before you lay down your cash.

MUSIC

It could be argued that New York is the ultimate city for music—most big stars wouldn't think of skipping it on tour, yet there are enough neighborhoods and local haunts to cultivate small-time bands and breakout artists. Going to see live music in New York can run the gamut from blow-out performances to cozy bars with awesome bands—check out *timeoutny.com* for the widest array of show listings. Other good resources include *gothamjazz.com* for the city's myriad jazz offerings, nyrock.com for rock, and ohmyrockness.com for a listing of performances at smaller, but established, venues like **Joe's Pub** (joespub.com) and the **Bowery Ballroom** (boweryballroom.com).

Having a few favorite spots is a good way to get a sampling of the city's offerings. **Carnegie Hall** (*carnegiehall.org*), **Lincoln Center** (*lincolncenter.org*), and the **Metropolitan Opera** (*metoperafamily.org/ metopera*) offer beautiful spaces, upscale experiences, and the best classical, jazz, and opera around. Well-respected small venues include the **Knitting Factory** (*knittingfactory.com*), Williamsburg's **Northsix** (*northsix.com*), and legendary rock club the **Bitter End** (*bitterend.com*). Jazz clubs are a major staple of the music scene as well; for A-list acts, check out the **Village Vanguard** (*villagevanguard.com*), **Blue Note** (*bluenote.net*), **Birdland** (*birdlandjazz.com*), and **Iridium** (*iridiumjazzclub.com*). For less expensive favorites uptown, check out **Smoke** (*smokejazz.com*), the **Lenox Lounge** (*lenoxlounge.com*), or **St. Nick's Pub** (*212-283-9728*).

DANCE

With its long and storied dance tradition, New York is home to some of the best dance companies in the world. Ballet enthusiasts probably already know about the **New York City Ballet** (*nycballet.com*), the **American Ballet Theater** (*abt.org*), and the **Dance Theater of Harlem** (*dancetheaterofharlem. com*). For contemporary dance, your best bets are **City Center** (*nycitycenter.org*), the **Brooklyn Academy of Music** (*bam.org*), and the **Joyce Theater** (*joyce.org*). For experimental choreography, check out the **Dance Theater Workshop** (*dtw.org*), the **Joyce SoHo Theater** (*joyce.org*), and **P.S. 122** (*ps122.org*). To find the most complete and up-to-date information, check the listings in Time Out or go to *nytimes.com/pages/arts/dance*.

FILM

Movies are made here all the time—visitors are sure to recognize neighborhoods, streets, parks, and buildings from some of their favorite films—so the budding festival scene should come as no surprise. Most are held annually: there's the **New York Film Festival** (*filmlinc. com/nyff*) in the fall, the **New Directors/New Films Festival** (*filmlinc.com*) in the winter, and most famously, the **TriBeCa Film Festival** (*tribecafilmfestival.org*) in the spring. Sign up for their newsletters to receive advance notice of what's showing, as well as the best deals. If you prefer the anti-establishment scene, check out the **NY Underground Film Festival** (*nyuff.com*), held in the spring, or **Arlene's Grocery Picture Show** (*filmsfilmsfilms.org*), the largest independent film festival in the city. Throughout the year, you an always see the latest blockbusters at **AMC/Lowes** (*they've merged—amctheaters.com*), but if you want something less mainstream, check out what's playing at **Lincoln Plaza Cinemas** (*lincolnplaza.moviephone. com*), the **Walter Reade Theater** (*filmlinc.com*), or **MoMA** (*moma.org*).

READINGS

Writers have always flocked to New York. As the home of some of the world's great literary magazines, the city is full of poetry, story, and nonfiction readings—many of which are reasonably priced or free to the public. The most renowned series and venues include the **Unterberg Poetry Series** at the 92nd Street Y (*92.org*), the **KBG Bar Readings** (*kbgbar.com*), the **St. Marks Poetry Project** (*poetryproject.com*), the **Bowery Poetry Club** (*bowerypoetry. com*), and the **Nuyorican Poetry Slam** (*nuyorican. org*). Don't be intimidated by the scene—everyone is surprisingly nice and approachable—but if you're overwhelmed, head to your local **Barnes & Noble** (*bn.com*) or **Borders** (*bordersstores.com*), which host free readings at least once a week.

In New York City, home of over 20,000 places to eat, the quest for the perfect restaurant is always ongoing. From hot dogs to foie gras, you could eat at a different place three times a day, seven days a week, 365 days a year, and it'd still take you 18 years to get through all of the city's offerings. For help finding your new favorite restaurant, flip through the pages of **Inside New York** *(you're holding it!), or turn to your native New Yorker friends and neighbors. Even asking strangers can yield excellent results. New Yorkers aren't rude, they're just busy; they're also foodies at heart, fiercely loyal to their favorite haunts. While their restaurant expertise may only extend a few blocks, years of experience have taught them what's good in all price ranges. As you're savoring the resulting meal, you'll be glad you asked.*

WHAT TO LOOK FOR

Eating out in New York isn't cheap—at least not always. In a city where a mid-range meal for two can cost upwards of $100, most people consider dining out a treat. If you're going to be laying out your cash, make sure you know what you're getting into before you go. In major tourist hubs like Times Square, themed restaurants, national chains, and $17 burgers dominate, but go just a few blocks west and you'll find dozens of tucked-away eateries on **Restaurant Row** (*46th between Eighth and Ninth*), all vying for your patronage with their tempting and reasonably priced three-course prix-fixe menus. No matter where you are in the city, you're only a short walk or subway ride away from a great bargain or amazing dining experience.

DINING'S GOLDEN RULES

Neighborhoods like Little Italy, Chinatown, and Curry Hill—and the rest of New York's neighborhoods, for that matter—are notorious for hit-or-miss food; for every great dining experience, there are dozens of restaurants that are just looking to capitalize on a neighborhood's reputation. With some common-sense dining tips, you can stay clear of tourist traps and underwhelming locales across the city.

⦿ **Check the Windows.** If it's dinner time and a restaurant seems empty, there's probably a reason. Keep walking until you find something well attended, but not overcrowded.

⦿ **Find the Lines**. It might seem counterintuitive at first, but if you're new to a neighborhood, trust the lines. New Yorkers aren't willing to wait for many things—if they're standing outside the door, odds are good the place is worth it.

⦿ **Follow the Chatter**. In an ethnic neighborhood, listen for the locals. The restaurant with the English-free menu and Cantonese staff may be the most authentic Chinese food on the East Coast.

⦿ **Know What You're Looking For**. Everyone likes being served by tuxedoed waiters once in a while, but often times such meals are more about ambiance than food. If you're looking for a truly great meal, holes-in-the-wall that have survived decades of intense competition are often just as good—or better—than their glitzy, pricey, and well-manicured contemporaries.

EATING BIG ON A SMALL BUDGET

One of the great things about eating in New York is that, occasionally, diners can splurge at one of the world's most famous restaurants. Celebrity chefs and boutique eateries are all the rage in foodie circles, with tables booked solid for months. Such meals can cost upwards of $400 per person—but if you know what you're doing, its easy to get in for a fraction of the cost.

ⓘ **Lunch: Learn to Love It**. The majority of New York's top dining establishments are open for lunch as well as dinner. For much less money and a much shorte wait, you can enjoy the same outstanding food as the dinner crowd.

ⓘ **Same Chef, Different Name**. Successful restaurants often spawn trendy cafés and bars that offer similar food for much less money. Jean George has Nougatine, Masa has Bar Masa, Per Se has Bouchon Bakery—the list goes on. They may not always share the same kitchen, but the quality is high and the cost unbeatable.

ⓘ **Restaurant Week**. For four weeks each year, New York's top chefs open their restaurants to the plebeians, serving up affordable and inclusive prix-fixe specials. Some, like Bobby Flay, revert to a "first come, first serve" policy, while others take reservations. Visit *nycvisit.com/restaurantweek* for dates and participating venues, then head to *opentable.com* to make your reservations.

AT THE RESTAURANT: TIPS AND TRICKS

ⓘ **Reservations.** Most nights of the week, it's a good idea to make reservations if you want to get a table at one of the city's more popular restaurants. But, before you go, keep a few things in mind. First off, know that your reservation time isn't always the time you'll actually sit down. Restaurants often run a bit behind schedule, so be sure to factor in the possibility of an additional wait. Also, remember that reservations are non-binding. Diners often forget that if they're unreasonably late, restaurants have the right to release tables to waiting customers. If you needed reservations in the first place, the restaurant is probably popular enough to survive without your business; call ahead if you're going to be more than a half-hour late.

ⓘ **Dress**. The old-school rules of dressing for dinner no longer apply to most everyday dining. Strict dress codes have been largely relaxed—expect to see dress jeans and open-collared shirts in places where such clothing used to be considered obscene. That said, at more upscale restaurants, be sure to check the dress code before you head out: Some places cling to tradition, and it's never pleasant to be turned away because of your attire. If you can sport it, always err on the dressier side—times may change, but men can't go wrong with a jacket and tie.

ⓘ **Tips, Hidden Charges, and Cash.** Tipping your server 15-20% is both normal and expected. Tip higher to reward superior service, but only drop lower if you're trying to send a message. Parties over five should know that many restaurants, especially those in tourist-heavy areas, will include an inconspicuous 18% gratuity that looks surprisingly like a tax on the final bill—when in doubt, ask the server. Finally, make sure you know whether your restaurant accepts credit cards before you sit down—the embarrassing last-minute dash to the ATM is no way to end an evening.

As the old saying goes, New York is the city that never sleeps—partly because entry-level investment bankers work 100-plus hour a week, but mostly because the nightlife is just that good. There's always a scene to fit your mood, so pick your poison: be it wine, liquor, beer, dancing, ice skating, or disco bowling, the Big Apple is where you want to be when the sun goes down.

BARS

New Yorkers aren't like other bar hoppers. Here, people flock to unexplored terrain—those unmarked bars so veiled in mystery they practically require a secret handshake to get in. But after a while, when the quest for the bar that's so-hot-it's-not-even-in-the-guidebooks grows tiresome, the nomad drinker longs for a barstool he can put a dimple in again and again. Until that perfect match is made, there are hundreds, even thousands of bars to scope out. Trial-and-error has never tasted so good.

Before selecting a destination, look into food and drink specials, happy hours, themes, clientele, music selection, and entertainment—the nightlife listings throughout this book are a good place to start. Want to try your luck at bar games? Seek out a spot that offers pool, foosball, darts, or pinball. Some bars are famous for more unusual draws like mechanical bulls or indoor bocce; others of-

fer live bands and DJ nights. To spice things up, many locations now offer themed evenings, from trivia games to margarita nights, attracting totally different crowds from one night to the next. In a city where every neighborhood feels like a self-contained town, you're sure to find a local bar where everyone knows your name, and, of course, your drink. Once you find the nightspots that suit you, whether they're the mellow post-industrial digs of Chelsea or the funky lounges of the Lower East Side, you'll enjoy the scene that much more.

CLUBS

The high-energy New York club scene—a mix of hipster, trendy, and exclusive party destinations—stands in marked contrast to the laid-back ease of a night at the bar. When choosing a place, you'll encounter everything from bouncing mega-clubs to serene lounges, but going out—and getting in the door—is always something of a production. Don't forget that bouncers and clubs go hand in hand; you won't find one without the other, so be prepared.

As with most of the world's party centers, any club experience in New York is shaped largely by the night of the week you go out. Some people stick to weekends, but there's no such thing as an off-night here—many clubs around the city schedule some of their hottest DJs to spin on Mondays, Tuesdays, and Wednesdays, turning the usual slow nights into primetime for tireless partiers. Bars and clubs also change their moods, styles, and even clientele from night to night, so be sure to do your homework and know what you're getting into.

Before you slip on your flip-flops or strap on

Neon Nightclub Sign

those heels, heed our tips for a successful night on the town:

HOUSE RULES

Ⓣ Bouncers at the city's more exclusive clubs are very selective about who gets in and who doesn't. The formula hinges on the three A's: attire, age, and attitude. If you want to make it past the velvet rope, dress up and carry yourself with an air of sophistication, but don't act too cool—nobody likes a poseur.

Ⓣ Dress comfortably, but remember that sneakers are never proper club attire. Wear jeans if you must, but make sure they look presentable. Designers are ok; grunge is not.

Ⓣ When approaching a bouncer, stand up straight and be confident. Act like you've got money to spend, even if you don't. If you're drunk, hide it; clubs consider the inebriated a liability, not an asset.

Ⓣ Some clubs charge a cover that can run from $5-30, but there are usually people at the door giving away complimentary or reduced-entry passes. Try to snag one if you can.

Ⓣ If you're underage and want to avoid a potentially embarrassing rejection, make sure you either have a really good fake, are extremely good-looking, or know a promoter or bouncer who can escort you inside. Remember, though, fake IDs are illegal, and depending on what kind of bouncer you encounter, yours will probably be confiscated if you're caught. At the very least, you'll be sent packing; if you're really unlucky, you'll gain the experience and insight that comes from a night in the slammer.

Ⓣ Most clubs have separate and shorter lines for those seeking bottle service—that is, those willing to drop $300 for a bottle that's worth $30 at the liquor store. For that amount of money, you'll get a table with minimal seating, various mixers, and a bottle of your choice—as well as some great new friends trying to mooch.

Ⓣ If you think you'll sweat when the bouncer gives you the once-over, just wait until you get inside—most clubs are hot and crowded. The trendiest spots are wall-to-wall flesh; before the night's over, expect to be covered in spilled drinks and body fluids that aren't necessarily yours.

Ⓣ Smart club-goers use the buddy system to repel unwanted grinders by pre-establishing a hand-signal or codeword that means "Help!" Mean club-goers agree to use the buddy system, then point and laugh when you're being crowded with unwanted attention. If you're stranded, tell your pursuer that you need to go to the bathroom and kindly excuse yourself from his or her grasp.

Ⓣ If you're hungry at 4 am after a night of drinking and dancing, snag some chicken fingers, pizza, or a kebab with your friends. Nothing tastes as good as grease when you're coming off that buzz, and the next morning, you'll be glad you put something in your stomach. Plenty of diners serve food all night long, and street vendors dish up sizzling nosh well into the wee hours of the morning.

Ⓣ Finally, BE SAFE. Never accept a drink unless you've watched it being made, and never let your drink out of your sight, even for a minute. Never assume your belongings will stay where you leave them, and don't walk or take the subway alone if it's late and the streets are deserted.

SHOPPING

Need something? Go shopping! Like the city itself, New York's shopping districts vary dramatically by neighborhood, each with its own individual style, vibe, and clientele to mirror the mood of its surroundings. Hardcore consumers can unearth something in any district, but if you stick to the neighborhood that suits you best—literally—you'll be set for the season.

FIFTH/MADISON AVENUES

Madison Avenue from the mid-50s to the mid-80s offers NYC's most upscale fashion destinations, with shoppers who reflect the merchandise—serious, and sometimes stuffy. The area is ripe with designer boutiques, fashion house flagships, and up-market chains that carry some of the world's most expensive labels. **Barney's New York** (*660 Madison Avenue at 61st*) is the area's golden child, combining classic favorites, cutting edge start-up designers, and a more fashion-forward attitude than many of its stodgy neighbors. Nearby **Fifth Avenue**, home to more designer flagships, is always heavy with tourists, but don't let them deter you from the area's mainstays: **Saks Fifth Avenue** (*611 Fifth Avenue at 50th*), **Henri Bendel** (*712 Fifth Avenue at 56th*), and **Bergdorf Goodman** (*754 Fifth Avenue at 57th*). All offer classically upscale duds to improve your closet, if not your bottom line. Before you leave the area, check out the sleek new 24-hour **Apple Store** (*767 Fifth Avenue at 59th*) and fashion standard **Bloomingdale's** (*1000 Third Avenue at 59th*), a few avenues over.

SOHO

Walking around this hip shopping district makes you feel cooler than you actually are; expect to see trendy/beautiful threads from designer shops, up-market boutiques, and national chains alike. The chic-boho **Anthropologie** (*375 West Broadway at Broome*) has a location here, as do **Prada** (*575 Broadway at Prince*), **Marc Jacobs** (*163 Mercer at Houston*), and Japanese basics emporium **Uniqlo** (*546 Broadway at Spring*). One-of-a-kind boutiques are peppered throughout the neighborhood; the most famous, the grandiose **Lounge** (*593 Broadway at Houston*), is where to go for European imports at an utterly offensive mark-up.

125TH STREET HARLEM

Harlem's recent development boom—some call it a second Renaissance, others character-draining gentrification—has resulted in the installation of multiple mega-chains along 125th, including **Old Navy** (*300 West 125th Street at Frederick Douglass*) and **H&M** (*125 125th Street at Malcolm X*). For the most authentic shopping experience, walk the corridor between St. Nicolas and Fifth Avenue—a hub of current urban styles, flashy shoes and jeans, and designer knock-offs. Don't miss **Jimmy Jazz** (*239 West 125th Street at Adam Clayton Powell*), a mainstay of neighborhood fashion.

HERALD SQUARE

The original **Macy's** (*151 West 34th Street at Broadway*) is Herald Square's main attraction, taking up an entire city block. Other area notables include the Spanish faux-designer chain **Zara** (*39 West 34th Street at Fifth*) and **Forever 21** (*50 West 34th at Sixth*), a guilty pleasure for the most serious of fashionistas. Put it all together and you've got all the amenities of a New Jersey Mall—just minus the food court.

NOLITA

This tiny, recently established retail neighborhood was a mere blip on the radar five years ago, but has lately made its mark with unique clothing emporiums and eclectic dress shops. Go to **May-le** (*252 Elizabeth Street at Prince*) for easy, bohemian pieces, or **Resurrection** (*217 Mott Street at Spring*) for vintage couture. Keep wandering and you'll come across a multitude of surprising finds, including enviable clothes and off-beat accessories you won't see on everybody else.

TIMES SQUARE

As the most ubiquitous city destination, Times Square is packed with literally millions of tourists refusing to walk faster than a snail's pace. Most city residents don't shop here with any regularity, although the neighborhood is home to a number of retailers that are attractions in and of themselves. The infamous outpost of **Toys "R" Us** (*1514 Broadway at 44th*) features an in-store ferris wheel, while the largely disappointing **MTV Experience Store** (*1515 Broadway at 44th*) is a magnet for out-of-towners. A contingency of affordable surf and skate chains, including **Quicksilver** (*3 Times Square at 42nd*) and **Billabong** (*1515 Broadway at 45th*), are actually worth a walkthrough.

WILLIAMSBURG

Just three subway stops from Union Square on the L, Bedford Avenue is the hub of hipster vintage; a walk along the thoroughfare, with detours along adjacent streets, provides trend-conscious shoppers with plenty of eye-candy. The color-coded racks and chaotic back rooms of **Beacon's Closet** (*88 North 11th Street at Wythe*), the city's most famous vintage store, hold treasures to suit all hipster tastes. **Buffalo Exchange** (*504 Driggs Avenue at North 9th*), which buys clothes from customers in exchange for store credit, offers similar fare— "gently used" clothing and accessories with some glittering costumewear thrown in. Many unique boutiques and workshops such as **Bittersweets** (*37 Broadway at Wythe*) offer goods by local designers; the area is especially heavy on neighborhood-based jewelry and furniture makers.

THE MEATPACKING DISTRICT

Cobblestone streets and converted meatpacking warehouses form the surprising backdrop of one of the most upscale fashion neighborhoods in New York City. Treasure-filled boutiques like **Girlshop** (*819 Washington Street at Gansevoort*) feature tomorrow's trends and a wide selection of hard-to-find designers, while **Jeffrey New York** (*449 West 14th Street at Washington*) carries the season's must-haves by the likes of Alexander McQueen and Helmut Lang. Several independent designers have recently opened their own boutiques in the area as well, including **Stella McCartney** (*429 West 14th Street at Ninth*).

LOWER MANHATTAN

In the shadows of old-school sailboats, **South Street Seaport** is littered with chain stores; **Pier 17 Mall** (*South Street at Fulton*) and the surrounding area feature standard fare like Abercrombie and Fitch and the Gap. The neighborhood's real draw, however, is **Century 21** (*22 Cortland Street at Church*), the best discount department store in NYC. Go for price-slashed European designer imports on the way down the fashion ladder; it's crowded on weekends, but the deals are worth it.

American Folk Art Museum

Folk art from the last three centuries is augmented by temporary exhibits in a variety of media, and a surprisingly quirky gift shop.

45 West 53rd Street (at Fifth). 212.265.1040. Tu-Sun 10:30-5:30, F 10:30-7:30, closed Monday. Adults $9, Students $7. folkartmuseum.org **B D F V** *to Rockefeller Center.*

Brooklyn Museum

Worldwide art from antiquity to today, the new Elizabeth A. Sackler Center for Feminist Art, and historical artifacts thrown in for good measure make up one of the most impressive collections in the city.

200 Eastern Parkway, Brooklyn (at Washington). 718.638.5000. W-F 10-5, Sat-Sun 11-6. Adults $8, Students $4 (suggested). brooklynmuseum.org **2 3** *to Eastern Pkwy/Brooklyn Museum.*

The Cloisters

Medieval Times it isn't. Gardens, medieval objets, and the famed unicorn tapestries combine for an other-worldy museum experience.

Fort Tryon Park (at Sherman). 212.923.3700. Tu-Sun 9:30-4:45 (Nov.-Feb.), 9:30-5:15 (March-Oct.), closed Monday. Adults $20, Students $10 (suggested). metmuseum.org **A** *to 190th St.*

El Museo del Barrio

Full of pieces from Latin America, Puerto Rico, and the Caribbean, el Museo also aims to educate visitors on issues of cultural representation and preservation.

1230 Fifth Avenue (at 104th). 212.831.7272. W-Sun 11-5, closed M-Tu. Adults $6, Students $4 (suggested). elmuseo.org **6** *to 103rd St.*

The Frick Collection

This slightly intimidating collection of old masters, housed in a magnate's former mansion, is an

The Cloisters

art history buff's dream.

1 East 70th Street (at Fifth). 212.288.0700. Tu-Sat 10-6, Sun 11-5pm. Adults $15, Students $5. frick.org **6** *to 68th St.*

Solomon R. Guggenheim Museum

Frank Lloyd Wright's conch shell-shaped building winds up (or down) with special exhibits lining the spiraling walls. Smaller permanent collections occupy off-set rooms.

1071 Fifth Avenue (at 89th). 212.423.3500. Sat-W 10-5:45, Fr 10-7:45, closed Th. Adults $18, Students $15. guggenheim.org **4 5 6** *to 86th St.*

International Center for Photography

The permanent collection of more than 100,000 photos, highlighting the 1930s and '40s, is available only by appointment, but is supplemented with public temporary exhibits.

1133 Sixth Avenue (at 43rd). 212.857.0000. Tu-Th 10-6, F 10-8, Sat-Sun 10-6. Adults $12, Students $8. icp.org. 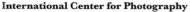 *A C E B D F V to 42nd St.*

The Jewish Museum

The extensive permanent collection of Jewish art and culture is augmented by special exhibits of notable Jewish artists.

1109 Fifth Avenue (at 92nd). 212.423.3200. Sat-W 11-5:45, Th 11-8, closed Friday. Adults $12, Students $7.50, free Saturday. jewishmuseum.org. 4 5 6 to 86th St.

Lower East Side Tenement Museum

This tours-only museum recreates life as lived by the immigrant population of the Lower East Side in the late 19th and early 20th centuries.

108 Orchard Street (at Allen). 212.431.0233. Tour times vary. Adults $15, Students $11. tenement.org. B D to Grand St.

Madame Tussaud's

Modern-day, Disney-fied Times Square is the perfect location for this museum devoted to wax replicas of celebrities, presidents, and sports stars.

234 West 42nd Street (at Seventh). 800.246.8872. Sun-Th 10-8, F-Sat 10-10. $29. nycwax.com. 1 2 3 7 N R Q W S to Times Square.

The Metropolitan Museum of Art

One of the world's greatest museums, from top (a roof garden with temporary installations) to bottom (the Costume Institute for fashion-lovers). In between, art by everyone from the Impressionists to ancient Greeks.

1000 Fifth Avenue (at 82nd). 212.535.7710. Tu-Th, Sun 9:30-5:30, Fr-Sat 9:30-9, closed Monday. Adults $20, Students $10 (suggested). metmuseum.org. 6 to 86th St.

Museum of Arts and Design

Going by the acronym *MAD*, this museum fittingly takes an idiosyncratic view of its subject: textiles, ceramics, and design ranging from jewelry to interiors.

40 West 53rd Street (at Fifth). 212.956.3535. Daily 10-6, Th 10-8. Adults $9, Students $7. madmuseum. org. V E to Fifth Ave.

Museum of Modern Art

The recently renovated MoMA offers a full range of modern art, with Picasso on one floor and video installations on another. Don't miss the sculpture garden, the upscale cafeteria, or the trendy-but-expensive Modern restaurant.

11 West 53rd Street (at Fifth). 212.708.9400. Daily 10:30-5:30, F 10:30-8, closed Tuesday. Adults $20, Students $12, free F 4-8. moma.org. V E to 5th/53rd.

American Museum of Natural History

This expansive institution is continually updated to include contemporary science. The Rose Center for Earth and Science is the splashiest addition, and the old-school dioramas and dinosaurs are still worth a visit.

Central Park West at 79th 212.769.5100. Daily 10-5:45. Adults $14, Students $10.50 (suggested). amnh.org. B C to 81st St.

The Museum of Sex

The name pretty much sums it up: a high-brow look at the history of sex, sexuality, and eroticism, meant to enlighten rather than titillate.

233 Fifth Avenue (at 27th). 212.689.6337. Sun-F 11-6:30, Sat 11-8. Adults $14.50, Students $13.50. museumofsex.com. N R 6 to 28th St.

The Museum of Natural History

Museum of Television and Radio

Rather than walk around and look at exhibits, visitors pick from a broad range of programs to watch at consoles. It's like real TV, but with more intellectual bragging rights.

25 West 52nd Street (at Fifth). 212.621.6800. Daily 12-6, Th 12-8, Closed Monday. $10 adults, $8 students. mtr.org. **B D F V** *to 47-50th Sts.*

National Museum of the American Indian

A part of the Smithsonian, the NMAI focuses on artifacts from history, art, and spirituality, with a look at contemporary art as well.

One Bowling Green (at State). 212.514.3700. Daily 10-5, Th 10-8. Free. nmai.si.edu. **4 5** *to Bowling Green.*

The New York Historical Society

A range of artifacts detail the history of the Empire State, along with an acclaimed permanent exhibit looking at slavery in New York.

170 Central Park West (at 77th). 212.873.3400. Tu-Sun 10-6, F 10-8, closed Monday. Adults $10, Students $6. nyhistory.org. **B C** *to 81st St.*

New York Transit Museum

Located in the decommissioned Court Street subway station, the collections, which include old-school subway cars, are devoted to the city's transportation history. Tours and special events are also worth checking out.

Court Street Station (Boerum Place at Schermerhorn). 718.694.1600. Tu-F 10-4, Sat-Sun 12-5, closed Monday. mta.info. **2 3 4 5** *to Borough Hall.*

South Street Seaport Pier 17

P.S. 1 Contemporary Art Center

Home not to elementary school students but contemporary art, P.S. 1 is a multimedia museum—part of MoMA—notable for its building almost as much as its art.

22-25 Jackson Avenue, Long Island City, Queens. 718.784.2084. Th-M 12-6. Adults $5, Students $2 (suggested). ps1.org. **V E** *to 23rd St.*

Queens Museum of Art

A museum within a museum, sitting next to the Unisphere on the 1964 World's Fair grounds. The scale-model version of the entire city of New York is incredible.

Flushing Meadows Corona Park, Queens. 718.592.9700. W-F 10-5, Sat-Sun 12-5 (Winter); W-Sun noon-6, F noon-8 (Summer); closed M-Tu. $5. queensmuseum.org. **7** *to Shea Stadium.*

The Skyscraper Museum

Exhibits and photographs allow visitors to explore the grandeur of the world's tallest buildings, without all the neck strain.

39 Battery Place (at 1st). 212.968.1961. W-Sun noon-6. Adults $5, Students $2.50. skyscraper.org. **1** *to Rector.*

South Street Seaport Museum

The city's history as a hub for trade comes to life through exhibits and a fleet of authentic ships lined up along the harbor.

12 Fulton Street (at Front). 212.748.8600. Hours vary by season. Aults $8, Students $6. southstseaport.org. **2 3 4 5 J M Z** *to Fulton.*

The Studio Museum in Harlem

Exhibits, in a variety of media, focus on African American artists.

144 West 125th Street (at Lenox). 212.864.4500. W-F noon-6, Sat 10-6, Sun noon-6, closed M-T. Adults $7, Students $3 (suggested). studiomuseum.org. **2 3 4 5 6 A C B D** *to 125th St.*

Whitney Museum of American Art

Concentrating on art from the 20th century, the museum's deep focus amounts to more than just the "greatest hits" of the century. The Biennial, a bi-annual showcase of current artists, is infamous.

945 Madison Avenue (at 75th). 1.800.WHITNEY. W-Th 11-6, F 1-9, Sat-Sun 11-6, closed M-T. Adults $15, Students $10, pay-what-you-wish F 6-9. **6** *to 77th St.*

New York is known around the world by its skyline—a fitting tribute to the city's rich and inimitable architectural tradition. Since its founding as a Dutch fur-trading outpost in the early 1600s, the convergence of immense wealth, modern engineering, and open land—at least for a time—ensured the city's status as a fertile breeding ground for great buildings. As overcrowding forced New Yorkers to build upwards, the vista began to resemble the iconic skyline we know today, with the skyscraper in all its various styles as the defining structure. Look closer, though, and you'll find a tradition that is as varied as it is long, encompassing a myriad of architectural styles.

COLONIAL AND POST-COLONIAL

New York is sadly short on **Georgian/Colonial**, architecture, and the few old gems that do survive can defy its characteristic straight-line symmetry. New York State's oldest surviving building, for instance, the **Wyckoff House** (*5816 Clarendon Road at East 57ᵗʰ, Brooklyn*), is a 1652 farmhouse more notable for its history than its architecture. The oldest building in Manhattan, **Fraunces Tavern** (*54 Pearl Street at Broad*), and the oldest public building, **St. Paul's Chapel** (*209 Broadway at Fulton*), are more typically colonial, with smooth columns and open entranceways. To enter the interior of each is truly to take a step back in time.

In the post-colonial era, architects of the vibrant young democracy both literal and figurative found their influences in the refined simplicity of the Greeks; **Greek Revivalism** is considered by many to be the first national movement. At Wall Street's **Federal Hall** (*26 Wall Street at Broad*), although much has been lost to development— including the original building—the stately columns and marble façade of America's first capitol remain. The Greek influence and the ideals that it represents have persisted throughout the years; the **New York City Supreme Court Building** (*60 Centre Street at Pearl*), built in 1919, is perhaps the city's most striking example of the style.

Another major style of the late 19ᵗʰ century, **Gothic Revivalism**, first emerged in New York's ecclesiastical community. **Trinity Church** (*74*

Trinity Place at Rector), **St. Patrick's Cathedral** (*Fifth Avenue at 50ᵗʰ*), **St. John the Divine** (*1047 Amsterdam at 112ᵗʰ*), and **Riverside Church** (*490 Riverside Drive at 120ᵗʰ*) all sport the heavily-adorned facades, delicate masonry work, and dark opulence that are so characteristic of the movement. For different interpretations on the same theme, see the

St. Patrick's Cathedral

Brooklyn Bridge or Central Park's **Tavern on the Green** (*Central Park West at 67th*), both of which fall into the tail end of the movement.

TURN OF THE CENTURY

By the turn of the 20th century, the technological breakthroughs of the Industrial Revolution had helped to transform architectural design. Inspired by the new possibilities that arose from steel construction, architects embarked on major projects, and buildings grew in both size and stature. Manipulating form, light, and shape as never before, firms built large, open rooms with interiors that exploded upwards. A variety of styles emerged during this period: **Romanesque Revivalism**, with its rounded arches and recessed entranceways, can be seen in **Temple Emanu-El** (*1 East 65th Street at Fifth*) and the **American Museum of Natural History** (*Central Park West at 79th*); **Beaux Arts Classicism**, characterized by lavish façade ornamentation, defines **Ellis Island**, the **Washington Square Arch**, **Macy's** (*Herald Square at 34th*), and **Grand Central Terminal** (*87 East 42nd Street at Park*); and the **Flatiron Building** (*175 Fifth Avenue at 23rd*), featuring an aesthetic of industrial simplicity, is typical of the **Chicago School**. Although these schools vary in design and philosophy, they are united by their grandeur—the products of a growing city, flush with possibility.

EARLY MODERNISM

The **Historicist** skyscrapers of the early 20th century, including the **New York Times Build-**

Grand Central Terminal

The Chrysler Building

as the typical iconic design of the period, which combines streamlining, rounded edges, and stylized representations of living forms. **Radio City Music Hall** (*1260 Sixth Avenue at 50th*), **Tiffany's** (*727 Fifth Avenue at 56th*), **Rockefeller Center** (*Fifth Avenue at 49th*), and the **Chrysler Building** (*405 Lexington Avenue at 42nd*) are the city's prime examples.

MODERNISM AND BEYOND

Formalism, **Futurism**, **Functional-Modernism**, **Brutalism**, **Expressionism**, **Post-Modernism**—only art history scholars really understand all the isms, but the styles born from them have changed the way the city looks. Since midcentury, improvements in metallurgy, construction, and engineering have allowed architects to do more with less. While supports and walls were once necessary to brace a 15-story building, the floor-to-ceiling windows of contemporary skyscrapers make them appear to be made entirely of glass. As buildings have grown, their footprints have also decreased in size. The **Seagram Building** (*375 Park Avenue at 53rd*), constructed in the mid-1950s, uses only 40% of its viable plot and hangs dozens of feet above the sidewalk, supported by beams. The glass tower of the **Hearst Magazine Building** (*951 Eighth Avenue at 47th*), built right on top of the Depression-era lobby, serves as perhaps the city's most poignant monument to how far building technology has come.

As the development of New York's skyline continues, expect to see the city's newest buildings play with smoothly sloping geometry and ultra-modern building materials. Developers have already broken ground on the new 1,776-foot **Freedom Tower** at the former site of the World Trade Center; upon completion, a tapered, prismatic tower of clear, untinted glass will become lower Manhattan's newest landmark. In Chelsea, the much-

ing (*229 West 43rd Street at Seventh*) and **One Times Square**, serve as a bridge between Revivalism and the early modern styles, rising in height but retaining characteristic detail. During the interwar period, **Art Deco** and **Setback** skyscrapers were products of a more streamlined and modern style, with less intricate detailing than their predecessors. Setback structures, such as the 1931 **Empire State Building** (*350 Fifth Avenue at 34th*), are often called "wedding cake" buildings because of their tiered design, narrowing as the height increases. Early Modern and Art Deco buildings have more gradual and graceful ascensions, as well beloved—and occasionally maligned—Frank Gehry has completed the new **InterActiveCorp Building** (*555 West 18th Street at West*), a complex of curved, white-tinted glass just feet from the Hudson River. Gehry is also in charge of Brooklyn's **Atlantic Yards**, a $4 billion project looking to revitalize the neighborhood with affordable housing and long-term economic investment. Whether projects like this should be called revitalization or gentrification is a question that has yet to be answered, with tensions and passions running high on both sides. Along with all the big names and big investments, however, New York's architects have quietly pioneered **green construction**; throughout the city, residential and commercial properties have adopted Earth-friendly building techniques and standards, both meeting and surpassing environmental benchmarks.

RESOURCES

For more information on New York's architectural heritage and future, visit the city's premier architecture site, *nyc-architecture.com*, and be sure to check with the Department of the Interior for more information on historic landmarks.

Seagram Building

MEDIA

TELEVISION STATIONS

NY1 (*Channel 1*) is New York's 24-hour local news channel. With up-to-the-minute news, weather, traffic, and sports, as well as political programs such as *Inside City Hall*, it's the best option in local TV news—all the info without the unnecessary glitz.

WCBS (*Channel 2*) is the local affiliate of CBS.

WNBC (*Channel 4*) is the local affiliate of NBC. Watch *Today in New York* for a lighter take on the day's most pressing stories.

WNYW (*Channel 5*) is the local affiliate of FOX. Newscasts like *Good Day New York* and *Fox 5 News at Ten* offer lightly-rendered city news that often goes the route of tabloid TV.

WABC (*Channel 7*) is the local affiliate of ABC.

WNET (*Channel 13*) is New York's commercial-free PBS flagship. Regular programming helps familiarize viewers with aspects of city life that commercial TV tends to skip, and the fascinating documentaries are the next best thing to leaving the house.

NYCTV (*Channel 25*) is a publicly-owned channel airing "Everything New York." Shows such as *Backdrop NYC* and *Eat Out NY* provide great info for those just getting to know the city.

RADIO STATIONS

WNYC New York Public Radio (*AM820 or 93.9 FM*)
City-owned WNYC is the most listened-to public radio station in the country for a reason, broadcasting NPR programs as well as award-winning local shows that reflect the great cultural depth of the metropolitan area.

WINS (*1010 WINS or AM1010*)
The first non-stop all-news station in the country, this frequency offers "All News, All the Time." As their slogan promises, "You give us 22 minutes, we'll give you the world."

WFAN Sports Radio (*AM660*)
This self-proclaimed "flagship station for New York sports" provides broadcasts of sporting events, updates on every major team in the state, and interviews with top sports personalities.

WHTZ (*Z100, 100.3 FM*)
"New York's #1 Hit Music Station" plays a steady stream of contemporary pop, rock, reggaeton, and R&B. As a Top 40 station, it has music to suit every taste, at least in theory—they rarely venture beyond the same rotation of current singles.

WQHT (*HOT97, 97.1 FM*)
New York's best station for hip-hop and R&B plays contemporary beats along with a handful of old school jams. Programming stays current and often includes interviews with big-name hip-hop stars.

WWRL (*AM1600*)
Known as "New York's Progressive Talk" destination, this Air America Radio affiliate offers everything from local news to ethnic programming, with a decidedly liberal slant.

NEWSPAPERS/MAGAZINES

The New York Times (*nyt.com*) is one of the most well-respected daily newspapers—and news sources, period—in the world, as well as the largest metropolitan paper in the country. The eminent Sunday Times has so much content, it takes all week to read.

The Wall Street Journal (*wsj.com*) is one of the premiere financial papers in the country, well read across the globe. Its take is usually conservative, but it's a must-read for finance buffs.

The New York Post (*nypost.com*) is the city's most widely-read tabloid. A 2004 study by Pace University rated this daily as the least credible major news source in New York, but the paper's distinctive voice and sensationalist style are always entertaining. Recently, its take on the news has grown increasingly conservative.

The Daily News (*nydailynews.com*) is another popular tabloid, filled with photographs and short news blurbs—the Post's more liberal rival.

Metro (*ny.metro.us*) and **amNY** (*amny.com*) are free papers given out at major subway stops during the morning commute. Grab both and you'll arrive at work fully prepared for water cooler chatter.

The L Magazine (*thelmagazine.com*) is a free bi-weekly magazine that publishes an extensive calendar of city events; they also keep an informative blog that focuses on Manhattan and Brooklyn.

The New Yorker (*newyorker.com*) is a nationally-revered literary institution that publishes weekly—a must-read for New York intellectuals and those who aspire to join their ranks. In addition to covering the wide scope of cultural life in the city, the magazine publishes fiction, literary criticism, reportage, and essays by eminent contemporary writers.

New York Magazine (*nymag.com*) is the best place to go each week for reviews of city restaurants, bars, clubs, and theaters. The quality of writing in the magazine has lurched upwards in recent years, and the cover stories are always worth reading.

Time Out New York (*timeoutny.com*) is an invaluable resource for visitors and city-dwellers alike. With comprehensive listings of weekly events, this is the source to consult when you're looking for a show, movie, concert, or special event in the city.

The Village Voice (*villagevoice.com*) is an alternative free weekly newspaper with a reputation as an arts-orientated tabloid; its greatest use is as a source of good conversation fodder.

New York Press (*nypress.com*) is another free alternative weekly, often eclipsed by The Village Voice, although their top-notch columnists and comprehensive music listings rarely disappoint.

The Brooklyn Rail (*brooklynrail.org*) is a free monthly journal that offers "critical perspectives on arts, politics and culture" in New York's five boroughs and beyond.

WEBSITES/BLOGS

Gothamist.com is an award-winning guide to everything New York; if you want to know what protest you just walked by or what movie's filming down the street, its frequent postings will most likely cover the details.

Gawker.com offers updates on city life that are heavy on snark, not to mention seriously entertaining to read. Celebrity and media gossip are its great contribution to the city blog scene, including the infamous Gawker Stalker.

Nonsensenyc.com keeps readers clued-in to the strangest events taking place in New York, from no-pants subway parties to ethnobotanical tours that teach you what plants you can eat in Central Park.

The New York section of **craigslist.com** is the go-to resource for apartment hunting, buying and selling cheap stuff, job searches, and surfing for anonymous sex. Ick?

Curbed.com is New York City's own real estate and neighborhoods blog, and a great source to consult when you're apartment-hunting.

New York City might just be the best place in the world to be gay. Whether you're kissing your boyfriend on a street corner or yelling prophesies outside Starbucks, no one gives a damn what you do, so feel free to do either. Even tourists, from middle-American sightseers to staunch Alabama Republicans, seem to adopt New York's Golden Rule when they're here: anything goes. Of course, it's not Fire Island—be careful in upper Manhattan and the more conservative areas of the outer boroughs, where resistance to so-called unconventional lifestyles can be strong; remember that there are always situations in which it's best to be discreet, whether gay, straight or anything in between. For the most part, though, if you're looking for an accepting, welcoming home where you can comfortably be yourself, you've come to the right place.

GOING OUT

If you're gay in New York, you can live, eat, and love almost anywhere you like—but you'll probably want to travel in order to go out at night. Certain neighborhoods are known for being saturated with gay culture, and although most areas of town have at least a few favorite gay bars, they're generally few and far between north of Midtown.

Hell's Kitchen

Hell's Kitchen is getting gayer, thanks to the concerted efforts of a few swanky lounge owners who have snuck their establishments across the northern border of Chelsea. Plop yourself on a leather bench at **Vlada** (*331 West 51st Street at Eighth*) for smooth music, one of over a dozen infused vodkas, French niblets, and men in ties. Or, if you'd prefer to stand, lean over the upstairs railing at **Therapy** (*348 West 52nd Street at Eighth*) and watch free nightly entertainment like the Electroshock Therapy Comedy Hour or the American Idol-esque "Cattle Call."

Chelsea

Chelsea sometimes seems to contain nothing but gay bars, many of which are sex-driven party scenes full of six-packed men and their admirers; go if you've got the body or are immune to intimidation. The raunchiest among them remains **Splash** (*50 West 17th Street at Fifth*), where

bartenders wear nothing but white briefs, sneakers, and athletic socks, and a rotating roster of sex-themed parties gets shirtless men to undulate en masse every night of the week. If you'd like

New York City Gay Pride Parade

to cruise without the distraction of erotic massage go-go specialists, try **g** (*225 West 19th Street at Seventh*). There's no lube dripping from the tables here—just clean, high-end fun. And if you're just in the mood to listen to (or sing) Broadway and cabaret favorites, pop into neighborhood hangout **Helen's** (*169 Eighth Avenue at 19th*).

West Village

In the heart of the West Village sits **Stonewall** (*53 Christopher St. at Seventh*), where a riot in 1969 spawned the Gay Rights Movement in America. Now more of an historical monument than a throbbing dance club, the bar sits quietly and proudly at the center of a veritable hurricane of gay culture. Lesbians in their 30s and 40s visit The **Cubbyhole** (*281 West 12th Street at West 4th*) for drinks and light music, while young, fish-netted vixens on the prowl head over to **Henrietta Hudson "Bar and Girl"** (*438 Hudson Street at Morton*) for award-winning nightly dance parties. Men looking to dance should visit **Mr. Black** (*643 Broadway at Bleeker*), where so-called "Gay Pimp" Johnny McGovern invites you to party with hot go-go boys and fierce trannies at *Boys Gone Wild*, his weekly Saturday night get-together.

East Village

In the now-legendary musical *Rent*, characters sporting every shade of gay cavorted through the streets of the East Village, drugged, penniless, and loving every second of it. The drugs are no longer quite as visible, and the East Village is no longer home to the penniless, but it still pulses with the same free-loving, boundary-less, dirty Bohemian energy—and it's got the bars and clubs to match. **Snapshot** (*Tuesday nights at Bar 13, 35 East 13th Street at University*) is fast becoming New York's favorite weekly lesbian party; it sports two separate dance floors, a roof deck, some prestigious DJs, and a house photographer who roams the party to document the chaos. If you're in the mood for a good old gay show, look up **Mr. Murray Hill** (*mrmurrayhill.com*), the self-billed "Hardest Working Middle-Aged Man in Show Business," who hosts frequent drag and burlesque shows at **Mo Pitkin's House of Satisfaction** (*34 Avenue A at East 3rd*).

Park Slope

In recent years, Park Slope has become a charming enclave for families with babies in strollers; expect to find a strong concentration of free-spirited lesbians and a few gay men peppered here and there for good measure. For a good taste of the scene, head to the **Cattyshack** (*249 Fourth Avenue at 14th*), a lesbian bar that even East Village and Harlem dwellers flock to on Saturday nights. Dance to hip-hop music behind the pool table downstairs, jump around to Madonna on the second floor, or smoke on the outdoor terrace as lesbians gather around the bar to watch new episodes of *The L-Word* with the rapt attention of the French during a soccer game.

MAKING A COMMUNITY

If it seems like there are few places in New York where straight people can commingle without the aid of alcohol, there may be even fewer for gays. If you're new to the city, the **LGBT Community Center** in Chelsea (*gaycenter.org*) is a good way to meet your neighbors (*gaybors?*). They've got a weekly discussion group for 20-somethings, monthly group outings, movie nights, and more.

If you're looking for a therapist who specializes in gay issues, the staff at the center can refer you to one—they keep a running list.

The **Audre Lorde Project** (*alp.org*) in Brooklyn also offers community events geared specifically to minority groups; or, check out **Urban Outings** (*urbanoutings.com*), a social club for gay men that eschews bars and nightclubs in favor of organized parties, hiking, and theater outings. The harmonically-inclined might want to audition for the **Stonewall Chorale** (*stonewallchorale.org*), a group for gays and lesbians that performs classical and contemporary arrangements.

LIVING AND EMPLOYMENT

If you're looking for a roommate and aren't having any luck on Craigslist, try **Rainbow Roommates** (*125 West 60th Street at Columbus*). A licensed apartment-sharing agent will set you up with someone whose lifestyle is compatible to yours, whether you're gay, bi, or transgender, messy or neat, introverted or a party animal.

Gays and lesbians seeking short-term employment should sign up with **Diversity Staffing** (*295 Madison Avenue at 41st, 16th floor*), a temp agency with a mission against discrimination.

WORSHIPPING

Primarily gay congregations thrive at many open-minded churches and temples throughout the city. Check out the **Metropolitan Community Church of New York** (*446 West 36th Sreet. at Tenth*), a nondenominational Christian Church; the **Broadway United Church of Christ** (*2504 Broadway at 93rd*); **Jan Hus Presbyterian Church** (*351 East 74th Street at First*); or **Congregation Beth Simchat Torah** (*296 Ninth Avenue at 28th*), a reform Shul. The many **Unitarian Universalist** (*uumetrony.org*) churches in the city are also famously gay-friendly.

If you're interested in exploring the issues involved in being both gay and religious, consider attending one of the many interfaith discussions or presentations sponsored by **Out & Faithful** (*at the LGBT Community Center; see above*), also backed by the Union Theological Seminary.

HEALTH SERVICES

Gay Men's Health Crisis (*119 West 24th Street at Sixth*) goes above and beyond mere health services. The non-profit organization offers HIV/AIDS support, including mental health assistance and nutrition services, as well as legal counseling, a public policy branch, a prevention advocacy group, and a women's institute for families coping with the disease. **Bailey House** (*275 Seventh Avenue at 26th, 12th floor*) has been providing services for HIV-positive clients since 1983, with a focus on housing, employment, healthcare, and independent living. The **Callen Lorde Community Health Center** (*356 West 18th Street at Ninth*) offers LGBT-focused primary health care to both insured and uninsured patients. For psychological support, **Gay and Lesbian Affirmative Psychotherapy** (*1841 Broadway at 60th*) offers treatments for youth, adults, couples, families, and seniors, with the recognition that problems aren't always related to one's sexual orientation.

CULTURAL INSTITUTIONS

The **Leslie/Lohman Gay Art Foundation** (*26 Wooster Street at Grand*) was established in 1990 with the mission of "preserving the visual legacy of gay men and women." It boasts a permanent collection and special exhibits in all media, with a focus on gay erotica. History buffs will want to visit the **Lesbian Herstory Archives** (*484 14th Street at Prospect Park West, Park Slope, Brooklyn*), which not only possesses a vast collection of recordings, news clippings, photographs, and memorabilia from times gone by, but also frequently hosts cultural events. The oft-changing exhibits at the **Museum of Sex** (*233 Fifth Avenue at 27th*), also frequently incorporates gay, lesbian, and transgender themes. If you're short on time, take the **Gay and Lesbian New York Gallery Tour** (*nygallerytours.com*), led once a month by the art critic for the *New York Blade*, which samples eight Chelsea galleries in two hours. Bibliophiles should make a visit to the **Oscar Wilde Bookshop** (*15 Christopher Street at Gay*), the self-proclaimed "world's oldest gay and lesbian bookstore," offering gay media of all kinds, including rare books, young adult fiction, and DVDs.

In the early summer, as **Gay Pride Month** and the anniversary of the Stonewall riots approach, gay-themed festivities pick up momentum. **NewFest** (*newfest.org*) has been hosting a LGBT film festival each spring for 19 years, and the world-famous **Gay Pride Parade** (*nycpride. org*) comes to Manhattan each June, bringing an eclectic array of gay and lesbian groups together to march down Fifth Avenue. In July, check out the cheekily-named **Fresh Fruit Festival** (*freshfruitfestival.com*), which sponsors theater, dance, and music performances at many locations throughout the city.

Greenwich Village

There's no reason to let the cost of living in New York deter you from fully experiencing the city. With a few tips, students and young professionals with perennially empty wallets can still enjoy the best musicals, museums, restaurants, events, and stores in town—all without breaking the bank.

THEATER

It's no secret that Broadway shows can be devastatingly expensive—but they don't have to be. The easiest way to see a show for cheap is by scoring **rush tickets** to individual productions, which are available for most same-day shows at about $25 each; go to *talkingbroadway.com/boards* for a list of theater rush policies. Those with sturdy feet should know that many of the larger productions offer discounted standing room tickets for sold-out shows—you'll have to stand in the back, but you'll be paying a lot less than everyone else.

Another option is **volunteer ushering**. Many theaters, including most Off-Broadway venues, allow ushers to sit in on shows for a bit of free labor. Individual theater policies vary—call the ones you'd like to visit and inquire. You'll have to dress in standard black and white and arrive early for training, but the job requires little more than courtesy and basic counting.

MUSEUMS AND ARTS

Savvy New Yorkers already know that many of the city's best cultural and historical centers allow patrons to roam through their hallowed halls for little or no charge, at least at certain times. Most museums have **admission-free hours** once a week, while many have similar times that are designated as "**pay what you wish**." Check out the **Bronx Museum of the Arts**, the **Guggenheim**, the **Brooklyn Museum of Art**, **MoMA**, and the **Whitney**.

Some museums operate on the ambiguous **suggested donation** system; at these institutions, it's "pay what you wish" all year long. The listed suggestion price is just that—a suggestion—although paying significantly less is highly frowned upon, sometimes literally, by the uptight ticket-sellers. No one will turn you away, though; participating museums include the **Metropolitan Museum of Art**, the **American Museum of Natural History**, the **Museum of the City of New York**, and the **Cloisters**.

Of course, some museums are just plain **free**. For a bit of no-cost education, go to the **National Museum of the American Indian**, the **Goethe Institute**, or the **Museum at the Fashion Institute of Technology**.

BEAUTY SERVICES

Just because you're on a tight budget doesn't mean you can't look like a million bucks. One good idea is to take advantage of the many training institutes at beauty salons throughout the city. Beauty school neophytes at places like **Bumble and Bumble** (*bumbleandbumble. com*), the **New York International Beauty School** (*nyibs.com*), and **Sephora** (*sephora.com*) are eager to practice their skills, often for free. If you're brave enough to be a lab rat, you can get a whole new look—just be sure to tip your stylist.

When it comes to dressing like a New Yorker, it helps to have a lot of disposable income;

if that's not an option, it's time to get creative. Check out the **sales listings** in Time Out New York (*timeoutny.com*) to see what big name stores are having sales each week. Some major events, like the **Barney's Warehouse Sale** each February, are not to be missed. For perennial good deals, head to the city's best discount stores: **Loehmann's** (*loehmanns.com*), **Marshall's** (*marshallsonline.com*), and, of course, **Century 21** (*c21stores.com*), where you can get designer duds at seriously discounted prices.

Another favorite option is to buy used clothes, but beware of the many so-called thrift

Knock-off Scarves, Chinatown

shops in the city—some are just expensive vintage stores in disguise, demanding $50 for that ratty old T-shirt. Stick with the classic, charity-driven shops instead of the sketchy for-profit stores; **Salvation Army** (*satruck.com*), **City Opera** (*222 East 23rd at Third*), and **Housing Works** (*housingworks.org*) are the city's best.

Finally, if your fashion conscience will allow it, vaguely illegal designer knock-offs can be found in abundance along Canal Street in Chinatown and on roadside tables throughout Midtown. It may not be ideal, but it's a lot less painful than spending two grand on the latest Fendi masterpurse.

FURNISHINGS

Internet-savvy New Yorkers should know that with luck, good timing, and a few clicks of the mouse, you can decorate your entire pad for less than the cost of one Ralph Lauren bed-sheet. If you have a way of transporting large household items from someone else's home to yours, many people will let you have their stuff at no charge, just for taking it off their hands. Check out the classifieds on **craigslist** (*craigslist.com*) and **Freecycle NYC** (*freecycle.org*) for the best deals in the city.

HEALTHCARE

One tried-and-true method for getting free specialized health care, and maybe getting some money in the process, is to become a human guinea pig. This can be as scary—or as fun, depending on how you look at it—as it sounds, but there's no cheaper way to see a doctor in the city. The cost of treatment and medication are usually covered, with the possibility of a small stipend. Paid psychological and clinical studies are the most common, so inquire at local hospitals or universities to see which need participants. Specific institutions that pay you to receive treatment include the **Columbia Presbyterian Medical Center Dermatology Department** *(212-305-6953)*, which conducts clinical trials for new skin medications regularly, and the **New York Headache Center** *(212-794-3550)*, which runs clinical trials on new treatments for migraines and other types of headaches.

Anyone who's ever been in college knows that paying for condoms is downright silly when there are so many programs that give them out for free—plan ahead, and you can save some of your money for the earlier part of the evening. The **NYC Condoms Program** *(nyc.gov/health/condoms)* distributes free city-brand condoms to hundreds of bars, restaurants, and stores throughout the metro area; check the website for specific locations, or go to your local **Planned Parenthood** *(plannedparenthood.org)* for free contraception that comes with free advice on sexual health. The **LGBT Community Center** *(gaycenter.org)* also readily provides free condoms, as well as free support groups and social activities. Or, if you're still in school, go to your university's health services center—the original and still best way to make sex a little cheaper.

If you didn't get one of those free condoms and start to have morning-after worries, remember that STD testing in major metropolitan centers is almost always available for

99 Cent Sign

free. Go to a city-run clinic like the **Central Harlem STD Clinic** *(2238 Fifth Avenue at 137th)* or **Chelsea STD Clinic** *(303 Ninth Avenue at 23rd)* to receive a free and confidential examination.

Finally, if you're really broke and need serious medical treatment, the **New York City Health and Hospitals Corporation** *(nyc.gov/hhc)* will take care of you no matter what. It's not a resource to be taken advantage of if you're just hoping to save some cash, but for those in serious need, it's a godsend.

FOOD

If you think there's no such thing as a free lunch, you're right—but if you look hard enough, it's not difficult to find ways to eat for cheap, or even for free, in the city. College students are already well-versed in scouring university-run events for free food; the same principle applies to the greater world. If you're shameless, don't be afraid to duck into art openings, alumni events at bars and hotels, and corporate-sponsored parties with distracted bouncers to score some free food and drink. If you're really desperate, take a big messenger bag and stock up.

Those not ready to resort to impersonations and petty theft can at least save money on groceries by skipping the specialty stores and buying in bulk at some of the city's better priced supermarkets—the reliable **Fairway** (*fairway-market.com*) is a perennial safe bet. For fresh fruits, vegetables, and herbs, head down to the open-air stalls in Chinatown, or buy from one of the fruit carts stationed at most major intersections, where you'll pay a fraction of what you would at the market. Or, if you prefer to dine out, check **Time Out New York** (*timeout-ny.com*) and **New York Magazine** (*nymag.com*) for the most comprehensive listings of cheap eats in the city—if you know where to go, dining out can be quite reasonable.

For cheap baked goods and prepared sandwiches, stop by bakeries and delis late in the day or right before closing. These stores can't sell today's food tomorrow, so you can often walk out with handfuls of cheap goodies at rock-bottom prices. **City Bakery** (*3 West 18th Street at Fifth*) and **Zabar's** (*2245 Broadway at 80th*) both regularly lower prices as the day goes on.

Finally, if you've exhausted all other resources—and funds—consider becoming a **Freegan**. The term, derived from the word vegan, refers to those who decry over-consumption by subsisting on food the rest of the world throws away. The Freegan community in New York is quite active and welcoming—check out freegan.info for info on the philosophy, as well as a list of supermarkets and restaurants that regularly leave food out on the street.

New York City Street Vendor

MAJOR LEAGUE TEAMS

New York City may seem like the antithesis of Middle America in many ways, but when it comes to sports, we all see eye to eye. Perhaps Gotham-dwellers refrain from showing their support with partial nudity and body paint, but that doesn't mean we're not diehard baseball, basketball, hockey, football, lacrosse, tennis, and soccer fans, with a number of professional teams to root for in the area. Tickets can be purchased from teams' websites, and are often costly—the Yankees franchise had to get its money somewhere. Cheap seats are available, though, if you're willing to sit in the back, go to less popular events, or support the minor leagues. **Ticketwood.com** is a useful website that compares the ticket prices of various online distributors, and **Ticketmaster** is always a reliable source for tickets, sports or otherwise.

FOOTBALL
New York Giants
Meadowlands, East Rutherford, NJ.
201.935.8111. giants.com. Load-and-go bus service from Port Authority.

New York Jets
Meadowlands, East Rutherford, NJ.
516.560.8100. newyorkjets.com. Load-and-go bus service from Port Authority.

BASEBALL
New York Yankees
Yankee Stadium, Bronx.
718.293.4300. newyork.yankees.mlb.com. **4 B D** *to 116ᵗʰ St./River Ave.*

New York Mets
Shea Stadium, Queens.
718.507.TIXX. newyork.mets.mlb.com. **7** *to Willets Point/Shea Stadium.*

BASKETBALL
New York Knicks
Madison Square Garden, Midtown.
212.465.6073. nba.com/knicks.com. **1 2 3 A C E** N Q R W **B D F V** *to 34ᵗʰ St.*

New York Liberty
Madison Square Garden, Midtown.
212.564.WNBA. wnba.com/liberty.com. **1 2 3 A C E** N Q R W **B D F V** *to 34ᵗʰ St.*

HOCKEY
New York Islanders
Nassau Veterans Memorial Coliseum, Uniondale, NY.
516.501.6700. islanders.nhl.com. LIRR to Hempstead, then N70/N71/N72 to Hempstead Turnpike.

New York Rangers
Madison Square Garden, Midtown.
212.465.6050. newyorkrangers.com. **1 2 3 A C E** N Q R W **B D F V** *to 34ᵗʰ St.*

SOCCER
New York Red Bulls
Meadowlands, East Rutherford, NJ.
201.583.7000. redbulls.com. Load-and-go bus service from Port Authority.

LACROSSE
New York Titans
Madison Square Garden, Midtown, and Nassau Veterans Memorial Coliseum, Uniondale, NY.
1.888.8TTTANS. nytitanslacrosse.com. **1 2 3 A C E** N Q R W **B D F V** *to Penn Station for MSG; LIRR to Hempstead then N70/N71/N72 to Hempstead Turnpike for Nassau Coliseum.*

TENNIS
U.S. Open
USTA Billie Jean King National Tennis Center, Queens.
718.760.6200. usta.com. **7** *to Shea Stadium/Willets Point.*

CLUB TEAMS

If you've recovered from the psychological trauma of Little League and you're ready to give team sports another go, join a New York City sports league. The leagues cater to grown-ups, athletically gifted and uncoordinated alike, who want to hone their skills, have fun, and stay fit. Playing sports is a great way to meet people, too—especially for teetotalers.

New York City Social Sports Club

With low-key group sports like ultimate frisbee, wiffleball, and dodgeball, this coed club brags that it puts "the social before the sport."
P.O. Box 111002, Brooklyn. 646.383.8508. nycssc.com. $30-125 per individual.

Zog Sports

The coed leagues run by Zog Sports have over 30,000 members; and profits go to charities chosen by winning teams.
225 West 34th Street (at Seventh), Suite 925. zogsports.org. $75-155 per individual. **1 2 3 A C E** *to Penn Station.*

New York Fast Pitch Softball League

Fourteen mostly male teams play hardcore softball on Central Park's Great Lawn to raise money for youth programs.
newyorkfastpitch.com. $1800 per team, per session.

Out of Bounds

This organization, which promotes LGBT recreational events, supports clubs such as the NYC Gay Hockey Association and the Metro Gay Wrestling Alliance.
P.O. Box 372, Times Square Station. oobnyc.org.

PERSONAL FITNESS

Though exercising outside is a pleasure in the spring and fall, a gym membership is a must for workout fanatics during those dog days of summer and those occasional blizzards. Lots of gyms offer great introductory packages, but expect to pay at least $50 per month—sometimes a few times that amount—for long-term membership.

Gold's Gym

Four locations in Manhattan and Brooklyn.
goldsgym.com.

Bally Total Fitness

Thirteen locations in Manhattan, Brooklyn, Bronx, and Queens.
1.800.515.2582. ballytotalfitness.com.

New York City Sports Club

Fifty locations in five boroughs.
nysc.com.

Crunch Fitness

Fifteen clubs in Manhattan and Brooklyn.
crunch.com.

Equinox Fitness Clubs

Eighteen clubs in Manhattan and Brooklyn.
212.774.6363. equinoxfitness.com.

NYC Fitness

3552 Broadway (at 146th). 212.368.1700. nycfitnessgym. com. **1** *to 145th St.*

NYC Adventure Boot Camp for Women

If you hate gyms but love punishment, sign up for this four-week fitness program that offers toning and fat loss for women of all shapes, sizes, and fitness levels.
448 East 78th Street (at First), Suite 3D. 212.426.4871. nycadventurebootcamp.com. $419 for four-week session.

While it's often easy to forget, this city of steel and skyscrapers is also a city of spectacular parks, winding trails, sandy beaches, and scenic vistas. From biking and hiking to skiing and boating, there are plenty of ways to enjoy the great outdoors, New York-style, no matter the time of year.

SUMMER

When the weather turns warm and the sun is shining, cooped-up city dwellers flock outdoors to sunbathe or picnic. The city's planners have found innovative ways to craft useable space where there previously was none, creating artificial beaches on abandoned wharfs and parks on traffic islands, so you'll never be deprived of suburban greenery just because you're living in an urban jungle.

Parks

At the center of summer activity in New York is the city's unmatched collection of parks. From the perfectly manicured lawns of iconic **Central Park** to the majestic trees of the Upper West Side's **Riverside Park**, each park, like each neighborhood, has a personality of its own. Arrive early in the morning to catch the locals practicing tai chi in Chinatown's **Columbus Park**, or challenge the always-ready-for-a-game chess players in Greenwich Village's **Washington Square Park**. From flying a kite

Central Park, Great Lawn

on a lighthearted date to tossing a football with a group of old friends, there's no more relaxing way to spend a steamy summer afternoon than lazing around in one of the city's giant public backyards.

Running

Forget the treadmill—New York was built for runners. Not only are city blocks evenly spaced, making it easy to chart your mileage and timing, but nearly every large or mid-sized park has a well-maintained jogging trail waiting for you to run it. The best of the best, most runners agree, is the **1.58-mile track** that rings Central Park's **Jacqueline Kennedy Onassis Reservoir** (*main entrance at East 90ᵗʰ Street; centralpark.nyc.org*). With stunning views of the New York skyline and frequent security patrols, the track lures everyone from serious athletes to little old ladies on mid-day power strolls. Just remember to run counter-clockwise, or risk a collision.

For a change in scenery, you can try any of the other loops in the park—swing by the **Road Runner's stand**, by the reservoir entrance, to pick up a useful map—or head over to the running paths that snake along much of Manhattan's shoreline. If you're seeking a little variation, contact **NYC Run** (*nycrun.com*), which offers guided running tours through some of the city's most interesting neighborhoods. Additionally, there are hundreds of public running groups operating throughout the five boroughs; check *craigslist .com* or *meetup.com* for existing groups, or get some friends together and start your own.

Biking

While thrill-seeking bikers can always risk their lives playing chicken with cabs on city thoroughfares, there are plenty of picturesque paths for bikers of all levels to ride freely without choking on exhaust fumes. **Free city cycling maps** are available from any bike shop, as well as any branch of the **New York City Public Library**. The biking site **A1 Trails** (*a1trails.com*) also provides a wealth of essential information for city cyclist. If you're a mountain biker, the best place to go is **Van Cortland Park** in the Bronx (**1** *to 242nd Street*), which offers 1,150 acres of beautiful forests and awesome hills. And don't forget that all of the city's bridges have biking and walking paths, as well, so you can enjoy the view without worrying about oncoming traffic.

Hiking

The **Urban Park Rangers** (*nycgovparks.org*) are the foremost authority on all things nature in New York City, leading hikes, walks, and nature trips through the five boroughs all year round. Many parks, including Central and Bryant, also run their own tours (*check websites for details*). For the best hiking in Manhattan, head north to **Inwood Park**, (**1** *to 191st Street*) where secluded trails will make you forget you're in the big city. If you want to walk with a group, sign up for **Walkny.org**'s mailing list—after all, hikes don't necessarily have to take place in the woods.

Horseback Riding

It's easier than you might think for the equestrian-minded among us to ride off into a New York sunset; just go to one of the stables throughout the boroughs that offer guided trail rides and lessons for all levels. **Pelham Bay Park** in the Bronx (*bronxequestriancenter.com*) provides a beautiful setting complete with marshes and woodlands; trail rides cost $30 per person for a one-hour ride, and private 30-minute lessons are $40. For a more central location, Prospect Park's **Kensington Stables** (*kensingtonstables.com*) and Central Park's **Bridle Paths** (*centralparknyc.org*) are both highly recommended.

Beaches

As a New Yorker, you are living on some of the world's most-sought after ocean-front property: If you're in search of sand and the sound of waves crashing ashore, you're in luck. From the concert hum resonating from the amphitheatre at Jones Beach to the bare bottoms at Sandy Hook, each beach draws a different surf-craving crowd. See page 49 for more details.

Watersports

From waterskiing to sailing, New Yorkers in the know can partake in just about any water sport imaginable somewhere within city limits. One of the best destinations for all things aquatic is the Bronx's **City Island** (*cityisland.com*). Classes in sailing and yachting take place in its many marinas, or you can rent a boat, charter a yacht, or join a fishing expedition for the chance at a great catch.

If you're in Manhattan and want to spend a perfect afternoon kayaking on the beautiful Hudson, the place to go is the **Downtown Boathouse** (*downtownboathouse.org*). With three different locations in Hudson River Park offering both one- and two-person kayak rentals and lessons, the boat house, which is open May-October, has a plethora of equipment and volunteers to prepare you for your journey. To make things even better, everything is 100% free of charge. Once you rack up some experience (and gather some courage), you can even join the volunteers on a free three-hour ride to the Statue of Liberty.

For a more romantic afternoon on the water, visit the **Loeb Boathouse** in Central Park (*thecentralparkboathouse.com*), where you can rent a rowboat or kayak on amiable March-October days for just $12 per hour. During the summer, the Boathouse also offers gondola rides in genuine **Venetian gondolas** for $30 per half hour—or for a bigger taste of Venice in New York, join the **Gowanus Dredgers Canoe Club** (*waterfrontmuseum.org/dredgers*) for a free canoe or rowboat ride through Brooklyn's picturesque canals.

Finally, if you've got a fishing rod and a little bit of patience, join the leagues of dedicated New York fishermen who spend many an hour awaiting a catch. True connoisseurs can charter a boat or join a scheduled outing—see *nycfishing.com* for more details—but it's much easier to just hang out with urban anglers on one of the city's docks or piers. The **107th Street Pier** and the **90th Street Dock**, both on the Upper East Side, are popular spots for catching East River bluefish, snappers, and stripers, and the docks on **Coney Island** are always lined with fisherman toting buckets of squirming catch. Just remember to catch and release, so the fishies will be around for someone else to catch tomorrow.

WINTER

Winter may bring with it gray winds and frigid skies, but the chilly months of December through March are also some of the city's most beautiful, with romantic flurries swirling overhead and holiday lights a-twinkling. Zip up your jacket and slip on your gloves, because with everything to see and do, there's plenty of reason to venture outdoors.

Sledding

Yes, it's silly, and yes, your friends may think you're regressing, but an afternoon sledding is a seriously fun way to relieve a week's worth of tension and reconnect with your inner child. Central Park (try **Pilgrim Hill** just past the 74th Street boat pond) and **Riverside Park** (enter at 91st or 108th for the best spots) both boast popular sledding hills where you can join legions slipping and sliding down the snow. For the ultimate sledding destination, make your way over to **Fort Greene Park** in Brooklyn, where you'll find multiple hills, ranging from near-straight drops (with obstacles!) to gentle slopes.

Skating

The most classic—not to mention most romantic—of outdoor winter activities, ice skating is New York City's favorite cold-weather pastime. The city operates numerous rinks throughout the boroughs, so there's always a patch of fresh ice to explore. The rink in front of **Rockefeller Center**, under the world-famous Christmas tree and soaring skyscrapers, is perhaps the most iconic in the city—but once you tire of the picture-snapping tourists and constant crowds, head over to Central Park's **Wollman Rink** (*East Side at 62nd*), the city's largest and most scenic. With Top-40 hits always blaring and horse-drawn carriages passing by periodically, it's the perfect place both to entertain out-of-towners and to spend an evening with that special someone. Another great place to skate in the city is New York's newest rink, **The Pond**, located in Bryant Park. Not only is the skating free—skate rentals are $7.50—but the rink tends to attract a smaller and more local crowd, so you'll actually have space to glide.

Skiing

While Manhattan may not boast Salt Lake City's urban mountains or Tokyo's indoor ski resorts, avid skiers in the city need not be disappointed. When the weather outside is frightful, many New Yorkers avoid walking through mush and slush by breaking out their **cross-country skis**. Pay close attention to the weather reports and wake up early, though, since most of that snow could be gone by midday.

If city streets and winding park paths just aren't your thing, New York State's Hudson Valley offers top-notch **downhill ski resorts**, many of which are just about an hour's bus ride away. **Hunter Mountain** (*huntermtn.com*), the largest area resort, boasts three separate mountains with a variety of terrain for skiers and snowboarders of all abilities, from wide-open, gentle slopes to moguls and steep drops. **Holiday Mountain** (*holidaymtn.com*) in **Monticello NY** is another popular destination, with 15 slopes and trails, seven lifts, and activities including go-karts, bumper cars, tubing, rock-climbing walls, and a potato sack slide. For a comprehensive list of the area's slopes, go to *Skicentral.com*.

Skating at Wollman Rink

CENTRAL PARK

Sometimes the best thing about the city is being able to escape from it; that's why Central Park exists. With 843 acres of green space, New York's most famous park spans the area from Fifth to Eighth Avenues east to west, and from 59th to 110th south to north. Over 20 million people flock to Central Park each year for its recreational facilities, outdoor arenas, and perfectly manicured natural splendor. Check out the following attractions for the best the park has to offer.

Wollman Rink

In the winter months, one of the city's most romantic activities is ice skating at Wollman Rink. Glide under a starry sky as you listen to Top 40 hits.
East Side at 62nd. 212.439.6900. M-T 10-2:30, W-Th 10-10, F-Sat 10-11, Sun 10-9. Adults $9.50; skate rental $5; lock rental $3.75.

Central Park Zoo

This urban oasis is home to more than 130 different species, living in habitats designed to mimic their natural environments. Polar bears, fairy blue birds, and red pandas are just some of the exotic creatures you'll find.
East Side at 64th. 212.439.6500. April-Oct: M-F 10-5, Sat-Sun 10-5:30; Nov-March: Daily 10-4:30. Adults $8.

Harlem Meer

The second-largest man-made body of water in the park is brimming with a vide variety of fish and turtle species—an uptown family favorite, surrounded by ginkgo, cyprus, and beech trees.
East Side at 110th.

The Delacorte Theater

Home to the famous annual "Shakespeare in the Park" series put on by the Public Theater, the Delacorte gives more than 80,000 New Yorkers the chance to see Shakespeare productions featuring the country's most well-renown actors free of charge.
Mid-park at 80th. 212.260.2400. publictheater.org.

Sheep Meadow

Along with the **Great Lawn** (*mid-park at 79th*), this meadow is one of the park's prime destinations for warm-weather picnickers, solitary readers, and Frisbee-players. Go for the people-watching, or just to hang out.
West Side at 68th.

Jacqueline Kennedy Onassis Reservoir

Joggers and walkers travel counterclockwise around the reservoir's 1.58-mile trail year-round; equestrians enjoy the bridle path further removed from the water.
Mid-park at 85th.

Bethesda Terrace

Home to the famous Angel of Waters statue, the geometrically splendid patio has been featured in numerous films; tourists and wedding parties are frequently photographed on the steps.
Mid-park at 72nd.

The Ramble

Offering a true taste of wilderness, these rugged paths constitute one of the few places in the park where you can truly forget that you're in the middle of a vast metropolis.
Mid-park at 79th.

Central Park Restaurants

If you want something fancier than a hot dog or pretzel from the park's many concession carts, check out the famously upscale **Tavern on the Green** (*West Side at 66th*), the outdoor-casual **Sheep Meadow Café** (*East Side at 69th*), or the waterfront restaurant at the **Loeb Boathouse** (*East Side at 74th*), where you can rent paddleboats and gondolas for a pre-meal float.

BEACHES

Jones Beach

This six-mile stretch of Long Island is the closest and most popular beach destination for city residents. There's a two-mile boardwalk, two public pools, and a summer concert series that draws big name-performers. Just be sure to arrive early in the day—the beach fills up quickly in good weather.

Ocean Pkwy (at Wantagh), Long Island. 516.785.1600. LIRR to Wantagh, then $3 shuttle bus to the beach. Jonesbeach.com.

The Hamptons

No longer just the ultra-exclusive playground of New York's elite, the Hamptons now offer something for everyone. Families enjoy the wide shores and clean waters of East Hampton's Main Beach, while trendsetters head to Gibson Beach in Sagaponack for a bikini-top-optional, celebrity-sighting good time. After the sun goes down, take advantage of the excellent nightlife—if you think your wallet can handle it.

Multiple destinations; see hamptons.com and hamptonjitney.com for travel information.

Rockaway Beach

This Queens destination, wryly referred to as the Irish Riviera, is the largest urban beach in the US (and the title of great Ramones' song). Go for the welcoming locals, the flat, clean sands, and the long boardwalk, or hit up the handball, paddleball, and basketball courts. If you're feeling bold, take off your suit and head to nearby **Federal Beach** for an innocent eyeful.

Cross Bay Pkwy (at Shore Front). 718-318-4000. A to Beach 25-116.

Coney Island

A quintessential New York landmark, Coney Island is currently in the midst of a makeover geared to change its face forever. Go now before they shut down Astroland (punks!) and build a Las Vegas-style mega hotel. By late 2008, the famous boardwalk, kid-friendly midway, and distinct local flavor will be changed forever

Brighton Beach, Brooklyn. N Q D F to Coney Island.

Sandy Hook

As a designated Federal Park, Sandy Hook is one of the rare public places in the tri-state area where patrons can be eat, drink and be naked all at the same time. Seven miles of oceanfront offer great swimming, the historic lighthouse is legendary, and the whole area has thankfully avoided over-commercialization.

Highlands, NJ. Seastreak ferry (1-800-BOATRIDE) from East 34th Street to Highlands. sandy-hook.com.

South Beach

Just a free ferry ride from Lower Manhattan, this Staten Island beach offer great views of the city skyline, free concerts and fireworks in the summer. Stroll along the FDR Boardwalk—it's the fourth-longest in the world.

Staten Island. 718-816-6804. From the Ferry, bus S51 to Father Capodanno Blvd. and Sand Lane.

Water Taxi Beach

Yes, it's artificial; yes, it's a publicity stunt; but it just might be one of the city's best beaches. Built on a Long Island City wharf by the New York Water Taxi Company, which imported 400 tons of NJ sand for the beach's creation, this 21-and-over, chill party spot on the East River is the place to come to hang out in the summer months. There's no swimming, but there's plenty of beer, cheap food, and fun in the sun.

Hunters Point (2nd Street at Borden), Long Island City. Free before 8, $3-5 after. watertaxibeach.com; nywatertaxi.com for stop locations.

CLASSES & WORKSHOPS

If you've ever wanted to learn how to do almost anything at all, New York is the place for you—the sheer number of classes and workshops offered within city limits is enough to fulfill your every self-enrichment need. This list, by no means exhaustive, is just the beginning; with a bit of research and a bit more grit, you can be an expert photographer, yoga master, culinary star, or nearly anything else in no time.

ARTS

The Acting Studio, Inc.
For over 21 years, this school has offered intensive short- and long-term classes in directing, monologue workshops, Shakespeare, and more.
244 West 54th Street (at Broadway), 12th Floor. 212.580.6600. actingstudio.com. Seminars and workshops $300-$1500. **B D E** *to Seventh Avenue.*

New York Institute of Photography
Offering courses for the casual shutterbug and aspiring professional alike, this Institute—almost as old as the medium it teaches—embraces both modern and traditional photographic techniques.
211 East 43rd Street (at Third), Suite 2402. 212.867.8260. nyip.com. Course prices vary. **4 5 6 7 S** *to Grand Central-42nd Street.*

CULTURE AND LANGUAGE

Alliance Française
Francophiles of all levels can improve their language skills at the largest French language center in the country.
22 East 60th Street (at Madison). 646.388.6612. fiaf.org Class prices vary. **4 5 6** *to 59th St.*

China Institute in America
America's oldest Chinese bicultural organization promotes awareness of culture, history, language, and arts through semester-long classes in language, calligraphy, painting, and more.
125 East 65th Street (at Lexington). 212.744.8181. chinainstitute.org Course prices vary; Admission $5. **6** *to 68th St.*

The Spanish Institute
Semester-long language classes, from "breakthrough-waystage" to "mastery," come with access to the institute's reference collection and reading room.
684 Park Avenue (at 68th). 212.628.0420. spanishinstitute. org $60 required membership fee; $430 per multi-week course. **6** *to 68th St.*

DANCE

Ballet Academy East
Adults who never got a chance to wear tutus during childhood get a second chance to learn the five basic positions (and more) at this academy.
1651 Third Avenue (at 92nd), 3rd Floor. 212.410.9410. baenyc.com. $14 per class. **6** *to 96th St.*

Manhattan Motion Dance Studios
Both children and adults can brush up on dance styles such as salsa, tap, belly dancing, and foxtrot, or even work on wedding choreography, in a fun, relaxed environment.
215 West 76th Street (at Broadway), 4th Floor. 212.724.1673. manhattanmotion.com. $16 per class. **1 2 3** *to 72nd St.*

MARTIAL ARTS

Aikido of Manhattan
This members-only dojo offers classes for students of all experience levels in the technique and philosophy of the art of "moving Zen."
60 West 39th Street (at Sixth), 3rd floor. 212.575.0151. aikidoofmanhattan.com. **B D F V** *to Bryant Park.*

MISCELLANEOUS

92nd Street YMCA

One of New York's most valuable cultural resources offers classes in art, dance, parenting, food and wine, foreign languages, and personal development.

1395 Lexington Avenue (at 92nd). 212.415.5500. 92y.org Course prices vary. **6** *to 96th St.*

Natural Gourmet Institute for Food and Health

This institute offers classes from culinary basics and macrobiotic cooking to raw food preparation and ayurvedic principles.

48 West 21st Street (at Fifth), 2nd floor. 212.645.5170. naturalgourmetschool.com. Class prices vary. **F V** *to 23rd St.*

Time's Up Bike Repair Workshop

Best known for organizing the Critical Mass rallies in which hordes of bikers flood city streets in protest of car-centrism, this environmental group also sponsors free bike repair and maintenance workshops.

49 East Houston Street (at Mott). 212.802.8222. times-up. org **B D F V 6** *to Bleeker.*

West Side Pistol and Rifle Range

Newbies learn how to take out paper bad guys from NRA-certified instructors at this underground gun range.

20 West 20th Street (at Fifth). 212.243.9448. westsidepistol-range.com. Beginner instruction $50. **1** *to 23rd St.*

WRITING

The Writers Studio

Aspiring authors and poets of all levels explore their craft in small workshops and one-on-one tutorials.

78 Charles Street (at 4th Street), Suite 2R. 212.255.7075. writerstudio.com. $345-$450 per seven-week class. **1** *to Christopher St.*

Gotham Writers' Workshop

Published writers teach classes in fiction, poetry, screenwriting, and other genres at seven Manhattan locations.

212.974.8377. writingclasses.com. Classes $125-$395. **1 2 3 A C E** *to Penn Station.*

YOGA AND MEDITATION

Jivamukti Yoga Center

The studio that first made yoga cool back in the eighties is still seeing the spirit in you.

jivamuktiyoga.com. $8-$17 per class. Passes valid at two locations. Downtown: 841 Broadway (at 13th), 2nd floor. 212.353.0214. **4 5 6 R Q W L** *to Union Square. Upper East Side: 853 Lexington Avenue (at 65th), 2nd floor. 646.290.8106.* **F** *to 63rd St.*

Life in Motion

Styles of yoga both vigorous and soothing are taught here, in addition to Pilates and aerobics classes.

2744 Broadway (at 105th), 3rd floor. 212.666.0877. lifeinmotion.com. $16 per class. **1** *to 103rd St.*

New York Zendo Shobo-ji

New Yorkers looking to escape urban chaos seek out this serene temple for classes in "zazen," or Zen mediation.

223 East 67th Street (at Third). 212.861.3333. daibosatsu. org. $5-$15 per class. **6** *to 68th St.*

Yoga Works

Classes of varying styles are geared toward all levels at this chain, with four locations in Manhattan.

yogaworks.com. $20 per class. Passes valid at all locations; see website for addresses.

When your insanely rich grandparents pay a visit to make sure you're surviving in the big city, you'll find no shortage of four- and five-star hotels to house them. Suggest the Ritz Carlton (50 Central Park South at Sixth) or the Four Seasons (57 East 57th at Madison), each of which runs about $650 a night, so you can take advantage of the room service. For the rest of your friends and relatives, the city offers a full range of economical lodgings—you just need to know where to look.

AFFORDABLE HOTELS

For visitors who aren't completely willing to sacrifice quality for cost, mid-range hotels are the way to go. New York hotel rooms, like apartments, tend towards the tiny—a $200 room in New York will almost certainly be smaller than a $200 room anywhere else in the country—although amenities are comparable; guests can generally expect internet access, housekeeping service, and fitness centers.

Rates listed here are for single rooms without taxes in the off-season. They are approximate, and change frequently throughout the year.

Americana Inn New York
From $100 nightly
69 West 38th Street (at Sixth). 888.468.3558. theamericanainn. com. **B D F V** *to Bryant Park.*

Best Western President Hotel
From $120 nightly
234 West 48th Street (at Broadway). 212.246.8800. bestwesternnewyork.com. N R W *to 49th St.*

Carter Hotel
From $120 nightly
250 West 43rd Street (at Seventh). 212.944.6000. hotelcarter. com. **1 2 3 7** N Q R W S *to Times Square.*

Chelsea Savoy Hotel
From $100 nightly
204 West 23rd Street (at Seventh). 866.929.9353. chelseasavoynyc.com. **1 C E F V** *to 23rd St.*

Da Vinci Hotel
From $100 nightly
244 West 56th Street (at Broadway). 212.489.4100. davincihotel.com. N R Q W *to 57th St.*

Days Hotel
From $100 nightly
215 West 94th Street (at Amsterdam). 212.866.6400. daysinn. com. **1 2 3** *to 96th St.*

Hotel Newton
From $120 nightly
2528 Broadway (at 95th). 800.643.5553. thehotelnewton. com. **1 2 3** *to 96th St.*

HOSTELS

Those looking for the cheapest possible lodgings should consider staying in a hostel. These small-scale establishments, catering to travelers on a budget, feature kitchens, shared bathrooms, dormitory-style bedrooms, and the occasional curfew. Though extras are sparse, many hostels are more than livable, and you'll feel just like you're finally taking that European backpacking vacation you've always talked about.

Rates listed here are per person, and vary according to season.

Broadway Hotel & Hostel
From $30 nightly
230 West 101st Street (at Broadway). 212.865.7710. broadwayhotelnyc.com. **1** *to 103rd St.*

Central Park Hostel
From $30 nightly
19 West 103rd Street (at Central Park West). 212.678.0491. centralparkhostel.com. **B C** *to 103rd St.*

Chelsea International Hostel
From $30 nightly
251 West 20th Street (at Eighth). 212.647.0010. chelseahostel. com. **1** *to 18th St.*

Flushing YMCA
From $30 nightly
138-46 Northern Boulevard (at Union), Flushing, Queens. 718.961.6880 ext. 133. ymcanyc.org. **7** *to Main Street-Flushing.*

The Gershwin Hotel and Hostel
From $40 nightly
7 East 27th Street (at Fifth). 212.545.8000. gershwinhotel.com. **6 R W** *to 28th St.*

Hostelling International New York
From $30 nightly
891 Amsterdam Avenue (at 104th). 212.932.2300. hinewyork.org. **1** *to 103rd St.*

Jazz on the City
From $15 nightly
201 West 95th Street (at Amsterdam). 212.678.0323. jazzhostels.com. **1 2 3** *to 96th St.*

Jazz on the Park
From $15 nightly
36 West 106th Street (at Manhattan). 212.932.1600. jazzhostels.com. **B C** *to 103rd St.*

Jazz on the Town
From $20 nightly
307 East 14th St. (at Second). 212.228.2780. jazzhostels.com. **L** *to First Ave.*

Loftstel Greene Avenue
From $40 nightly
580 Greene Avenue (at Tompkins), Bedford-Stuyvesant, Brooklyn. loftstel.com. **G** *to Bedford-Nostrand.*

Loftstel Jefferson Avenue
From $40 nightly
397 Jefferson Avenue (at Throop), Bedford-Stuyvesant, Brooklyn. loftstel.com. **C** *to Kingston-Stroop.*

Wanderers Inn Hostel East
From $30 nightly
179 East 94th Street (at Lexington). 212.289.8083. wanderersinn.com/east. **6** *to 96th St.*

Wanderers Inn Hostel West
From $25 nightly
257 West 113th Street (at Frederick Douglas). 212.222.5602. wanderersinn.com/west. **B C** *to 110th St.*

VACATION RENTALS
A less-common option for visitors on a budget is to rent lodging in a private home. New Yorkers frequently sublet their apartments—or at least parts of them—to vacationers for short periods of time, and a number of online services provide listings for short-term sublets in a wide range of prices. In addition to the following resources, consult sites like **craigslist**, **couchsurfing. com**, and **vrbo.com** (**Vacation Rentals by Owner**) when you need a place to crash.

Bed and Breakfast of New York
From $75 daily (with 25% deposit)
800.900.8134. bedandbreakfastnetny.com.

New York Urban Living
From $100 daily
281 Fifth Avenue (at 30th). 212.689.6606. new-york-apartments.com. M-Sat 9:30-7:30. **R W** *to 28th St.*

Sublet in the City
From $50 daily
85 Fifth Avenue (at 16th), 7th floor. 212.924.9694; after hours 646.236.7055. subletinthecity.com. M-F 9-8, Sat-Sun noon-5 **N R Q W 4 5 6 L** *to Union Square.*

ADDRESSES

Fifth Avenue divides Manhattan lengthwise into the East Side and West Side. On numbered east-west streets, building address numbers start at 1, beginning at Fifth Avenue, and increase outward from there. Buildings with low address numbers are closest to Fifth, near the middle of the island, while those with high numbers are closer to the shores. The resulting system is one in which very different buildings can have confusingly similar addresses—312 East 34th Street and 312 West 34th Street, for instance, are decidedly not the same place, although each is about the same distance from Fifth Avenue.

For many streets, it's possible to use just the address of a building to determine the surrounding avenues.

On the East Side, building address numbers 1-49 are between Fifth and Madison, 50-99 between Madison and Park, 100-149 between Park and Lexington, 150-199 between Lexington and Third, 200-299 between Third and Second, 300-399 between Second and First, and 400-499 between First and York.

On the West Side below 59th Street, numbers 1-99 are between Fifth and Sixth, 100-199 between Sixth and Seventh, 200-299 between Seventh and Eighth, 300-399 between Eighth and Ninth, 400-499 between Ninth and Tenth, and 500-599 between Tenth and Eleventh.

On the West Side between 59th-110th Streets, numbers 1-99 are between Central Park West and Columbus, 100-199 between Columbus and Amsterdam, 200-299 between Amsterdam and West End, and 300-399 between West End and Riverside Drive.

Determining location based on address in other areas of town is less straightforward. Determining the nearest street from an avenue address is a task that skirts the borders of human reason, involving a complex algorithm that is explained, in great detail, at *ny.com*.

AREA CODES

New York City uses four area codes. The most ubiquitous (read: oldest) is **212**, used for all phone numbers in Manhattan that are at least a decade old. In the late nineties, to accommodate growing demand, **646** was added as a second Manhattan code, and is given to most new numbers today. The addition provoked an interesting and altogether meaningless minor uproar among city residents: Seen as less "prestigious," reception to 646 was chilly, and discussion of the resulting area code envy made it all the way to an episode of *Seinfeld*.

The outer boroughs share the area codes **718** and **347**. The newest code, **917**, covers cell phones and pagers throughout the city, plus a few Manhattan landlines. Due to the high volume of calls in the metropolitan area, you must dial an area code before every call placed to a city number.

BANKING

The number of bank locations in New York is second only to the number of Starbucks—fitting, since the city is full of reasons to withdraw money. In Manhattan and the more populated parts of the boroughs, you're never more than a few blocks from an ATM at a bank branch, a drug store, convenience store, or restaurant; ask any store clerk if you need to be pointed in the right direction. The major banks in the city, with the most ATM locations, are **Citibank**, **Washington Mutual**, **Wachovia**, **Commerce Bank**, **Bank of America**, and **Chase**, which has an ATM in every Duane Reade. There are also a number of smaller banks, including some from other regions of the country, with just a few branches in the city.

Once you've chosen a bank as your own, it's worth making a note of the ATMs in your area—fees for using competitors' machines can add up quickly. If you're in a tight spot and can't get to one of your own bank's ATMs, go with one from another major bank instead of a no-name machine like the ones that often sit at the front of small convenience stores. Scams where unaffiliated machines steal account information are rare but not unheard of, and it's always best to have the accountability of a big-name bank behind your withdrawal.

BUSINESS HOURS

Are the doors to the city that never sleeps always open?

Almost. Office buildings work the typical schedule of 9am-6pm. Shops, including the big department stores, tend to open and close later—10am-8pm is typical, although schedules vary. Hours of service-oriented stores like salons and dry cleaners vary dramatically by location, although many open early (7am) and close late (9pm) to accommodate the before- and after -work crowds. Libraries usually shut their doors by 6pm, with restricted hours on weekends. Museums open anywhere from 9-11am and usually close by 5:30pm, although many stay open until 8 or 9pm on certain days, and most close at least one day per week.

Most of the city's more expensive restaurants are open only for dinner, serving from 5 or 6pm until 11pm or midnight. Those that serve lunch do so from about 11:30am-3pm and close for a bit before the dinner rush; some offer brunch on the weekends from 10am-3pm. Lower-end restaurants tend to serve continuously throughout the day, with many diners and delis open 24 hours. All ATMs, many drugstores, and certain grocery stores are also 24-hour—as is, thankfully, public transportation.

Bars tend to open around 5pm for happy hour and don't close until 4am; clubs open anywhere from 8 to 10pm and, depending on the night, can still be hopping when the sun comes up at 7am.

CLIMATE AND SEASONS

Like most parts of the northeastern United States, New York has four distinct seasons with varying lengths.

Winter usually starts in November and can last into March, with temperatures averaging in the 30s. Snowfall is common but does not usually exceed a foot at a time—thanks to its costal location, NYC gets less snow than many major cities in the north, and much less than you'll find upstate.

Spring is arguably the most pleasant time of year, although it always seems to be the shortest of the four seasons—temperatures can soar into the 80's and above as early as May.

Summer-like weather begins in May or June and is characterized by waves of oppressive heat and humidity, which can stretch into August or even September. New Yorkers with vacation homes—or rich friends—tend to flee the city in summer; the heat can be intense, so spring for an air conditioner if you're going to be hanging around.

Autumn, like spring, is pleasant and altogether too brief, although with mild temperatures, low humidity, and frequent sunny days, it's the perfect time to host visitors.

Rain patterns in New York are comparable to the rest of the Atlantic Coast. Expect wet days on occasion (about 120 days of precipitation each year, usually in groups of a few days at a time), but don't worry if you're caught unprepared; in heavy-traffic areas of the city, umbrella sellers emerge like magic at the day's first drops.

COUNSELING SERVICES

Life in New York—just like life everywhere—can be trying; thankfully, the city has a myriad of mental health treatment options available for those in need.

Counseling services in the city run the gamut, including 24-hour hotlines, private practitioners, and support groups. If ever you're feeling in need of someone to talk to, the **Samaritans of New York** run a confidential suicide prevention hotline (*212-673-3000*), as does the **US Department of Health and Human Services** (*1-800-273-TALK*). You can also call the **Mental Health Organization of New York** (*1-800-LifeNet*), where someone is always available to speak with you about family problems, relationship issues, drug and alcohol abuse, or anxiety and depression, as well as to give you advice on how to help family members or friends you feel may be at risk.

If you're a student, all major universities have psychological health centers and psychiatrists; contact your school's health services office for help navigating the system. If you're not a student, it can be hard to choose from among the thousands of doctors in the city. Go through your primary care provider or an insurance company to narrow down the field, as well as to increase the likelihood of matching up with a doctor who accepts your insurance plan, as private practitioners can be pricey. An hour of therapy in New York can cost anywhere from $100-350, and insurance hardly ever covers the full cost; for a more affordable alternative, consult the **National Institute for the Psychotherapies Training Institute** (*nip-inst.org*), where therapists-in-training and new therapists offer one-on-one counseling for anywhere from $20-50 an hour, based on a sliding scale.

Local support groups are another economical option. The **NYC Depressive and Man-Depressive Group** (*917-445-2399*), for example, offers free support groups for those suffering from depression. The country's premier eating disorder center, the **Renfrew Center** (*11 East 36th Street at Fifth*), also has an outpost in Manhattan that offers extensive inpatient and outpatient services. You can also visit one of the city's many free and confidential health clinics; call the **NYU Medical Center** (*917-544-0735*) for more information.

For a more extensive directory of mental health resources as well as accurate information about diagnoses and treatments, turn to the **New York State Office of Mental Health** (*omh.state.ny.us*). And of course, in the case of any health emergency, dial **911**.

DIETARY RESTRICTIONS

Diners who follow restricted diets, whether based on religion, medical conditions, or lifestyle choices, need not fear eating out in New York.

A city whose population is about 13% Jewish has no choice but to abound with kosher restaurants and delis; go to *shamash.org/kosher* for the web's most extensive list of certified dining spots. For those who prefer to cook at home, most supermarkets and grocery stores offer a limited selection of kosher products—**Fairway** (*fairwaymarket.com*) and **Zabar's** (*zabars.com*) have particularly good selections. For the widest array, head over to one of the many large kosher supermarkets in Brooklyn, or shop online at *kosher.com*. Muslims who adhere to Islamic dietary law also have a myriad of options in the city; the website *zabihah.com* has an extensive list of halal restaurants and markets in all five boroughs.

Those with medical dietary restrictions like lactose intolerance or celiac disease know that most restaurants worth their salt offer options to accommodate any condition, although there are many eateries in New York with specialized menus as well. The Upper West Side restaurant **Josie's** (*josiesnyc.com*) is famously dairy-free, and the seven city locations of the burrito mini-chain **Block-head's** (*blockheads.com*) tout their ability to make any dish lactose-free. For those who can't take the wheat, *glutenfreerestaurants.org* has a list of around 40 restaurants in the city that specialize in non-gluten based foods.

New York is also a veritable paradise for vegetarians and vegans. Nearly every restaurant offers some vegetarian options, usually including at least one entrée, but don't hesitate to ask your waiter if you want reassurance; some dishes may look vegetarian on the menu, but have hidden ingredients like gelatin, beef stock, and fish sauce that can upset your best efforts. To be completely certain, go to one of the many restaurants in the city that specialize exclusively in meatless fare; the local blog *supervegan.com* has the best list of vegetarian and vegan restaurants around.

For carnivores who still want to eat with a clean conscience, most high-end restaurants in New York are increasingly using organic and locally-produced ingredients—just ask your server if it's not already noted on the menu. There are also many restaurants that serve only organic cuisine; visit *lowimpactliving.com*, which has a searchable database of organic restaurants nationwide, to find one nearby. For the cook-at-home crowd looking for the freshest untreated produce around, check with the **Council on the Environment of New York City** (*cenyc.com*) to find a schedule of farmer's markets throughout the boroughs.

The dining reviews throughout the neighborhood sections of this book include many restaurants with specialized menus; each review is clearly marked.

EMERGENCY PHONE NUMBERS

911: Emergency Services
311: City Government Info and Non-Emergency Services
Child Abuse Report Line: 800-342-3720
Crime Victims Hotline: 212-577-7777
Gas Leak Report Line: 212-683-8830
Domestic Violence Report Line: 800-621-4673
NYPD Switchboard: 646-610-5000
NYPD Tip Line: 800-577- TIPS
Poison Control: 800-222-1222
Sex Crimes Report Line: 212-267-RAPE
Suicide Prevention: 212-673-3000

GOVERNMENT

With a population rivaling that of most states and some countries, New York City's municipal government can be as confusing as it is complex. At the top, the office of **Mayor Michael Bloomberg** and the 51-member **City Council** govern as the executive and legislative branches, respectively. As New York's mayors are notoriously hands-on, His Honor tends to draw much of the media spotlight away from the City Council, although it remains a powerful force in local politics. As the city's law-making body, the Council approves city budgets, monitors city agencies, and decides on matters of land use, among other legislative tasks. Council seats are distributed geographically throughout the five boroughs. Elections, which tend to be local affairs within individual communities, are held every four years; all elected officials, including Councilmembers and the Mayor, are limited to two terms of office. Currently, the Democratic Party has a majority in the Council, whereas recent mayors (Rudy Giuliani, 1994-2001; Bloomberg, 2002-present) have been moderate Republicans—at least until Bloomberg jumped ship to become an Independant. Both administrations worked closely with the Council on matters of security, reform, and quality of life.

Much of the Mayor's actual power resides in his **appointments**, including the Education Chancellor (Joel Klein) and Police Commissioner (Ray Kelly). The municipal government as a whole controls most city agencies through such a network of appointees and elected officials. Exceptions include the **MTA** (Metropolitan Transit Authority) and **Port Authority**, which, as "public-benefit corporations" chartered by the state itself, run independently of the city government.

THE GRID SYSTEM

The southern part of Manhattan can be difficult to navigate without a map or significant experience; below Houston, streets are named rather than numbered, and between Houston and 14th, the combination of numbered and named streets is equally confusing. Thanks to the famous **Commissioner's Plan of 1811**, however, most of the land above 14th street is laid out in a fairly mathematical, easy-to-follow pattern of intersecting streets and avenues. With a bit of knowledge, you can rely largely on intuition to get you where you need to go.

Numbered streets (1st-220th) cut east and west across the island, with numbers increasing from south to north. While some major streets have two-way traffic (14th, 23rd, 34th, 42nd, 57th, 125th), most are one way. Traffic on odd numbered streets runs west, while traffic on even numbered streets runs east.

Avenues, which are both numbered and named, run north-south down the length of Manhattan. Avenue numbers (First–Twelfth) get larger from east to west. On the West Side, traffic on odd numbered avenues runs downtown, while traffic on even numbered avenues runs uptown. On the

City Hall

East Side, just to keep things interesting, the rule reverses. Most named streets are two-way, at least in certain sections. Notable exceptions are Lexington, which runs downtown, and Madison, which runs uptown.

GROCERIES

In a city where the diversity of food markets mirrors the diversity of the population itself, shopping for groceries can be downright thrilling. Small, independent grocers abound, adding their charm-

The Commissioner's Plan of 1811

ing character to the culinary landscape; every neighborhood has at least one local favorite where the faces are familiar and the prices are almost as good as at the big chains. As you explore your new home, ask around to learn what your neighbors recommend, then get to know your grocers—you'll be seeing a lot of them.

In addition to the smaller independents, there are a few large supermarkets with outposts throughout the city. The no-frills chains **C-Town** (*ctownsupermarkets.com*) and **Gristedes** (*gristedes.com*) have locations scattered throughout New York's residential areas, and offer competitive prices on staples and base-level groceries. The **Food Emporium** (*thefoodemporium.com*) and **D'Agostino** (*dagnyc.com*) are slightly more upscale versions of the same basic idea, offering a more pleasant atmosphere and better quality products at higher, but still reasonable, prices. **Morton Williams** (*mortonwilliams.com*) has ten small markets in Manhattan and the

Bronx; each is tailored to the neighborhood so it doesn't feel like a chain, but prices are relatively high for what you get.

If you're planning a major shopping trip, it's worth it to go to **Fairway** (*fairwaymarket.com*), the undisputed best all-around supermarket in the city. The mini-chain has three spacious locations (Upper West Side, Harlem, and Redhook, Brooklyn), each selling all the basics you'd expect along with a wide variety of gourmet items and a staggering amount of fresh produce—a veritable foodie's paradise. The Harlem location even has a multi-room walk-in freezer where meats and cold products are stored, and provides customers with heavy coats to wear as they shop. (What will you find in your grocer's freezer? Yourself!). Best of all, they've got some of the lowest prices in the city. The closest downtown equivalent is **Trader Joe's** (*142 East 14th Street at Irving*), a national chain known for high quality and reasonable prices, which just opened up a location in Union Square. Go for the famed "two buck chuck" wine, although it costs a bit more than it used to.

For discerning customers, New York's upscale markets are the most gourmet option, but also the most expensive. The four Manhattan locations of the national chain **Whole Foods** (*wholefoodsmarket.com*) each offer a huge selection of natural and organic foods in a full-service atmosphere, and have recently become shopping destinations for the up-market crowd. **Citarella** (*citarella.com*) and **Dean and Deluca** (*deandeluca.com*), whose locations are peppered throughout Manhattan, offer smaller stores with more selective product lines and gourmet prepared foods. There's also **Zabar's** (*2245*

Broadway at 80th), an old-school New York institution in a class of its own. The aisles are tiny and crowded, but the experience is a must-have.

Of course, if you can't make it out, *FreshDirect.com*, *netgrocer.com*, or *urbanorganic.com* will make your life that much easier by bringing the groceries to you.

HOSPITALS

24-hour emergency rooms are available at the following hospitals if you find yourself in need.

DOWNTOWN WEST
St. Vincent's Hospital and Medical Center
153 West 11th Street (at Seventh; **1 2 3** to 14th)
212-604-7998

DOWNTOWN EAST
Beth Israel Medical Center
281 First Avenue (at 16th; **L** to First Avenue)
212-420-2000

MIDTOWN WEST
St. Luke's-Roosevelt Hospital Center
425 West 59th Street (at Columbus; **1 A C B D** to Columbus Circle)
212-523-4000

MIDTOWN EAST
NYU Medical Center
550 First Avenue (at 33rd; **6** to 33rd)
212-263-7300

UPTOWN WEST
St. Luke's-Roosevelt Hospital Center
1111 Amsterdam Avenue (at 113th; **1** to 116th)
212-523-4000

Columbia Presbyterian Medical Center
622 West 168th Street (at Broadway; **1 A C** to 168th)
212-305-2500

UPTOWN EAST
Lenox Hill Hospital
100 East 77th Street (at Park; **6** to 77th)
212-434-2000

Mount Sinai Medical Center
1190 Fifth Avenue (at 100th; **6** to 103rd)
212-241-6500

INTERNET

Home internet is a veritable necessity in our modern age. Unfortunately, connecting can be both expensive and a hassle. If your computer has wireless capabilities and you live in a busy area, it's possible that your apartment is close enough to a wireless hotspot—or an unwitting neighbor—to get internet for free at home. If not, it's easy to find **free wireless** as long as you're willing to lug around your laptop. Most major parks, universities, and libraries offer it, as do many cafés and hotel lobbies. Go to *jiwire.com* for a list and maps of specific locations.

If you find yourself having to pay for internet access, the city's major high-speed providers are **Time Warner**, **Optimum**, **Verizon** and **RCN**. Expect to pay $30-50 per month, although you can save a little money if you buy a package that bundles internet with cable or phone service. Go to *newyorkutilities.com* to compare rates and plans available in your neighborhood.

LIQUOR LAWS

Although liquor laws are less strict in New York than they are in many areas of the country, there are a few things you need to know if you want to party in the city.

Drinking in public is illegal, although these laws are loosely enforced. The standard fine is

$25, conveniently payable by mail. The most commonly-caught offenders are those who bring paper bag-covered concoctions into the subway; watch out for undercover cops whose job it is to ticket miscreants.

Sale of beer and liquor is forbidden in New York State on Sundays before noon and after 9pm, as well as on Christmas Day. If Christmas Day falls on a Sunday, it's also forbidden on the following Monday. These rules, however, are often ignored, especially at independently owned convenience stores looking out for their bottom lines. Teetotalers can take comfort in the fact that it is forbidden for an establishment that sells beer or liquor to be located within 200 feet of the front entrance of a church, synagogue, or other place of worship.

Laws prohibiting possession of alcohol by a minor are inconsistently enforced. Police officers are not authorized to make arrests for possession alone, and have been known to ignore it altogether. The maximum punishment is 30 hours of community service. Purchase or attempted purchase of alcohol by a minor is more serious, resulting in up to 30 hours of community service and an additional fine of up to $100.

With its enormous bar and club industry, New York City is naturally haven to a thriving underground market dealing in false identification. Be warned, though; possession of a fake ID is a felony that could result in serious jail time, due in part to the growing concern over the use of false identification to aid terrorist plots. Over the past few years, the city has been cracking down on fake ID use, and the NYPD has been known to raid college bars frequented by underage drinkers. Fear of steep fines and lost liquor licenses has, in turn, caused clubs and bars to crack down at the door; underage partiers should be prepared for that thick-skulled bouncer to be armed with an ID scanner or blacklight.

If you have the misfortune of being underage in a bar that gets raided and a cop asks for your identification, seasoned party-goers—and probably your lawyer—would advise that you show your real ID. According to underground wisdom, if you deny that you presented a fake upon entry, the bar will take the heat instead of you. If your ID is confiscated by a bouncer, don't hang around—he's not allowed to detain you, and the longer you wait, the more likely you are to get arrested.

PANHANDLING

Homelessness continues to be a major problem in New York City. Despite Mayor Bloomberg's best efforts, around 35,000 people stay in shelters each night, in addition to the thousands who sleep on the streets rather than endure deplorable shelter conditions. The desperate cycle is hard to escape; only about 17% of the city's homeless are employed, a trend that is difficult to reverse due to rampant mental illness, lack of permanent addresses, and the difficulty of acquiring presentable clothes for interviews.

Though New York City is home to a wide variety of public and private aid organizations that provide food and shelter, panhandling is as common as ever. Though beggars are rarely dangerous, it's best not to open wide your wallet in front of them. If you do chose to give, keep a few singles or some change in your front pocket for the purpose. Some panhandlers are more aggressive than others; if you feel uncomfortable, just walk away.

Before you give to those on the street, however, keep in mind that around half of the city's homeless are victims of chronic mental illness, and many suffer from a dependence on drugs or alcohol. To ensure that your money doesn't go to support harmful behavior, consider giving food instead of money, or bypass panhandlers altogether and donate to a reputable aid organization instead.

PETS

New York offers a unique set of obstacles to would-be pet owners. If you can't do without your four-legged best friend, be prepared to include him or her in your apartment search—many buildings have strict policies prohibiting large breeds, pets with fur and/or claws, or even pets in general. If you do find an acquiescent landlord, providing your pet with enough space to live free can be rough in a city where each square foot of apartment space costs hundreds of dollars. To make things easier, consider investing in a **dogwalking service** so that Buddy doesn't have to stay cooped up while you're at work all day. **Obedience schools** can

A Manhattan Dog Walker

help you house train your pet, and some even offer socialization classes and pet therapy. Go to *downtownpets.com* for a full list of resources.

Small pets are another alternative; caged animals and fish save both space and hassle. National stores like **PetCo** (*petco.com*) or the tri-state area chain **Petland Discounts** (*petlanddiscounts.com*) have locations throughout the city and knowledgeable staffs that can help you set up your new habitat. Those set on having a dog or a cat should consider adopting from the **ASPCA** (*424 East 92nd at First; 212-876-7700*). You'll not only be adopting a friend, but probably saving an animal's life while you're at it. The center also offers low-cost spaying and neutering, and free advice.

If your pet gets sick, check out *downtownpets.com* for a list of veterinarians and animal hospitals in your area. Many, like **Heart of Chelsea Animal Hospital** (*257 West 18th Street at Eighth*), offer extended hours and a holistic approach to animal medicine, while others, like **Urban Vets** (*212-674-6200*), do 24-hour housecalls in dire situations.

SAFETY

Though high crime rates in the '70s, '80s and '90s gave New York a reputation as one of the country's most dangerous cities, former mayor Rudy Giuliani's controversial hard-line crackdown on crime helped turn the tide. In the past decade, crime rates—including rates of murder, assault, and burglary—have dropped dramatically. With the lowest crime rate among America's 10 largest cities, New York is actually a very safe place, with the same overall crime rate as Boise, Idaho. Manhattan and Staten Island are the safest boroughs, with the exception of North Central Harlem, which joins south Bronx and central Brooklyn as the city's murder hotspots. It's important to take simple precautions to ensure your safety no matter where you go, but be extra vigilant in dangerous areas to avoid being pickpocketed, robbed, or worse.

To ward off pickpockets and purse-snatchers, carry your wallet in your front pocket, and keep a hand on your bag when you're in a crowded area. Be especially aware in large subway stations, bars, clubs, and other environments where constant contact with other people makes it easier for thieves to grab your wallet.

Though random muggings now happen much less frequently than in years past, it's never a good idea to carry large amounts of cash on your person. Despite the perceived inconvenience, it's better to make frequent stops at any of the city's thousands of ATMs than to have all your cash lost or stolen—you can find one in nearly any bank or drug store, and most are open 24 hours.

When traveling at night, keep to well-lit areas and major avenues rather than side streets. If you're alone or unfamiliar with the neighborhood, consider taking a cab instead of public transportation. If you do ride the subway, try to get into the same car as the train conductor.

If at all possible, stick to yellow cabs when taking taxis—unlicensed gypsy cabs are unregulated and potentially dangerous. If there are no yellow cabs and you're in a tight spot, negotiate the price up front—gypsy cabs are almost universally unmetered—and keep an eye on where the driver is taking you. If you begin to feel uncomfortable, ask the driver to pull over in a well-lit area and let you out.

On the whole, the best way to avoid becoming a victim of crime is to act confident and secure at all times. Never look lost or confused, even if you are. Your parents always warned you that criminals can smell fear, and they can—a bewildered tourist is like a wounded baby wildebeest to the predatory petty criminal. Don't make yourself an obvious target, use common sense, and you'll have much less reason to worry.

SALES TAX

The sales tax in New York City currently stands at **8.375%**, the combination of a **4% state sales tax** and a **4.375% city sales tax**. Not everything you purchase, however, will be subject to taxation. The frequently-changing laws are at the discretion of the powers that be, although generally, the precedent calls for tax exemption on basic necessities like simple food and clothing, and full tax on luxuries and non-essentials.

Non-prepared foods are tax-free, meaning that you're safe on most of your grocery store purchases. Certain beverages, however, are taxed, including soft drinks, alcoholic beverages, and juice drinks with less than 70% real fruit juice. Prepared foods like sandwiches and heated products are also subject to taxation—in general, expect to pay tax at restaurants and for any prepared food bought at a grocery. Farmers are notably exempt from this rule; all purchases made at streetside farmer's markets will be tax free.

Since April 2006, tax is only applied to indi-

NYPD Cars

vidual items of **clothing or footwear** that cost $110 or more. The cost of your total bill doesn't matter—as long as no single item exceeds the $110 cap, you can charge up a storm and still avoid paying tax. Accessories and luxury items, however, such as handbags, watches, umbrellas, and clothing for pets and dolls, are always taxed, regardless of their cost.

Most other material goods are taxed, with the exception of periodicals, glasses, hearing aids, medicine, medical equipment, and prosthetic limbs.

Services follow the same general rule. Tanning, manicures, hair salons, beauticians, electrolysis procedures, massages, private investigators, bodyguards, gyms, and health clubs are all subject to tax; laundering services, shoe repair, and veterinary services are not.

SMOKING

Although cigarette smoking as an urban phenomenon is amply ingrained into the American cultural philosophy, New York is not a smoker-friendly city. Ever since the **state-wide smoking ban** of 2003, all bars, restaurants, clubs, and workplaces are non-smoking—smoke in the street or the park if you will, but don't even think about lighting up indoors unless you're in a private home and have the express permission of the owner.

As a result of the ban, the front doorways and surrounding areas of most of the city's hotels, restaurants, and office buildings have transformed into social smoking spots. As a general rule, though, it's a good idea to take a few steps away from others before indulging—New Yorkers tend to be easily irritated by second-hand smoke, and won't have any problem letting you know. If nothing does it for you like smoking indoors, a limited number of "cigarette bars" around the city, such as **Circa Tabac** (*32 Watts Street at Sixth*), allow you to eat, drink, smoke, and be merry all at the same time, just like in the days of yore.

A word to the wise: if you can, buy your cancer sticks outside of the city, as the average pack will cost you just under $8.

TELEPHONES

In these days of widespread cell phone use and inexpensive calling plans, home phone service in the city is becoming less and less necessary. Companies like **Verizon** and **AT&T Wireless** have good cell coverage all over the five boroughs and offer competitive pricing, but steer clear of **T-Mobile**, whose service in the city can be spotty, even in Manhattan. If you must have a home phone, companies like **Verizon**, **RCN**, and **Time Warner** offer service in the area; go to *newyorkutilities.com* to compare rates and plans available in your neighborhood.

For cheap international rates, buy a **phone card** from your neighborhood drug store, convenience store, or newsstand. You can use it to connect anywhere in the world through a local or toll-free phone number, and a $10 card will get you 2-10 hours of talk time, depending on where you're calling. If you don't mind talking through your computer's speakers and microphone, download **Skype** (*skype.com*), a popular internet-to-phone program, and use it to call anywhere in the world for about two cents a minute.

TELEVISION

TV and cable services in New York are equivalent to those throughout the US. The city's major service providers—**Time Warner, Optimum, DirecTV**, and **RCN**—provide packages that cost an average of $50-70 a month for a few hundred channels—less for basic packages, more for premium channels and perks. Most companies also offer bundled packages, which save money when you purchase cable in conjunction with Internet or home phone service. Time Warner is by far the most prominent company in the city, but coverage varies by neighborhood, so check out *newyorkutilities.com* for a list of providers and packages available in your area.

Man on cell phone in New York

TIPPING

The rules of tipping in New York are similar to those in the rest of the country, with a few urban additions. Although the decision of just how much to tip is based on the quality of service received, it is almost never optional, except in cases of truly abominable service.

Personal care and **service providers**, such as employees at salons and spas, expect 15-20% of the service's base cost as gratuity.

At **restaurants**, a good rule of thumb is to double the tax for the **server**'s tip, plus a bit extra if you're happy with the service. **Sommeliers** should receive 15-20% of the wine bill at upscale restaurants and wine bars. **Coat check**, **valet**, and **bathroom attendants** should be tipped $1-2 for each item or visit.

At **coffee shops** and restaurants with counter service, drop your change in the tip jar near the checkout, and add a dollar or two if you're pleased with the service.

At bars and clubs, tip **bartenders** $1-2 for drinks at the bar, or 15-20% of the total bill on a tab. If you plan to order multiple drinks at a crowded spot, tip a base sum up front to ensure speedy service, then add on throughout the evening; bartenders will often ignore bad tippers, especially when there's a crowd.

At hotels and airports, **porters**, **bellmen**, and **skycaps** should be tipped $1-2 per bag—more if the luggage is especially heavy or fragile. Concierges should be tipped a dollar or two for hailing a cab, and around $5 if they help with loading or unloading luggage. Room service waiters should be tipped around 15% of the bill.

Taxi drivers should be tipped around 15% of the total fare. For short trips, round up to the nearest dollar plus one—never tip less than a buck, unless the ride was particularly offensive.

ZIP CODES

All zip codes in New York, Pennsylvania, and Delaware begin with the number one; those in New York State begin with 10-14, while those in NYC proper begin with 10 or 11. There are multiple codes for each borough: **Manhattan** has 10001-10282; **Staten Island**, 10301-10314; the **Bronx**, 10451-10475; and **Brooklyn**, 11201-11256. Just to make things more interesting, there are some gaps in the numerical sequence—especially in **Queens**, which uses the codes 11101-11109, 11351-11385, 11411-11436, and 11691-11697. Areas that have similar zip codes (10026, 10026, and 10027, for instance) tend to be located near each other geographically, although as population grows unevenly and new codes are created to fit the needs of the post office, that tendency has almost as many exceptions as not. There's no reliable formula for determining location by code, or vice versa.

As in other areas of the country, New York zip codes can be status symbols. Recent announcement of the post office's plans to break up 10021, the country's 13th richest zip code, into three parts—effectively reducing the number of residents by two-thirds—caused an uproar, albeit a well-mannered one, among the Upper East Side elite.

JANUARY

New York Times Arts & Leisure Weekend
Early January
The Gray Lady rings in the new year by assembling famous musicians, authors, and actors to discuss their work.
888.698.1870. artsandleisureweekend.com. Ticket prices vary.

New York National Boat Show
Early January
Motor yachts, performance boats, and other watercrafts go on display at the Jacob K. Javits Convention Center.
Javits Center (655 West 34th Street at Twelfth). 212.216.2000. newyorkboatshow.com. Adults $15, Kids $8.

Martin Luther King Jr. Day
Third Monday in January
The city celebrates our nation's greatest civil rights leader with a parade of over 25,000 people.
Fifth Avenue from 61st to 86th.

Winter Restaurant Week
Late January
The city's finest restaurants offer three-course meals for beautifully reduced prices.
212.484.1222. Lunch $24.07, nycvisit.com; Dinner $35 (not including beverage, tax, or tip).

FEBRUARY

Chinese New Year Festival
Late January or Early February
Chinatown struts its stuff with a ten-day festival to ring in the new year, on a date determined by the lunar cycle.
212.431.9740.

Mercedes-Benz Fashion Week
Second week of February
Models, designers, fashion journalists, and couture fanatics of all kinds congregate to preview the fall season's collections.
Bryant Park (Fifth Avenue at 42nd). mercedesbenzfashionweek.com.

Westminster Kennel Club Show
Mid-February
More than 2,000 dogs of 169 breeds and varieties compete for Best in Show.
Madison Square Garden (34th Street at Seventh). 800.455.3647. westminsterkennelclub.org; General admission: one-day $40, two-day $75; Reserved seating: $125.

Annual Urban Pillow Fight
Late February
Hundreds of New Yorkers grab their downiest cushions, clobber one another, and blot out the sky out with feathers.
Union Square (14th Street at Union Square East). 516.312.0693. newmindspace.com.

International Art Expo
Late February to Early March
Art of all kinds attracts dealers, publishers, interior designers, and other professionals to the Javits Center.
Javits Center (655 West 34th Street at Twelfth). 800.827.7170. artexpos.com.

MARCH

St. Patrick's Day Parade
March 17
Irish expats and beer lovers from all nations celebrate all things green—and the conversion of the pagans in the 5th century AD.
Fifth Avenue from 44th to 86th. 212.465.6741. saintpatricksdayparade.com.

Easter Day Parade
Easter Sunday
Old-fashioned fashionistas show off their flamboyant bonnets at this free-form procession.
Fifth Avenue from 49th to 57th. 212.484.1222.

Blades Over Broadway
Late March
Skaters take to the ice, moving to the sounds of Broadway standards.
Riverbank State Park (145th Street at Riverside). 646.698.3440. figureskatinginharlem.org Suggested donation $5.

JFK Runway Run
April
Joggers regress to childhood and pretend they're airplanes while running this 5K charity race on the JFK runways.
John F. Kennedy International Airport. 718.244.5140. jfkrunwayrun.org

Annual Urban Pillowfight

Night of A Thousand Gowns

April

A drag-heavy charity ball benefits God's Love We Deliver, which brings food to individuals with AIDS and other life-threatening diseases.

212.501.4797. imperialcourtny.org

The Big Swim

Mid-April

Schoolchildren race in the Delacorte pool, while Olympic swimmers wait for them at the finish.

Asphalt Green (555 East 90th Street at East End). 212.369.8890. asphaltgreen.org

Dachshund Spring Fiesta

Late April

The Dachshund Friendship Club celebrates the beloved cylindrical canines.

Washington Square Park (West 4th Street at MacDougal). 212.475.5512. dachshundfriendshipclub.com.

TriBeCa Film Festival

Late April-Early May

Robert DeNiro's labor of love attracts movie buffs for screenings of new and independent films at venues throughout Lower Manhattan.

212.941.2400. tribecafilmfestival.org Ticket prices vary.

MAY

Great Five Boro Bike Tour

Early May

Over 30,000 bikers roll through the boroughs from Manhattan to Staten Island, covering over 42 miles and five bridges.

Battery Park (Battery Place at State Street). 212.932.0778. bikenewyork.org

Ninth Avenue International Food Festival

Weekend after Mother's Day

Stands set up shop in Hell's Kitchen to hawk street food from all around the world.

Ninth Avenue from 37th to 57th. 212.581.7217.

Fleet Week

Late May

New York City celebrates service on the sea as 3,000 sailors from the U.S. Navy and Coast Guard interact with locals and show off the latest in military equipment.

fleetweek.navy.mil.

Washington Square Outdoor Art Exhibit

Late May-Early June

Over 200 painters, sculptors, photographers, jewelry-makers, and craftspeople descend upon Washington Square Park for an annual exhibit started by Jackson Pollock and Willem DeKooning.

Washington Square Park (West 4th Street at MacDougal). 212.982.6255. washingtonsquareoutdoorartexhibit.org

JUNE

Puerto Rican Day Parade

Second Sunday of June

Three million people celebrate to the sounds of salsa, meringue, and plena at the world's largest single-day celebration of Puerto Rican culture.

Fifth Avenue from 44th to 85th. 718.401.0404. nationalpuertoricandayparade.org.

Museum Mile Festival

Second Tuesday in June

NYC's biggest museums welcome visitors for free as live bands, street performers, and musicians replace the usual traffic on Fifth Avenue.

Fifth Avenue from 82nd to 105th. 212.606.2296. museummilefestival.org

Lesbian, Gay, Bisexual, and Transgender March

Last Sunday in June

Over 10,000 people come out for the city's flashiest parade, commemorating the anniver-

sary of the Stonewall Riots.

From Fifth Avenue at 52nd to Christopher Street at Greenwich. 212.807.7433. nycpride.org

Shakespeare in Central Park
June through August
The Public Theater offers free performances of the Bard's works—usually featuring big-name stars—to anyone willing to wait for tickets.

Delacorte Theater, Central Park (mid-park at 80th). 212.539.8750. publictheater.org

JULY

Lincoln Center Festival
Last Three Weeks in July
The arts hub hosts a variety of performing artists from around the globe.

Lincoln Center (65th Street at Columbus). 212.546.5103. lincolncenter.org. Ticket prices vary.

Tap City
Mid-July
The biggest tap festival in the world offers classes geared towards all levels, along with evening performances by leading tap artists.

646.230.9564. atdf.org. Class and ticket prices vary.

International Dance Festival
Late July
Dance troupes from around the world perform traditional and modern dances.

Dicapo Opera Theater (184 East 76th at Third). 212.233.2323. internationaldancefestival.org. Ticket prices vary.

Summer Restaurant Week
Late July
Once again, the city's finest restaurants offer three-course meals for beautifully reduced prices.

212.484.1222. Lunch $24.07, nycvisit.com; Dinner $35 (not including beverage, tax, or tip).

AU-GUST

Harlem Week
Throughout August
The Greater Harlem Chamber of Commerce celebrates the neighborhood's culture and history with workshops, performances, and festivals.

212.862.7200. harlemweek.harlemdiscover.com.

Lincoln Center Out-of-Doors
Throughout August
A month-long series of free, interactive workshops and performances for families is held near Lincoln Center.

Damrosch Park (62nd Street at Amsterdam). 212.875.5108. lincolncenter.org

New York International Fringe Festival
Mid-August
Over 20 venues in the Lower East Side feature theater, musicals, dance, and comedy as part of the largest multi-arts festival on the continent.

212.279.4488. fringenyc.org

U.S. Open
Late August-Early September
The final event of the tennis season brings racqueted superstars and their fans to Flushing's Arthur Ashe Stadium.

USTA Billie Jean King National Tennis Center (Flushing Meadows Corona Park, Queens). usopen.org.

SEPTEMBER

Big Apple Performing Arts Festival
September
Theater, music, and dance meet the carnival in this most expressive of street fairs.

Seventh Avenue from 47th to 57th. 212.809.4900. nyc-streetfairs.com.

Olympus Fashion Week
Mid-September

Fashionistas converge for a prelude of the coming spring's designs.

Bryant Park (Fifth Avenue at 42nd). 617.780.2243. bryantpark.org. Ticket prices vary.

Broadway on Broadway
Mid-September

A free outdoor concert revue presents previews of upcoming musicals and performances from old Broadway favorites.

Times Square (Broadway at 42nd). broadwayonbroadway.com.

New York Film Festival
Late September to Mid-October

This 17-day showcase of new international cinematic endeavors, which accepts submissions from filmmakers of all experience levels and genres, comes to Lincoln Center.

Frederick P. Rose Hall (Broadway at 60th). 212.875.5050. filmlinc.com.

OCTOBER

Columbus Day Parade
Second Monday in October

He might have enslaved the Native Americans and left a legacy of violence in his wake, but at least we all get a day off work and a chane to make merry with a parade in celebration of Italian culture.

Fifth Avenue from 44th to 79th. 212.249.2360. columbuscitizensfd.org.

Rockefeller Center Tree Lighting

International Vintage Poster Fair
Mid-October
Over 25 vendors sell tens of thousands of original posters from the 19th century to the 1980s.
Metropolitan Pavilion (123 West 18th Street at Sixth). 800.856.8069. posterfair.com.

Greenwich Village Halloween Parade
October 31
The nation's largest public Halloween party brings two million costumed revelers to the Village.
Sixth Avenue from Broome to 23rd. halloween-nyc.com

NOVEMBER

New York Comedy Festival
Early November
Over fifty of the biggest names in stand-up comedy perform throughout the city in this five-day event.
nycomedyfestival.com.

Chocolate Show
Mid-November
Chocolatiers and pastry chefs come together for a weekend of mouthwatering innovation.
Metropolitan Pavilion (123 West 18th Street at Sixth) and Altman Building (125 West 18th Street at Sixth). 646.638.0771. chocolateshow.com. Adults $28 per day.

Christmas Tree Lighting at Rockefeller Center
Late November
Top-40 performers serenade a tightly-packed crowd before the famed tree is illuminated.
Rockefeller Center (Fifth Avenue at 50th). 212.632.3975. rockefellercenter.com.

Macy's Thanksgiving Day Parade
Fourth Thursday in November
Wide-eyed children marvel at the mammoth floats and marching bands that pass through Midtown's closed-off streets.
Central Park West at 77th to Seventh Avenue at 34th. 212.695.4400. macysparade.com

New York City Marathon
Early November
World-class athletes and weekend warriors do their best to tough out all 26.2 miles.
Fort Wadsworth, Staten Island, to Central Park. 212.423.2249. ingnycmarathon.org.

DECEMBER

Radio City Christmas Spectacular
Mid-November to December
Families flock to watch the Rockettes and their eerily synchronized legs.
1260 Sixth Avenue at 50th. 212.307.7171. radiocity.com. $40-100.

The Nutcracker
Late November to December
The dancers of the New York City Ballet tell the story of Marie's magical Christmas gift.
Lincoln Center (Columbus Avenue at 63rd). 212.870.5570. nycballet.com. $20-96.

Emerald Nuts Midnight Run
December 31
Exercise fanatics ring in the New Year with a 5 K race through Central Park.
Central Park at 72nd St. 212.860.4455. nyrr.org.

Times Square New Year's Eve Bash
December 31
Join the countdown and watch the ball drop at the city's biggest bash of the year.
Times Square. 212.768.1560. timessquarenyc.org.

DOWNTOWN

FINANCIAL DISTRICT

The Staten Island Ferry docks, the commuter trains pull in, and a sea of yellow cabs open their doors. It's another early weekday morning, and the suit-and-briefcase crowds are already on the way to making their first million. Against the backdrop of imposing glass monoliths, the daily feeding frenzy—buying and selling, making and breaking—is about to begin. The morning bell is poised to ring.

Located on the southern tip of Manhattan, the Financial District is the epicenter of the nation's economy—and the world's. Because of its easy access to both the Atlantic and the mainland, Manhattan's downtown harbor flourished from its earliest days, making the island the biggest center of commerce in North America. Shipping eventually gave way to finance as the neighborhood's driving industry and marinas ceded ground to larger and larger buildings, culminating in the cathedrals of commerce that define today's city skyline.

Downtown has become especially well known following September 11th, 2001; the eerily empty space of Ground Zero, a reminder of where the Twin Towers once stood, still draws flocks of people coming to pay their respects.

The neighborhood is also home to some of the city's most spectacular parks, from lush Bowling Green to gorgeous Wagner Park. The development of Battery Park City on the west side of southern Manhattan has brought luxury high rises, gourmet delis, and a much-needed residential feel to the area.

On Wall Street at night, the Financial District becomes a ghost town—but soon enough, the cabs will descend, the sun will rise over the skyscrapers, and the center of the capitalist world will be reborn.

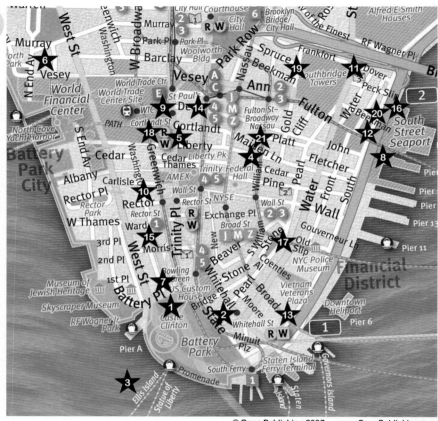

© Opus Publishing 2007 — www.OpusPublishing.com

FINANCIAL DISTRICT

SIGHTS
1. Battery Park
2. Castle Clinton
3. Ellis Island
4. Federal Reserve Bank
5. Ground Zero
6. Irish Hunger Memorial
7. National Museum of the American Indian
8. South Street Seaport

9. St. Paul's Chapel
10. The Wall Street Bull

DINING
11. Bridge Café
12. Harbour Lights
13. Harry's at Hanover Square
14. Les Halles
15. Mangia

16. Seaport Café
17. Smorgas Chef

SHOPPING
18. Century 21
19. J&R Music and Computer World
20. Neighborhoodies
21. Strand Annex

Sights/Attractions

Battery Park

This park, which derives its name from the battery of cannons placed on the site to fend off the British during the Revolutionary War, is filled with many important monuments and statues, including the nation's first WWI memorial and an eternal flame to honor the victims of September 11th.

State Street at Broadway. batterypark.com. **1** *to South Ferry.*

Castle Clinton

This former Revolutionary War fort is primarily used today as a waiting area and rest stop for tourists taking the ferry to the Statue of Liberty and Ellis Island. The circular, roofless structure, renamed in 1817 to honor former mayor DeWitt Clinton, houses a small exhibit space detailing the history of the fort, as well as a preserved section of the Battery Wall, but don't expect too much—come more for the atmosphere than the amenities.

Battery Park (State Street at Pearl). 212.344.7220. nps. gov/cacl. Daily 8:30am-5pm. **1** R W *to Rector St.*

Ellis Island and the Statue of Liberty

A single ferry ride and fare will take you to both Ellis Island and the Statue of Liberty, two of the city's most popular attractions. As the city's first immigration center, the infamous Ellis Island was the port of welcome for all immigrants to New York City from 1892-1932. Visitors can trace the immigrants' path from the baggage registry rooms, view the American Immigrant Wall of Honor, and search for their own ancestors among the center's archives. The Statue of Liberty, perhaps the city's most recognizable icon, was

The Statue of Liberty

BATTERY PARK CITY

Although technically part of Manhattan, this add-on neighborhood can feel very far from the city—partly because 50 years ago, it didn't exist. A planned community designed to create a sense of suburban life within a massive urban metropolis, the 92 acres upon which Battery Park City was built are man-made, installed in the Hudson River from land primarily excavated during the construction of the original World Trade Center in the 1960s. Today, there's no way to tell where Manhattan used to end—it's as seamless as if the addition were a natural part of the land.

If you're roaming around lower Manhattan and want to know what it feels like to stand on new ground, head over and walk, bike, skate, or jog along the **ESPLANADE**, which runs the length of Battery Park City along the Hudson River. While you're there, covet the yachts of the area's wealthiest residents at **NORTH COVE** (*385 South End Avenue at Liberty*), or check out the rock wall in tiny **TEARDROP PARK** (*North End Avenue at Murray*). Then visit the **MUSEUM OF JEWISH HERITAGE** (*36 Battery Place at 1st*) or the **SKYSCRAPER MUSEUM** (*39 Battery Place at 1st*), a sleek space whose design mirrors its subject matter. Limit your visits to the daytime hours, though; the area is highly residential, and tends to shut down at night.

given by the French government in 1886 to commemorate the bond between the two nations. Since September 11th, 2001, the crown has been closed to tourists—the torch has been closed since 1916, due to the Black Tom Explosion, a little-remembered act of sabotage during WWI on an American arms reserve in New Jersey—but you can still climb to the top of the pedestal for a somewhat better view.

Ferries depart from Castle Clinton in Battery Park every 30 minutes. 212.363.3200. nps.gov/elis. Daily 9:30am-5:15pm. Adults $11.50. **1** R W *to Rector St.*

Federal Reserve Bank of New York

If you want to know how it feels to stand on $140 or so billion dollars, head to the Federal Reserve, reported to hold roughly one-third of the world's gold reserve in its subterranean vaults. The bank's informative displays and free hour-long tours lead visitors into the gold vault, and are worth the trip, but be sure to plan ahead—reservations must be

made at least a month in advance.

33 Liberty Street (at William). 212.720.6130. ny.frb. org. Tours M-F 9:30am-2:30pm. **1** R W *to Rector St.*

Ground Zero

Visitors flock to the former site of the World Trade Center towers to commemorate the victims of the September 11th, 2001 terrorist attacks and to see the ongoing construction of the Freedom Tower, a 1,776-foot-tall building that will emit light from its peak. Cranes and crumbled earth fill the fenced-off space where the towers once stood, with large photographs taken on September 11th displayed near a memorial that records the names of those who died.

Church Street at Liberty. buildthememorial.org. **1 2 3 A C** *to Chambers St.*

Irish Hunger Memorial

Uniquely designed to provide a bit of the rural Irish landscape amid skyscrapers and cement, this memorial to those who died in the mid-19th century Irish Potato Famine is reached by walking through a dark covered walkway as a voice recording recalls the tragedy of the millions of lives lost. Continue walking, and a gate leads visitors back outside and up a large, winding hill with plants and stones from various counties in Ireland, ending with a view of the river.

290 Vesey Street (at North End). batteryparkcity.org. **1 2 3 A C** *to Chambers St.*

National Museum of the American Indian

Marvel at the traditional Native American clothing, weaponry, jewelry, tools, and games that make up the impressive collection of artifacts at this branch of the Smithsonian. In addition to the historic collections, work by contemporary Native American artists and artisans attempt to connect the modern with the traditional in Native American culture. Go for a free movie screening, or to attend a powwow.

One Bowling Green (at State). 212.514.3700. nmai. si.edu. Daily 10am-5pm, Th 10am-8pm. Free. **4 5** *to Bowling Green.*

South Street Seaport

The pier and cobblestone streets of this historic port have acquired a few additions over the past 30 years, including clothing stores, boutiques, and a mini-mall, which make it decidedly more tourist-friendly than during its former life. Even without the shopping, it's the perfect place to spend a few hours with family or friends; catch a bite at one of the area's many seafood restaurants, or buy a ticket to the South Street Seaport Museum ($8) for access to the three historic ships permanently docked in the harbor. The Seaport also hosts events, including concerts, throughout the summer; with stunning views of

South Street Seaport

FAST FACTS

Scenic Stroll: The Esplanade

Major Subway Stations: Bowling Green (**4 5**), Broadway-Nassau (**A C**), Fulton Street (**J M Z**, **2 3**, **4 5**), Wall Street (**4 5**)

Urban Oasis: Battery Park

Notable Buildings: Castle Clinton, City Hall, U.S. Customs House

Neighborhood Landmarks: Ellis Island, Ground Zero, New York Stock Exchange, South Street Seaport, Wall Street Bull

Best View: Statue of Liberty

Best Deal: Century 21

Quintessential Neighborhood Event: Wall Street Market Opening Bell at 9:30am

Famous Historical Moment: On April 30, 1789 George Washington was inaugurated as the first U.S. president at Wall and Nassau Streets.

Kid-Friendly Place: Teardrop Park

---

the East River, it provides a literal breath of fresh air to stressed urban dwellers.

South Street at Fulton. 212.SEAPORT. southstreetseaport. com. **2 3 4 5 J M Z** *to Fulton St.*

St. Paul's Chapel

Completed in 1776 when the Financial District was nothing but a grassy field, St. Paul's Chapel holds the distinction of being Manhattan's oldest public building in continuous use; presidents from George Washington to Bill Clinton have sat in its white-painted pews. Trinity Church, based out of the chapel, has been serving the local Episcopalian community for 200 of those years, but took on its most crucial role in the wake of the September 11th terrorist attacks, when the church served as a refuge for thousands of rescue and recovery workers who slept and mourned under its roof during the following year.

209 Broadway (at Fulton). 212.233.4164. saintpaulschapel.org. **A C E** *to Chambers St.*

The Wall Street Bull

This 7,000-pound bronze statue, also called the "Charging Bull," is an icon of the Financial District, money, power, and New York itself. Artist Arturo Di Modica was reportedly inspired to create the beast as an encouraging tribute to American Capitalism after 1987's Black Monday, the day of the largest stock market losses in history. At a personal cost of $360,000, the sculptor created the uncommissioned, unfinanced statue and placed it in front of the Stock Exchange building illegally, where it quickly attracted attention. When the police hauled it away, the public protested; because of the resulting outcry, the city dropped its plans to impound the statue, installing it at its current location instead.

Broadway at Bowling Green. **2 3 4 5** *to Wall St.*

Dining
UPSCALE

Harry's at Hanover Square *Steakhouse*
If you're in the mood for suits, cigars, and meat, this Wall Street hangout is the place to go. Order a martini or a glass of scotch as you enjoy one of Harry's sumptuous steaks, or, if you're not into red meat, go for the equally exquisite lobster or swordfish. The wine list is extensive, including a good selection of after-dinner ports. It's all typical steakhouse fare, but with a lower Manhattan, power-player atmosphere that makes it worth the trek.

1 Hanover Square (at Pearl). 212.425.3412. Daily 11am-midnight. Appetizers $8-16, Entrées $26-43. **R W** *to Whitehall St.*

MID-RANGE

Bridge Café *New American*
Drenched in mystery and lore, the menu at Bridge Café is as haunting as the restaurant's history. Established as New York's first drinking establishment in 1855, the wooden bar has long been a popular stomping ground for pirates, former mayors, ladies of the evening, and even ghosts. Stop by for an evening of good food, great ambiance, and possibly apparitions—with a vast wine list, liberal portions, and colorful tableside tales spun by owner Adam Weprin, guests are in for an infinitely memorable meal. Whet your appetite with the warmed blue cheese soufflé served with grapes in port syrup, or select the jumbo soft shell crabs, perhaps the best in the neighborhood. The velvety chocolate indulgence is precisely that, but well worth the calories.

279 Water Street (at Dover). 212.227.3344. Sun-M 11:45-10, T-F 11:45am-11pm, Sat 5pm-midnight. Appetizers $8-15, Entrées $20-30. **2** *to Fulton St.*

Harbour Lights *Seafood, New American*
After spending a day exploring the South Street Seaport, there's no better place to give your legs a rest and your eyes a treat than this gem by the water. The raw bar is a nice way to settle into the meal, followed by perfectly cooked steaks and fish fresh from the sea. The food is a bit overpriced and the clientele a bit touristy, but the spectacular view makes it all worthwhile.

South Street Seaport Pier 17 (South Street at Fulton), 3rd floor. 212.227.2800. Daily 10am-midnight. Appetizers $9-14, Entrées $22-32. **2 3 4 5 6 A C J M** *to Fulton St.*

Les Halles Downtown *French, Steak*
Housed in a nearly 100-year-old building, warm lighting and a beautiful wood interior combine to form a warm ambiance at this quality French Bistro. Start your meal with a delectable steak tartare, prepared tableside by the wait staff, and continue with a melt-in-your-mouth "American beef, French style" entrée. The steak frites—the restaurant's most popular dish—is also a crowd pleaser. A hotspot for corporate lunches and after-work dinners, you'll leave full of good meat, and even with a little money left in your wallet.

15 John Street (at Broadway). 212.285.8585. Daily 8am-midnight. Appetizers $6-18, Entrées: $15-28. **2** *to Fulton St.*

Smorgas Chef *Scandanavian*
If you like being served succulent Swedish meatballs by tall Scandinavian waitresses, head to Smorgas Chef for fresh, hearty, balanced fare. Come for the food, but stay for the drinks—three of the creations were finalists in the Sidewalk Café Cocktail Competition, with fresh fruit and spices combined in innovative mixes that are worthy of the honor.

53 Stone Street (at William). 212.422.3500. Daily 10:30am-10:30pm. Appetizers $8-15, Entrées $11-$28. **2 3** *to Wall St.*

CASUAL

Mangia *Mediterranean*
Gourmet Mediterranean cuisine and a friendly waitstaff make Mangia alluring to crowds from

nearby businesses, galleries, and museums. With a diverse selection of pastas, sandwiches, and entrées—including an "antipasto table" with an impressive selection ranging from paella to rare tuna—expect a thrilling sit-down meal. You can also stop by the downstairs café for equally delicious take-out.

40 Wall Street (at Nassau). 212.425.4040. M-F 7am-4pm. Appetizers & Entrées $4-11. R W to Rector St.

Seaport Café *American*
The menu at this open-air café includes fresh pastas, sandwiches, and wraps, along with gourmet coffees and desserts, perfect for casual diners who don't want generic fast food or an expensive tab. The outdoor table area is great for people-watching, ensuring that diners won't miss any of the action at the lively pier: Enjoy a scrumptious pastry while taking in the fantastic view.

89 South Street (at Pier 17). 212.964.1120. M-Sat 10am-9pm, Sun 11am-8pm. Appetizers and Entrées $7-20. 2 3 4 5 6 A C J M to Fulton St.

Nightlife
As a nightlife destination, the Financial District has dwindled over the years. Nevertheless, if you're in the neighborhood in the evening and in dire need of refreshment, check out the super "pubby" **Irish Pub Ulysses** (*25 Pearl Street, 212.344.0800*), or **MacMenamin's Pub** (*89 South Street, 212.732.0007*), a saloon with frozen drinks and a full menu. Order one of the special 32-once Styrofoam buckets of beer at **Jeremy's Ale House** (*228 Front Street, 212.964.3537*), and if you're still craving ale but short on cash, head up to **The Patriot Saloon** (*110 Chambers Street, 212.748.1162*) for $5 pitchers of beer.

Shopping
Century 21
This often-overwhelming discount department store is not for the weary; with five levels of merchandise and crowds that rival Times Square, be prepared to battle it out with other bargain hunters for $70 Prada frocks or $25 pairs of DKNY jeans. If you can make it on a weekday, the crowds will be more manageable—but if you can handle the mess, the deals are always worth the effort.

22 Cortlandt Street (at Church). 212.227.9092. c21stores.com. M-F 7:45am-8:30pm, Sat 10-8, Sun 11-7. 2 3 A C to Fulton St.

J&R Music and Computer World
This downtown megastore, occupying almost an entire city block, is known for its low prices on electronics, computers, cameras, and music. Although the extensive selection can be hard to navigate, the knowledgeable staff will help you find what you need, and the prices can't be beat.

23 Park Row (at Beekman). 212.238.9000. jr.com. M-F 9am-7:30pm, Sat 9am-7:30pm, Sun 10:30-6:30. R W to City Hall.

Neighborhoodies
This unique clothing shop in the South Street Seaport specializes in customized hoodies, allowsing customers to quite literally wear their hometown allegiances on their sleeve. Create your own T-shirt with the name of your native borough, or choose from the store's pre-made designs.

89 South Street, 2nd Floor (at Beekman). 212.608.7285. neighborhoodies.com. M-Sat 10am-9pm, Sun 11am-8pm. 2 3 4 5 J M Z to Fulton St.

Strand Annex
This little sibling of the Village's famed Strand Bookstore is the Financial District's best discount bookseller. Browse the humble aisles for great book bargains, including many for less than $1, in categories ranging from "Modern Classics" to "Firefighting and Safety."

95 Fulton Street (at William). 212.732.6070. strandbooks.com. M-F 9:30am-9pm, Sat-Sun 11am-8pm. 2 3 4 5 A C J M Z to Fulton St.

SOHO

Famed fashion mag *Vogue* may keep its office in Times Square, but it clearly draws inspiration from the streets of SoHo. The narrow, often cobblestoned streets are packed with rail-thin models sporting the latest fashions and street vendors hawking the hottest accessories, side-by-side with chi-chi bars, indie cinemas, and spacious galleries.

SoHo, short for South of Houston Street—just don't pronounce the latter like a Texas town unless you want your inner tourist to show—was once a haven for struggling artists who couldn't make the Midtown rent. The area's spacious lofts proved to be ideal workspaces, and the starving bohemian set began discreetly moving into the area; although residing in a light-manufacturing zone was illegal, initially landlords turned a blind eye. But as more and more "illegal" lofts materialized, legalization became inevitable; laws slowly changed to fully accommodate more and more of the resident artists who were living here anyway.

In 1971, SoHo was designated as the first mixed-use zone for artist housing, and an Artist Certification Committee was formed to ensure that SoHo housing went only to artists. The committee still operates today, but has no enforcement power; both residents and landlords now routinely ignore the old artists-only policies.

Now, 5pm sees a changing of the guard at the Prince Street subway station, as those who work in SoHo, but could never afford to live here, pass by the Wall Street raiders returning home.

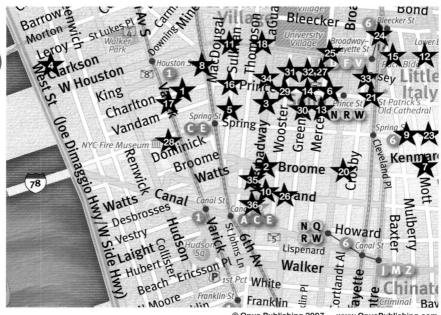

© Opus Publishing 2007 — www.OpusPublishing.com

SOHO/NOLITA

SIGHTS/ATTRACTIONS
1. Charlton Street
2. Haughwout Building
3. Little Singer Building
4. Trapeze School of New York

DINING
5. Fiamma Osteria
6. Mercer Kitchen
7. Public
8. Ama
9. Ceci-Cela
10. L'Ecole
11. Once Upon a Tart
12. Rialto
13. Woo Lae Oak
14. Zoë

NIGHTLIFE
15. Botanica
16. The Cub Room
17. Culture Club
18. Madame X
20. Ñ
21. Pravda
22. SoHo Grand Bar
23. Sweet and Vicious
24. Temple Bar

ARTS
25. Angelika Film Center

26. Deitch Projects
27. Joyce Soho
28. New York Fire Museum
29. New York Earth Room

SHOPPING
30. Anna Sui
31. Betsey Johnson
32. Face Stockholm
33. Housing Works Used Books Café
34. Prada
35. Scoop
36. Soho Antiques Fair and Flea Market

Sights/Attractions

Charlton Street
The stretch of Charlton Street filled with Federal-style redbrick townhouses provides the best modern approximation of what SoHo looked like before the cast iron boom of the mid-19th century. Built in the 1820s and '30s, these row houses are considered to be among the finest surviving examples of early New York architecture.

Charlton Street between Sixth and Greenwich. **C E** *to Spring St.*

Haughwout Building
Don't let the Staples store downstairs fool you; this building is an architectural masterpiece, as well as the first building ever to install a commercial passenger elevator. Designed in 1857 by John Gaynor, who drew his inspiration from a 16th-century Venetian library, the stunning cast iron façade earned the building its reputation as the "Parthenon of New York's Iron Age."

488-492 Broadway (at Broome). **N R Q W** *to Canal St.*

Little Singer Building
This building's steel, glass, and terracotta façade is considered architect Ernest Flagg's greatest achievement. Delicate ornamentation and innovative use of mixed building materials has made this 1904 structure an emblem of SoHo; come to remember the glory that was the Singer Tower, this building's older brother, demolished in 1967.

561 Broadway (at Prince). **N R W** *to Prince St.*

Trapeze School of New York
Since 2002, young thrill-seekers have been getting in touch with their inner acrobats at this most unusual of educational institutions. Harnesses and a complicated net system guarantee that you won't break your neck, and the shouted encouragement of fellow classmates and instructors ensures that expanding your exercise regimen and conquering your fear of heights all at once is at least as fun as it is terrifying. "Forget fear. Worry about addiction." read T-shirts sold in the small shop adjacent to the equipment; if students' fits of giggles are any indication of addiction, the slogan is right on the mark.

Pier 40, Hudson River Park (West Street at Clarkson). 917.797.1872. newyork.trapezeschool.com. Classes daily, weather permitting. $47-75. **1** *to Houston St.*

Dining
UPSCALE

Fiamma Osteria *Italian*
The impressive décor of this Stephen Hanson eatery—he also owns Ruby Foo's and Blue Water Grill, among others—is heavy with leather and oak, the perfect setting for both current and future power players to indulge in hearty Italian fare. Ride to one of the three floors on a unique glass elevator, then sit down to food presentations that are creative, colorful, and daring: Imagine a white chocolate crème brulée basking in rhubarb shaved ice and raspberry sorbet, all nestled in a caramelized sugar shell. While a few of the dishes take the presentation too far, the penne pasta with a butter truffle sauce and smoky prosciutto is particularly memorable, and the bigeye tuna rubbed with coriander is not to be missed.

206 Spring Street (at Sullivan). 212.653.0100. Lunch M-F noon-2:30pm; Dinner M-Th 5:30pm-11pm, F-Sat 5:30pm-midnight, Sun 5pm-10pm. Appetizers $10-$16, Entrées $18-26. **C E** *to Spring St.*

Mercer Kitchen *New American, French*
Tucked in the basement of the Mercer Hotel, Kitchen's sidewalk-ceilings of cast iron and glass, exposed brick arches, and warm ambient lighting make plush booth seating all the more enjoyable. An open kitchen compliments the inviting atmosphere, but don't be fooled—this place is uber-trendy. Some diners come to be seen, but the smart ones come for the food; chef Jean-Georges Vongerichten combines diverse flavors to create innovative dishes like the black sea bass carpaccio with lime and mint, and raw tuna and wasabi pizza. Devote more attention to your food than your glittering neighbors, because you won't be tasting its like again for a while.

99 Prince Street (at Mercer). 212.966.5454. Lunch

FAST FACTS

? Scenic Stroll: Charlton Street, West Broadway between Grand and Houston

? Major Subway Stations: Broadway-Lafayette (B D F V), Prince St (R W), Spring St (6, C E)

? Urban Oasis: The New York Earth Room

? Kooky Corner: La Casa Verde, New York Trapeze School

? Notable Buildings: Haughwout Building, Little Singer Building

? Neighborhood Landmarks: Angelika Film Center, The Puck Building

? Best Deal: SoHo Antiques Fair and Flea Market

? Celebrity Hangouts: Don Hill's, Prince Street

? Kid-Friendly Place: Playground at Mulberry Streets and Spring Streets

? Community Issues: Gentrification in other areas is sometimes called the "SoHo effect," after artists were famously out-priced here in the '80s.

M-F noon-3pm, Sat-Sun noon-4pm; Dinner M-Th 6pm-midnight, F-Sat 5:30pm-1am, Sun 5:30pm-11pm. Appetizers $9-17, Entrées $18-39. N W to Prince St.

PUBLIC *Fusion*

The owners of this crowded hotspot describe the cuisine as "free-spirited fusion," although a quick glance at the menu makes it clear that their influences are primarily Asian. The most successful dishes and drinks make novel use of ginger to create complex flavor combinations, including a clear ginger cosmopolitan and a ginger-infused New Zealand snapper. If you're up for a different kind of adventure, the grilled kangaroo is a favorite. Closely-packed tables and a bustling bar area have a tendency to overwhelm, but the subtle and sophisticated food is worth braving the uber-trendy atmosphere; for a more low-key contrast,

start the evening next door at the Monday Room, Public's acclaimed wine lounge.

210 Elizabeth Street (at Prince). 212.343.7011. Brunch Sat-Sun 11am-3:30pm; Dinner M-Th 6pm-11:30pm, F-Sat 6pm-12:30am, Sun 6pm-10:30pm; Bar Sun-Th 6pm-1am, F-Sat 6pm-2am. Appetizers $10-19, Entrées $20-28. N W to Prince St.

MID-RANGE

Ama *Italian (Puglian)*

With a name that means love in Italian, Ama's moniker may well be derived from the genuine affection with which chef Turibio Girardi approaches every dish. Freshness is the modus vivendi here; homemade pastas like eggplant-filled Mezzelune di Melenzane are produced in a kitchen of largely-imported Italian ingredients. Start off with the insalata delizia, a cleverly composed salad of mouth-watering lump crab, chilled avocado, and tomatoes. The stuffed quail that's offered as a main course displays the same close attention to presentation as the décor does—precisely placed mirrors combine with clean oak furnishings to open up what could have been a tight space, and ensure that your senses are not distracted from the well-crafted regional fare. It's not a bargain, but head here if you're looking for refined Italian food, served with a SoHo swagger.

48 MacDougal Street (at King). 212.358.1707. Lunch Daily noon-3pm; Dinner daily 5:30pm-11:00pm. Appetizers $10-13, Entrées $17-25. **1** *to Houston St.*

L'École *Contemporary French*
Take a seat in this warm and spacious dining room where New York's newest gastronomic talents show off their schooling. This teaching restaurant at the French Culinary Institute features dishes by current students, and while their zeal can sometimes carry them in odd directions, the results are often unique and delicious. When ordering the five-course, student-prepared prix fixe (a good deal at $40), expect one dish to confuse your palate, one to blow your mind, and a few others in between. You can arrive earlier for the four-course prix fixe prepared by the instructors (at the same price), but to do so would be something of a cop-out; go for the students, as nowhere else offers the exciting opportunity of experiencing the nuances of tomorrow's culinary superstars today.

462 Broadway (at Grand). 212.219.3300. Lunch M-F 12:30pm-2pm; Dinner M-Sat 5:30pm-7pm (instructors' menu) and 8pm-9pm (students' menu). Lunch prix fixe $26.50, Dinner prix fixe $39.95. **6 J M Z** N R Q W *to Canal St.*

Rialto *New American, Italian*
First-time visitors are consistently wowed by the understated ambience and first-rate Italian/Continental food at this gastronomically ambitious NoLIta eatery. Neighborhood types visit time and again, and the magnificent garden out back is consistently booked for private parties. You won't mind eating inside, however—the décor is light and elegant, and the food comes in portions big enough to make you forget the outdoors altogether. Keep your eye on the soup of the day, often a heavenly mix of Italian ingredients with an American twist.

265 Elizabeth Street (at East Houston). 212.334.7900. Lunch daily 11am-4:30pm; Dinner daily 5pm-1am. Appetizers $9-17, Entrées $12-28. R W *to Prince St.*

Woo Lae Oak *Korean*
Tucked deep into chaotic SoHo streets, this stylish restaurant is the perfect blend of traditional Korean barbecue and chic modern fare; upon descending the stairs to the cavernous dining room, visitors pass under an ornate awning and by a steaming fountain to find a Zen-like interior. In true Korean style, each table comes equipped with its very own grill; do-it-yourself meat selections are plentiful, ranging from the traditional *Bul Go Gi* (sliced beef rib eye) to the uncommon *Ta Jo* (ostrich), all perfectly marinated and seasoned before arriving at the table. The service, often inattentive, is a major drawback, although the high-quality food at least partially makes up for it.

148 Mercer Street (at Prince). 212.925.8200. Sun-Th noon-11pm, F-Sat noon-11:30pm. Appetizers $10-14, Entrées $15-32. N R W *to Prince St.*

Zoë *New American*
Elegant décor and a well-designed layout make Zoë an appealing stop for world-weary shoppers and neighborhood explorers; comfortable booths line the walls and tables are set far apart, offering everyone the maximum level of privacy. Colorful dishes, thrilling for eyes and taste buds alike, are consistently tasty but subtly flavored. Try the organic salmon or the innovative polenta fries. If you're having trouble deciding, the attentive, well-timed waitstaff is happy to suggest its favorites.

90 Prince Street (at Mercer). 212.966.6722. Lunch daily 11:30am-3:30pm, Dinner T-Th 6pm-10:30pm, F-Sat 5:30pm-11pm, Sun 5:30pm-10pm. Appetizers $10-15, Entrées $18-30. N R W *to Prince St.*

CASUAL

Ceci-Cela *Bakery, Café*

Homemade sorbet and café au lait evoke the Cote d'Azur at this charming patisserie perched on the edge of Little Italy. The chat room in the back is oh-so-perfect for nibbling on petit-fours, and the chocolate gateau and croissants are famous throughout the city. The service can be slow, so come on a lazy afternoon to enjoy the sweets if you've got some time to spare.

55 Spring Street (at Mulberry). 212.274.9179. M-Sat 7am-10pm, Sun 8am-8pm. Pastries $1-6. **6** *to Spring St.*

Once Upon A Tart *Bakery, Café*

The delectable pastries at this lighthearted café are both savory and sweet; and they're not only much tastier than the standard coffeecakes in Manhattan's corporate espresso bars, but much cheaper as well. Everything is made on-site each morning, earning the eat-in bakery a loyal clientele and a full house almost every day for brunch. If you enjoy the baked goods as much as the locals do, pick up a copy of the Once Upon a Tart cookbook, which contains recipes for all the bakery's classics.

135 Sullivan Street (at Houston). 212.387.8869. M-F 8am-7pm, Sat 9am-7pm, Sun 9am-6pm. Baked goods $1-8. **C E** *to Spring St.*

Nightlife

Botanica *Bar*

Botanica's Afro-Cuban décor and playful, friendly bartenders make this one of the neighborhood's most comfortable places to get sloppy. There's a full bar and a decent selection of draft beers, but don't ask for anything too complicated unless you're prepared to take the heat.

47 East Houston Street (at Mulberry). 212.343.7251. Daily 5pm-4am. Drinks $3-10. **B D F V** *to Broadway-Lafayette.*

The Cub Room *Lounge*

After the dinner crowd clears out of this upscale New American restaurant, the space transforms itself into a swanky yet unpretentious lounge that draws a classy, well-dressed crowd. The cocktails, with names like the Cary Grant and the Rita Hayworth, are as reliably satisfying as their namesakes. Reserve a romantic table in front of the elegant backroom's fireplace to make like Bogey and Bacall, or try the so-called chef's table for a larger affair.

131 Sullivan Street (at Prince). 212.677.4100. M-W 11am-2am, Th-Sat 11am-4am, Sun noon-2am. Drinks $12. **1** *to Houston St.*

Culture Club

This is the place for your ultimate '80s escape; pull on those leggings, tease that hair, and let yourself go at this bi-level club. Reagan-era pop hits are the standard soundtrack, but when you get tired of dancing, entertain yourself by looking around: Murals of your favorite '80s artists grace the walls, and there's even a DeLorean worthy of Marty McFly.

179 Varick Street (at Charlton). 212.243.1999. Th 9pm-2am, F-Sat 9pm-4am. Cover $0-20. **1** *to Houston St.*

Madame X

This cozy lounge, spread over two floors, features an eclectic décor that mixes bright red lighting, art exhibits, and comfy antique couches. Visit weeknights for a laid-back atmosphere, or stop by on the weekend when the emphasis moves from the "Madame" to the "X" as the club packs up, spinning DJs and all.

94 West Houston Street (at Thompson). 212.539.0808. M-F 6pm-4am, Sat-Sun 7pm-4am. $5 Cover on weekends. **1** *to Houston St.*

Ñ

This unique tapas bar is worth visiting any night of the week, but come on Wednesday nights between 8 and 10pm to down pitchers of sangria as professional flamenco dancers shake their castanets all around the room. Order a few small plates to snack on, but be warned that the space is as small as the portions; smart drinkers stake their place early and camp out all night.

33 Crosby Street (at Broome). 212.219.8856. Sun-Th 5pm-2am, F-Sat 5pm-4am. Drinks $5-7. **6 J M Z N R W** *to Canal St.*

Pravda *Vodka Bar*
Despite the fact that this bar's name evokes shades of the USSR, Pravda embodies neither post-Soviet mayhem nor hard-core proletariat boozing. Nevertheless, the 80 types of vodka (including mango and raspberry), caviar, and rust-tinted décor almost justify the moniker.

281 Lafayette Street (at Prince). 212.226.4944. M-Th 5pm-1am, F-Sat 5pm-3am. Drinks $6-12. **6** *to Bleecker St.*

The SoHo Grand Bar *Hotel Bar*
This bar, located in the SoHo Grand Hotel, is growing ever more popular for its famed martinis; sophisticated SoHoustonians head here for the most reliable nightcap in town.

310 West Broadway (at Canal). 212.965.3588. Daily 6am-2am. Drinks $8-18. **A C E** *to Canal St.*

Sweet and Vicious *Bar*
This NoLIta hotspot lives up to its Jekyll-and-Hyde name: Austere brick and plenty of wood combine with pink bar lights and quirky chandeliers, resulting in a hip, irreverent, and comfortable vibe. Patrons pack in, sipping G&Ts and shooting tequila like it's their job in small and large groups alike. If the night is clear, check out the smoker's garden in the back.

5 Spring Street (at Bowery). 212.334.7915. Daily 4pm-4am. Drinks $4-6. **6** *to Spring St.*

Temple Bar *Power Hour*
Leather seating and thick curtains make this mahogany-heavy bar the perfect place for an intimate gathering, with a wide selection of vodkas, wines and cocktails to sip as you revel in your seclusion. The space itself, which feels like it could have come out of an elegant, turn-of-the-century train station, is as beautiful as it is dignified; don't go to get sloshed, unless you want to lose your inhibitions among the crowd of suit-clad power players. Grab a martini, order some shrimp toast, and pretend you could afford to do this every day.

332 Lafayette Street (at Bleeker). 212.925.4242. M-Th 5-1, F-Sat 5pm-2am. Drinks $8-15. **6** *to Bleecker.*

Arts

Angelika Film Center
Don't buy popcorn at this independent movie theater—it would prevent you from spending hours conversing with other indie film lovers over the fresh pastries and coffee at the stylish café. With everything from foreign hits to Sundance winners, this is the place to go if you want to get away from the mainstream and gain some culture cred.

18 West Houston Street (at Mercer). 212.995.2000. angelikafilmcenter.com. **B D F V** *to Broadway-Lafayette.*

Deitch Projects
Serious exhibits and more ambitious-but-quirky ones compete for space in this large, white square gallery. Specializing in modern art, the space has featured work from artists as varied as Yoko Ono, Keith Haring, and Robert Rauschenberg, to name just a few; now it holds fascinating themed exhibitions, usually including the work of less well-known artists.

76 Grand Street (at Wooster). 212.343.7300. deitch. com. T-Sat noon-6pm. **A C E** *to Canal St.*

Joyce SoHo
Considered downtown's premiere dance performance space, this branch of the Joyce is a venue for everything from contemporary to international ethnic dance, including a good deal of experimental works. Performances take place Thursday through Sunday, with tickets usually available 30 minutes before curtain for those who can't plan ahead. Rehearsal space is also available for independent choreographers and non-profit dance companies.

155 Mercer Street (at Prince). 212.431.9233. joyce.org. **N R W** *to Prince St.*

New York City Fire Museum

If you spent even a little time telling people that you wanted to be a firefighter when you grew up, then the museum of the FDNY is worth a visit. The renovated 1904 Beaux-Arts firehouse is home to every imaginable firefighting artifact, from 18th century signal lamps and trumpets to old fire trucks and a permanent September 11th memorial. Tours are guided by real firefighters, and are sure to make you feel like a little kid again. On your way out, check out the gift shop's impressive selection of firefighting paraphernalia.

278 Spring Street (at Hudson). 212.691.1303. nycfire-museum.org. T-Sat 10am-5pm, Sun 10am-4pm, closed Monday. Adults $5, Students $2. **C E** *to Spring St.*

The New York Earth Room

If you've ever wondered where you could find the weirdest room in New York City, ring the doorbell to this walk-up on Wooster Street and find out. Climb a narrow staircase, and discover an interior earth sculpture by Walter de Maria that consists of nothing but 280,000 pounds of dirt. Even though you're not allowed to touch, walk on, or photograph the dirt, just standing in the room is bound to be an experience you'll never forget: the humidity and the smell are overwhelming, and the sculpture will either make you question your relationship with nature, as the artist intends, or wonder why you just wasted your energy on those stairs.

141 Wooster Street (at Prince). 212.989.5566. earth-room.org. W-Sun noon-6pm (closed 3-3:30). N R to Prince St.

Shopping

Anna Sui

This cozy, dimly lit boutique offers everything from casual printed tees to eccentric eveningwear. The red floors and purple walls, cluttered with rock band and movie posters, are watched over by sultry salespeople; at times, it can feel more like a swank Parisian café than a SoHo boutique. Although the clothes may seem expensive, the price

is worth it to dress like a fashion-conscious rock 'n' roll star. Don't leave before checking out Sui's cosmetics and the seductive cabaret-style lingerie section hidden in the back of the store.

113 Greene Street (at Prince). 212.941.8406. annasui. com. Sun-W 11:30am-7pm, Th-Sat 11am-8pm. N R W to Prince St.

Betsey Johnson

You may feel like you've walked into your little sister's closet at this small ultra-feminine boutique. Floral patterns cover just about everything in the store; the wallpaper, couches, and dressing room curtains are adorned in extremely girly patterns that make the atmosphere almost sickly sweet. The part-babydoll, part-hippie clothing found here ranges from girl-next-door cute skirts to glamorous evening dresses, worn by the likes of Paris Hilton and Beyoncé (with price tags to match).

138 Wooster Street (at Prince). 212.995.5048. betsey-johnson.com. M-Sat 11am-7pm, Sun noon-6pm. N R W to Prince St.

Face Stockholm

This Swedish make-up chain supplies you with everything you could ever need for your mug. Products are available in a wide array of colors, sure to include the exact shade of eyeshadow or blush that you've been looking for, and the knowledgeable staff will gladly shower you with personal attention until you find what you're after. The space, both small and airy, has an upscale vibe that makes the reasonable prices come as a pleasant surprise.

110 Prince Street (at Greene). 212.966.9110. facestock-holm.com. M-Sat 11am-7pm, Sun noon-6pm. N R W to Prince St.

Housing Works Used Book Café

Spiral staircases and mahogany paneling welcome you to this beautiful bookstore run by Housing Works, a non-profit organization dedicated to serving NYC residents affected by AIDS. While it has a limited selection of new material, the real draw is the often-changing collection of rare and used books. Coffee tables are scattered throughout, and high ceilings give the space an open feel; sit down with a book or just observe the local hipsters browsing while you enjoy the café's delicious coffee and desserts. Readings, concerts, and other special events are held here frequently, so check the calendar online before you visit.

126 Crosby Street (at Jersey). 212.334.3324. housingworks.org. M-F 10am-9pm, Sat-Sun noon-7pm. **N R W** *to Prince St.*

Prada

Don't let the fact that you probably won't be able to afford anything inside stop you from visiting Prada's flagship store, designed by hip Dutch architect Rem Koolhaas of OMA. The building housed the SoHo branch of the Guggenheim

Coffee Break

in a former life, and if you treat the store like a museum, you'll probably more feel comfortable amid the exuberantly priced clothing—some of which is even kept behind glass. Even if you aren't interested in the clothing, the store's modern décor make it worth a visit. Take a ride in the circular glass elevator and check out the changing rooms—the sliding glass doors allow the changer to see outside, but keep other customers from seeing in.

575 Broadway (at Prince). 212.334.8888. prada.com. M-W 11am-7pm, Th-Sat 11am-8pm, Sun noon-7pm. **N R W** *to Prince St.*

Scoop

This 10,000-square-foot megastore is a top destination for trendy New Yorkers. Self-described as "the ultimate closet," there truly is something for everybody here—at least everybody wealthy—whether it's a stylish little sister or a fashion-conscious dad. It's not uncommon to see Manhattanite families shopping alongside solo hipsters in this spacious and chic space, browsing the $50 T-shirts and $250 jeans. Check the back of the store for sales if you're in the mood for something cheaper.

473-475 Broadway (at Grand). 212.925.3539. scoopnyc.com. M-Sat 11am-8pm, Sun 11am-7pm. **6** *to Canal St.*

SoHo Antiques Fair and Flea Market

Although it's not as large as other New York street markets, the size turns out to be a good thing, making it more manageable than the other mammoth mazes of old stuff. If you've got a little time and patience, seek out more than just the usual collectibles; it's not uncommon to chance upon some retro-trendy clothing that would cost three times as much in the boutique next door. Try to come early, when the street is not as crowded and more dealers are displaying goods.

Broadway (at Grand). Sat-Sun 9am-5pm. **6** *to Canal St.*

CHINATOWN/ LITTLE ITALY

The growth of Chinatown has helped turn neighboring Little Italy into Very Little Italy—walk south for a couple of blocks and the marinara sauce becomes duck sauce, the espresso replaced with Chinatown's famous bubble tea. In a sense, it's fitting that the two neighborhoods run together geographically: Each offers a uniquely singular ethnic vibe, a phenomenon seldom found in Manhattan. In America's greatest melting pot, these neighborhoods truly are enclaves of ethnicity.

Of course, this is New York, and anything that can be sold, will. That authentic ethnic feeling can't remain uncommercialized forever—and indeed, to many Italian Americans, Little Italy seems insultingly false. It's often said that the last person you'll ever find in Little Italy is a real Italian, and that's mostly true. In large part, the old, founding community has been pushed aside in favor of a tourist-driven theme park.

Chinatown has not yet gone the tourist route, at least partially due to the fact that American society never quite developed the same trend-driven cultural obsession with China that it has with many other countries, Italy included. Here, you can still find authentic food, cheap prices, and people speaking languages that you probably don't understand. Due to much growth over the last 50 years, it's now the largest Chinese community in the Western world. The street-side stalls are filled with shining fish eyes, porcelain tea kettles, wizened ginseng roots, and tiger-penis aphrodisiacs—a bizarre bazaar, indeed.

© Opus Publishing 2007 — www.OpusPublishing.com

CHINATOWN/LITTLE ITALY

SIGHTS/ATTRACTIONS
1. Chatham Square
2. Columbus Park and Five Points
3. Confucius Plaza
4. Fung Wah Bus
5. Mahayana Buddhist Temple
6. Manhattan Bridge

DINING
7. Almond Flower Bistro
8. Café Gitane
9. Golden Unicorn
10. Grand Sichuan
11. Great New York Noodletown
12. Joe's Shanghai
13. Lombardi's Pizza
14. O'nieals Grand Street
15. Paris Sandwich Shop
16. Puglia
17. Tai Pan Bakery

NIGHTLIFE
18. Double Happiness
19. Happy Ending Lounge
20. Mulberry Street Bar
21. Shebeen
22. Winnie's Karaoke

ARTS
23. Asian American Arts Center

SHOPPING
24. Asia Market
25. Dynasty Supermarket
26. Hung Chang Imports Inc.
27. Pearl Paint
28. Pearl River Mart
29. Ten Ren Tea and Ginseng Co.

Sights/Attractions

Chatham Square

This central neighborhood meetingplace is formed by the convergence of seven of Chinatown's principle streets—Bowery, East Broadway, St. James Place, Mott Street, Oliver Street, Worth Street, and Park Row. The square is home to several important landmarks, including the Kimlau Memorial Arch, erected in 1962 in memory of the numerous Chinese-American soldiers who died in WWII, and a statue of Lin Tse-Hsu, a 19th century Chinese officer whose anti-drug policies led to the First Opium War against Britain in 1839.

Bowery at East Broadway. **F** *to East Broadway.*

Columbus Park & Five Points

Once a dangerous slum defined by the violent gang wars between Irish and German immigrants that terrorized the neighborhood—an uncomfortable bit of city history recently depicted in the Martin Scorsese film *Gangs of New York*—this area near the formerly infamous Five Points neighborhood is now home to Columbus Park, a charming, modest green space in one of the busiest sections of Chinatown. Grab a pork bun to go from any nearby Chinese bakery, then drop by to watch gaggles of old men huddled around intense games of Chinese checkers, teenagers playing pick-up games of basketball and soccer, and children frolicking in the cooling mist of the park's sprinkler. In an emergency, Columbus Park has one of the few public bathrooms in the city—most, including those in subway stations, have been shut down over the years to cut back on maintenance costs and to discourage public bathing by the city's homeless.

67 Mulberry Street (at Bayard). **6** *to Canal St.*

Confucius Plaza

Standing tall in the shadow of multi-story restaurants and high-rise apartments, a 15-foot granite statue of one of East Asia's greatest thinkers, philosophers, and teachers watches over the frantic masses with a calm serenity. The statue's inscription, an excerpt from Confucius' Chapter of Great Harmony, describes a perfect society in which all citizens' needs are fulfilled.

Bowery at Division Street. **6** *to Canal St.*

Fung Wah Bus

For a cheap way to get to Boston that's also a New York experience in and of itself, a few so-called Chinatown bus companies—Fung Wah is the most well-known—offer one-way trips every hour on the hour from 7am to 10pm. Line up on Canal Street near Bowery, just blocks from the Manhattan Bridge, with the rest of the city's bargain-seekers waiting for the next departure. Take care, though: the Fung Wah bus is notoriously dangerous, with occasional delays and even crashes due to poorly maintained buses and fatigued, overworked drivers.

139 Canal Street (at Bowery). 212.925.8889. Chinatown-bus.com. **B D** *to Grand St.*

Mahayana Buddhist Temple

For an escape from Chinatown's colorful, crowded chaos, pass between the two golden lions that guard the entrance of the Mahayana Buddhist Temple and enter a world of bright, neon spirituality. In the small, ornate lobby, incense burns in golden urns as worshippers bow in prayer; in a room farther back, a 16-foot golden statue of the Buddha sits atop a lotus, framed by the glow of blue neon rings. Buy a fortune scroll for $1 or visit over the

weekend to attend an elaborate public service featuring traditional drums and bells.

133 Canal Street (at Bowery). Daily 8-6, public services Sat and Sun 10am-noon. **6 J M Z** N R Q W *to Canal St.*

Manhattan Bridge

This suspension bridge, built in 1909, isn't as pretty or as famous as its southern sister in Brooklyn, but it's more attractive to city motorists who appreciate the fact that it has no toll. Pedestrians can get a nice view of the bridge's arches, columns, and deflection cables from the intersection of Cherry and Pike in Manhattan; there's also a footpath on the bridge's south side. Though the roar of traffic, the rumble of the N, Q, B, and D trains, and the whir of power tools never disappear, you can enjoy fabulous views of Chinatown, the Financial District, and the Brooklyn Bridge through the blue railings—if you can handle the vertiginous thrill of standing hundreds of feet above the surface of the East River.

Bowery at Canal. **F** *to East Broadway.*

Dining
MID-RANGE

Almond Flower Bistro *New American, Chinese*
Tin ceilings, crisp white tablecloths, fresh grass centerpieces, and exposed red brick are the backdrop to this inventive Chinese-American fusion restaurant with mouthwatering food, nestled unexpectedly in the middle of a busy block. Appetizers are perfectly prepared and beautifully presented, paving the way for delicious entrées like the *char sui* blackened cod—a specialty of the chef since his days at Nobu—and an amazing Peking duck served on a bed of pancakes. The dessert menu features a large chocolate fortune cookie packed with light mint crème, drizzled with a rich caramel sauce that will keep you coming back for seconds.

96 Bowery (at Grand). 212.966.7162. Daily 11:30am-11pm. Appetizers $7-12, Entrées $ 16-24. **B D** *to Grand St.*

Café Gitane *French, Mediterranean*
Like Francis I in the Italian War of 1542, France is invading Italian territory, this time armed with an authentic bistro menu and an aloof waitstaff. Gitane boasts the perfect ambience for flipping through fashion mags, sipping cappuccinos, and posing, but also comes through with the cuisine. Try the goat cheese with pomegranate syrup to start your meal with a zing. The crowd can get thick on the weekends, but it's comforting to have bodies to hide behind, just in case of an Italian counterattack.
242 Mott Street (at Prince). 212.334.9552. Daily 9am-noon, 5:30pm-11:30pm. Entrées $5-13, cash only. N R W to Prince St.

Golden Unicorn *Chinese*
Cleaner and more polished than most Chinatown dim sum houses, this chandeliered restaurant has become especially popular among tourists and local businessmen hosting lunch meetings. Delicious dim sum is served Hong-Kong style, stacked on metal carts piloted by vigorous employees. The array of choices is impressive, meriting a return visit to sample new selections. Many like to say it's dim sum—and then some.
18 East Broadway (at Catherine). 212.941.0911. Daily 9am-4pm. Dim Sum $2-$35. B D to Grand St.

Grand Sichuan *Chinese*
You have to love a restaurant with a menu featuring a prominent section called "Chairman Mao's Favorite Dishes." But note, when they say "hot & spicy" at this authentic Sichuan favorite, rest assured they mean it. Don't be surprised when the harmless-sounding sautéed pork with szechuan bean sauce is served on a bed of more than a dozen chopped jalapeños; it's positively mouth-melting. Despite the intense heat, the food is delicious—a real treat in an era when General Tso's chicken threatens to destroy authentic Chinese regional cuisine in America.
125 Canal Street (at Bowery). 212.625.9212. Daily 11:30am-11pm. Appetizers $3-4, Entrées $8-16. 6 J M Z N R W to Canal St.

Great New York Noodletown *Chinese*
Away from the touristy center of Chinatown, you'll stumble on this affordable and cozy restaurant where you're guaranteed to find a dish to excite your taste buds. Soup lovers can rejoice in 20 different varieties, providing a chance to sample authentic soups from across the region; in-season seafood specials like the crab are must-trys, as is the barbecued chicken, duck, and pork combo.
28 Bowery (at Bayard). 212.349.0923. Daily 9am-4am. Entrées $7-15, cash only. B D to Grand St.

Joe's Shanghai *Chinese*
Tourists and locals flock to this deservedly popular eatery year-round for a taste of the famous crabmeat buns. If you're in the mood for something a little more involved, try the soup

Open-air grocery shopping

dumplings filled with juicy crabmeat and pork in a flavorful broth. With a reputation as one of the best authentic restaurants in the neighborhood, the friendly service and savory fare keep customers coming back for more. Though the tourists can be a bit of a turn-off at times, a few recommendations from those in the know will ensure that you end up with dishes delicious enough to outweigh distraction.

9 Pell Street (at Mott). 212.233.8888. Daily 11am-11:15pm. Appetizers $3-9, Entrées $12-$38, cash only. **6 J M Z** N R W *to Canal St.*

Onieal's Grand Street *American, Italian*
A turn-of-the-century tavern, rumored to have been frequented by Teddy Roosevelt during his tenure as police commissioner, retains its old-world charm even though today it caters to bankers, architects, models, and celebrities. The food is a combination of hearty American fare and flavorful Italian twists, and it matches the atmosphere nicely. The restaurant also features a traditional Irish breakfast and transforms into a popular lounge at night. The drinks pack a punch, but taste so good you'll enjoy the hit.

174 Grand Street (at Baxter) 212.941.9119. Lunch daily 11:30am-4pm; Dinner M-Sat 6pm-11pm; Lounge menu Th-Sat 11pm-1am. Appetizers $9-13, Entrées $13-29. **B D** *to Grand St.*

Puglia *Italian*
Elvis fans will be delighted by the impersonator working his magic on a little Casio keyboard in the corner, though on some nights he's relieved by Frank Sinatra and other celebrity singer wannabes. The tables are large and communal, encouraging a loud and social dining experience—whether you want it or not. On par with other quality restaurants in the neighborhood, the food will leave you feeling satisfied.

189 Hester Street (at Mott). 212.226.8912. Sun-Th noon-midnight, F-Sat noon-1am. Appetizers $5-11, Entrées $10-24. **6 J M Z** N R W *to Canal St.*

CASUAL
Lombardi's Pizza *Pizza*
Established a hundred and two years ago, this beloved pizzeria is a landmark in its own right. Owners call it the first pizzeria in the nation—a far more reliable claim than their highly touted, "best pizza in the world." With a limited menu, the pizza is sold fresh and only by the pie. Tasty but not spectacular, you'll find as many tourists as locals gathered in a newly expanded and refurbished dining room.

32 Spring Street (at Mott). 212.941.7994. M-F 11:30am-11:00pm, Sat 11:00am-midnight, Sun 11:30am-10:00pm, cash only. **6** *to Spring St.*

Paris Sandwich Shop *Vietnamese*
This might be the best lunch deal in the city. For $3.50, purchase one of 12 varieties of delicious *bahn mi*, a Vietnamese sandwich prepared on a fresh-baked baguette with any of a variety of meats, from grilled pork to meatballs to stewed sardines, and topped with cilantro, crisp carrots, and spicy peppers. Instead of a soft drink, try a cup of Vietnamese coffee, brewed with beans imported from Vietnam and served with sweetened condensed milk. The green tea waffles—sweet, hot, and floral—are another delicious treat. Brightly lit and colorful, this small eatery also does a brisk to-go business, with patrons taking their sandwiches to munch in nearby Columbus Park.

113 Mott Street (at Hester). 212.226.7221. Sun-Th 8am-8pm, F-Sat 8am-8:30pm. Appetizers $1-2, Entrées $3-5. N R Q W *to Canal St.*

Tai Pan Bakery *Chinese, Bakery*
The pastries at this popular bakery make the long weekend lines tolerable. Serving Chinese delicacies as well as a selection of standard European desserts, the custard tarts and pearl milk tea drinks are particular favorites. If you're looking for something a little more substantial, the fish burgers are sure to please the adventurous diner.

194 Canal Street (at Mulberry). 212.732.2222. Daily 7:30am-8:30pm. Baked goods $1-5, cash only. **6 J M Z** N R W *to Canal St.*

Nightlife

Double Happiness *Bar*

Friendly bartenders and an excellent mix of house and organic grooves attract a hip, young, and unpretentious crowd to this basement bar. With ample floor space for dancing and hidden, candle-lit alcoves, Double Happiness is perfect either for a casual first date or a boisterous night out with a group of friends. The bar menu features Pan-Asian cuisine with an Italian accent.

173 Mott Street (at Broome). 212.941.1282. Sun–W 6pm-2am, Th 6pm-3am, F-Sat 6pm-4am. Drinks $5-11. **6** *to Spring St.*

Happy Ending Lounge *Lounge*

Previously an "erotic massage parlor," this lounge has recently become far less risqué, though the current owners did maintain the original private,

Lunar New Year Celebration

white-tiled rooms downstairs—complete with waist-high showerheads—that emit a faint spa-like scent. Upstairs, lounge in red velvet booths alongside young and attractive club-goers and revel in the fact that you didn't have to pay a cover charge. The hottest night of the week here is Tuesday, when the lounge hosts two Britpop parties on separate floors—an indie and New Wave party "Disco Down," and the post-punk *Six Six Sick* upstairs.

302 Broome Street (at Eldridge). 212.334.9676. happyendinglounge.com. T 10pm-4am, W-Sat 7pm-4am, closed Sun-M. Drinks $7-12. **B D** *to Grand St.*

Moomia Bar & Lounge *Club*

With King Tut, Anubis, and Osiris-themed martinis and walls covered with large Egyptian paintings and hieroglyphics, it's clear that this isn't your typical nighttime destination. Open for nearly two years, the bar has a (fairly) strict no hip-hop policy; the music is mostly house, with occasional Russian dance music nights. Lounge on low couches and watch the belly dancers as you inhale liquorish-flavored hookah as you sip on a tart passionfruit martini. They also have a full Asian-themed menu. Though the decoration is a bit gaudy, this off-the-beaten track lounge might be just the dance hall you need for an experience as bizarre as the surroundings.

157 Lafayette Street (at Grand). 212.219.4006. moomiany.com. Daily 5pm-4am. $6-13. **6 J M Z N R Q W** *to Canal St.*

Mulberry Street Bar *Bar*

This is one of the area's last authentic Italian bars. Gape at the huge photo of Frank Sinatra, then go get yourself a drink at the back bar, which has been there since it opened as social club Mare Chiaro in 1908. Known simply as Tony's by the locals, this place has been featured on shows like *The Sopranos*.

176 Mulberry Street (at Broome). 212.226.9345. Daily 11:30am-3am. Drinks $5-9, cash only. **6** *to Spring St.*

Shebeen *Lounge*

Walk through a virtually unmarked storefront,

and enter a room with dim lights and a minimalist color scheme. But don't be fooled by the bar's aesthetic—the drinks offer all the excitement you need for one night. This bar has specialty martinis without the sugary extras others rely on; for a refreshing summer treat, try the watermelon martini, made of pureed watermelon and vodka. Other treats include margaritas infused with unlikely flavors, including maple syrup.

202 Mott Street (at Spring). 212.625.1105. Sun-W 6pm-2am, Th-Sat 6pm-4am. Drinks $9-12. **6** *to Spring St.*

Winnie's Karaoke *Bar*

After the vendors have closed their shops and the carts of vegetables and smelly fish have been packed away, a different Chinatown emerges, as the city's night owls head to this neighborhood icon for a late-night snack, a lychee martini, or some good old-fashioned karaoke fun. The eclectic crowd belts out everything from classic rock to Mandarin pop, but be careful not to butcher those classics too badly—the Manhattan Criminal Courthouse is right next door.

104 Bayard Street (at Mulberry). 212.732.2384. Daily noon-3am. Drinks $6-7, cash only, two-drink minimum. **6 J M Z** N Q R W *to Canal St.*

Arts

Asian American Arts Centre

By featuring works ranging from traditional folk art to post-modern sculpture—as well as playing host to frequent Asian American dance performances—this museum and cultural center aims to represent and support artists of Chinese, Japanese, and Korean backgrounds. It has an extensive historical archive, documenting the evolution of Asian American art since 1945; visit in February for its annual Lunar New Year Folk

Fish Market

Arts Festival, which features performances and hands-on arts and crafts demonstrations.

26 Bowery (at Bayard). 212.233.2154. artspiral.org. M-W, F 12:30pm-6:30pm, Th 12:30pm-7:30pm, closed Saturday-Sunday. **B D** *to Grand St.*

Shopping

Asia Market

Asian groceries of every imaginable variety are sold at this modestly sized store, which carries produce and food products from Thailand, Indonesia, Japan, Korea, the Philippines, Malaysia, China, and beyond. Prices are low and produce is high quality, although for meat or fish, you'll have to go next door.

71½ Mulberry Street (at Bayard). Daily 8am-7pm. **6** *to Canal St.*

Dynasty Supermarket

This full-service grocery with an exotic flair carries all the essentials for Asian cooking and more, including quality cuts of meat for ridiculously low prices. The attitude here is strictly "waste not, want not"—adventurous eaters can get perfectly good pig's blood, cow hearts, or sheep intestines that more squeamish shoppers ignore. Dozens of large fish tanks also hold seafood not often found in chain grocery stores, including eel, bass, buffalo carp, conch, and snails.

68 Elizabeth Street (at Hester). 212.966.4943. Daily 9:30am-8:30pm. **B D** *to Grand St.*

Hung Chang Imports Inc.

Bargain prices attract local restaurant owners and their chefs to this culinary equipment supply store, where friendly and knowledgeable employees are more than willing to give advice to the amateur buyer. The wide selection of professional-quality equipment includes a vast array of Chinese chef's knives—heartier and cheaper than Wusthofs and Henckel—and more varieties of woks, pots, pans, and utensils than even the most creative chef could ever use.

14 Bowery (at Pell). 212.349.3392. Daily 9am-7pm. **6** *to Canal St.*

Pearl Paint

Serious artists in need of high quality supplies know that Pearl Paint is the place to go. Six floors of art supply madness are organized by medium; one entire floor is devoted to canvas frames and stretching, another contains only paper, while others hold paint, stationary, and sculpture supplies.

308 Canal Street (at Mercer). 212.431.7932. pearlpaint.com. M-F 9am-7pm, Sat 10am-6:30pm, Sun 10am-6pm. **1 6** *to Canal St.*

Pearl River Mart

Shoppers who can't handle the madness of Canal Street—but who still long for cheap bric-a-brac—flock to this soothing oasis, filled with products to satisfy every whimsical need. In an air-conditioned warehouse, lamps and kitchen supplies sit next to Samurai swords and musical instruments; the sounds of soothing Chinese guitar and the gurgle of an enormous fountain put your shop-weary mind at ease. Before you leave, be sure to head downstairs and check out the selection of old-school metal wind-up toys—the clicking gears and cheerily whirling wheels are enough to bring out the kid in any hardened shopper.

477 Broadway (at Grand). 212.431.4770. pearlriver. com. Daily 10am-7:20pm. **6** *to Spring St.*

Ten Ren Tea and Ginseng Co.

Those who take the time to chat with the helpful employees at this vast tea emporium will soon lose the feeling of intimidation that surfaces upon first seeing the enormous variety of styles and flavors; with a little assistance, it's not difficult to find a few brews that are well-suited to your palette. From $12 per pound for bargain teas to $130 per pound for "King's Tea," there's something for every kind of tea drinker.

75 Mott Street (at Canal). 212.349.2286. tenren. com. Sun-Th 11am-11pm, F-Sat 11am-midnight. **6** *to Canal St.*

LOWER EAST SIDE

Rock music blares out of bar windows, setting the beat for foot traffic along Ludlow Street. Young locals contend for sidewalk space on Orchard and Rivington, past designer boutiques and ramshackle shops crammed with wedding dresses and roasting pans.

Once one of the most overpopulated neighborhoods in the world, the Lower East Side was the first stop for free black farmers and 19th century immigrants in the population boom of the mid-to-late 1800s. Infamous for providing the worst housing conditions in the city, the neighborhood was filled with tenements and immigrants who could afford nothing better.

Great spirit, however, arose out of poverty. During the early part of the 20th century, Yiddish theater flourished along Second Avenue, area newspapers grew into forums for academic debate as performers like George Gershwin, Irving Berlin, and the Marx Brothers cut their teeth in front of their first paying audiences.

Although the neighborhood was plagued by drugs and decline in the '60s and '70s, it stabilized in the '80s after an influx of Puerto Rican and Dominican immigrants arrived. Many have since dubbed the area *Loisaida*, according to the Spanish pronunciation of "Lower East Side."

Even now, the cultural tides continue to shift. Crowds of young professionals and black-clad creative types rush east from SoHo and Tribeca to live as well as work, but the historic *Lower East Side* remains immortalized by many of the neighborhood's most august institutions; Katz's Delicatessen is a timeless neighborhood staple, as are the old-timers who still ply their wares on Orchard Street on Sundays. East of Suffolk Street, the neighborhood retains its original flavor, as trendy boutiques and bars give way to home cooking, colorful murals, and salsa music.

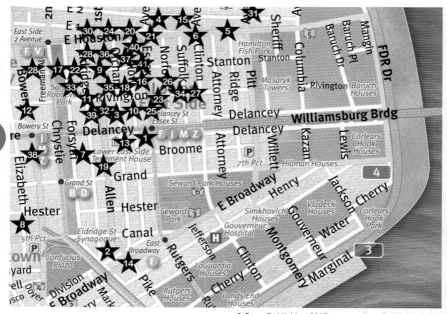

LOWER EAST SIDE

SIGHTS/ATTRACTIONS
1. Bargain District
2. Eldridge Synagogue
3. Lower East Side
   Tenement Museum

DINING
4. Buenos Aires
5. El Maguey Y La Tuna
6. Frankie's
7. Little Giant
8. Nelson Blue
9. Stanton Social
10. Teany
11. Verlaine

NIGHTLIFE
12. BLVD

13. Gallery
14. Good World
15. Identity
16. 'inoteca
17. Kush
18. Libation
19. Lolita
20. Max Fish
21. Mercury
22. People
23. Rewind
24. Tuts
25. Verlaine Bar
26. Whiskey Ward

ARTS
27. ABC No Rio
28. Dixon Place

29. Fusion Arts
30. Landmark Sunshine
    Cinema
31. Nuyorican Poets Café
32. Participant, Inc.
33. Smith-Stewart

SHOPPING
34. Alife Rivington Club
35. Babeland
36. Bluestockings
37. Hudson Street Paper
38. Lighting by Gregory
39. Mooshoes
40. Organic Avenue
41. TG-170

Sights/Attractions

Bargain District

In contrast to the neighboring high-end boutiques, where hipsters drop thousands of dollars on the latest fashions, the shops in the so-called Bargain District, which centers around main drags Orchard and Rivington, offer far less glitz and far lower prices. Just don't expect garments to last very long—those shirts are $2.99 for a reason. Most of the narrow stores in the area are too packed with cheap luggage, baseball caps, leather jackets, and perfumes to allow much movement indoors; expect to see vendors sitting on crates on the sidewalk outside, waiting for you to stop in. Outdoor racks offer $3 blouses and plus-sized dresses, while inside walls are lined with headless white torsos clad in spangled halters. If you need cheap clothes, sunglasses, or bags, or if you're just sick of the attitude found within so many nearby stores, these blocks will give you just what you're looking for.

J M Z F to Essex.

Eldridge Street Synagogue

Standing on a section of Eldridge Avenue with awnings full of Chinese characters, the rose window and Stars of David of this temple stand out, to say the least. Commissioned in 1886, the Spanish-style house of worship was a major cultural institution for Orthodox Jewish immigrants in the early 20th century. Since its designation as a National Historic Landmark in 1989, the synagogue has offered historical tours and hosted music, arts, and literary events. Today, the inside of the church is closed for renovations (set to reopen in 2008), but the outside's Moorish arches look just as glorious as ever.

12 Eldridge Street (at Canal). 212.219.0888. eldridgestreet.org. Adults $5, Students $3 (for tours). F to East Broadway.

Lower East Side Tenement Museum

This tours-only museum serves as a reminder of what the Lower East Side was back in the days before shiny glass apartment buildings and boutique shops. Start out at the visitor's center, which, in addition to a gift shop, has a makeshift theater showing a History Channel program about the area; then follow an "educator" through the tenement apartments themselves, built in 1863 by a German tailor. As you're taken through the apartments, guides tell the stories of families who lived there in the late 19th and early 20th centuries. Though the adolescent tourists dragged along by their parents look bored out of their minds, history buffs and any of the one in four Americans who can trace his lineage to the Lower East Side will appreciate this careful reconstruction of turn-of-the-century immigrant life.

108 Orchard Street (at Delancey). 212.431.0233. tenement.org. M 11am-5:30pm, T-F 11am-6pm, Sat-Sun 10:45am-6pm. Adults $15, Students $11. B D to Grand St.

Dining

UPSCALE

Little Giant *New American*

A philosophy of simple purity pervades the dining room at this cozy eatery where "love" is listed as an ingredient in several of the award-winning desserts. Nestled in a turn-of-the-century tenement building, the restaurant uses fresh, seasonal produce to create innovative variations on American classics. The menu changes often based on the availability of local ingredients, which are allowed to speak for themselves; items like scallop and artichoke are just seasoned enough to enhance the natural flavors. Complete with a small bar and small-town charm, this place brings healthy, hearty, and refined cuisine to the neighborhood.

85 Orchard Street (at Broome). 212.226.5047. Brunch Sun 1pm-4pm; Dinner M-Th 6pm-11pm, F-Sat 6pm-midnight, Sun 6pm-10pm. Appetizers $7-14, Entrées $17-27. J M Z F to Essex St.

The Stanton Social *Tapas*

The owners of two Manhattan hotspots—Tao and Happy Ending—joined forces to open this three-story restaurant and lounge in 2005, billed as the "sexiest" place on the Lower East Side. Designed by the award-winning firm Avroko, the interior is pure 1940s glamour, with swanky wood tables, lizard skin banquets, and brown, belt-strapped pillows. Dishes are miniaturized versions of both classic and innovative foods; the Kobe beef burgers, red snapper tacos, and crab cake corn dogs are so cute you almost won't want to eat them (almost). Though the portions are small, the food is deliciously rich, so a couple of plates make for a very satisfying meal.

99 Stanton Street (at Orchard). 212.995.0099. Brunch Sat-Sun 11:30am-4pm; Dinner Sun-T 5pm-2am, W-Sat 5pm-3am. Tapas $6-19. F V to Lower East Side.

MID-RANGE

Buenos Aires *Argentinean Steakhouse*
You can enjoy a delicious steak at this Argentinean steakhouse with none of the pomp that seeps from many of the stuffy Midtown establishments—with a smaller price-tag as well. The steak is tender and juicy, but don't be afraid to branch out into their other options, like the perfectly grilled sausages. TVs are tuned to international soccer matches, fostering an enthusiastic, South American sports bar vibe in the red-brick dining room. Given its close proximity to nearby bars, this is the ideal place to gobble up a hearty meal before a big night out.

513 East 6th Street (at Avenue A). 212.228.2775. M-Th 1pm-midnight, F-Sat noon-1am, Sun noon-midnight. Appetizers $4-10, Entrées $10-25. **6** *to Astor Place.*

El Maguey Y La Tuna *Mexican*
Down-home décor breaks through the East Side, and the neighborhood's pretensions crumble into flaky forkfuls of banana piñata pastry at this authentic Mexican eatery. Traditional family recipes evoke the aromas and hues of the

owners' hometown, Puebla; try the signature enchiladas covered in a homemade mole sauce, thick with ground nuts, spiced cocoa, and subtle fruit flavors. Brilliant flags festoon the ceiling and the Vírgen de Guadalupe watches from the wall to complete the transformation from Manhattan to Mexico.

321 East Houston Street (at Ridge). 212.473.3744. T-Sun 11am-11pm, closed Monday. Appetizers $6-10, Entrées $8-20. **F V** *to Second Ave.*

Frankie's Spuntino *Italian*

Serving up *spuntinos* (snacks) in a friendly, romantic atmosphere, this cute Italian eatery provides quality normally associated with the Upper East Side, without the stuffiness of most of that area's restaurants. The dishes are small, so order a little bit of everything: fresh and hearty soups, eclectic salads, and any one of the great variety of cheeses. Be sure to check out the assortment of *crostini*—roasted slices of Italian bread piled high with mushrooms and truffle oil, or with cannelini, capers, and lemon. Organic produce, locally bought, is just one more reason to give this place a try.

17 Clinton Street (at Houston). 212.253.2303. Sun-Th 11am-midnight, F-Sat 11am-1am. Appetizers $6-11, Entrées $8-17. **J M Z F** *to Essex St.*

Kuma Inn *Southeast Asian, Tapas*

At the top of a steep flight of stairs lies an intimate and tranquil dining area where patrons at Kuma Inn feast on over 30 different small plates of innovative Asian fusion. Owner King Phojanakong, the child of a Filipino mother and a Thai father, creates signature nightly specials that steal the show: astonishingly fresh bigeye tuna tartare, pan-fried pork tonkatsu with watercress salad and lime butter, and tamarind-glazed Atlantic salmon in Thai coconut curry. Pair your meal with a flight of three sakes for $15 for a fun and savory experience.

113 Ludlow Street (at Rivington), 2nd Fl. 212.353.8866. T-Sun, 6pm-midnight, closed Monday. Tapas $5-11, cash only. **J M Z F** *to Essex St.*

Nelson Blue *New Zealand Grill*

This welcoming, intimate new eatery brings the tastes and style of New Zealand to a relaxed, casual dining experience. The funky, authentic décor features a wall of fine wines from Down Under, creating an atmosphere best suited for casual dates or a low-key night out. For a tasty starter, try the Tasman Bay crabcake, a great example of the chef's use of unusual yet perfectly paired sauces and sides; you can also choose from a variety of delectable skewers that will satisfy your wallet far better than a vacation south of the equator. Supplement the food with something from the impressive wine list; the restaurant also offers a host of original cocktails, including the flirtatious "panty-dropper."

233-235 Front Street (at Peck Slip). 212.346.9090. Daily 11:30am-2am. Appetizers $8-12, Entrées $12-18. **2 3** *to Fulton St.*

CASUAL

TEANY *Vegetarian Café*

Despite its hip clientele, Moby's pet project feels like a friendly community coffee shop—except here, the staggering variety of loose teas clearly takes precedence over espresso. The café serves lattes and mochaccinos, but it's the tea-based beverages, such as the stellar foamy and belly-warming "candied apple teanychino," that are the real standouts. The edibles are better than average café fare, and some dishes, like smoky gazpacho tempered with hunks of avocado and mango, are darn near-perfect. Adventurous eaters might like the vegan quiche; served with a tomato sauce laced with bits of soy sausage, it may not resemble the real McCoy, but has a mild flavor and pleasant texture thanks to cornbread dressing. For dessert, don't miss one of the best carrot cakes in the city, with an absurdly moist crumb and fluffy vegan icing.

90 Rivington Street (at Orchard). 212.475.9190. Sun-Th 10am-11pm, F-Sat 10am-1am. Food $4-8, Tea $3-8, cash only. **J M Z F** *to Essex St.*

Nightlife

'inoteca *Food and Drink*

This popular Italian wine and tapas bar takes its vintages seriously: thousands of bottles deck the walls and an eight-page wine list covers all bases. The staff is more than friendly, and is as accommodating to non-connoisseurs as to wine snobs. The open atmosphere—think wall to wall windows—is filled by eclectic music and dressed-to-impress 20-somethings both artsy and working class, making it ideal for a college student looking for a place to sit and talk.

98 Rivington Street (at Ludlow). 212.614.0473. Daily noon-3am. Drinks $8-12. J M Z F *to Essex St.*

BLVD *Club*

A combination dance club and restaurant, this high-class establishment stands out among the traditionally seedy places along the Bowery. It offers a little of everything, with a Latin American restaurant, private "green" rooms, ultra-private "white" rooms for celebrity parties, a performance area, and plenty of floor (and table) space to dance. After a long night of drinking, the café upstairs conveniently opens at 5am to help you sober up before you start another day.

199 Bowery Street (at Spring). 212.982.7767. M-Sat 10pm-4am, closed Sunday. J M Z *to Bowery.*

Gallery *Bar*

This unique locale combines an art gallery and a bar into an enjoyably unpretentious union of the two. But perhaps most importantly, it's a welcomed addition to the ever-growing art scene. To further this club's hybrid aesthetic, it features two floors, each offering separate and unique atmospheres, and often hosting different events and DJ's simultaneously. The main level, possessing a refreshingly intelligent vibe, pays homage to the works of different emerging artists, with new exhibits opening regularly. Down in the basement you'll find a more intimate, lounge-like feel, as well as the bar's permanent art collection, which features work from various artists; the graffiti mural by renowned street artist Wombat is especially notable.

120 Orchard Street (at Delancey). 212.529.2266. M-Sat 1pm- 4am, Sun 1pm-7pm. Drinks $12-$25. J M Z F *to Essex St.*

Good World Bar *Bar*

Tucked away in an unlikely setting, Good World is a true neighborhood bar. Technically there isn't a dance floor, but that's never stopped anyone in the mixed crowd from Chinatown and the Lower East Side from shaking their stuff—everyone meshes just fine once they've tasted the decadent Truffle Martini.

3 Orchard Street (at Canal). 212.925.9975. Daily 11am-4am. Drinks $5-11. F *to East Broadway.*

Identity *Lounge*

A seemingly ironic clean-cut dive, this lounge thumps techno and house music while a glittery disco ball rotates overhead and bartenders chatting in French. The bar does have an exotic *je ne sais quoi* quality, with excellent *caiphroska* blending the *caipirinha* of Brazil with vodka, blond sugar cane, fresh orange juice, and lime. For eats, try the Cypriot sausage and smoked kasseri cheese, which just might make you want to pack your bags and head for the Mediterranean.

511 East 6th Street (at Avenue A). 212.995.8889. Daily 1pm-4am. Drinks $7-11. N R W *to 8th St.*

Kush *Lounge*

This relaxed, Middle Eastern lounge is a good place to meet someone new—especially if you're looking for a European. Kush holds themed nights, so call to find out what's in store for the evening you're going; you can also entertain a private hookah party with flavors ranging from mint to peach. The custom-made Bombay Gunpowder, made with ginger ale, is one in a host of drinks that complement the atmosphere.

191 Christie Street (at Stanton). 212.677.7328. M-Sat 7pm-4am, closed Sunday. Drinks $7-12. F V *to Lower East Side.*

Libation *Club*

Don't be intimidated by the exclusive appearance of velvet ropes, black clothing-clad bouncers, and clipboard-toting girls at the door: the same old, laidback LES crew is still inside and the cover is only five bucks (on Saturday, $15 for guys). This dark, hip, three-floored enormity with spiraling ceilings and a more intimate mezzanine is home to a diverse crowd of mid-20 and 30-somethings both in couples and participating in a vibrant singles scene. On the weekends, NYU kids make their presence known, contributing a rowdy element to the air of unpretentious glamour this super-club usually exudes. In line with that vibe is the specialty drink menu ($10-$12), featuring fresh fruit martinis that still allow you the choice of vodka or gin. Later in the night, ascend the hidden stairs to the third-level dance floor where the music gets progressively louder and the bodies pack progressively tighter.

137 Ludlow Street (at Rivington). 212.529.2153. M-F 5pm-4am, Sat-Sun noon-4am. Drinks $7-10pm. J M Z F *to Essex St.*

Lolita *Bar*

On weekends, expect to find an abundance of stylish Lower East Siders at the bar and looking for love at this secretive neighborhood spot. On weekdays, though, Lolita remains fairly empty and is an excellent place to go for happy hour, which occurs daily from 5-8pm and offers amazing drink specials.

266 Broome Street (at Allen). 212.966.7223. Daily 5pm-4am. Drinks $6-7. J M Z F *to Essex St.*

Mercury Lounge *Music*

Once a headstone shop, the Mercury Lounge has established itself as a premiere venue for "just-breaking" bands. A high stage, excellent

A view of the Lower East Side

sound system, and standing room-only for three to five acts per night—featuring acoustic, alternative, and rock acts—ensures the lounge is alive and kicking.

217 East Houston Street (at Essex). 212.260.1214. Daily from 7pm; Shows M-Sat 7:30pm-1am. Drinks $4-7. **F V** *to Lower East Side.*

People Lounge *Lounge*

As the name would imply, everything at people is designed to incourage sociability. Two floors of lounge space provide ample room for mingling and meeting and comfortable couches and upholstered stools. Dim, warm lighting and high ceilings create the perfect socializing atmosphere, while the DJs eclectic hip-hop mix and the delicious infused-vodka drinks will have you and your crew meeting and greeting like there's no tomorrow.

163 Allen Street (at Stanton). 212.254.2668. T-Th 5:30pm-midnight, F 5:30pm-3:30am, Sat 7pm-3:30am, Sun 7-midnight, closed Monday. **F V** *to Lower East Side.*

Rewind *Lounge*

Serving brunch and an Italian-meets-New American dinner menu, Rewind is relatively new but starting off strong as a diverse crowd pleaser. Try the deliciously crafted mango mojito; the drink provides a good intro to the lounge's great look, solid service, and loads of ambition.

137 Essex Street (at Rivington). 212.779.7923. T 5pm-4am, Th-Sat 8pm-4am, closed Sun-M. Drinks $6-13. **J M Z F** *to Essex St.*

Tuts *Club*

This chic yet cozy hookah bar and club—luxurious decorations share the space with belly dancers on the weekend and music playing on the big screen—serves great food with delicious cocktails. The bar and lounge also serve authentic North African-tinged Middle Eastern food; complement the dishes with one of the over 15 flavors of deliciously smooth hookah.

196 Orchard Street (at Houston). 212.961.7507. Daily 7pm-4am. Drinks $6-10. **J M Z F** *to Essex St.*

Verlaine *Tapas, Asian*

A multicultural crowd of laid-back and friendly twenty-somethings makes this LES lounge a choice after-work destination. With dim lighting, subtle hip hop, and red-tinged décor, the space represents the marriage of earth and industry, with the hum of constant chatter only adding to the vibe. The menu, composed entirely of Southeast Asian tapas, includes extensive vegetarian options; the pan-seared salmon and vegetable curry puffs are excellent. The most ordered item, though, is the Hanoi Martini. The drink has a loyal and adoring fan base, due either to its $4 price during happy hour (5-10pm daily) or the lychee at the bottom of the glass. Though not a quick-stop spot—the service is less than timely—one look at the cocktail menu and its homemade hot pepper-infused vodka and ginger-infused sake, and you'll be in no rush to leave.

110 Rivington Street (at Essex). 212.614.2494. Sun-W 5pm-1am, Th-Sat 5pm-4am. Tapas $7-10. **J M Z F** *to Essex St.*

Whiskey Ward *Whiskey Bar*

Cheap beer, a jukebox blasting rock-and-roll, and a refreshingly mixed crowd attract a growing group of regulars, from hipsters and college students to an older sort who actually drinks whiskey. Decked out with exposed brick walls and handmade furnishings, the bar stocks dozens of whiskeys, six taps, and 20 types of bottled beers. While not ideal for dancing, a friendly staff and a bustling vibe make this a great place to catch up with some friends and shoot some pool.

121 Essex Street (at Rivington). 212.477.2998. Daily 5pm-4am. Drinks $3-16. **J M Z F** *to Essex St.*

Arts

ABC No Rio

The name of this "collectively-run community center for art and activism" is spray-painted above a mural of a pink bird on the building's front side, next to a sculpture incorporating large metal gears. Inside, there is a darkroom (though photographers must provide their own paper), a 'zine library, a computer center, and silkscreen equipment for aspiring Warhols. Events include open poetry readings and weekly concerts—local punk bands on Saturdays, experimental jazz on Sundays. The center also hosts Food Not Bombs, a popular weekly vegan lunch held in Tompkins Square Park.

156 Rivington Street (at Suffolk). 212.254.3697. abcnorio.org. Hours and prices vary. J M Z F *to Essex St.*

Dixon Place

This small venue is known as a jumping-off point for experimental and avant-garde theatre and dance groups—Blue Man Group, for instance, was discovered at an open mic series here. The theater's legal capacity is 75, although it looks full with just a few dozen audience members; it also sponsors shows at larger venues around the city. Throughout its 21-year history, the theatre has fostered new works and works-in-progress, with an emphasis on minority, feminist, and gay and lesbian themes. Come see one of the almost nightly performances to get a sense of truly artist-driven work—but catch it soon, before a move to 161 Chrystie in late 2008.

258 Bowery (at Stanton), 2nd Floor. 212.219.0736. dixonplace.org. Tickets free-$15. F V *to Lower East Side.*

FusionArts Museum

You can't miss this museum's entrance—plastered with bicycle tires, car hubs, and multicolored wiring, it showcases the historically quirky and alternative character of the Lower East Side. Run by the non-profit Converging Arts Media Organization, the museum is dedicated to exhibiting and archiving contemporary "fusion art," self-defined as "a merging of painting, sculpture, light, sound, video projection, photography, performance, and the written word." Before you leave, make sure to check out the 3-D art in the bathroom,

considered to be just another gallery space.

57 Stanton Street (at Eldridge). Tu-W 1pm-6pm, Sun and Th 1pm-7pm, M and F by appointment only, closed Saturday. F V *to Lower East Side.*

Landmark Sunshine Cinema

Located where the Houston Hippodrome cinema stood over fifty years ago, the Sunshine is today one of the most popular independent movie theatres in the city, with a sleek design to complement the hip flicks—a mix of high-quality, low-budget independent films, classic throwbacks, and current blockbusters. Gourmands will be pleased by concessions ranging from standard popcorn, accompanied by free gourmet popcorn seasonings, to Fizzy Lizzy sodas, nut brittles, and Japanese Pocky. Stadium seating and a serious audience aversion to talking through films ensure an enjoyable experience once the lights go down.

143 East Houston Street (at Eldridge). 212.330.8182. landmarktheatres.com. $10.75. F V *to Lower East Side.*

Nuyorican Poets Café

This bar and concert venue is famous for its slam poetry performances, and it doesn't shy away from that reputation: the outside façade is painted with a gargantuan mural of the face of Pedro Pietri, the late slam artist who frequently performed his satirical material here. Inside, a motley crew of stools and folding and wooden chairs cluster around small tables in front of the low stage. If you want to see a slam, visit on Friday nights; if you think your own poetry is worthy, come on Wednesdays for the open slam. Or, stop by on Thursday to see a 17-piece salsa band perform. Unfortunately, aside from the talent and the reputation, though, the nightspot is fairly unremarkable.

236 East 3rd Street (at Avenue C). 212.505.8183. nuyorican.org. F V *to Lower East Side.*

Participant, Inc.

With avant-garde and occasionally bizarre performances and exhibits, this gallery has been providing a nurturing environment for contemporary artists since 2001. Exhibitions tend to be heady, and the group's focus on artists' interests means that laypeople might feel left out in the cold. Intellectuals and creative types, however, will love the gallery's premise: "artists produce significant work through a deep relationship with an organization whose focus is its committed collaborations with them."

95 Rivington Street (at Ludlow). 212.254.4334. participantinc.org. W-Sun noon-7pm, closed M-T. **J M Z F** *to Essex St.*

Smith-Stewart

This fledgling gallery is easily outshone, literally, by the wildly sculptured exterior of the neighboring FusionArts Museum, but its exhibits are easily just as interesting. The simplicity of the studio itself doesn't detract from the art; curator Amy Smith-Stewart, whose resumé includes a curating stint at P.S. 1, plans to exhibit the work of international, intergenerational artists of all media. "Art is supposed to be part of the everyday," says Smith-Stewart, who wants the art here to be a piece of the local culture, rather than cordoned off from people's lives. The gallery may be small—about the size of an artist's studio—but the artistic talent is substantial.

53 Stanton Street (at Eldridge). 212.477.2821. smith-stewart.com. W-Sun noon-6pm, closed M-T. **F V** *to Lower East Side.*

Shopping

Alife Rivington Club

Fans of elitism and leopard-print high-tops will fall head over heels for the room behind the all-but-hidden exterior of 158 Rivington, where nothing but a small plaque indicates the shop's existence. Customers must be buzzed in to get inside and see the merchandise—a collection of goods that's lifeblood for the young, urban, moneyed men who make up the club's clientele. Sit on the black leather sofa and admire the expensive limited-edition Nikes, Pumas, and New Balances of all colors and patterns, displayed in illuminated cubbyholes, as loud hip hop music reverberates throughout the store. This is the kind of place where awestruck clients cradle shoes as though they were made of crystal—sneaker fanatics will feel right at home.

158 Rivington Street (at Clinton). 212.375.8128. rivingtonclub.com. M-Sat 11am-7pm, Sun noon-7pm. **J M Z F** *to Essex St.*

Babeland

The sign on the door, requesting that customers show respect for the privacy and dignity of all patrons, indicates that this is hardly your stereotypical sleazy sex shop. Formerly (and famously) known as Toys in Babeland, this shop sells books, condoms, lubricant, candles, bath oils, party games, and sex toys of all shapes, colors, materials, and sizes. With plenty of helpful signs to explain the occasionally puzzling merchandise, and lots of educational pamphlets describing proper sexual technique, the store seems to be on a mission to make sex toys accessible to everyone. Thankfully, the space is clean, the dance music soundtrack is fun, and the employees are knowledgeable and respectful.

94 Rivington Street (at Ludlow). 212.375.1701. babeland.com. Sun-W noon-10pm, Th-Sat noon-11pm. **J M Z F** *to Essex St.*

Bluestockings

Much friendlier than you'd expect a radical, anti-patriarchal bookstore to be, Bluestockings offers progressivist books, novels, socialist pamphlets, T-shirts, and magazines such as *Off Our Backs: The Feminist Newsjournal.* It may also be the only bookstore in the world that sells reusable menstrual cups and pads—look for them, inexplicably, below the DVDs. The small fair trade café serves coffee drinks, vegan cookies, and organic chocolate bars; during quieter hours, patrons like to sit on the plastic chairs by the window, drink coffee, and read beneath Japanese lanterns. Frequent store events include readings, magazine and book release parties, and film screenings.

172 Allen Street (at Stanton). 212.777.6028. bluestockings.com. Daily 11am-11pm. **F V** *to Lower East Side.*

Hudson Street Paper

The owner of this geographically-misnamed stationery store claims to have the best selection of greeting cards in the city. Much of the merchandise has a city theme—look out for everything from cards featuring photos of hot dogs with "New York" written on them in mustard to those with NYC-themed political cartoons—but the sheer volume of cards and card shop-esque gifts ensures that you'll find whatever you're looking for.

149 Orchard Street (at Rivington). 212.229.1064. M-Sat noon-8pm, Sun noon-7pm. **J M Z F** *to Essex St.*

Lighting by Gregory

A tall person's nightmare and a stoner's dream, endless metal chains hang from the ceiling of this lighting emporium, each attached to a working lamp. A series of small, connected rooms containing ceiling fans, bathroom and bookshelf lamps, outdoor lanterns, shelf lighting, and, inexplicably, the offices of the people who work here, this maze of a store is fun to wander around in, especially for people who really like turning on and off light bulbs. Much (if not most) of the merchandise here is affordable and intended for everyday use, but don't miss the room of jaw-dropping crystal and glass chandeliers, whose centerpiece is a $16,789 custom-made Schonbek.

158 Bowery (at Broome). 212.226.1276. lightingbygregory.com. M-F 8:30am-5:30pm, Sat-Sun 9am-5pm. **J M Z** *to Bowery.*

Mooshoes

The vegan proprietors of this small shoe store don't sell anything made with animal products, and although some of the canvas slip-ons look just as frumpy as you'd expect them to, other items, like the cute Novacas pumps, are surprisingly stylish. The employees are laid-back and helpful, and pet lovers will be delighted to find the friendly resident cats reclining on the counter. The boutique also sells belts, T-shirts, vegan cookbooks, and bags with prices comparable to their non-vegan counterparts; lots of free pamphlets on living vegan in the city are available in the window.

152 Allen Street (at Rivington). 212.254.6512. mooshoes. com. M-Sat 11:30am-7:30pm, Sun noon-6pm. **F V** *to Lower East Side.*

Organic Avenue

This strange mix of clothing boutique and café sells only organic products, including juice blends, soups, salads, and raw desserts to fill your stomach, plus shirts, dresses, and pants to cover it. Also look out for raw food bamboo serving ware, cookbooks, vitamins and supplements, and natural makeup. Clothing styles are simple and classy, but natural fibers don't come cheap: Expect to pay $62 for a cotton T-shirt. If you live and breathe organic, become a member for $40 a year to get discounts on merchandise.

101 Stanton Street (at Ludlow). 212.334.4593. organicavenue.com. Daily noon-10pm. **F V** *to Lower East Side.*

TG-170

This extremely trendy women's-only boutique sells a large selection of funky and girly dresses, tops, jeans, bags, and jewelry by lesser-known designers seasons before they get picked up by Barneys. Styles range from casual to dressy; prices from about $150 to several times that. Men who find themselves waiting as their girlfriends try on the entire store can play with the owner's three West Highland Terriers.

170 Ludlow Street (at Stanton). 212.995.8660. tg170.com. Daily noon-8pm. **F V** *to Lower East Side.*

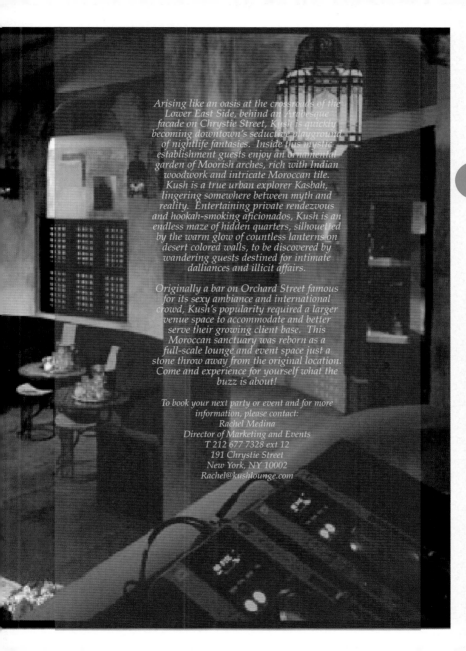

Arising like an oasis at the crossroads of the Lower East Side, behind an Arabesque facade on Chrystie Street, Kush is quickly becoming downtown's seductive playground of nightlife fantasies. Inside this mystic establishment guests enjoy an ornamental garden of Moorish arches, rich with Indian woodwork and intricate Moroccan tile. Kush is a true urban explorer Kasbah, lingering somewhere between myth and reality. Entertaining private rendezvous and hookah-smoking aficionados, Kush is an endless maze of hidden quarters, silhouetted by the warm glow of countless lanterns on desert colored walls, to be discovered by wandering guests destined for intimate dalliances and illicit affairs.

Originally a bar on Orchard Street famous for its sexy ambiance and international crowd, Kush's popularity required a larger venue space to accommodate and better serve their growing client base. This Moroccan sanctuary was reborn as a full-scale lounge and event space just a stone throw away from the original location. Come and experience for yourself what the buzz is about!

To book your next party or event and for more information, please contact:
Rachel Medina
Director of Marketing and Events
T 212 677 7328 ext 12
191 Chrystie Street
New York, NY 10002
Rachel@kushlounge.com

GREENWICH VILLAGE

The West Village a neighborhood brimming with charm. With a landscape of countless bars, restaurants, bakeries, and boutiques, and a history of sheltering generations of artists, writers, and revolutionaries, Greenwich holds court in New York as the elder statesman of hip.

During New York's 19th-century explosion, Greenwich Village thrived as residents commissioned famous architects and artists to design and ornament their buildings. As the art scene increased in importance early in the 20th century, the Village's distance from the financial concerns of Midtown's Broadway theaters and publishing powerhouses resulted in the development of the neighborhood's own distinctly bohemian culture. Experimental theater, galleries specializing in avant-garde art, and irreverent magazines exploded onto the scene. Wild parties, candlelit tearooms, novelty nightclubs, and bizarre boutiques soon followed.

Historically home to a strong gay community, the area was the site of the first stirrings of the Gay Liberation movement with the 1969 Stonewall Riots. The community was also hard hit by the AIDS epidemic in the '80s, which spurred local activists to take a leading role in combating the spread of the disease through education and awareness.

The central axis of Bleecker and MacDougal Streets—also known as Bourbon Street North—hosts a cluster of cafés by day, and transforms into a bustling thoroughfare of bars and cheap eats by night. Stray from the main drags and you'll stumble upon quieter streets, like Waverly Place and Bedford Street, with quaint restaurants and shops. Take a break at Sheridan Square, and explore corner jazz clubs, trendy bars, and NYU dorm parties. Here, anything goes—from pink hair to size-13 stilettos.

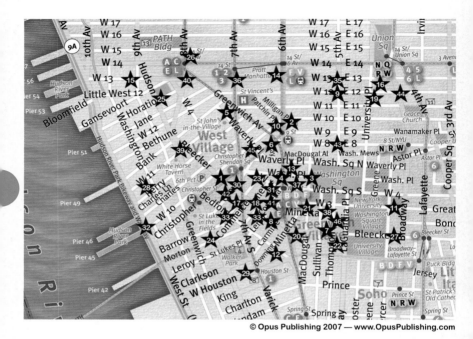

© Opus Publishing 2007 — www.OpusPublishing.com

GREENWICH VILLAGE

SIGHTS/ATTRACTIONS
1. Bleeker Street
2. Stonewall Inn
3. Washington Square Park

DINING
4. Blue Hill
5. Bone Lick Café
6. Corner Bistro
7. Cuba
8. Famous Joe's Pizza
9. Gotham Bar & Grill
10. Gusto
11. Leela Lounge
12. Mas
13. Pasita
14. Salam
15. Spice Market

NIGHTLIFE
16. Bar 13
17. Barrow Street
18. Blind Tiger Ale House
19. Bowlmor Lanes
20. Café Wha?
21. Club Groove
22. Cubby Hole
23. Down the Hatch
24. Henrietta Hudson
25. Hudson Bar and Books
26. Manor
27. Mr. BLACK
28. The Otherroom
29. S.O.B.s
30. Village Vanguard
31. Vol de Nuit

ARTS
32. 401 Projects
33. Cherry Lane
34. Cornelia Street Café
35. Forbes Galleries
36. The National Museum of LGBT History

SHOPPING
37. American Apparel
38. Bleecker Bob's
39. Marc by Marc Jacobs
40. MXYPLYZYK
41. The Pink Pussycat
42. Reiss
43. Rugged Sole
44. The Strand
45. Three Lives & Co.
46. Village Chess Shop

Sights/Attractions

Bleeker Street

Once the center of 1960s New York bohemian life, Bleecker has gone upscale in recent years—long gone are the days when $30 paid your rent. A major artery of downtown life, the street winds through the Village, lined with stores. For shops and record stores from the area's heyday, you'll have to head east of Seventh Avenue; if your desire for designer goods is stronger than your desire for authenticity, the western section of Bleecker, where the street starts running north, is peppered with up-market fashion shops.

A C E **B D F V** *to West 4th.*

Stonewall Inn

On June 28, 1969, police raided this gay bar on Christopher Street; such raids were common in the '60s, usually resulting in arrests of patrons and the closing of the bar for the night. At Stonewall, though, something happened—accounts vary—that sent the crowd over the edge. The rioting that broke out, in which both police and protesters were injured, lasted for days, and marked the beginning of the Gay Liberation movement. While the Stonewall Inn has gone through many transformations in the years since, its legacy remains, and for that alone it's well worth a visit.

53 Christopher Street (at Sixth). 212.647.8258. stonewall-place.com. **1** *to Christopher St.*

Universities: Cooper Union, New School, New York University

Three universities call Greenwich Village home, ensuring that the neighborhood retains its reputation as epicenter of all things young and hip. Most of the buildings around Washington Square Park belong to NYU, the largest private university in the country, while Cooper Union is centered on Astor Place; the New School's buildings are spread throughout the Village. The universities often host public talks by academic, artistic, or public figures, and each of these schools has strong arts programs—shows at NYU and art exhibitions at the New School's Parsons School of Design can be as good as anything you'll find uptown.

cooper.edu, newschool.edu, and nyu.edu.

Washington Square Park

This park is more village square than green space; on any given day, the area is filled with chess players, NYU students, current hippies, ex-hippies, musicians, and visitors from around the world. The park's iconic monument, the Washington Arch, is a 77-foot-tall marble monument designed by architect Stanford White and built in 1892 to mark the 100-year anniversary of George Washington's arrival in New York. Come on a nice day to sit on a bench by the central fountain and watch street performers entertain the crowd. For a more morbid tour of the park, be sure to stop by the "hanging elm," famous for being the site of public executions in the 1800s.

West 4th Street at MacDougal. washingtonsquarepark.org. **A C E** **B D F V** *to West 4th St.*

Dining

UPSCALE

Blue Hill *New American*

Muted earth tones, artfully recessed lighting, and high-end decorator touches permeate the intimate dining room at this understated and sophisticated eatery. The menu is simple, but strikingly thoughtful; favorites include the asparagus and poached egg and the pork tenderloin with pork jowl. The wine list is comprehensive and refreshing, with useful notes about flavor characteristics printed on the menu. If in doubt, ask the sommelier for an artful pairing of wine by the glass with each course.

75 Washington Place (at 6th). 212.539.1776. M-Sat 5:30pm-11pm, Sun 5:30pm-10pm. Appetizer $10-16, Entrées $28-34. **A C E** **B D F V** *to West 4th St.*

Gotham Bar and Grill *New American*

Everything reaches great heights at this legendary eatery: the acclaim for chef Alfred

Portal, the ceilings and cream cloth chandeliers, the garden-view windows, the glass carafes of grappa on the bar, the pyramid of exquisite food that balances precariously on your plate—and, of course, the prices. While you probably won't become friends with your waiter, the theatrical setting is perfect for its elegantly attired clientele. the chocolate cake sums up the dining experience perfectly: warm, inviting, divinely prepared, and rich.

12 East 12th Street (at Fifth). 212.620.4020. Lunch M-F noon-2:15pm; Dinner M-Th 5:30pm-10pm, F 5:30pm-11pm, Sat-Sun 5pm-11pm. Appetizer $13-115, Entrées $32-48. **4 5 6 L N R Q W** *to Union Square.*

Gusto Ristorante *Italian*

Like a scene out of late 1950's Italian cinema, Gusto's sexy, black velvet booths, shining ebony table tops, and white ceramic floors envelop diners in a world of sleek and simple sophistication. Buffalo mozzarella served with fresh tomatoes makes for a light and refreshing start, but it's the rustically inventive main dishes, like the perfectly cooked Malfati pasta and the Sicilian meatballs, that make this menu truly memorable. Begin the night with a bubbling prosecco cocktail at the long, glowing bar, or sit at a candlelit table on the outdoor terrace and watch the people strolling by. Thanks to the attentive waitstaff, attention to detail, and exquisite presentation, you'll leave feeling like you've experienced something truly special.

60 Greenwich Avenue (at 6th). 212.924.8000. Lunch M-F noon-3pm, Sat-Sun noon-4pm; Dinner Sun-Th 5:30pm-11pm, Fri-Sat 5:30pm-midnight. Appetizers $8-$16, Entrées $16-$39. **A C E B D F V** *to West 4th St.*

Washington Square Park

WEST VILLAGE LITERARY LANDMARKS

The Village has a long history as a hub for literary greats, and many of the haunts where these icons spent their time are still around today. **THE WHITE HORSE TAVERN** (*567 Hudson Street, 212-989-3956*) has hosted Dylan Thomas, Norman Mailer, James Baldwin, and Jack Kerouac, who became here infamous for causing scenes. **CHUMLEY'S** (*86 Bedford Street, 212-675-4449*), a one-time speakeasy, has seen writers from the Lost Generation to the Beats; the walls are covered with pictures and book covers of the authors who have visited. If you need help navigating the neighborhood's labrynth-like streets, check out a **LITERARY PUB CRAWL** (*Sat 2pm, White Horse Tavern, 212-613-5796*) walking tour, guided by local actors.

Mas (farmhouse) *New American*
This classically cool restaurant is intimate and fun, with outstanding eco-friendly food. Hippies and liberals will appreciate the local produce and sustainable farming techniques used by chef Galen Zamarra, but even the staunchest Republican won't be able to resist the sumptuous $68 tasting menu. The décor is New York chic with touches of the French countryside ("Mas" means farmhouse in French). The wine list has the breadth and depth of the most elite restaurants in the world, and the Fanny Bay oysters, served with a rose champagne, are definitely worth a try. For those on a budget, the after-hours menu is more reasonable, with beer and hot gruyere cheese under 10 dollars, and a fun late-night bar scene.
39 Downing Street (at Bedford). 212.255.1790. M-Sat 6pm-4am. Appetizers $14-21, Entrées $32-36. **1** *to Houston St.*

Spice Market *Asian Thai*
Entering renowned chef Jean-Georges Vongerichten's most dramatic New York eatery—one of his eight city offerings—feels like stepping onto the street of a bustling Thai market. The exciting atmosphere sets the perfect tone for a unique dining experience inspired by Asian street food. Start the night at the ultra-trendy and conversation-friendly bar before taking a seat upstairs, where the small plates menu will stun and delight your palette. There are no wrong choices to make when ordering, though the shaved tuna is a must. To get the full effect, wash down the satisfying spices with a Pattaya champagne cocktail.
403 West 13th Street (at Ninth). 212.675.2322. Lunch M-Sat noon-4pm; Dinner Sun-W 5:30pm-midnight, Th-Sat 5:30pm-1pm; Bar daily noon-2am. Appetizers $9-15, Entrées $18-36. **A C E** L *to 14th St.*

MID-RANGE

Pasita *Venezuelan*
At this neighborhood tapas bar, the chatter of the crowd—a mix of locals and Village visitors—competes with funky background music, mixing into a varied cacophony of animated noises that exemplify the atmosphere of definitive cool. An inlaid oak bar, mock chandeliers, warm brick walls, and an open kitchen decorate the space so well, you'd never guess the food is so affordable. Kick off the evening with a free wine tasting (T-Sun 5-7), followed by a hefty platter of *pasapalos*—an assortment of fried Latin American tapas served with guacamole and green pepper salsa. Grab a few small plates to round out the meal, or try the *ropa vieja*, complemented by caramelized onion and red pepper, if you need something more filling. Finish it off with a glass

of tamarind sangria, an innovative twist on the perennial classic.

47 Eighth Avenue (at West 4th street). 212.255.3900. T-W, Sun 5pm-11pm, Th-Sat 5pm-midnight. Appetizers and Entrées $3-16. **A C E L** *to 14th St.*

Leela Lounge *Indian*

Exposed brick and clear glass welcome trendy guests to this superbly innovative haute Indian restaurant and lounge, where beautiful faces gather for colorful signature cocktails like the Chaitini—which combines Indian spiced chai with Baileys and vodka—and the Sex in Goa. While most Indian restaurants limit their menus to a particular region, the food here is inspired by all the tastes of the Indian diaspora, creating bold, richly flavored dishes. The Bharta bruschetta—baked bread served with spiced fire-roasted eggplant—is bursting with flavor. For the main course, try the ginger-infused spinach and cottage cheese koftas; even if you're not a vegetarian, the delicious combination of fresh, savory spices and sweet plum tomato sauce is impossible to resist. Best of all, the food is prepared without using heavy cream, butter, or ghee, so it won't leave you feeling weighed down.

1 West 3rd Street (at Broadway). 212.529.2059. Daily noon-midnight. Appetizers $7-$25, Entrées $14-$24. **A C E B D F V** *to West 4th St.*

Salam *Middle Eastern*

Follow the smell of spices into this low-lit restaurant where everything, including the food, earth tones, and delicately painted porcelain, summon Arabian air into New York nights. The interior is cozy enough for a date, and the waitstaff will advise you to order a number of small dishes, so take your time to appreciate them. The wide range of *meze* include some stellar offerings: mild Syrian goat cheese, flaky fried zucchini, and aromatically spiced samosas. The *ouzi*—crusty fillo dough filled with meats or vegetables—are also highly recommended. End with intriguing Syrian desserts or the intoxicating cinnamon ice cream.

104 West 13th Street (at Sixth). 212.741.0277. M-F

5pm-11pm, Sat-Sun noon-11pm. Appetizers $4.50-$7.50, Entrées $13 - $20. **1 2 3 B D F V** *to 14th St.*

CASUAL

Bone Lick Park *American Barbecue*

The sidewalk tables at this barbecue pit are perfect for watching the constant stream of Village characters who pass by. If you can't get a seat by the curb, enjoy nicely spaced tables in the dimly lit interior, filled with friendly regulars enjoying beers and spicy wings. Sip on a refreshing $3.50 mojito as you decide between the baby back ribs and pulled pork—both, as the moniker suggests, are bone-licking good. Though the key lime pie is delightfully tangy, you'll probably be too stuffed from your generously sized entrée, side dish, and cornbread to indulge.

75 Greenwich Avenue (at Seventh). 212.647.9600. Daily 11:30am-11pm. Appetizers $5-8, Entrées $12-19. **1 2 3** *to 14th St.*

Cuba *Cuban*

From the salsa dancers performing between tables to the antique cigar roller sitting in the window, there's nothing if not atmosphere at this new restaurant and bar. Authentic tapas creations are paired with exotic mojitos and sangrias, as well as a wide selection of superb desserts bursting with Cuban flavor. Check out the live band four days a week, or for a quieter dining experience, escape to one of the intimate rooms in the back.

224 Thompson Street (at Bleeker). 212.420.7878. Daily noon-midnight. Appetizers $6-13, Entrées $16-23. **A C E F V** *to West 4th St.*

Famous Joe's Pizza *Pizza*

This is arguably the best pizza joint in the city—at least, according to Ben Affleck. Their not-too-greasy, perfectly baked thin-crust pies are topped with sweet tomato sauce and just enough cheese; but don't expect a place to sit. Instead, eat your slice on a bustling Village sidewalk and quietly take in the flavors.

7 Carmine Street (at Bleecker). 212.255.3946. Daily 9am-4am. Slice $2, Pies start at $17. **A C E B D F V** *to West 4th St.*

Nightlife

Bar 13 *Club*

On sweaty summer nights, this club's rooftop patio serves as a tropical summer escape in the middle of bustling Midtown, packed with an animated crowd perched on white plastic furniture against a backdrop of plastic palm trees. During the school year, you'll find yourself jostling for drinks alongside hip NYU students, but with two spacious floors of comfortable, low-level black couches and several secluded corner sofas, you can still find an intimate spot for a quiet chat. The music changes drastically every night – there are poetry slams on Mondays, hip hop parties on Saturdays, and rock and punk performances by local bands at Sunday's popular SHOUT! parties.

35 East 13th Street (at University). 212.979.6677. Hours and cover charge vary daily. **4 5 6** N R Q W L *to Union Square.*

Blind Tiger Ale House *Tavern*

The bartenders seem to know everything about Blind Tiger Ale House, and they pride themselves on great beers, small portions, and creative freedom. Beer Cocktails are the newest trend here, blending beer flavors with unexpected ingredients to lure those who usually stick to cosmopolitans and mixed drinks. Try the Kentucky Derby, which combines chilled beer with mint and sugar cane to mimic a julep. Many a Villager is drawn in by the large open windows that are kept open even as the weather cools; a working fireplace is used in the winter months, and provides the perfect setting for chowing down on a variety of good pub snacks.

281 Bleecker Street (at Jones). 212.462.4682. Daily 11:30am-4am. Drinks $15-25. **1 2 3** *to Christopher St.*

Bowlmor Lanes *Bowling*

Forget the party hats and five pin lanes with inflatable bumpers in the gutters—this bowling alley features a velvet rope at the door, waitress service to each lane, and way more shooters than bowling pins. The cocktail list equals almost any bar in town; try the crisp but potent apple martini and the liquid cookie shot, which tastes uncannily like the oatmeal variety. There's also an extensive food menu with a huge selection of appetizers—try the chicken tenders, tangy buffalo wings, or the light and crispy vegetarian spring rolls served with a spicy chili plum sauce for a very un-bowling alley option. On Mondays, Night Strike gets you unlimited bowling, plus rental of those so-awful-they're-fun shoes, from 10pm until 2am for $22; just be prepared for a long wait. With two floors of bowling, 48 lanes, a live DJ, and excellent service, it's no wonder Bowlmor has managed to hang around since 1938.

110 University Place (at 12th). 212.255.8188. Daily 11am-1am or later, closed Sunday. **4 5 6** N R Q W L *to Union Square.*

Café Wha? *Music*

The exposed-brick walls of this Greenwich Village veteran hold the most eclectic and enduring house band in the city; the "Wha Band" will play anything from Bob Marley to Santana, with the occasional *Since U Been Gone* thrown in. The lively beats are designed to get you out of your seat and dancing, and you won't be lonely if you do; dance space is tight, and the floor tends to get crowded. The café also showcases comedy acts on Friday and Saturday nights. The intimate seating and the signature Alabama slammers help create a friendly setting, while the promptly served *whappetizers* will leave your stomach—and possibly your soul—singing.

115 MacDougal Street (at Bleecker). 212.254.3706. Sun, T-Th 8:30pm-2:30am, F-Sat 8:30pm-4am, M 9pm-3am. Cover $5-15. **A C E B D F V** *to West 4th St.*

Club Groove *Music*

Only a few steps from the famed club Blue Note in the heart of the West Village, Club Groove feels like it's in an entirely different city. The "Home of Rhythm and Blues," it's also home to a small

FAST FACTS

ⓘ Scenic Stroll: Bleeker Street

ⓘ Major Subway Stations: Christopher St-Sheridan Square (**1**), West 4th St (**A C E**, B D F V), 8th Ave-14th St (**A C E**, L), 14th St (**1 2 3**)

ⓘ Kooky Corner: MXYPLYZYK

ⓘ Neighborhood Landmarks: Chumley's, C.O. Bigelow Chemists, Washington Square Park

ⓘ Quintessential Neighborhood Event: Annual Village Halloween Parade

ⓘ Famous Historical Moment: Stonewall Riots in 1969

ⓘ Celebrity Hangouts: Florent, Pastis, SoHo House, Spice Market

ⓘ Notable Residents: E.E. Cummings, Theodore Dreiser, Henry James, Edna St. Vincent Millay, Eugene O'Neill, Mark Rothko, Dylan Thomas

ⓘ Schools: Cooper Union, The New School, New York Univeristy, Yeshiva University's Bejamin N. Cardozo School of Law

number of tight house bands, all of which play an innovative mix of original and cover R&B, soul, and hip-hop, both originals and covers. Guest artists pop in occasionally, but the place really belongs to a few artists-in-residence who, with a highly entertaining combination of music and banter, keep guests wishing they could get up and dance—there's no dance floor—until their sets end at 2 or 3 in the morning.

125 MacDougal Street (at West 3rd). 212.254.9393. Call for show schedule. Drinks $6-10, two-drink minimum. Cover F-Sat $5. **A C E B D F V** *to West 4th St.*

Corner Bistro *Bar*

A bar that once saw fleets of sailors and travelers arriving from abroad now welcomes a clientele clad in anything from suits to baseball hats;

come-as-you-are is key at this classic bohemian structure that dates back to the 1800s. The Corner Bistro specializes in good, inexpensive, and cold beer, along with great burgers, but if you can divert your eyes from the mouthwatering food, be on the lookout for local jazz celebrities who drop in occasionally. While the front area is small, there's plenty of room in the back for the groups of friends this place was made for.

331 West 4th Street (at Jane). 212.242.9502. M-Sat 11:30am-4am, Sun noon-4am. Drinks $3-5. Cash only. **A C E** *to 14th St.*

The Cubby Hole *LGBT*

The concept is refreshingly simple: casual good times at a charming neighborhood drinking spot. While technically a lesbian bar, Cubby Hole was one of the first mixed bars in the area, and it welcomes an eclectic cross section of patrons with no discrimination or attitude towards any gender, age, or sexual orientation. TV screens play cartoons, and the ceiling and walls are host to some outrageous décor, most notably a wild collection of paper lanterns. While the bar doesn't serve food, they do have a binder filled with take-out menus, and will order upon request if you are feeling peckish.

281 West 12th Street (at 4th). 212.243.9041. M-F 4pm-4am, Sat-Sun 2pm-4am. Drinks $5-10. cash only. **1 2 3** *to 14th St.*

Down The Hatch *Bar*

This basement dive, where the rafters are adorned with Christmas lights and the beer flows like eggnog, pays homage to college frat parties with a gum-stained and beer-soaked wooden floor and long lines for Beirut and Foosball tables. Rowdy and excitable students and recent grads watch sports games on flat screen TVs, while deafening hip hop and rock blares from the speakers. There are daily and hourly rotating drink specials (including half-priced drinks M-F 2-8pm) and on the weekends (Sat-Sun 1-6pm), you can get all-you-can-eat wings and three pitchers of beer for a mere $19.

179 West 4th Street (at Jones). 212.627.9747. Daily noon-4am. Drinks $3-6. **A C E B D F V** *to West 4th St.*

Henrietta Hudson *Lesbian Bar*

For wall to wall women and strong drinks with an attitude, head to this always packed lesbian bar, famous throughout the city. A smaller space, thoughtfully laid out with a dance floor between two bars and plenty of places to sit on the edges, this dive reminds you that you're on women's turf from the moment you step up to the bouncers at the door.

438 Hudson Street (at Morton). 212.924.3347. M-F 4pm-4am, Sat-Sun 2pm-4am. Drinks $7-$9. **1** *to Houston St.*

Hudson Bar and Books *Cigar Bar*

A true West Village gem, and one of the few places in the city where you can still legally smoke indoors. A robust cigar and scotch menu provides real substance for this quaint literary-themed bar, although the $15 cocktails are well-made and justify the price—you'll only need one or two before you start writing the next great American novel yourself. Come after work or late in the evening; you won't be disappointed in the trendy yet classic contradiction that is Hudson Bar and Books.

636 Hudson Street (at Horatio). 212.229.2642. Daily 5pm-3am. Drinks $15. **A C E** *to 14th St.*

The Manor *Club*

The ever-present line outside this Meatpacking District hotspot betrays what the subtle and simply marked exterior doesn't: hidden behind the dark, heavy doors is one of the hottest (and coolest) lounges in the city. The former home of Pink Elephant wears its $2 million makeover well, with an interior with inspirations ranging from old English, heavy with masculine leather, to Japanese, with a sleekly geometrical polished-wood bar. The mood, energetic but convivial, sucks you in from the moment you walk in the door; lounge in the Trophy Room for a bit of r&r, or hit the dance floor and move to a mix of house, rock, and R&B with the up-market downtowners who make up the crowd.

73 Eighth Avenue (at 14th). 212.463.0022. T-Sat 10pm-4am, closed Sun-M. Drinks $8-12. **A C E L** *to 14th St.*

Mr. BLACK *LGBT*

With wildly uninhibited dancers shaking to bass-thumping beats, what appears to be a tiny hole in the wall is actually what some call the best gay club in the East Village, frequented by a young, hip crowd. The dark dance floor is lit by glimmering '80s-style disco balls, and music pumps throughout. The signature Mr. Black Smash, which combines gin, juices, and champagne, is a noteworthy choice among an expensive, but tasty, drink selection; you'll be served by friendly and charming waiters, albeit ones who prance around sporting ass-less chaps.

643 Broadway (at Bleeker). 212.253.2560. T, F-Sun 10pm-6am, W-Th 10pm-4am, closed Monday. Cover $5 weeknights, $10 weekends. **6** *to Bleecker.*

Village Vanguard *Music*

Founded in 1935, the Vanguard earned its current status as a renowned jazz club during the late '50s and early '60s, when Sonny Rollins, John Coltrane, and Bill Evans released acclaimed albums of their live performances here. Since then, the Village Vanguard has become a mecca for jazz musicians who later go on to record their own live albums. Despite its fame, the club retains the small, slightly run-down triangular performance space that it has had for years; most nights the club features two sets, one at 9pm and one at 11pm, with an occasional third on Saturday nights at 12:30am.

178 Seventh Avenue South (at Perry). 212.255.4037. Doors open at 8pm. M-Th $30, F-Sun $35, including $10 drink minimum. **1 2 3** *to 14th St.*

Vol de Nuit *Beer Garden*

This beer garden, also known as the Belgian Beer Bar, may rival the best spots in Brussels. An unmarked red door leads customers into a wide garden; pass picnic tables filled with merry drinkers snacking on pomme frites, climb a small wooden staircase, and you'll end up in a space lit by a red glow, containing long wooden tables, noticeably aged furniture, and worn plaster walls. Beer enthusiasts will be thrilled to find that Stella Artois is the lowest quality beer on tap; the lengthy menu includes beers ranging from Chimay and Duvel to more esoteric selections. Try the Delirium Tremens, a classic European refreshment popular among college students that will astound those used to Rocky Mountain foil.

148 West 4th Street (at Sixth). 212.979.2616. Sun-Th 4pm-2am, F-Sat 4pm-4am. Drinks $5-10. **A C E B D F V** *to West 4th St.*

Arts

401 Projects

Founded in 2006 by Mark Seliger, chief photographer of *Rolling Stone*, this non-commercial gallery features photography by both new and established artists. In the exhibition room, the brilliant photographs stand out against white, pipe-lined walls; the gallery is set up in a former car showroom, converted to serve as an exhibition and gathering space for photographers of all levels. Every show is supplemented with a program such as a lecture or panel discussion, designed to bring the art into further focus.

401 West Street (at 10th). 212.633.6202. 401projects. com. W-Sun noon-6pm, closed M-T. **1** *to Christopher St.*

Cherry Lane

Founded in the 1920s by the poet Edna St. Vincent Millay and her literary circle, Cherry Lane is the city's oldest continuous off-Broadway theater. Presenting the century's best avant-garde pieces since its inception, the theater has premiered plays by F. Scott Fitzgerald, W.H. Auden, T.S. Eliot, Samuel Beckett, Edward Albee, Sam Shepard, and David Mamet, and continues to produce works by new and established playwrights. In addition to its main stage theater, Cherry Lane also has a studio theater showcasing young playwrights through a mentoring program that words with established authors.

38 Commerce Street (at Bedford). 212.989.2020. cherrylanetheater.org. **1** *to Christopher St.*

Cornelia Street Café

Since it was opened by three artists in 1977, this bohemian café has maintained its support for local artists by holding readings, performances, and exhibitions. Jazz musicians regularly play in Cornelia Street's small downstairs area, while locals and tourists feast on delicious meals in the homey, brick-walled dining rooms at street level. Performances are held at night, and during the day patrons can soak up the neighborhood from the sidewalk seating

MEATPACKING DISTRICT

Widely regarded as one of the city's most fashionable neighborhoods, the Meatpacking District has only become a hotspot within the last decade. At night, Jimmy Choo-shod models stumble along the cobblestone streets, brusque bouncers corral crowds with velvet ropes, and peckish after-partiers attempt to ward off hangovers at the popular 24-hour upscale diner, **FLORENT** (*69 Gansevoort Street at Washington*). During the day, after the morning stench has cleared from the 30-odd functioning packing plants that remain in the area, beautiful people amble from designer boutiques to cutting-edge galleries, often stopping for a late lunch at **SPICE MARKET** (*402 West 13th Street at Ninth*).

Of course, it wasn't always this way. At one time, as the home of 250 meat-processing plants and an underworld of alternative sex lairs, the Meatpacking District was one of Manhattan's grittiest neighborhoods. Stretching east-west from Hudson Street to the Hudson River and north-south from 15th Street to Gansevoort, the neighborhood used to be known as Gansevoort Market, the name of an open-air produce market that opened in 1884, with meat, poultry and dairy products sold in a nearby building. In 1949, the city built the Gansevoort Meat Center on the market's original site, cementing the meat industry's foothold on the district.

Today, in the wee hours of the morning, as straggling partiers enter waiting cabs, the remaining meatpacking plants come alive. The result is a vibrant neighborhood in transition, a mix of blue-collar and star-studded industries.

---

beneath a red-and-white-striped awning.

29 Cornelia Street (at Bleecker). 212.989.9318. corneliastreetcafe.com. **A C E B D F V** *to West 4th St.*

Forbes Galleries

Walking past the neoclassical building that houses Forbes Magazine, you'd never suspect that it also houses a small, charming gallery of toys and collectibles. The rooms of the gallery are themed, from a nautical room that holds the glass panels of old ships and more than 500 toy boats, to a showcase of thousands of toy soldiers arranged to represent different periods in history.

62 Fifth Avenue (at 12th). 212.206.5548. forbesgalleries. com. T-Sat 10-4, closed Monday. **4 5 6 N R W L** *to Union Square.*

Independent Cinema

The antidote to an endless cycle of big-budget Hollywood sequels, Greenwich Village is one of the best places in the country to see independent, foreign, classic, and documentary films that can't get a mainstream release. **Film Forum** (*209 West Houston Street at Sixth, 212-727-8110*), an independent, nonprofit movie house that was founded in 1970 with one projector and several folding chairs, is the best known of the Village cinemas; today it has matured into a full, three-screen theater. The Waverly Theater, where The Rocky Horror Picture Show debuted in 1975, may be gone, but its spirit lives on in the **IFC Center** (*323 Sixth Avenue at West 3rd, 212-924-7771*), which took over its space in 2005—cult classics are shown every Friday and Saturday at midnight. For a piece of history, visit **Cinema Village** (*22 East 12th Street at University Place, 212-924-3363*), the oldest continuously running movie theater in the Village, which focuses on independent and foreign features.

The National Museum of LGBT History

This archive and library space rotates art and photography created by both new and established queer artists, and touches on the artistic pulse of the West Village's gay community. An abundance of donated photographs, historical articles, and avant-garde art embraces pluralistic points of view and waits to be explored.

208 West 13th Street (at Seventh). 212.620.7310. gaycenter.org. Daily 9am-11pm. **1 2 3** *to 14th St.*

American Apparel

If you've spent more than a day in the city, you've undoubtedly seen American Apparel's in-your-face ads full of sulking and/or coy hipsters wearing little more than striped leg warmers. For the last few years, this L.A.-based chain has been helping to add some quirkiness to New York style with its bold-colored leggings and metallic unitards. If the glaring white lights and explicit photos don't lure you in, the brand's classic, comfortable pieces, and sweatshop-free all-American philosophy should convince you to pay a visit.

373 Sixth Avenue (at Washington). 646.336.6515. americanapparel.net. M-Sat 11am-9pm, Sun 11am-8pm. **A C E B D F V** *to West 4th St.*

Bleeker Bob's

Opened in 1967, Bleecker Bob's is a Village landmark, known for carrying hard-to-find records. The inside appears gloriously cluttered at first, so full of CDs that even the walls are covered with them, but the store is actually meticulously well-run. Hand-written cardboard dividers mark out minute genre distinctions, and the staff is fairly helpful, especially when you're looking for rare (and expensive) vinyl. It's the quintessential New York record store, still selling pipes from the '70s ("for tobacco only"), alongside punk and metal from the shop's early days further down Bleecker.

118 West 3rd Street (at MacDougal). 212.475.9677. bleeckerbobs.com. Sun-Th 11am-1am, F-Sat 11am-3am. **A C E B** D F **V** *to West 4th St.*

Marc by Marc Jacobs

Vintage shoppers, downtown fashionistas, uptown socialites, and hip Chelsea residents alike all praise the name of Marc for clothing that's become the unofficial uniform of the city's chic-est. Expect to pay steep prices for anything from this über-trendy fashion line, launched by Marc Jacobs in 2001—a piece can cost more than $200, and accessories more than $75—although you'd have to pay much more for the designer's premier line.

403-405 Bleecker Street (at 11th). 212.942.0026. marcjacobs.com. M-Sat noon-8pm, Sun noon-7pm. **1 2 3 A C E** L *to 14th St.*

MXYPLYZYK

Any shop named after a Superman villain, especially this one, is bound to be quirky. MXYPLYZYK (mix-ee-pliz-ik) doesn't disappoint, selling everything from a Pinocchio-shaped toilet brush to clocks constructed out of books. The goods and décor both emphasize whimsical, retro-hip design, and the small shop takes on the hues of its merchandise: a chic-ly cartoonish blend of bright green, orange, and polished wood.

125 Greenwich Avenue (at 13th). 212.989.4300. mxyplyzyk.com. M-Sat 11am-7pm, Sun noon-5pm. **A C E** L *to 14th St.*

The Strand

How many books can you fit into one bookstore? A lot, apparently. The Strand famously claims to hold "18 miles of books" in and around its dusty shelves, and you really can spend hours browsing its never-ending collection of rare, new, used, and out-of-print books—just don't go looking for something specific, as the staff is notoriously unhelpful. Before you leave, make sure you browse the stacks of $1 books, kept outside.

828 Broadway (at 12th). 212.473.1452. strandbooks. com. M-Sat 9:30am-10:30pm, Sun 11am-10:30pm. **4 5 6** N R Q W L *to Union Square.*

Three Lives & Co.

The antithesis of overwhelming mega-bookstores, the owners of Three Lives & Co. describe this charming shop as a "living room." This small bookshop caters mainly to gays, lesbians, and women, with a staff that's incredibly well-read and helpful—they don't just find the book you're looking for, they'll tell you what book you should be looking for. An extensive collection of fiction, poetry, and non-fiction is offered at reasonable, though not cheap, prices; the staff and the charm make paying a little extra worthwhile.

154 10th Street (at Waverly). 212.741.2069. M-T noon-8pm, W-Sat 11am-8:30pm, Sun noon-7pm. **A C E B** D F **V** *to West 4th St.*

Village Chess Shop

A mecca for chess fans since its opening in 1972, the Village Chess Shop offers a place to both play and talk over the finer points of the game. A match is almost always going on at the tables—the store rents them for $1.50 per hour—and players can get advice and tips while they're here. Those not playing can wander the shop's museum-like collection of elaborate themed sets, ranging from Bauhaus to Lord of the Rings; the more practically-oriented can pick out a standard tournament clock to practice with at home.

230 Thompson Street (at West 3rd). 212.475.9580. chess-shop.com. Daily 11am-midnight. **A C E B D F V** *to West 4th St.*

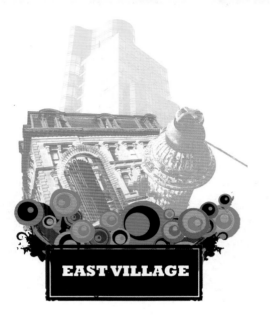

EAST VILLAGE

Once the bohemian home of beatniks and punk, the East Village is now known for its trendy designer shops, bargain-bin second-hand stores, and endless supply of bars and restaurants. Every week, a new drinking hot-spot or hip restaurant rises from the ashes of one that has recently closed—you could spend a year here and never use the same fork or chopstick twice.

Much of the mythology that hovers around the 14 blocks and six or seven avenues that now make up the East Village stems from its beatnik past. Throughout the 1960s, colorful characters like Bukowski, Ginsberg, and Baraka advanced a lifestyle of artistic exploration, radical politics, and anything-goes bohemia that infused the neighborhood with an edgy aura of cool.

The hard drug use of literary luminaries like William S. Burroughs, however, opened a crack into the neighborhood's dangerous side. When the economic plunge of the '70s pushed downturn into despair, the drug traffic exploded. Residents, feeling threatened by dealers, repeatedly demanded police protection and government funding for their dilapidated tenements, but the aid received was insufficient. Eventually, locals banded together to reclaim vacant lots and abandoned buildings from urban decay.

The most defining moment of recent neighborhood history occurred in 1988, when police attempted to enforce a new curfew at Tompkins Square Park. The goal was to oust the homeless who had moved onto the grounds, but many locals, hostile towards government regulation, protested. The ensuing riot was brutally quelled by the police, scarring the neighborhood and resulting in the park's closure. After numerous marches and additional violent protests, it finally reopened in 1992, but the rupture between the law and the community remains an open wound to this day.

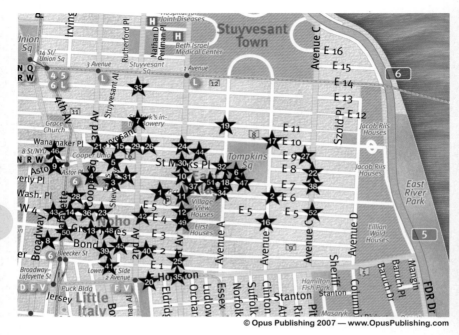

© Opus Publishing 2007 — www.OpusPublishing.com

EAST VILLAGE

SIGHTS/ATTRACTIONS
1. Curry Row
2. Community Gardens
3. Little Ukraine
4. McSorley's
5. St. Mark's Place
6. Tompkins,

DINING
7. Bar Carrera
8. Bond Street
9. Butter
10. Caracas
11. Caravan of Dreams
12. Counter
13. Hedeh
14. Indochine
15. La Paella
16. Le Souk
17. Life Café
18. Yuca Bar

NIGHTLIFE
19. 11th Street
20. 288-Tom and Jerry's
21. Angel's Share
22. baraza
23. Bbar and Grill
24. Coyote Ugly
25. DBA Exotic Beer
26. Decibel
27. Esperanto
28. Fish bar
29. Louis 649
30. Lunasa
31. McSorley's
32. Niagra
33. Nightingale
34. Pyramid
35. Sutra
36. Swift Hibernian Lounge
37. WCOU
38. Zum-Schneider

ARTS
39. Amato Opera House
40. Anthology Film Archive
41. Bowery Poetry Club
42. La MaMa
43. Merchant's House Museum
44. Performance Space 122
45. Rivington Arms

SHOPPING
46. Astor Place Hair
47. Bodanna
48. Dave's Quality Meat
49. Dual Specialty Store
50. Screaming Mimi's
51. Shape of Lies
52. Recycle a Bicycle

Sights/Attractions

Community Gardens

It's impossible not to notice the series of small, lush "Community Gardens" that are speckled throughout the East Village. One of the largest and most intriguing, which sits on the corner of 6th Street and Avenue B, contains an enormous wooden sculpture by the late Village eccentric Eddie Boros. Rising well above the garden fence—it's a whopping 65 feet high—the hodgepodge of wooden beams, random knicknacks, and weathered stuffed animals seems barely able to stand on its own, yet has become an unusual and unexpected neighborhood landmark.

evpcny.org. **6** *to Astor Place.*

Curry Row

If you're craving vindaloo, there's no better place to get it than the section of East 6th Street between First and Second Avenues known as India Row. Over a dozen Indian restaurants of all qualities and prices line the block, each striving to differentiate itself from the others. For the best deals, arrive between 11am and 3pm, when many of the restaurants feature lavish lunch buffets for $10-12. Don't expect a truly authentic cultural atmosphere, though; the food is top-notch, but if you're looking for a real Indian enclave, you're better off with Jackson Heights.

East 6ᵗʰ Street between First and Second. **6** *to Astor Place*

Little Ukraine

Though not the bastion of Ukrainian culture that it once was, the East Village still provides a glimpse of the old country on 6th and 7th Streets between Second and Third Avenues. **St. George Church** (*30 East 7ᵗʰ Street at Third*), with its Ukrainian-Byzantine domes and mosaics, is the centerpiece of the community. Less than a block away, the **Surma Store** (*11 East 7ᵗʰ Street at Third*) proudly proclaims to have "served the Slavic community since 1918," providing Ukrainian gifts and goods. To learn a little more about the history of that nesting doll in the store's window, stop by the **Ukrainian Museum** (*222 East 6ᵗʰ Street at Third*), which shows exhibits on Ukrainian cultural heritage.

East 6ᵗʰ and 7ᵗʰ Streets between Second and Third. **6** *to Astor Pl.*

McSorley's Old Ale House

Sawdust covers the dark wood floor of the oldest Irish pub in New York City, opened in 1854, just as the institution's history covers the walls; look around to see newspaper clippings and photos of historic notables who once visited the ale house, from Abraham Lincoln to John Lennon. Of course, the world has changed since the era of Honest Abe, and McSorley's has grown with the times—albeit reluctantly. As one of the last surviving single-sex places of business in the country, the pub famously barred women from its premises until 1970, when a Supreme Court order mandated that they abolish the policy. Today, the owners gently poke fun at the backward-thinking proprietors of yore, and happily serve anyone who walks in the door. As always, beer comes in only two varieties—"light" and "dark"—which, at today's prices, will run you $4.50 for two half-pints (one of each type). And while the pub attracts a sizeable crowd of history-minded tourists, frequent visits by neighborhood locals help to maintain its homey, friendly atmosphere.

15 East 7ᵗʰ Street (at Third). 212.474.9848. mcsorleysnewyork.com. M-Sat 11am–1am, Sun 1pm–1am. **6** *to Astor Place.*

St. Mark's Place

In the 1960s, this colorful and vibrant stretch of East 8ᵗʰ Street was home to radicals and revolutionaries from Lenny Bruce to Leon Trotsky. With a reputation as a stronghold of the alternative downtown community, it retains traces of those counterculture roots, although recent decades have also witnessed its transformation into an unconventional hub of shopping and dining. Hip stores and ethnic restaurants are literally piled on top of each other here—be sure to look above and below street level to avoid missing any of the dozens of tattoo parlors, record shops, and vintage clothing retailers that target the students and 20-somethings who flock to the area. The wide variety of dining options has a more universal appeal, with offerings that include cheap falafel, authentic Afghan cuisine, trendy Thai fare, and a wide variety of Japanese food.

East 8ᵗʰ Street between Second and Third. **6** *to Astor Place.*

Tompkins Square Park

Many of the trees in this humble 10-acre park—a neighborhood favorite because of its basketball courts, chessboard tables, playgrounds, and two off-leash dog runs—are over 150 years old. One elm in the center of the park is even considered a religious site by followers of the Hare Krishna religion—in 1966, the first chanting session outside of India was held underneath its branches. This popular urban oasis is probably most famous, however, as an oft-used meeting ground for activists and protesters. From the 1870s, when residents rioted over the poor economy and lack of jobs, to the 1980s, when they demonstrated against the newly-instituted park curfews that displaced the homeless who camped there at night, the Lower East Side has always relied on Tompkins Square Park for both personal enjoyment and public expression.

East 7ᵗʰ Street at Avenue A. nycgovparks.org **6** *to Astor Place.*

Skater at Tompkins Square Park

Dining
UPSCALE

Bond St. *Japanese*

Classic Japanese tradition meets modern Manhattan luxury at this townhouse-turned-eatery. The décor is dreamy—semi-translucent fabrics in light, clean colors frame windows, doors, and hallways. The lighting is dim enough to set the mood, but bright enough to see the colorful plates that are the main attraction at this highly-respected establishment. If your wallet can handle it, try the tasting menu, an exquisite selection of the chef's creations ranging from live lobster sashimi, to Stilton-dusted tuna sushi, to creamy foie gras with toro. For dessert, try a layered cup with cream, pastry, Japanese mountain peach sorbet, and a whole fruit garnish.

6 Bond Street (at Broadway). 212.777.2500. M-Sat 6pm-midnight, Sun 6-11pm. Appetizers $10-28, Entrées $25-34. **B D F V** *to Broadway-Lafayette.*

Butter *New American*

The long walkway into the dining area of this hotspot might as well be a catwalk—even the Olson twins are known to frequent the scene. There is so much social energy pulsating through the place that it's almost easy to forget you came for dinner. Nonetheless, the food is as exciting as the clientele; the chef's imaginative seasonings complement the base of each meal without overpowering the natural flavors of the meat or fish. Try to appreciate the subtly prepared dishes before getting caught up in the anything-but-subtle eye-candy.

415 Lafayette Street (at Astor). 212.253.2828. M-Sat 5:30pm-11:30pm, closed Sunday. Appetizers $10-21, Entrées $19-36. **6** *to Astor Place.*

MID-RANGE

Bar Carrera *Tapas*

So small that the bathroom sink is left out in the hallway, this trendy tapas destination boasts no tables, just two bars lined with Moroccan tiles and tightly packed chairs. With only a couple of electric griddles serving as a kitchen, big crowds mean long waits—but the time passes quickly when sipping one of a fine assortment of sherries. If you're lucky, you can grab the seat closest to the chef and watch him as he masterfully navigates the cramped quarters to turn out plate after beautifully manicured plate. The neatly prepared jamón serrano and an assortment of chorizo dishes are stellar standouts. But be sure to check your neighbor's selections: for the same price, certain menu items are conspicuously larger and far more filling than others, though it's still hard to go wrong.

175 Second Avenue (at 11th). 212.375.1555. Daily 5pm-2am. Tapas $3-7. L *to Third Ave.*

Caravan of Dreams *Vegetarian*

The décor of this East Village mainstay may be eccentric—a jazz trio playing in the corner juxtaposes the décor's Bedouin-chic—but the food has a clear mission. All dishes are vegan, many are raw, and a local Rabbi supervises kosher preparation. The restaurant used to host yoga classes in its back room—expect your server to be pretty mellow. That laid-back attitude accounts for what may be the restaurant's greatest idiosyncrasy: a large line of hungry New Yorkers all waiting happily outside.

405 East 6th Street (at First). 212.254.1613. M 5pm-11pm, T-Sun 11am-11pm. Appetizers $5-13, Entrées $12-17. N R *to 8th St.*

Counter *Vegan/Wine Bar/Raw Food*

Another vegetarian/vegan great in the East Village, this bistro and organic wine and martini bar features a slick interior complete with color-changing mood lighting, giant three dimensional flower portraits, and a romantic bathroom (think red lighting and Billie Holiday singing in

the last stall). The menu is full of exotic flavors, but remains unexpectedly comforting. Try the bast'eeya, a fantastic pastry of basmati rice, vegetables, and a hint of citrus baked into a cinnamon-dusted fillo crust, and the caprese, an almost-convincing goat-cheese facsimile, all the more amazing because it's "raw food" (which at other spots often tastes uniformly of ground nuts). By the time the decadently rich desserts arrive, you'll have long forgotten that you're eating meat.

105 First Avenue (at 6th). 212.982.5870. M-Th 5pm-midnight, F 5pm-1am, Sat 11am-1am, Sun 11am-midnight. Appetizers $8-15, Entrées $13-19. F V *to 2nd Ave.*

Hedeh *Japanese*

Hedeh manages to keep up with New York's hottest Japanese restaurants by abandoning image concerns and simply focusing on the food. This emphasis becomes immediately apparent when you sit down to some of the best foie gras the city has to offer. The sushi is likewise phenomenal—particularly the dragon roll—and the prime filet and black cod are stars among the entrées. Desserts are not too sweet, but give a light, almost breathy end to the meal. Come here for cuisine, not to be seen.

57 Great Jones Street (at Bowery). 212.473.8458. M-Sat 5pm-1am, closed Sunday. Appetizers $8-14, Entrées $18-26. 6 *to Bleecker St.*

La Paella *Tapas*

The most difficult part of dining at La Paella is getting in the door—or rather, locating it. Finding the awning is easy, but first-time diners may feel like they're pulling a reverse Rapunzel through a French window rather than walking through the front door; there's no hostess or entry space, just tables as soon as you enter. But once you've settled into this dimly-lit space with Don Quixote jousting at windmills on the wall and flowers hung from the ceiling, you'll know that getting in was well worth the trouble. The staff is friendly and welcoming, and amply-portioned

FAST FACTS

- Scenic Stroll: St. Mark's Place

- Major Subway Stations: Astor Place (6), 8th St-New York University (R W)

- Urban Oasis: Community Gardens

- Kooky Corner: Sculpture at 6th St and Avenue B Garden, Dave's Quality Meat

- Neighborhood Landmarks: The Alamo at Astor Place, McSorley's Old Ale House, Tompkins Square Park

- Neighborhood Foods: Samosas and other spicy delights on Curry Row

- Best Deal: $14 haircuts at Astor Place Hair

- Quintessential Neighborhood Event: Howl! Festival of East Village Arts

- Famous Historical Moment: In August 1988, police tried to enforce a newly-passed curfew for Tompkins Square Park, resulting in what became widely known as the Tompkins Square Park Police Riot.

- Notable Residents: Beastie Boys, John Coltrane, Bob Dylan, Allen Ginsberg, Jack Kerouac, Norman Mailer, Charlie Parker, William S. Burroughs

plates are superb. The seafood and vegetable dishes are especially good, running the gamut from basic olives soaked in oil to baked asparagus wrapped in salmon—perhaps the perfect complement to the almost-mandatory tapas bar sangria.

214 East 9th Street (at Third). 212.598.4321. Sun-Th 5pm-11pm, F-Sat 5pm-midnight. Tapas $6.50-12. R W to 8th.

Le Souk *Middle Eastern*
An enthusiastic staff and loyal customers pack into this candle-lit dive outfitted with tiled tables and Moroccan lamps. Although patrons are seated a bit too close to each another in the small quarters, the experience is worth the mild claustrophobia. A three-tiered *meze* appetizer platter offers a sampling of North

African flavor featuring traditional dishes sizzling with spice, prepared in a giant clay oven. Try the *merguez*, an authentic Tunisian sausage, or the grilled fish prepared with Moroccan spices (a very popular choice); but avoid the dry chicken dishes. Belly dancers and hookahs round out the atmosphere.

47 Avenue B (at East 4th). 212.777.5454. Sun-Th 5:30pm-midnight, Fri-Sat 5:30pm-2am. Appetizers $5-8, Entrées $13-22. F V to 2nd Ave.

Life Café *Southwestern*
The famous setting of the groundbreaking musical Rent, this eclectic source for nutritious Cal-Mex platos is an East Village landmark thanks largely to its laid-back creativity. The cheap brunch menu is full of good ways to start a weekend morning, and

the dinner specials always include several vegetarian options. Check out the rotating exhibits by local artists, best viewed during the weekday happy hour from 5-9pm. Even the restrooms provide an extra, unexpected venue for innovative artwork.

343 East 10th Street (at Avenue B). 212.477.8791. Sun-Th 10am-midnight, F-Sat 10am-2am. Entrées $13-17. L *to First Ave.*

Yuca Bar *Latin*
Whether it's the lively music or the incredible food, something about this Latin American bistro makes you want to dance like you've never danced before. Every night, the street corner outside fills with a hipster crowd braving a definitely-worth-it hour wait. The food is so top-notch and authentic you'll almost be convinced that you've flown to South America for supper. To remind you that you're still in Manhattan, the menu and the cocktails have a fusion twist, combining traditional American and South American flavors into great dishes like guava BBQ short ribs. With a constantly changing menu, you never know what surprises you'll find; but one thing's for sure: your meal will be a hit.

111 Avenue A (at 7th). 212.982.9533. Lunch M-F 11:30am-5pm, Dinner M-F 6pm-11:30pm, Sat-Sun 6pm-1:30am. Appetizers $5-10, Entrées $13-28. 6 *to Astor Place.*

CASUAL

Caracas Arepa Bar *Latin*
With only a handful of small two-person tables and some of the most authentically home-cooked Venezuelan food in the city, this modest *taguarita* (roadside restaurant) is both cramped and very popular; expect a long line, especially for outside tables during nice weather. This may not be the perfect restaurant for a fancy date or a posh outing, but the food is sure to satisfy those whose patience endures. Be sure to sample the *arepas*—corn flour bread, stuffed like pita pockets with traditional meats and sauces.

91 East 7th Street (at First). 212.228.5062. M-F 5:30pm-10:45pm, Sat noon-10:45pm, Sun noon-9:45pm. Food $4-12. 6 *to Astor Place.*

Nightlife

B Bar and Grill *Bar*
Many patrons are turned off by the vibe of self-determined elitism in this up-market drinkery; with unfriendly service, self-important bouncers, and fewer celebrity sightings than in its heyday as the Bowery Bar, some say that this place has gotten too cool for its own good. The self-important attitude, however, doesn't keep people from flocking here in droves; nor does it make the martinis any weaker. If you're in need of a good stiff drink and don't mind the scene—or, if you're actually hip enough to hang out here—come by to lounge in the 3,000-square-foot outdoor garden, shake it on the backroom dance floor, and look at all the pretty people.

40 East 4th Street (at Bowery). 212.475.2220. Daily 11:30am-4am. Drinks $9-13. N R *to 8th St.*

Coyote Ugly Saloon *Country-Western*
By now, we've all seen the movie—but in case you're the kind of person who could never admit that in public, feign ignorance if you're ever asked the definition of a "coyote ugly," the term used to sum up a series of unfortunate events that starts with a drink and ends with a severed limb. The situation isn't pretty—and neither is this East Village mainstay, the original location in the series of sexed-up country-western bars that took the nation by storm a few years back. At least the spunky, jean-miniskirted bartenders aren't so bad, depending on what you go for.

153 First Avenue (at 10th). 212.477.4431. M-Th 2pm-4am, F-Sun 12:30pm-4am. L *to First Ave.*

Esperanto *Latin*
You'll feel like you've just stepped off a Brazilian beach instead of an East Village sidewalk when you enter this club. Wooden booths and turquoise walls, lined with tile and tropical kitsch, recreate a seaside hut. An envy-inducing contingent of very good (and attractive) dancers moves to live Latin beats; order one of the six-dollar capirinhas and join them on the floor.

145 Avenue C (at 9th). 212.505.6559. Sun-Th 6pm-midnight, F-Sat 6pm-1am. Drinks $5-8. L *to First Ave.*

Louis 649 *Jazz*

This jazz bar in Alphabet City is cool, laid-back, and relatively quiet—perfect for those who prefer good conversation to deafening music. Order a glass of inexpensive but carefully-selected wine or an imported beer and soak up some jazz, played here seven nights a week. The music, drinks, and hand-crafted art deco bar remind you that you're out on the town, but the relaxed and easy atmosphere makes you feel right at home. Just don't get so comfortable that you forget about the no cell phone rule—music fans do not take kindly to invasive ringtones.

649 East 9th Street (at Avenue B). 212.673.1190. Daily 7pm-4am. L to First Ave.

Pyramid *LGBT*

The worn black exterior and neon sign on the outside of this storied gay dance club can be off-putting, but don't be deterred; step inside for a party full of pop-tastic '80s hits that make it hard to pry yourself away from the dance floor. The drinks are small and a bit overpriced, but the scene here isn't about getting tanked anyway—it's about dancing, drunk or not, in a frenzied mess of pure fun. If you're not looking for anything more than a great night of dancing, bring your friends, gay and straight, and let your body move to the music.

101 Avenue A (at Sixth). 212.228.4888. M 11pm-4am, T-W 8pm-1am, Th 9pm-4am, F-Sat 10pm-4am, Sun 8pm-1am. Cash only. F V to 2nd Ave.

Sutra Lounge *Club*

Though not quite the Kama Sutra brought to life, there's an undeniably sexy vibe at this spacious bar and lounge. The two-story, red-toned, and incense-filled club offers friendly service and fantastic music, with neo-Caribbean and Brazilian beats that attract an eclectic and fashionable mix of all ages. Come to dance with the city's most stylish, or to take advantage of the free salsa lessons, offered every Tuesday.

16 First Avenue (at 1st St). 212.677.9477. W-Th 10pm-4am, F-Sat 9pm-4am, closed Sun-T. F V to 2nd Ave.

Hipster culture in the East Village

Swift Hibernian Lounge *Beer Hall*

Beneath the dreamlike painting that stretches the length of this long beer hall, drinkers down sweating mugs of ale imported from all over the world. Head over here for a brew if you're in the mood to toss down a drink or two in the loud company of friends and neighbors.

34 East 4th Street (at Bowery). 212.260.3600. Daily 11:30am-4am. Drinks $4-8. **B D F V** *to Broadway-Lafayette St.*

Tom & Jerry's *Neighborhood Bar*

NoLIta artists and filmmakers make this relaxed hangout their regular drinking hole on weeknights, grabbing a Guiness—the bar's drink of choice—and soaking up the low-key vibe. Listen to the jukebox bang out country and classic rock hits as you admire the owner's collection of memorabilia from the classic cartoon duo that serves as the inspiration for the place's nickname—the dull official name, 228 Bar, is derived from its address.

288 Elizabeth Street (at East Houston). 212.260.5045. Daily noon-4am. Drinks $5-7, cash only. **F V** *to Broadway-Lafayette St.*

Arts

Amato Opera House

Just next to the late CBGB, the thin, white, four-story building marked "Amato Opera House" fits in so perfectly with its surroundings, you'd expect it to be a cheeky rock club. But the name isn't ironic—it might not be as magnificent as the Met, but the Amato is one of the city's most acclaimed opera houses. Founded in 1948 with the goal of making opera more accessible both by charging minimal ticket prices and giving budding performers a chance to prove themselves, Amato puts on five operas a year with ticket prices that are cheaper than anything you'll ever find uptown.

319 Bowery (at Bond). 212.228.8200. amato.org **6** *to Bleecker St.*

Anthology Film Archive

In addition to the obvious—11,000, in case you were wondering—the Anthology Film Archive is a museum, a library, and a venue for experimental cinema. If you're not a researcher, the best way to access the Archive's collection of rare movies is to attend a screening, shown in the converted courthouse-turned-theater. The seats aren't very comfortable and the space feels old, but you'll never get another chance to see most of the films shown here.

32 Second Avenue (at 2nd St). 212.505.5181. anthologyfilmarchives.org **F V** *to 2nd Ave.*

Bowery Poetry Club

The expansiveness of the daily line-up at this renowned neighborhood center is consistently astonishing; writing workshops, spoken word slams, and readings by established poets are just some of the three-to-six events held each day. Poets can also sell their self-published work in the Club's consignment bookshop—one of only a few in the city—complete with a café for reading, brooding, and post-poem conversation.

308 Bowery (at 1st St). 212.614.0505. bowerypoetryclub.com. **F V** *to 2nd Ave.*

La MaMa

From its origins as a tiny basement theater forty-five years ago to its current incarnation as a three-stage complex and affiliated art gallery, this experimental theater club has maintained its mission to showcase new and original work from artists around the globe. Runs tend to be short and very popular, so try to get tickets in advance. If you get shut out, consider attending an evening of the "Coffeehouse Chronicles," a running series of live conversations in which those involved in La MaMa's early years take the stage to publicly reminisce.

74A East 4th Street (at Second). 212.475.7710. lamama.org **6** *to Bleecker St.*

Merchant's House Museum

Built in 1832 and occupied by the same family for nearly a century, this three-story Greek Revival building is the only 19th century home in the city to be preserved both inside and out. Some visitors say that going through the museum is the closest thing to time travel that exists in New York; the rooms, decorated with their original furniture and belongings, can feel downright eerie, and rumors of ghosts abound. After emerging—intact—from the home's interior, take a few moments to wander through the symmetrical designs of the 19th century garden.

29 East 4th Street (at Lafayette). 212.777.1089. merchantshouse.com. Th-M noon-5pm, closed T-W. Adults $8, Students $5. **6** *to Astor Place.*

Performance Space 122

One of the oldest off-off-Broadway theaters in New York, P.S. 122, which takes its name from the abandoned school that serves as its home, maintains its commitment to showcasing new and original works that are unlikely to be supported by mainstream theaters—check out their website for a full listing of eclectic performances and workshops.

150 First Avenue (at 9th St). 212.353.1315. ps122.org. **6** *to Astor Place.*

Rivington Arms

A small gallery that packs a big punch, Rivington Arms' contemporary art exhibits are usually of high quality—a relatively safe bet in a city of hit or miss art. If you can swing it, try to go to one of the frequent openings; when the gallery is flooded with artists, students, collectors, and connoisseurs, the energy in the air becomes palpable. If you happen to fall in love with any of the art you see on display, you're in luck: the gallery features mostly young and budding artists, and prices are relatively low.

4 East 2nd Street (at Bowery). 646.654.3213. rivingtonarms. com. M-F noon-6pm, closed Saturday-Sunday. **6** *to Bleecker St.*

Students continue the long tradition of protest in the East Village.

Shopping

Astor Place Hair

Unlike anywhere you've ever been before, Astor Hair is one of those places that could only exist in New York. Just below street level, and behind an unassuming façade, lies an enormous space—several thousand square feet—that teems with dozens of stylists. The clientele ranges from students to executives, all of whom appreciate the quality, conversation, and price—$14 plus tip—for a standard haircut. The ever-busy stylists, of course, are hit-or-miss; the best way to ensure a good cut is to keep up a lively conversation so that yours won't want to stop working.

2 Astor Place (at Broadway). 212.475.9854. M-Sat 8am-8pm, Sun 9am-6pm. R W *to 8th St.*

Bodanna

Tailor-made for the socially conscious gift-giver, 100% of the money made from product sales at this pottery shop and community center goes to support classes for inner-city youth. Aiming to foster responsibility and a strong work ethic, programs at the center teach pottery as a trade, combining crafting classes with hands-on business experience in the store. The product's not bad either: Mugs, tableware, and vases are practical and elegant.

125 East 7th Street (at Avenue A). 212.388.0078. bodanna.org. M-F 10am-6pm, Sat-Sun noon-6pm. 6 *to Astor Place.*

Dave's Quality Meat

A shoe store that looks nothing like one, this unusual shop is designed to resemble a meat market, complete with hanging hooks and a refrigerator filled with packages of foam and saran wrap; luckily, there's no blood, and those refrigerated packages are filled with T-shirts instead of T-bones. Go for hard-to-find Nikes and other rare sneakers, all of which are priced as high as you'd expect.

7 East 3rd Street (at Bowery). 212.505.7551. davesqualitymeat.com. M-Sat noon-7pm, Sun noon-5pm. 6 *to Bleecker St.*

Screaming Mimi's

A vintage store that's so well-established it's practically vintage itself, Screaming Mimi's is an East Village icon. This isn't your typical thrift store; the clothes here are exquisitely organized and the selection is incredible. The store prides itself on finding unique, stylish, one-of-a-kind pieces so you don't have to, but all that effort doesn't come cheap; be prepared to pay for the clothes as if they were new.

382 Lafayette Street (at 3rd). 212.677.6464. screamingmimis.com. M-Sat noon-8pm. Sun 1pm-7pm. 6 *to Bleecker St.*

Shape of Lies

One of the last Mom and Pop joints left in the East Village, Shape of Lies sells historic jewelry—based on artifacts found at the world's great museums and handmade in the back of the store—for far less than you'd pay at any gallery shop (pieces here average $70). Stop by to browse and talk to the owners about the specific history of any individual piece.

127 East 7th Street (at Avenue A). 212.533.5920. solnyc.com. W-F 3pm-8pm, Sat-Sun noon-8pm. 6 *to Astor Place.*

Recycle-a-Bicycle

A used bike store with a charming green-and-yellow storefront, this shop has an admirable mission: to provide after-school bike programs and equipment to high schoolers, and to educate students about bike repair and environmentalism. The shop itself is little more than an outlet of the program, but you can still stop by to have your two-wheeler repaired or to buy a used bike in excellent condition.

75 Avenue C (at 5th). 212.475.1655. recycleabicycle.org T-Sat noon-7pm, closed Sun-M. F V *to 2nd Ave.*

boucarou lounge

an urbane me
transplante

tamorphosis of this dignified spirit
d and actualized in our modern reality

TRIBECA

After angry objections, near-brawls at community board meetings, and plenty of melodramatic pouting, the artists who pioneered TriBeCa's minimalist, neo-industrial aesthetic have been forced to throw in their well-decorated towels. In another iteration of the classic New York story, the chic restaurants and luxury co-ops are in, and the bohemians are out.

Beginning modestly in 1813, TriBeCa was a major point of transfer for the increased shipping and commerce moving through Lower Manhattan by the mid-19th century. Its cast-iron facades and spacious five- and six-story buildings were factories and storage facilities, as TriBeCa joined SoHo in becoming an extensive light-manufacturing zone.

In the '70s, the area's population jumped from 243 to more than 5,000. Development continued into the '90s, and illegal lofts were quickly converted into luxury residences, but with the important distinction that unlike those in SoHo, they were open to non-artists as well as the creative class.

At the peak of its re-development, the name of the area—Washington Market—was deemed too uncouth for the loft-living crowd. And so TriBeCa was born, a name that refers to the *Triangle Below Canal Street*, despite the fact that the area, roughly bounded by Canal, Broadway, Warren, and West, is in the shape of a trapezoid.

During the '90s, TriBeCa kicked and scratched its way into the Manhattan elite with the help of a healthy dose of celebrity. Most famously, Robert De Niro moved here and launched the TriBeCa Film Center and TriBeCa Grill in hopes of revitalizing the neighborhood after September 11th. Young Wall Street types with fat wallets are drawn to the neighborhood for its proximity to the Financial District and abundance of amazing apartments, while yuppie families enjoy TriBeCa's renewed parks and child-friendly shops.

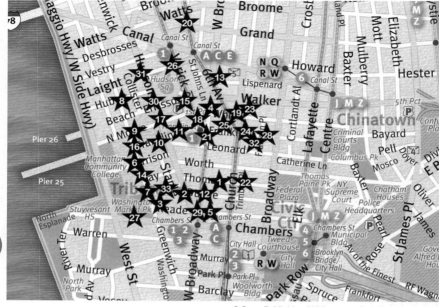

© Opus Publishing 2007 — www.OpusPublishing.com

TRIBECA

SIGHTS/ATTRACTIONS
1. AT&T Long Lines Building
2. Duane Park
3. Washington Market Park

DINING
4. Cercle Rouge
5. Fresh
6. The Harrison
7. The Hideaway
8. Il Mattone
9. Ivy's Bistro
10. Mai House
11. Nobu, Next Door
12. Rosanjin

13. Thirty-Five
14. Viet-Café
15. Walker's
16. Yaffa's Tea Room

NIGHTLIFE
17. Brandy Library
18. Bubble Lounge
19. Church Lounge
20. Circa Tabac
21. Grace
22. Kimono Lounge

ARTS
23. Apex Art
24. Collective: Unconscious

25. The Flea Theater
26. TriBeCa Cinemas
27. TriBeCa Performing Arts Center

SHOPPING
28. Collector's Toy Den
29. Gotham Bikes
30. Issey Miyake
31. Just Scandinavian
32. Steven Alan
33. TriBeCa Girls

Sights/Attractions

AT&T Long Lines Building

Built in 1974, this windowless skyscraper is one of New York's most distinctive high-rises. The industrial granite façade masks 18-foot-high floors—built that way in order to house telephone switching equipment—and although some consider the imposing edifice an eyesore, others feel it brings character to the neighborhood. Don't expect to be able to enjoy the view from the top, however; a security desk will stop you at the ground floor, and even the pleasant courtyard east of the building is off-limits to the public. For another nearby example of imposing, technology-sheltering architecture, check out 32 Sixth Ave., one of a handful of "interconnection powerhouses" (or "switch hotels") in the city.

33 Thomas Street (at Broadway). **1 2 3 A C** *to Chambers St.*

Duane Park

This quirky triangular island in the middle of Duane Street is the second-oldest public park in the city—and also one of its smallest. Two rows of curved benches donated by local residents and businesses snake through hellebores and other flowers, with tall trees to provide ample shade in the summertime. The surrounding brick-paved streets have a European air about them, and the park's flagpole, bearing the Stars and Stripes, may be the only reminder that you're not in Amsterdam or Paris. Relax among locals, have a cup of coffee, and enjoy the surrounding architecture.

Duane Street (at Hudson). duanepark.org. Open daily, dawn-1am. **1 2 3 A C** *to Chambers St.*

Washington Market Park

Yuppie parents and their designer-clad offspring love this park for its well-kept spaces and sparkling red playgrounds. The park's pristine grounds come at a price, though: signs warn, "No blankets allowed. Blankets kill grass." (Bicycles, skateboards, chairs, loud music, pets, and alcohol are also prohibited). Don't miss the small flower garden, with its inviting stone path and benches at the north end of the park. The wi-fi is free, thanks to the neighboring Borough of Manhattan Community College, but expect to pay a fee if you want to have a party in the blue and white gazebo.

Entrance on Greenwich Street (at Duane). washingtonmarketpark.org. Daily, 8am-dusk. **1 2 3 A C** *to Chambers St.*

Dining

UPPER TIER

Fresh *Seafood, American*

A modern take on seaside nostalgia, the main dining room at this refined seafood eatery is decked out in a soothing, impressionistic color palate, split by a classical colonnade. Serving only the freshest fish, the restaurant also distributes its daily catch to several of New York's finest, including Per Se and Le Bernadine. With executive chef Kento Komoto at the helm, the kitchen, visible from the dining room through frosted glass, delivers an ever-changing but always enticing selection. Simple ingredients enhance rather than mask the savory seafood. The soft shell crab with mango relish is phenomenal, while the yellowfin tuna on a bed of rock shrimp risotto expertly balances smooth texture and rich flavors. For those craving a memorable experience, the six course prix fixe ($90) is a must.

105 Reade Street (at West Broadway). 212.406.1900. Lunch M-F 11:30am-2:30pm; Dinner M-Sat 5pm-10pm, Sun 4pm-9pm. Appetizers $11-20, Entrées $19-36. **1 2 3 A C** *to Chambers St.*

The Harrison *American*

Served in a dining room evocative of an old-time wooden ship, the seafood at this Tribeca classic is as delectable as it is finely presented. The service, seemingly choreographed, runs like clockwork; the staff is knowledgeable and eager to advise diners on the most seasonable choices to suit their desires. A large banquet room in the wine cellar makes this restaurant a fine choice for large parties, while the cozy atmosphere upstairs and the outdoor seating area make it perfect for intimate groups as well.

355 Greenwich Street (at Harrison). 212.274.9310. M-Th 5:30pm-11pm, F-Sat 5:30pm-11:30pm, Sun 5pm-10pm. Appetizers $10-$16, Entrées: $21-$34. **1** *to Franklin St.*

Mai House *Vietnamese Fusion*

This hip former warehouse has yet to truly catch on, but with good cuisine and chic décor, it is only a matter of time. Linger on the appetizers, like cuddlefish (sic) with sweet and sour kiwi sauce, or spicy beef salad, which artfully integrates traditional Vietnamese influences with pan-Asian undertones. For mains, the kafir lime duck with daikon pancakes is the best option, while the inventive two-part cocktail list provides delightful accompaniment. Two favorites include the "tiger

tail," which balances sugar and spice by mixing passion fruit with Thai chile, and the *red river*, a sweeter blend of grapefruit, hibiscus, and ginger. Come late for the unbeatable $10-after-ten deal (M-Th), featuring more than 20 dishes at a bargain price.

186 Franklin Street (at Liberty). 212.431.0606. M-Sat 5:45pm-midnight, closed Sunday. Appetizers $10-13, Entrées $14-28. **1** *to Franklin St.*

Mr. Chows Tribeca *Chinese*

A veritable pop-culture mecca, this iconic space revitalizes the forgotten tradition of glamorous Chinese cuisine that flourished at the turn of the twentieth century. White marble and black columns echo the staff dress code of tuxes only, while glass panel lighting and inlaid mirrors don't distract from the Mr. Chow portrait—an authentic Warhol, of course—hung on the wall. Come with a fat wallet and a celebrity fetish, but

Rosanjin sashimi

know that the extravagantly priced fare offers only a slight upgrade from the realm of glorified Chinese takeout. But if you're willing to splurge, snag a glass of champagne as it rolls past your table and toast to the high life. Traditional dishes with a modern twist, like salt-and-pepper prawns, fiery buffalo, or the crispy duck are par for the course, always tasty but rarely spectacular. End the night on the wraparound porch, with drink in hand, and enjoy the view.

121 Hudson Street (at North Moore). 212.965.9500. Daily 6pm-11:30pm. Appetizers $5.50 to $25, Entrées $26 to $36. **1** *to Franklin St.*

Nobu, Next Door *Japanese*

Nobu, Next Door—little sister to über-trendy hotspot Nobu—is a hit with those who want the subtly Latin-inspired Japanese dishes that made its namesake famous without the long waits and stratospheric prices. The sushi, of course, is top quality; but to make your visit worthwhile, stick to the genius hot and cold dishes, the true highlight of the restaurant. The no-reservations policy that applies to parties smaller than six means that at times, you'll have to wait for a table, but once you're seated the attentive staff will spring to your aid straightaway. Unlike the austere Nobu, the décor is elegant yet casual, and because it's tightly packed in a modestly-sized space, expect noise that can border on deafening.

105 Hudson Street (at Franklin). 212.334.4445. M-Sat 6pm-midnight, Sun 6pm-11pm. Appetizers $8-18, Entrées $18-34. **1** *to Franklin St.*

Rosanjin *Japanese*

Prepare for a finely-tuned aesthetic experience at this purveyor of *kaiseki*—the traditional, elaborate, Zen Buddhist meal based primarily on fresh fish and vegetables. Overseeing a menu that changes daily, owner Jungjin Park promises

Cercle Rouge

you will never eat the same dish twice no matter how many times you visit; expect alternately hot and cold courses built around impeccably fresh ingredients, perfectly combined. Every detail, down to the cedar chopsticks, house-blended soy-sauce, and handmade ceramic serving dishes has been carefully considered. It's not a relaxing dining experience—you are expected to give your full attention to the food, and to eat it properly—but given the chef's dexterity with flavor and texture combinations, your task should be quite enjoyable.

141 Duane Street (at West Broadway). 212.346.0664. M-Sat 6pm-11pm, closed Sunday. Nine-course prix fixe menu $150 non-vegetarian, $105 vegetarian, plus beverages. **1 2 3 A C** *to Chambers St.*

MIDDLE TIER

Cercle Rouge *French*

Scores of loyal fans come to this traditional French bistro again and again looking for a hearty meal in an old-world setting. Once seated in the artfully decorated dining room, start off with the unique Cercle Rouge chicken wings—the best French take on traditional American fare you're likely to find in the city—then ask the chef, who often roams the dining room striking up conversations, what to sample next. If he's stuck in the back and can't offer advice, go with the duck served in cassis sauce, a sweet and savory masterpiece. For dessert, the molten chocolate cake will send you home beaming from ear to ear.

241 West Broadway (at North Moore). 212.226.6252. M-Th noon-midnight, F-Sat noon-1am, Sun 4pm-midnight. Appetizers $8-18, Entrées $20-28. **1** *to Franklin St.*

The Hideaway *American*

The crowd at this tiny neighborhood hangout—a single room with a staff of three—consists mostly of regulars who return again and again for upscale food in a laid-back, welcoming atmosphere. Grab a beer or fancy cocktail and watch the game from the bar, or bring the kids to one of the 12 tables for an easy, yet refined, night out. The menu, characterized by upscale twists on classic American comfort foods, is startlingly limited—five appetizers, five entrées, and one rotating dessert only—but everything is exquisitely prepared by the one-man show that is the owner/manager/chef, who knows many of his customers by name. The pulled pork and duck sloppy joe sliders, served on mini burger buns, are more filling than they look (and, at $2 each, an excellent deal); the grilled cheese, made with cheddar, brie, tomato, and bacon, is one of the most indulgent you'll ever try.

185 Duane Street (at Greenwich). 212.334.5775. Dinner daily 5pm-11pm; Bar Sun-Th 5pm-midnight, F-Sat 5pm-3am. Appetizers $5-7, Entrées $9-24. **1 2 3 A C** *to Chambers St.*

Il Mattone *Italian*

A variety of Italian fare is available at this simple eatery, but locals keep coming back for the pizza, available both for eat-in and delivery. After experiencing the taste—the crust is somehow crispy on the outside and soft and steaming on the inside, and toppings are simple, fresh, and perfectly proportioned—it's easy to see why. The décor matches the pizza: simple exposed brick and concrete, clean lighting, and spartan wood furnishings are combined to create an environment both crisp and cozy. Though the specialty drink menu is still being perfected, the bar is well-stocked and offers creative twists on classic cocktails that tend toward the sweet and chocolaty.

413 Greenwich (at Hubert). 212.343.0030. M-W 11am-10pm, Th-F 11am-11pm, Sat 5pm-11pm. Appetizers $4-13, Entrées $15-28. **1 2 3** *to Canal St.*

Ivy's Bistro *Italian and American*

This quaint bistro features plush seating, candlelight, smooth Spanish guitar, and simple, appealing food with a presentation to match. Soak up the photographs of Italian architecture on the walls, taken by the owner himself, as you feast on pesto garlic bread and hearty entrées. Save room for dessert, though—the 20-minute wait for the warm soft-in-the-middle chocolate cake is well worth it.

385 Greenwich Street (at North Moore). 212.343.1139. M-F 7am-11pm, Sat-Sun 10am-11pm. Appetizers $8-12, Entrées $13-23. **1** *to Franklin St.*

Thirty-Five *Thai*

Ideal for a first date, this authentic Thai spot boasts a trendy and romantic ambiance; hot pink lights radiate on traditional Thai wall tapestries, mirroring the westernized streets of modern Bangkok. Service is extremely friendly, and the chefs are willing to cater each dish to your spice preferences. Try an innovative Thai cocktail from the full bar in the back, like the whiskey with iced green tea, and enjoy the artfully presented curries in rich coconut milk. The lunch special, including an entrée and an appetizer, is a steal, but even a full meal won't empty your wallet.

35 Lispenard Street (at Church). 212.226.8123. M-Sat 11am-11pm, closed Sunday. Appetizers $4-9, Entrées $8-20. N Q R W *to Canal St.*

VietCafé *Vietnamese*

With lacquered wooden tables, exposed brick walls, and soft golden lighting, this Vietnamese treasure perfectly combines modern chic with cozy warmth to make it the perfect winter dinner or date spot. Begin with crispy spring rolls, or try the Ha Noi pillow dumplings with crab, shrimp, pork, scallions, and jicama root. The roasted sesame beef and the roasted chicken breast, served with a ginger-citrus sauce, are both delicately flavored and sweetly savory. With ten entrées under $10 and a menu that combines the tastes of Northern, Southern, and Central Vietnam, this is one of those rare spots in the city where you can linger over a glass of wine and enjoy the experience of an upscale meal without having to watch your wallet or the clock. Stop by the Gallery Vietnam, located next door, to savor the sights of the island after enjoying its tastes.

345 Greenwich Street (at Harrison). 212.431.5888. M-Th 11am-10pm, F 11am-11pm, Sat 5pm-11pm, closed Sunday. Appetizers $6-12, Entrées $6-24. **1** *to Franklin St.*

Walker's *American*
This neighborhood favorite is an unusual hybrid of Irish pub and formal dining room; soft candlelight fades into the glow of neon bar signs in the windows, while flower arrangements coexist with flat screen TVs. The low-key vibe is appealing to the repeat after-work crowd, and the meat-and-potatoes menu ranks well above your standard pub fare. Befitting the setting, the offerings aren't completely devoid of innovation: warm herb goat cheese and roasted shallots rejuvenate classics appetizers like bruschetta, and cornmeal-crusted Willapoint oysters (served with Cajun tartar sauce) provide a marked contrast to standard wings and chicken tenders.

16 Moore Street (at Varick). 212.941.0142. Daily 11:45am-1am. Appetizers $4-11, Entrées $10-20. **1** *to Franklin St.*

LOWER TIER
Yaffa's Tea Room *Mediterranean*
Come to this classic tea room, decorated in burgundy velvet and antique crystal chandeliers, for a delightful meal at any time of day; the breakfast offerings are a delectable way to start your morning, and the lunch fare is fresh and healthy. Reservations are required for High Tea ($20), served every day but Sunday from 2-5pm, and it's a worth-while experience (if you've got the time to spare). This throwback to classic English elegance is accentuated by the attentiveness of the friendly waitstaff.

353 Greenwich Street (at Harrison). 212.274.9403. Daily 8:30am-4am. Appetizers $6-9, Entrées $10-18. **1** *to Franklin St.*

Nightlife
The Brandy Library
The Brandy Library, a small, cozy room awash with warm golden light, has a gigantic leather-bound binder for a menu, containing more varieties of brandy and cognac than you ever knew existed—and an impressive selection of scotches and whiskies as well. Classy and refined, the bar embodies all of the glamour (but none of the debauchery) of a 1920's speakeasy, attracting well-dressed financiers and their beautiful companions. The effect is amplified by the friendly bartenders' dress—think suspenders, cufflinks, and arm-bands—and expert knowledge of the spirits. Don't pass up the molten-centered Valhrona chocolate cake just because you're at a bar—the dessert goes wonderfully with a tasting tray of cognacs or single-malt-scotches.

25 North Moore Street (at Hudson). 212.226.5545. Sun-W 5pm-2am, Th-Sat 4pm-4am. Drinks $9-13. **1** *to Franklin St.*

Bubble Lounge
An i-banking, BWM-driving clientele enjoys this lounge's champagnes and sparkling wines, possibly the best selection in the city. The posh interior provides a great setting to impress a first date with some bubbly and caviar, so long as you don't mind dropping your whole wallet in the process.

228 West Broadway (at North Moore). 212.431.3433. M-W 5pm-2am, Th 4pm-2am, F-Sat 5pm-4am, closed Sunday. Drinks $13. **1** *to Franklin St.*

Circa Tabac
The self-described 1930s art deco décor and dim lighting create an inviting atmosphere at Circa Tabac, one of the few cigarette bars left in the city. The menu boasts 125 different brands of cigarettes and bidis from all parts of the world, including Armenia, Indonesia, Malaysia, Canada, China, and others. Tobacco enthusiasts can puff the night away while sipping classic cocktails at the bar or a personal table, where a menu in the shape of

a matchbook lets everyone know what's important here. For a unique twist on the traditional tasting menu, try the package that includes a cocktail, an appetizer, and a pack of cigarettes to complement the flavors.

32 Watts Street (at Sixth). 212.941.1781. M-Th 5pm-2am, F-Sat 5pm-3am, Sun 5pm-1am. Drinks $8-14. **1 A C E** *to Canal St.*

Kimono Lounge

With blood-red walls and plush white couches, the Kimono Lounge has a great view of neighbor Megu's fabric-draped dining room. Fortunately, that spot's long lines, expensive bottle service, and ogre-ish bouncers don't plague the pack of travelers who visit this lounge nightly. More of a pre-bar than a bar, go prior to dinner or a night out; it's also a great space for private parties. If you're lucky, you'll catch the DJ spinning new pop remixes and sing-along oldies, and maybe even a few models enjoying small plates from Megu's kitchen.

62 Thomas Street (at Church). 212.964.7777. Sun-Th 5pm-11pm, F-Sat 5pm-4am. Drinks $5-20. **1 2 3 A C** *to Chambers St.*

Arts

Apex Art

Though you would never guess from its easy-to-miss façade, this gallery is home to some of the most exciting contemporary art exhibits in the country. Every year since 1994, this non-profit organization has displayed eight group visual exhibitions, hosted up to 10 foreign artists in its residency program, and arranged scores of lectures, film screenings, and performance art pieces. The directors encourage outside contributions and even accept unsolicited proposals for exhibits each season. The exhibits and events tend to be

Old factories in TriBeCa

serious, provocative, and cerebral, with an aim to "encourage thought and commentary and to stimulate public dialogue about contemporary art," but even non-art snobs can appreciate free art of this quality when accompanied by the informative and easy-to-handle brochures, written by the curator for each exhibit.

291 Church Street (at White). 212.431.5270. apexart. org. T-Sat 11am-6pm, closed Monday. Free. **1** *to Franklin St.*

Collective: Unconscious

Its maximum occupancy may be 74 people, but this "all-ages, volunteer-run, non-profit, multi-use performance venue" is one of the best places in the city for developing musicians to show off their stuff and get scouted by indie labels. The upstairs houses a small auditorium for musical acts and plays, while the downstairs is currently home to the Tank, a non-profit organization that hosts film, comedy, music, dance, public affairs, new media, and theater events. It's got quite a following among artists and loyal audience members, one of whom, a feng shui expert, recently spiffed up the downstairs with lights and new furniture.

279 Church Street (at White). 212.254.5277. wierd.org **1** *to Franklin St.*

The Flea Theatre

Jim Simpson—otherwise known as Mr. Sigourney Weaver—directs a resident company of actors, known as "The Bats," at this friendly off-off-Broadway theater space. Productions include both contemporary works and familiar masterpieces, in addition to the frequent dance troupes and musical acts to which the venue plays host. There are two small auditoria—a downstairs black box and a larger convertible theater one floor up—allowing for up to three performances in a single evening. Reserve tickets early to avoid sitting on the floor.

41 White Street (at Broadway). 212.226.2407. theflea.org N Q R W *to Canal St.*

Tribeca Cinemas

Not only is it the primary home of Robert DeNiro's Tribeca Film Festival, this multifaceted establishment on TriBeCa's northern border is also one of the city's hottest venues for cocktail parties, film screenings, and other social functions. Available spaces include a dining room, two lounges, a loft, a gallery, and, of course, two movie theaters; stroll around the block and relish walking in the steps of the innumerable celebrities who have graced this space with their presence. Though some screenings are closed to the public—or have tickets that run for hundreds of dollars—others, such as the monthly Channel 102 television pilot contest, are free for all.

54 Varick Street (at Laight). 212.941.2400. tribecacinemas.com. **1** *to Canal St.*

TriBeCa Performing Arts Center

Though it is housed in the Borough of Manhattan Community College, the Tribeca PAC has been devoted to serving the entire area community since 1983. It has multiple performance spaces, including one of the largest theaters downtown (capacity 913), and accommodates film screenings, theater, live music, and more. Highlights include a the Lost Jazz Shrines concert series, celebrating the history of jazz in New York City, as well as college productions, occasional free performances, and shows for children.

199 Chambers Street (at West). 212.220.1460. tribecapac. org **1 2 3** *to Chambers St.*

Shopping

Collector's Toy Den

Whether it's a Raggedy Ann 90th anniversary commemorative doll, a *Terminator 2* bobble head, or the *Shrek* Barbie that your collection has been missing, Collector's Toy Den is the place to find it. This shop is chock full of toys, dolls, games, posters, cookie jars, and other collector items that can be described as retro, new, classy, and, on occasion, just plain weird. Adults and kids alike delight in rare toys, like a Harry Potter Extreme Quiddich action figure ($44.95) and a Beatles Yellow Submarine pin-ball game ($7.50). Most prices are reasonable, but particularly hard-to-find pieces go for well upwards of $100.

85 Franklin Street (at Broadway). 212.334.0409. collec-torstoyden.com. M-Sat 11am-7pm. **1** *to Franklin St.*

Gotham Bikes

Whether you're a hardcore Tour de France buff or haven't been on a bike since grade school, anyone can enjoy an afternoon pedaling along the paths of the Hudson River Park—just stop by this multi-purpose bike shop to rent a hybrid for reasonable rates. They also sell bikes, locks, gloves, jerseys, water bottles, sports bars, along with a multitude of unexpected accessories to fill all your cycling needs. And in the sad case that your beloved ten-speed hasn't been working up to snuff, the knowledgeable staff also does repairs.

112 West Broadway (at Reade). 212.732.2453. gotham-bikes.com. M-Sat 10am-6:30pm, Sun 10am-5pm. Rentals: $10/hr, $30/day. **1 2 3 A C** *to Chambers St.*

Issey Miyake

The flagship store of this Hiroshima-born clothing designer, famous for his innovative use of pleats, was designed by Frank Gehry—a good reason to stop by, even though chances are you can't afford the clothes. The colorful fashions, though fun and light, have price tags to match the designer's renown; expect to pay $1225 for a top. Still, it's a shopping experience not to be missed: The space, often infused with lively bossa nova, houses not only Miyake's eight clothing collections (two for men, six for women), but also work by local artists. Don't be intimidated if you're not a fashionista—the friendly staff welcomes window shoppers, and even keeps dog treats behind the counter for visits from neigh-borhood mutts.

119 Hudson Street (at North Moore). 212.226.0100. tribecaisseymiyake.com. M-Sat 11am-7pm, Sun noon-6pm. **1** *to Franklin St.*

Just Scandinavian

The furniture and housewares here are funkier, fresher, and far more expensive than what you'll find at that other Scandinavian furniture store. From blue and white curtains with drawings of French houses to a rubber "washing-up bowl," the items sold here don't shy away from playfulness or bright colors. The pieces, all by Finnish, Swedish, Norwegian, and Danish designers, are ergonomic, durable, and hard to find anywhere else in the country. During the winter, which sometimes seems to last here as long as it does in Oslo, you'll be glad you invested in that bright yellow plastic carpet.

161 Hudson Street (at Laight). 212.334.2556. justscandi-navian.com. T-Sat 11am-7pm, Sun noon-6pm. **1** *to Canal St.*

Steven Alan

A couture-meets-outdoorsman atmosphere prevails in this lauded designer's downtown location; as you walk in the door, you're greeted by a loud R&B soundtrack, a gargantuan leather bench, and a pair of stuffed brown-and-white birds. Once you're in, you can find clothing for men and women, bags, shoes, vintage watches, European skincare products, and candles. Each of the dressing stalls, draped with blue curtains, contains a strip of uncovered light-bulbs; be prepared to see the unvarnished truth of how you look in that $200 shirt dress.

103 Franklin Street (at Broadway). 212.343.0692. steve-nalan.com. Daily 11:30am-7pm, Th 11:30am-8pm. **1** *to Franklin St.*

TriBeCa Girls

In TriBeCa, according to a salesclerk here, "People are not looking for the Gap." The success of this not-unridiculous boutique proves it. TriBeCa Girls offers "urban contemporary and European fash-ion" to the heretofore Gap-clad market of girls as young as 12 months old. With T-shirts, shoes, and dresses from such lines as IKKS, Sally Miller, and Diesel, the store attracts downtown girls with a sense of style and a disposable income. If you're too young to shop here, don't despair: infants can amuse themselves with blocks and toys as their older sisters max out Daddy's AmEx.

171 Duane Street (at Hudson). 212.925.0049. tribeca-girls.com. T-Sat 11:30am-7pm, Sun noon-6:30pm. **1 2 3 A C** *to Chambers St.*

MIDTOWN

CHELSEA

Gorgeous brownstones line one side of the street and towering projects occupy the other in this neighborhood where boutiques are nestled between untidy bodegas, and beautiful, bronzed gods descend to walk amongst men.

Although today, it is largely associated with the hard-bodied, gym-going, look-at-me-not-looking-at-you gay men who call it home, Chelsea was once one of the city's premier shipping ports. When Chelsea Piers opened in 1910, designed by the same team responsible for Grand Central Terminal, they soon became the prime docking space for both passenger and military ships. During the 1950s and '60s, the piers served as a cargo terminal, but soon thereafter fell into disrepair and decay. It wasn't until the 1990s that the pier was overhauled and rebuilt, saving it from joining the ranks of other forgotten New York relics.

Chelsea also boasts a rich history of artistic movements. As one of the stops on the Theater District's uptown crawl from SoHo to Times Square, the neighborhood enjoyed a brief tenure as the premier place to catch a live performance of classics new and old. In the first half of the 20th century, the Chelsea Hotel was home to some of the modern era's greatest writers, actors, and musicians. The 1990s art boom saw an influx of studios and galleries move into the neighborhood, as artists were priced out of more traditional visual art enclaves such as SoHo.

Today, residents and visitors alike wine, dine and unwind in the area's many coffee shops, chic lounges and restaurants, or peruse the ultra-sleek, ultra-hip art galleries, all in the shadows of the neighborhood's history as a bustling center of the working class.

CHELSEA 163

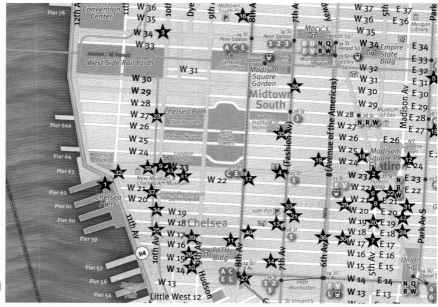

© Opus Publishing 2007 — www.OpusPublishing.com

CHELSEA

SIGHTS/ATTRACTIONS
1. Chelsea Piers
2. Flatiron Building
3. The High Line
4. The Hotel Chelsea

DINING
5. Artisanal Fromagerie and Bistro
6. Aspen
7. BLT Fish
8. Duvet
9. Izakaya Ten
10. Markt
11. Matsuri
12. Shake Shack
13. Tello's
14. Westside Market
15. Yakiniku Juju
16. Zipper Tavern

NIGHTLIFE
17. Barracuda
18. The Cutting Room
19. Dusk Lounge
20. Flatiron Lounge
21. G Lounge
22. Live Bait
23. Marquee
24. Old Town Bar
25. Park
26. Passerby
27. The Plumm
28. Rebel
29. Slate
30. Splash Bar
31. Strata

ARTS
32. Chelsea Art Museum
33. The Dance Theatre Workshop
34. The Kitchen Center
35. Museum at the Fashion Institute of Technology
36. Rubin Museum of Art,
37. 192 Books

SHOPPING
38. Balenciaga
39. Chelsea Market
40. Chisholm Larsen Poster Gallery
41. Comme Des Garçons
42. Fishs Eddy
43. Printed Matter

FAST FACTS

⑦ **Scenic Stroll: Chelsea Piers**

⑦ **Major Subway Stations: 23rd St (C E, F V, 1), 28th St (R W, 1)**

⑦ **Urban Oasis: The High Line**

⑦ **Kooky Corner: Mugs with "Brooklynese" phrases at Fishs Eddy**

⑦ **Notable Buildings: Flatiron Building**

⑦ **Neighborhood Landmarks: Chelsea Market**

⑦ **Celebrity Hangouts: Hotel Chelsea**

⑦ **Neighborhood Foods: Brownies at Fat Witch Bakery**

⑦ **Notable Residents: Jimi Hendrix, Edie Sedgewick, Andy Warhol, Tennessee Williams**

⑦ **Schools: Fashion Institute of Technology (FIT)**

Sights/Attractions

Chelsea Piers

This famous 30-acre waterfront sports and entertainment complex contains a bowling alley, golf club, ice skating rink, rock climbing wall, athletic training center, and large recreational spaces open for rental, all complemented by an amazing view of the Hudson.

23rd Street and the Hudson River. 212.336.6666. chelseapiers.com. Entrance fees vary by activity. **1 C E** *to 23rd St.*

Flatiron Building

This distinctively triangular 21-story structure, designed by architect Daniel Burnham, was one of the tallest buildings in the city when it was completed in 1902, and is one of the most famous in the world today. With its limestone façade and steel frame, it is considered one of the first skyscrapers ever built; visit to gawk at its odd shape, designed to fit the mid-street plot of land on which it sits.

175 Fifth Avenue (at 23rd). **6 R W F V** *to 23rd St.*

The High Line

This 1.45-mile elevated railway, stretching through Chelsea from Hell's Kitchen to Greenwich Village, was once used to transport goods along the Hudson River. Trains stopped running in 1980, and since then, it's become a grassy, trash-filled no-man's land—a literal urban jungle. When then-mayor Rudolph Giuliani hoped to raze the High Line in 2001, the newly formed Friends of the High Line coalition—backed by high-profile celebrity spokespeople and money brought in by David Bowie's annual High Line Festival—pushed for its preservation. After a few years of indecision, it was finally determined that the site would be converted into an elevated public park; construction began in the spring of 2006, and is currently scheduled to be completed by the summer of 2008.

34th Street to Gansevoort Street, between Tenth and Eleventh. 212.206.9922. thehighline.org **A C E L** *to 8th Ave.*

The Hotel Chelsea

Several of the most well-known writers, actors, and musicians in American history—including Mark Twain, Arthur Miller, Tennessee Williams, Edie Sedgewick, Bob Dylan, and Jimi Hendrix—have lived in this Chelsea landmark. The city's first co-op apartment in 1884, this 12-story brick building has served as an arena for intellectual and creative thought throughout the 20th century; cameos in work ranging from Warhol's 1966 film *Chelsea Girls* to songs by Bob Dylan, Joni Mitchell, and the Counting Crows testify to its lasting impression on contemporary culture. The hotel has also been the site of tragedy: Room 100 infamously played host to the brutal slaying of groupie Nancy Spungen by her notoriously unhinged boyfriend, ex-Sex Pistols bassist Sid Vicious.

222 West 23rd Street (at Seventh). 212.243.3700. hotelchelsea.com. **1** *to 23rd St.*

Dining
UPSCALE

Artisanal Fromagerie *French*

This lively, spacious, and densely-packed bistro is a cheese-lover's paradise that caters to an upscale crowd. But don't worry if you're neither; Artisanal's knowledgeable, attentive waitstaff are happy to provide you with information on any cheese you can—or can't—pronounce. Try one of four creamy fondues with an assortment of *baigneuses* for dipping, like kielbasa and crudités, though the hearty breads do just fine. A basket of addictive *gougères* (puffed cheese bread) is an absolute must, and the parmesan gnocchi with wild mushrooms and spring vegetables is another favorite. For a unique experience, call ahead to reserve a table in "the cave," a temperature- and humidity-controlled room that literally surrounds you with cheese.

2 Park Avenue (at 32nd). 212.725.8585. Brunch Sat-Sun 11am-3pm; Lunch M-F noon-5pm; Dinner M-Th 5pm-

11pm, F-Sat 5pm-midnight, Sun 5pm-10pm. Appetizers $9-25, Entrées $20-36. **6** *to 33rd St.*

BLT Fish *Seafood*

From the Vermont cheddar biscuits with maple syrup-soaked butter to the exceptional Baked Alaska, this seafood mecca always hits the spot. Downstairs, an upscale version of a New England clam shack serves up basic but well-prepared seafood specialties and drinks at a bar decorated with life preservers and other nautical flair. Upstairs, formality is the name of the game in the dining room that provides an elegant setting for meticulously crafted and flavorful dishes, though the raw bar fails to impress. Ask the encyclopedic sommelier to guide you through the expansive wine list if you have any trouble on your own. BLT Fish may be a little noisy, but the charm of the exposed kitchen and upbeat music coalesce for a lively, sophisticated evening.

21 West 17th Street (at Fifth). 212.691.8388. M-Sat 5:30pm-11:30pm, closed Sunday. Appetizers $9-23, Entrées $27-36. **4 5 6** **N R Q W L** *to Union Square.*

Duvet *Seafood*

You'll be sure to have your date in bed before you even pay for dinner at this trendy spot, where diners lounge on beds while nibbling food served on Lazy Susans. Pillows provide ample comfort, and each diner is given slippers to don for ultimate relaxation. While everything tastes excellent, be sure to sample seafood specialties like the dragon roll or Fuji apple and salmon. As expected, the drinks are sultry and seductive, especially the Duvet Sin.

45 West 21st Street (at Fifth). 212-989-2121. Dinner T-Sat 5:30pm-11pm; Lounge Th-Sat 11pm-4am. Appetizers $12-18, Entrées $24-34. **F V** *to 23rd St.*

MID-RANGE

Aspen *New American*

Deer heads mounted above the bar of this luxurious ski lodge-style restaurant might make you feel like you've returned from a day swooshing down the slopes instead of tromping through the urban jungle. Take your cue from the trendy 20-

somethings and professional types with money to burn and gather around the fire pit. The small plates are meant for sharing and include everything from juicy bison sliders to elk sausage and scrumptious trout tacos; the cuisine is decidedly American, but the wine list covers the globe, including affordable selections from Austria and Slovenia. Finish off your meal with snow-capped cupcakes or warm chocolate cake, and enjoy a breather from urban life.

*30 West 22nd Street (at Fifth). 212.645.5040. M-Sat 6pm-4am, closed Sunday. Small Plates $9-16. **F V** to 23rd St.*

Izakaya Ten *Japanese*

Built around an exotic drink menu, this unusual tavern pushes traditional sake and Shochu (Japanese vodka) the way American bars sell local and home-brewed beer. Expect to wait for a table and don't forget to bring your spirit of adventure, because there are few familiar dishes on the elaborate, well-crafted menu. From the shrimp avocado *age*—deep-fried avocado with a creamy, fruity center, topped with a crunchy shrimp tempura helmet—to the succulent ginger pork belly served in-skillet, each dish is more innovative than the last. The quiet, well-lit environment serves as the perfect backdrop for any occasion, and the Japanese pop music only adds to the authenticity.

*207 Tenth Avenue (at 23rd). 212.627.7777. M-Sat 5pm-midnight, Sun 5pm-10pm. Appetizers $4-8, Entrées $8-15. **1** to 23rd St.*

Markt *Belgian*

There's a saying that the Belgians eat as well as the French and as much as the Germans. See for yourself at this large, loud, and authentic bistro that rivals any on the Grande Plaza in Brussels. Rustic dark-wood décor, open café seating, an incredible array of Belgian beers, and a helpful, svelte waitstaff make this a good choice for a group or a date. Try the dewy-fresh Belgian endive and mache salad or the nectar-like cold tomato soup with sweet red onions, and finish with a French press coffee and the warm Belgian chocolate tart

with homemade pistachio ice cream.

*401 West 14th Street (at Ninth). 212.727.3314. Brunch Sat-Sun 10am-4:30pm; Lunch daily 11:30am-4:30pm; Dinner daily 5:30pm-midnight. Appetizers $7-20, Entrées $14-36. **1 2 3 A C E** to 14th St.*

Matsuri *Japanese*

Marked by a red door but barely visible from the street, this traditional Japanese restaurant draws both trendy diners and Japanese nationals looking for a little taste of home. You won't find any innovative rolls at this sushi joint, but the authentic menu combines fresh ingredients with stellar presentation. Fish is served traditionally, with the head and tail fried after the filet has been picked clean. The softshell crab tempura, fried to perfection, and the thinly sliced kobe beef, lightly salted and delightfully velvety, are both excellent choices. In contrast to the food, the décor is playfully modern, with large misshaped lanterns eclipsed by rows of electric lights.

*369 West 16th Street (at Eighth). 212.243.6400. Sun-W 6pm-midnight, Th-Sat 6pm-1am. Appetizers $8-17, Entrées $19-27. **1 2 3 A C E** to 14th St.*

Tello's *Mediterranean, Italian*

With a classic Italian look and charming, friendly waiters, this traditional find will make you feel right at home. The menu is home-style and hearty, with a refreshingly deep selection of accompanying wines. To start, try the intricate mix of shrimp and salmon baked in a soft pasta shell, so good you might want to forget the entrée and order seconds. Classic love songs and a cozy interior set the mood for a romantic evening that should always end with the eatery's trademark homemade ice cream.

*263 West 19th Street (at Seventh). 212.691.8696. Brunch Sat-Sun 11am-4pm; Dinner daily 5pm-midnight. Appetizers $4-9, Entrées $14-25. **1** to 18th St.*

Zipper Tavern *American, Eastern European*

Heavy on atmosphere, this industrial-chic duplex restaurant is the latest addition to the Zipper Factory's lounge and off-Broadway theater. Expansive, but never overwhelming, dark hues and gritty lighting contribute to the comfortable and trendy ambiance. A new face in the emerging "Gastropub" culinary movement, think haute cuisine done informally. Friendly and attentive service makes this welcomed addition to the Garment District a fantastic place to spend an evening before or after a show.

336 West 37ᵗʰ Street (at Eighth). 212.695.4600. M-Th noon-11pm, F noon-midnight, Sat-Sun 5pm-11pm. Appetizers $10-15, Entrées $15-25. **1 2 3** N R Q W **S 7** *to Times Square.*

CASUAL

Shake Shack *American*

In a city where diners routinely pay $29 for burgers dolled up with foie gras and black truffles, it's surprising to find out that the most talked-about burger in town is actually flipped at this stand in Madison Square Park. Topped with American cheese, lettuce, tomato, and special "shack sauce," the burgers are unpretentious, unassuming, and utterly satisfying. Save room for a delicious frozen custard, available daily in vanilla and chocolate, along with a rotating flavor du jour. Enjoy it in a simple cone or cup, slurp it as a shake or creamsicle, or try a "concrete"—a formidable tub of custard blended solid with a slew of toppings. Be prepared for a long line of foodies, suits, and chattering 20-somethings.

Madison Square Park (Madison Avenue at 23ʳᵈ). 212.889.6600. Daily 11am-11pm. Burgers $3.50-9. **6** N R W **F V** *to 23ʳᵈ St.*

Nightlife

Barracuda *LGBT*

With no sign outside and a single red light bulb over the entrance, this Chelsea icon has often been mistaken for a bordello. Have no fear, though: The place is packed with the friendliest New Yorkers you'll ever meet. The vintage-Vegas-themed décor is a little seedy, but the gorgeous bartenders and the riotously funny comedy shows will make you feel right at home—assuming your home comes with dancing drag queens. Go for a healthy selection of attractive and welcoming folk to please even the most jaded New Yorker.

275 West 22ⁿᵈ Street (at Eighth). 212.645.8613. Daily 4pm-4am. Drinks $5-11, cash only. **C E** *at 23ʳᵈ St.*

The Cutting Room *Music*

One of the city's best destinations for a night out, The Cutting Room offers live music, an amazing jukebox, attractive patrons, great drinks, and food that comes complete with homemade ketchup for the burgers and fries. There are live performers almost every night, including comedians, musicians, and saxophone players, and it's not unusual to spot a celebrity or two.

19 West 24ᵗʰ Street (at Broadway). 212.691.1900. M-Sat 5pm-1am, closed Sunday. Drinks $9-13. **1** *to 23ʳᵈ St.*

Flatiron Lounge *Lounge*

The speakeasy craze has afflicted many a downtown watering hole—if you've seen one nameless door, you've pretty much seen them all—but there's a light at the end of the tunnel in Flatiron Lounge. The low-tunneled entrance leads to classy red banquets and bona fide antique cocktails, with recipes ranging from the 1895 "Corpse Reviver" to a classic New York Sour circa 1930. The original drinks are just as inspired, incorporating flavors such as juniper, lychee, and hibiscus. The décor is subdued and lovely, as are the people, who are content to sip and savor their drinks as if Prohibition were still on.

37 West 19ᵗʰ Street (at Fifth). 212.727.7741. Sun-W 5pm-2am, T-Sat 5pm-4am. Drinks $12-13. **1** *to 18ᵗʰ St.*

g Lounge *LGBT*

Despite some flaws in the décor, this lounge is a mainstay of the gay bar scene. A huge circular bar dominates the room, perfect for seeing and being seen, but when the crowd is light it makes the space empty; leather ottomans up front interfere with foot traffic, and there's rarely a place to sit in the rear lounge when the crowd swells. Stay for a drink to get a feel for the scene, but know that the crowd is older than you might expect.

223 West 19th Street (at Seventh). 212.929.1085. Daily 4pm-4am. **1** *to 18th St.*

Marquee *Club*

It's one of the hottest clubs in NYC, so the door policy is strict: Dress to impress. Assuming you get inside, this place is pretty much all it's cracked up to be—both levels are packed with beautiful people, and each has a large bar so it's never too hard to get a drink—although those drinks aren't cheap. The design is simple, but the atmosphere is great.

289 Tenth Avenue (at 27th). 646.473.0202. T-Sat 10pm-4am, closed Monday. Cover $20. **C E** *to 23rd St.*

Old Town Bar *Bar*

Don't count it out as just another of the ubiquitous "oldest bars in New York," and don't call it worn, either: This bar is a classic, with just as much dive as a young, professional clientele is willing to risk. Come in for a drink after work in the gritty splendor of dusty stained glass and antique booths, or grab a burger, which some patrons call the best in the city. If you order one, watch as your waitress flexes her muscles to haul it from the upstairs kitchen on a dumbwaiter—the oldest such machine in the city.

45 East 18th Street (at Broadway). 212.529.6732. M-Sat 11:30am-1:30am, Sun noon-midnight. **4 5 6 N Q R W L** *to Union Square.*

Passerby *Bar*

The signless door and flashing red, yellow, and blue checkered floor suggest just another trendy bar, but with nary a martini glass in sight, this low-key watering hole favors locals over supermodels any day. Stick to beer and chat with an ever-changing crowd of gallery employees, yuppies, geeks, artists, and loners.

436 West 15th Street (at Ninth). 212.206.6847. M-Th 6pm-2am, F-Sat 8pm-4am, closed Sunday. **A C E** *to 14th St.*

The Plumm *Club*

Don't even try to get into this ripe joint without a reservation; if you're not on the list, the club is always at capacity. Once you're in, there's actually plenty of room to lounge—the club forgoes a traditional dance floor, and plays old favorites to break up the dance music. An older crowd pours drinks from Grey Goose bottles while stunning girls dance on the tables, but the well-stocked bar has plenty for everyone to afford. Pretentious? Definitely—but if you can get on the list, The Plumm is worth a taste.

246 West 14th Street (at Eighth). 212.675.1567. W-M 10pm-4am, closed Tuesday. **L** *to 8th Ave.*

Rebel *Club*

On any given night, expect to find a death metal band downstairs performing for suburban Jersey kids with thrashing dreadlocks, while a flashy urban crowd stands around upstairs, refusing to

The Flatiron Building

dance. In a similar dichotomy, you can either get a table with a $300 bottle of vodka, or drink from plastic cups at the bar. Either way, you can go for a smoke on the new roof deck afterwards.

251 West 30th Street (at Seventh). 212.695.2747. Th-F 10pm-4am, Sat 11pm-4am, closed M-W. Cover $5-25. **1 2 3 A C E** *to Penn Station.*

Slate *Pool Hall*

The former home of Chelsea Billiards, this pool hall has been revamped to become New York's swankiest, with blue lights and an amniotic glow inside. There's surprisingly little attitude for this part of town, and the new Mediterranean fusion menu is a fantastic addition to a night of pool-playing.

54 West 21st Street (at Fifth). 212.989.0096. Daily noon-1am. Drinks $7-8. **4 5 6** N Q R W L *to Union Square.*

Splash *LGBT*

This outrageous gay club boasts Musical Mondays for the theatrically inclined, and a dance floor for weekend partygoers who don't want to shell out 30 bucks for a night at the Roxy. It's a fun place for loud house music and some very outrageous go-go dancing, but since the crowd is a little bit older (25 and up), the dance floor isn't usually as crowded as some might like it to be.

50 West 17th Street (at Fifth). 212.691.0073. Daily 4pm-4am. $5-20 cover. **4 5 6** N Q R W L *to Union Square.*

Strata *Lounge*

Feel free to sink into the comfort of the lush decor and kick back with cocktails and appetizers in this unique celebrity-sighting hotspot—just be wary of your bill. Slightly more polished and pricey than the other Gramercy lounges, Strata attracts a young, early-to-mid-20s crowd; on weekends, it transforms into a club dominated by thumping hip-hop and house music.

915 Broadway (at 21st). 212.505.7400. F-Sat 10pm-4am, closed Sun-Th. Cover $10-15. N R *to 23rd St.*

Arts

Chelsea Art Museum

This bold, red, three-story museum next to Chelsea Piers is devoted to promoting relatively unexplored 20th and 21st century artists, including celebrated internationals who usually receive scant attention in the U.S. The museum, which hosts frequent special events, artist panel discussions, chamber music concerts, and family workshops, also presents exhibitions that include work by standout students at Parsons and The New School.

566 West 22nd Street (at Eleventh). 212.255.0719. chelseaartmuseum.org. T-Sat noon-6pm, Th noon-8pm. Closed Sun-M. Adults $6, Students $3. **C E** *to 23rd St.*

The Dance Theater Workshop

Dedicated to developing and showcasing passionate and talented dancers, this organization hosts intensive programs designed to initiate new artists into the professional realm. Check its calendar for a list of public performances, which often focus on exploring and redefining artistic and media boundaries.

219 West 19th Street (at Seventh). 212.691.6500. dtw.org. Standard ticket $20. **1** *to 18th St.*

The Kitchen Center

This experimental performing arts center, founded in 1971 by a group of avant-garde artists, has grown into an internationally recognized organization, unafraid to take creative risks in its exploration of video installations, music, and dance. In addition to the gallery—an open, two-floor space that allows visitors to roam freely around the randomly placed displays—the Kitchen Center presents regular performances, readings, panel discussions, and even public street fairs.

512 West 19th Street (at Tenth). 212.255.5793. thekitchen.org. T-F noon-6pm, Sat 11am-6pm, closed Sun-M. Free. **1** *to 18th St.*

Museum at the Fashion Institute of Technology

These two small galleries exhibiting items from

GALLERY-HOPPING IN CHELSEA

To get an idea of the three-hundred-plus small art galleries that give Chelsea its reputation as a center of the New York art world, stroll down any street in the 20s between Tenth and Eleventh Avenues. You'll encounter dozens of galleries to kick off your visit; or, just follow our advice for a good sampling of the neighborhood's offerings.

A good place to start your tour is the **MATTHEW MARKS GALLERY** (*522 West 22nd Street, 212-243-0200*), which shows contemporary photography in an eerily industrial space reminiscent of a renovated factory. Next, cross the street to the local outpost of **PACEWILDENSTEIN**—one of three in the city—which showcases large, hanging sculptures constructed with metalwork and a variety of experimental materials (*545 West 22nd Street, 212-989-4258*).

For a taste of more established artists, head either north or south to one of the two Chelsea branches of the famed **GAGOSIAN GALLERY** (*522 West 21st Street, 212-741-1717 and 555 West 24th Street, 212-741-1111*), which show renowned 20th century works by Jackson Pollock, Cindy Sherman, and Pablo Picasso.

Finally, stop into **JIM KEMPNER FINE ART** (*501 West 23rd Street, 212.206.6872*), an architecturally inventive gallery space composed of a two-story viewing area and an inner stone courtyard that exhibits American prints and works on paper. Before you leave, catch a bird's eye view of the fascinating, bustling streets of Chelsea from behind the large panel window on the second floor.

FIT's permanent collection—an accumulation of over 50,000 costumes from 1700-2007, plus an even greater number of 6th-21st century textiles—are open to the public free of charge. Exquisite Chanel couture, Oscar de la Renta gowns, and ornate handbags are carefully displayed under dim lighting and against black walls. A third room adjacent to the main viewing gallery is dedicated to work by the Institute's students.

Seventh Avenue (at 27th). 212.217.5800. fitnyc.edu. T-F noon-8pm, Sat 10pm-5pm, closed Sun-M. Free. **1** *to 28th St.*

The Rubin Museum of Art

Established in 2004, this 70,000-square-foot museum is dedicated to increasing public awareness and appreciation for the art, history, and culture of the Himalayas; the vast collection of Himalayan sculptures, textiles, and paintings from the 12th century to the present is one of the most comprehensive in the world. The Rubin also presents regular workshops, theater, films, and parties at its new K2 Lounge, as part of a larger mission to enhance the presence of Himalayan literature, poetry, and music in the city.

150 West 17th Street (at Sixth). 212.620.5000. rmanyc.org. M, Th 11am-5pm, W 11am-7pm, F 11am-10pm. Sat-Sun 11am-6pm, closed Tuesday. Adults $10, Students $7. **1** *to 18th St.*

Shopping
192 Books

Come to this cozy bookstore for author signings, lecture series, and group discussions with authors such as Salman Rushdie, Kiran Desai, and Alice Munro, or check out one of the frequent art exhibits, chosen to relate to themes of selected texts.

192 Tenth Avenue (at 21st). 212.255.4022. 192books. com. Tu-Sat 11am-7pm, Sun-M noon-6pm. **C E** *to 23rd St.*

Balenciaga

Enter through a bright red door, then follow an irregular pathway of white-washed brick walls into the cavernous main space of this famed Spanish designer boutique. Mannequins are perched atop artificial rocks and clad in a rich assortment of dresses and fashionable tops; don't miss the chance to wonder among them, San Sebastian-style.

542 West 22nd Street (at Tenth). 212.206.0872. balenciaga.com. M-Sat 11am-7pm, Sun noon-5pm. **C E** *to 23rd St.*

Chelsea Market

With old brick walls and corrugated steel scaffolding, this industrial warehouse-turned-gourmet marketplace contains a wide array of mouth-watering bakeries, sweet shops, and restaurants. Feast on the moist, chewy brownies at Fat Witch Bakery, and peer into the kitchen of the very popular Amy's Bread to watch as chefs effortlessly bake fresh, savory loaves for their doting customers. Trendy, upscale restaurants such as Morimoto and Buddakan, as well as flower and fruit markets, an extensive kitchenware supply store, a wine vault, and a gelateria, fill the rest of the space.

75 Ninth Avenue (at 16th). chelseamarket.com. M-F 9am-10pm, Sat-Sun 10am-6pm. **A C E** L *to 8th Ave.*

Chisholm Larsen Poster Gallery

This well-established store boasts a collection of over 35,000 vintage posters dating as far back as the 1890s. Designs include quirky advertisements, original movie promotions, fashion design, and political flyers. Come to browse one of the largest selections of European film posters in the world, or search through the gallery's easy-to-navigate online catalog.

145 Eighth Avenue (at 17th). 212.741.1703. chisholm-poster.com. T-F 11am-7pm, Sat 11am-5pm, closed Sun-M. **A C E** L *to 8th Ave.*

Comme des Garçons

You can't miss the Chelsea branch of this Tokyo-based boutique: the metallic cave-like entrance, a standout on brick-heavy 22nd Street, leads shoppers into a fascinating white interior of irregular spaces and protruding walls, reminiscent of the Japanese fashion brand's trendy clothing. Founded by Rei Kawakubo in 1973, the brand plays with irregular cuts and a range of vibrant colors and materials—with irregular prices to match, at about $1000 for a light jacket. If you don't feel like foregoing next month's rent for a new look, come to admire the architecture, which is always free.

520 West 22nd Street (at Tenth). 212.604.9200. T-Sat 11am-7pm, Sun noon-6pm, closed Monday. **C E** *to 23rd St.*

Fishs Eddy

Owned by husband-and-wife antique collectors, this haphazard home store feels more like a friendly small town shop than a big city boutique. An assortment of cute knick-knacks, dishware, and necessary household products form the bulk of a terrific inventory; wooden cabinets hold formal glassware alongside colorful stacks of china teacups and bowls. Prices are reasonable, the environment is fun, and the selection can't be beat.

899 Broadway (at 19th). 212.420.9020. fishseddy.com. M 10am-9pm, T-Sat 9am-9pm, Sun 10am-8pm. **to 23rd St.

Westside Market *Gourmet Supermarket*

Any craving for obscure ingredients can be satisfied by the gourmet maze of fresh and reasonably priced produce that is Westside Market. If you're in a rush, grab a salad, some sushi, or a delicious prepared treat. Sweet-tooths be warned: the dessert section will surely fuel your habit. Come here for quality ingredients for any meal, and if the urge to cook fails you, you can always place an order with their highly-esteemed catering service.

77 Seventh Avenue (at 15th). 212.807.7771. Daily 7am-midnight. **1 2 3** *to 14th St.*

FROM CHILLI TO HOT WINGS

WE'VE GOT WHAT YOU'RE HUNGRY FOR.

From the best of what's fresh and seasonal to finely aged cheese, tasty prepared foods and exceptional catering, Westside Market is the gourmet market where you'll find all this and more.

Getit@"theMarket"

77 7th Avenue @ 14th Street, New York, NY
212.807.7771 www.wmarketnyc.com

Free Delivery within a 10 block radius, $25 minimum. Extra Charge for Deliveries outside of range.

THE MANOR OFFERS A PIED-A TERRE FOR AFTER DARK ENJOYMENT, SPARING NO EXPENSE TO AFFORD GUESTS AN ARISTOCRATIC LEVEL OF INDULGENCE.

DISCREETLY LOCATED ON EIGHTH AVENUE NEAR 14TH STREET, THE MANOR IS OPEN FIVE NIGHTS A WEEK FROM 10PM-4AM AND OFFERS AN ECLECTIC VARIETY OF MUSIC FROM HOUSE, TO HIP-HOP, TO CLASSICS AND ROCK.

THE VENUE IS CAPABLE OF HOSTING PRIVATE EVENTS FROM INTIMATE SCREENINGS TO COCKTAIL PARTIES FOR UP TO 350 GUESTS.

GRAMERCY/MURRAY HILL

Don't be fooled by the stone fountain, perfectly manicured English garden, and rows of carved niches overlooking lush flowerbeds. You're still in Manhattan: Gramercy Park, to be exact. It is among the city's most beautiful, tranquil spaces—and unless you are one of the select millionaires with keys, you're not allowed in.

Take a stroll around the park and you'll see some of the most beautiful homes in the city, a mixed bag of Southern-style architecture and posh high-rise apartments, nestled on cool, leafy streets—a welcome oasis from the insanity that is nearby Union Square and Baruch College. Although originally a swamp, this area has long been considered one of the most fashionable addresses in New York City. In 1831, Samuel Ruggles, long-time trustee of Columbia College, drained the marsh and laid out 66 English-style lots around the now-famous private park.

Thanks to its intellectual residents at the turn of the century, Gramercy has historically been called an American Bloomsbury. Past residents include James Harper, founder of the Harper Collins publishing house, Theodore Roosevelt, Edith Wharton, Eugene O'Neill, and O. Henry, who wrote *The Gift of the Magi* in Pete's Tavern, a local restaurant. Today, the residents are low-key modern aristocrats, the calm of the neighborhood attracting everyone from aging movie stars to bird-boned models tired of public celebrity.

In the last few years, nearby Murray Hill has become the affordable housing choice of middle-income hipsters in search of a good deal, but wary of the great leap to Brooklyn or Queens. The neighborhood has become particularly popular with the UN crowd—they can walk to work at 46th Street easily from here, making for some interesting conversations in the bars around 5pm.

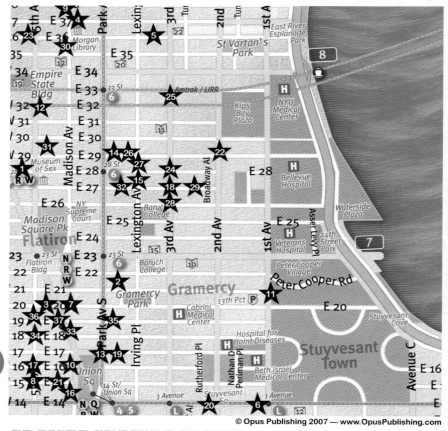

© Opus Publishing 2007 — www.OpusPublishing.com

GRAMERCY/MURRAY HILL

SIGHTS/ATTRACTIONS
1. Flower District
2. Gramercy Park
3. National Arts Club
4. Polish General Consulate
5. Sniffen Court Carriage Houses
6. Stuyvesant Town
7. Theodore Roosevelt Birthplace National Historic Site

DINING
8. 15 East
9. Asia de Cuba
10. Blue Water Grill
11. Ess-a-Bagel
12. Hangawi
13. Olives New York
14. Pinch-Pizza by the Inch
15. Pongal
16. Tavalon
17. Tocqueville
18. Turkish Kitchen
19. Zen Palate

NIGHTLIFE
20. Beauty Bar
21. Belmont
22. Failte Irish Whiskey Bar
23. Ginger Man
24. Maker's Bar
25. Patrick Kavanaugh
26. Red Sky Bar
27. Rocky Sullivan's
28. Rodeo Bar & Grill
29. Stone Creek

ARTS
30. Morgan Library
31. Museum of Sex
32. Repertorio Español (Gramercy Arts)

SHOPPING
33. ABC Carpet & Home
34. Books of Wonder
35. Cavalry St. George's Vintage Furniture
36. Revolution Books
37. Trixie + Peanut

Sights/Attractions

Empire State Building

A true New York staple, this 102-story Depression-era giant is as majestic today as it was when it was built 75 years ago. With a variety of ticket packages and attractions, it's worth a trip even for the most seasoned New Yorkers. If you're new to the city, bring a map—using it while on top is a great way to familiarize yourself with Manhattan's neighborhoods, many of which are visible from the storied observation deck. Just be careful: lines for the petite elevators can stretch across the building and out the door.

350 Fifth Avenue (at 34th). esbnyc.com. Daily 8am-2am. Adults $20-35. N R Q W **B D F V** *to Herald Square.*

Flower District

During the day, men on the sidewalks of this stretch of Sixth Avenue assemble rose bouquets against a backdrop of dreary wholesale warehouses. Around 4 am, though, the district really comes to life—daily shipments of flowers and plants are delivered, and local entrepreneurs converge to buy vegetation for their shops and businesses. Come to watch the hubbub, pick up vases, ribbon, baskets, bamboo, and peacock feathers for homemade arrangements, or just to stroll amid potted palms.

Sixth Avenue at 28th. **1** *to 28th St.*

Gramercy Park

The towering trees, honeysuckles bushes, and green benches may be lovely, but don't expect to be able to tread on the grey gravel paths of the oldest private park in America. The cast-iron gates remain closed to all but über-wealthy local residents, and sneaking in isn't an option—park employees secure the chains on the gates behind every authorized visitor. Though it was a swamp in Manhattan's feral days, today the park is the picture of tidiness; gawk through the bars at a statue of Edwin Booth (brother of John Wilkes),

Flower District

pagoda-shaped birdhouses, and unassuming young heirs and heiresses toddling behind their parents.
East 20th Street at Gramercy Park West. **6** *to 23rd St.*

The National Arts Club

Originally a forty-room Victorian Gothic mansion—and currently a national historic landmark—this ornately decorated copper-colored brownstone is home to the city's most renowned society of artists and patrons. Inside, five public galleries display frequently changing exhibits. Club membership, available by invitation only, grants access not only to the galleries, but to high-society parties and exclusive events. The atmosphere of the whole place is decidedly upper-crust, so dress up if you're going to look at the art—or to visit one of the old-money socialites who inhabit the apartments on the building's upper floors.

15 East 20th Street (at Broadway). 212.475.3424. nationalartsclub.org. M-F 10am-5pm. **6** *to 23rd St.*

Polish General Consulate

Built in 1906 as a residence for a wealthy copper financier, this Beaux-Arts mansion is now home to the Polish Consulate, complete with a red-and-white flag hanging over the door. The gorgeous architecture, featuring rusted copper-trimmed mansard roofs and old-fashioned lanterns on either side of the entrance, is a great distraction while you're waiting for your visa.

233 Madison Avenue (at 37th). 212.561.8160. polishconsulateny.org. M-T, Th-F 9am-1pm, W noon-6pm, closed Sat-Sun. **6** *to 33rd St.*

Sniffen Court Carriage Houses

It's easy to walk right by this courtyard without batting an eyelash, but that would be a shame; it is, as a plaque to the side unabashedly notes, "an unusually picturesque and charming area." The quadrangle, complete with converted horse stables, still looks like the essence of the Victorian era, complete with stones paving the ground. Low stoops, small trees, and window flower boxes set the scene, and when the sun cuts romantically across the ivy-covered left-hand façade a few hours

before dusk, you can almost hear mares behind the gate.
East 36th Street (between Third and Lexington). **6** *to 33rd St.*

Stuyvesant Town

Built in the mid-1940s to provide civil servants with affordable housing, this vast complex contains apartments that originally rented for as low as $50 per month. The affordability persisted until recent years; the development was sold for $5.4 billion in late 2006, much to the chagrin of the rent-controlled tenants who had been renting at less than half market value. Though the identical brown brick buildings are aesthetically similar to housing projects, the parks of Stuy Town are some of the most serene outdoor spaces in the city, tucked away from the din of traffic. Couples, children on skateboards, hipsters from the Village, and solitary middle-aged men alike enjoy the large lawns, tall trees, and majestic fountain.

East 14th at First. 866.302.0709. stuytown.com. **L** *to 1st Ave.*

Theodore Roosevelt Birthplace National Historic Site

Speak softly and carry a big camera while visiting the reconstructed brownstone that marks the childhood home of America's 26th president. The library, parlor, dining room, master bedroom, and nursery, accessible via guided tour, have been refurnished to their 19th century glory, and the gallery on the ground floor is enough to satisfy anyone's yen for Teddy nostalgia.

28 East 20th Street (at Broadway). 212.260.1616. nps.gov/thrb. T-Sat 9am-5pm, closed Sun-M. $3. **R W** *to 23rd St.*

Dining
UPSCALE
15 East *Japanese*

Top-quality sushi is the order of the day at this sleekly-designed, humbly-sized hotspot. With impeccably delicate presentation, respectful but attentive service, and a sashimi menu that contains more cuts of fish than you ever knew existed, 15

CURRY HILL

This cleverly-named section of Murray Hill, centered around Lexington Avenue just south of 30th Street, is a home to all things Indian. Check out grocery stores like **SPICE CORNER** (*135 Lexington Avenue at 29th*), with its huge display of sweets and spices, or **KALUSTYANS** (*123 Lexington Avenue at 28th*), where chutney pots in tin and brass hang above the cash register. Apparel stores, including **NEERA SAREE PALACE** (*121 Lexington Avenue at 28th*), sell tunics, saris, scarves, and sequined wraps, or go into one of the area's small storefronts to buy DVDs, magazines, and CDs for a Bollywood fix. For the tired and peckish, there's no shortage of sub-continental cuisine—restaurants advertising dosai, roti rolls, biriyani, and Indo-Chinese curries abound, but **CURRY IN A HURRY** (*119 Lexington Avenue at 28th*) remains the most popular spot, attracting the most diverse group of diners.

Lexington Avenue between 26th and 30th. **6** *to 28th St.*

East is the pinnacle of Japanese haute cuisine. Dynamite roll-lovers beware: you won't find any of the typically Americanized fare on this authentic menu. Instead, get ready for simple, fresh fish, ranging from *namadako* (billed as *live octopus*, even though it's not) to *uni* (sea urchin), whose natural flavor is unblemished by additional flavors or ingredients. A limited number of prepared dishes are also available, ranging from duck breast to squid-ink risotto so rich it could be on the dessert menu. Order a pleasant but generally lackluster cocktail if you must, or stick with sake pairings if you know what you're looking for. Finish the evening with the sweet almond tofu, an unexpected treat that's easily the most delectable item on the menu.

15 East 15th Street (at Fifth). 212.647.0015. M-Sat 5:30pm-10:30pm, closed Sunday. Appetizers $8-22, Entrées $24-45, Sushi à la carte $4-7 per piece. **4 5 6 N R W L** *to Union Square.*

Asia de Cuba *Asian Fusion*

This beautifully decorated space, designed by Phillippe Stark and located in the Morgans Hotel, is home to one of New York's most widely discussed restaurants. This notoriety is due mostly to the fantastic atmosphere—a mix of young beauties, social climbers, and old tycoons dining side by side. A balcony with a sleek lounge overlooks the bustling restaurant floor, and while the scene can be intoxicating, but most of the dishes, including Latin-inspired spring rolls, don't stray far from average. Adventurous appetizers, like calamari salad flavored with bananas, are your best bet. In general, go for the vibe, not the cuisine—if you're looking for a great meal, steer clear, but if you're looking to see and be scene, you won't be sorry you came.

237 Madison Avenue (at 37th). 212.726.7755. M-W noon-11pm, Th-F noon-midnight, Sat 5:30pm-midnight, Sun 5:30pm-11pm. Appetizers $18-28, Entrées $23-69. **6** *to 33rd St.*

Blue Water Grill *Seafood*

With unusual extras like live jazz, an oyster bar, and high ceilings—leftover from the space's past life as a bank—this delightful seafood proprietor is perpetually full of all things beautiful and hip. The nouveau cuisine relies on fresh seafood of the finest quality, with an oyster list that can't be matched and imaginative offerings like nori-crusted bigeye tuna garnished with bok choy salad and açai vinaigrette. Be sure to sample innovative sushi like the coconut shrimp roll or the tempura

BBQ eel; for those on a budget, the $24 prix-fixe lunch is a must. Check out the jazz downstairs, or reserve a sidewalk table for a satisfying session of people watching.

31 Union Square West (at 16th). 212.675.9500. Lunch M-Sat 11:30am-4pm; Dinner daily 5pm-midnight, . Appetizers $8-14, Entrées $24-37. **4 5 6** N Q R W L *to Union Square.*

Hangawi *Korean/Vegetarian*

Expect to remove your shoes before you enter this so-called "vegetarian shrine in another space and time," but don't worry, the food is better than the shtick. Shimmy into a seat on the floor, then order a glass of brisk ginseng juice to keep you awake. The best bet for dinner is the prix fixe menu—at $37.95, it's one of the cheapest in town for the quality. If you're up for some minor assembly work, go for the *emperor's rolls*, an appetizer of six julienned vegetables served with crêpe-like wrappers, each small enough to fit in your palm of your hand. No matter what you order, however, expect your food to be presented impeccably by some of the most attentive and genuinely enthusiastic servers in Manhattan.

12 East 32nd Street (at Fifth). 212.213.0077. Lunch M-F noon-3pm, Sat-Sun noon-5pm; Dinner M-Th 5pm-10:30pm, Sun 5pm-10pm. Appetizers $5-$16, Entrées $16-$25. **6** *to 33rd St.*

Olives NY *Mediterranean*

This desperately trendy hotspot in the lobby of Union Square's W hotel is a place to be seen, with prices to match. An attractive clientele enjoys expertly-presented modern American cuisine infused with Mediterranean undertones; celebrity chef Todd English's culinary genius is especially apparent in his preparation of non-traditional meats, like lamb porterhouse with pistachio vinaigrette or brick oven-roasted swordfish with garlic chips and mint butter. Amid cream-colored walls and arched windows, mingle among New York's elite—you may leave with a lighter wallet, but for both food and atmosphere, it's worth the hype.

201 Park Avenue South (at 17th). 212.353.8345. Brunch Sun 11am-2pm; Lunch daily noon-2:30pm; Dinner daily 6pm-10:30pm. Appetizers $13-16, Entrées $24-32. **4 5 6** N Q R W L *to Union Square.*

Tocqueville *French New American*

The design of Marco Moreira's award-winning restaurant—a champagne interior juxtaposed against dark chairs and classic white linen—creates the perfect setting for this archetypal culinary experience. The innovative French dishes, however, are anything but simple: Presentation approaches the baroque, and the extraordinary care given to each dish assures a memorable experience. Signature plates like the spiced honey-glazed Peking duck and the 60-second seared dry aged sirloin are consistently impressive. As expected, a fleet of waiters ensures that the service is attentive rather than intrusive—although, as expected, it doesn't come cheap.

1 East 15th Street (at Fifth). 212.647.1515. Brunch Sun 11am-2pm; Lunch daily 11:45am-2:00pm; Dinner daily 5:30pm-10:30pm. Appetizers $14-22, Entrées $29-40. **4 5 6** N Q R W L *to Union Square.*

MID-RANGE

Incredi Fusion *Pan-Asian/Fusion*

This brand-new restaurant, specializing in pan-Asian cuisine, is already popular with students from local universities, which isn't surprising; its warm wooden décor, 1920s soundtrack, and huge front windows make it a cozy people-watching or casual-date location. The menu is impressive in its own right, with four pages stuffed full of Thai, Malaysian, Vietnamese, and Japanese specialties, but where it really shines is in its attention to detail. The quality of ingredients is echoed in the fresh and clean taste of every dish. Saigon Rolls feature sweet and juicy mango, while the meat in the Massaman Curry is cooked and spiced to perfection. Adventurous eaters can try one of the specialty rolls made fresh at the sushi bar, while those looking for comfort food can hunker down with one of the many stews or curries, all served in large portions at very reasonable prices.

363 Third Avenue (at 26th). 212.532.2848. Sun-W 11:30am-11pm, Th-Sat 11:30am-11:30pm. Appetizers $4-9, Entrees $8-20. **6** *to 28th St.*

Pongal *Kosher, Indian*

The best Indian restaurant on a block with some of the best Indian restaurants in New York, Pongal's authentic South Indian vegetarian dishes make it the perfect choice for a Southeast Asian or kosher-friendly meal. A bargain by city standards, the fact that the majority of entrées hover around nine dollars undoubtedly fuels the restaurant's ever-increasing popularity; be sure to order samosas and *dosai* to increase the chances you'll be taken for a local. Be warned: everyone else wants in on the great deal too, so long lines and less-than-expedient service are the norm. If getting to Murray Hill is too much of a trek, check out its sister location on the Upper East Side.

110 Lexington Avenue (at 27th). 212.696.9458. Lunch M-F noon-3pm; Dinner M-F 5pm-10:30pm, Sat-Sun noon-10:30pm. Appetizers $2-9, Entrées $9-12. **6** *to 28th St.*

Tiffin Wallah *Southern Indian*

In India, a *tiffin wallah* is the person who delivers the *tiffin*, or mid-day meal, to people at work. The delivery signals a much anticipated opportunity to enjoy a home cooked meal with colleagues. This casual Curry Hill eatery captures the experience to a tee with décor of banana-leaf green, metallic "tiffin carriers," and cozily compact tables. The community feel is enhanced by the fact that a good portion of customers are native Indians that seem to have befriended the personable owner. Specializing in rare South Indian fare, the menu is all vegetarian and also includes delicious North Indian favorites. Must haves include the *masala dosa*, a curry-filled crepe larger than your upper body, and *idli*, rice cakes. If you're of the meat-eating persuasion and are convinced that those who don't eat meat have never known flavor, this place is bound to make you reconsider. If you're an herbivore, well, you've struck gold. Even better—cheap gold.

127 East 28th Street (at Lexington). 212.685.7301. Lunch daily 11:30am-3pm; Dinner daily 5pm-10pm. Appetizers $2-8, Entrées $8-14. **6** *to 28th St.*

CASUAL

Ess-A-Bagel *Bagels*

Bargain prices and filling fare lure a diverse slice of the city, from hipsters to doctors, to this humble shop. Earn the respect and admiration of your coworkers by picking up a baker's dozen ($9) on your way to work—go for the pumpernickels, chock-full of raisins, and some always-fresh cream cheese. The fare is hearty and the lines are always long; if you're on a diet or tight on time, don't even bother stopping by.

359 First Avenue (at 21st). 212.260.2252. Bagels $1-3, Sandwiches $5-7. **6** *to 23rd St.*

Pinch—Pizza By the Inch *Pizza*

Size matters at this unique pizza joint, where, as the name implies, pizza is ordered by the inch—anywhere from four to a whopping 36. While conforming to a standard size may be cliché, the 24-inch provides a deliciously happy medium between discipline and gluttony, and is filling enough for two. (Inches refer to the length of a relatively thin strip, not diameters.) While the ordering process can get a little arduous, the staff is friendly and always willing to guide first timers; finish your meal with a refreshing gelato after savoring just the right amount of New York's unofficial favorite food.

416 Park Avenue South (at 29th). 212.686.5222. Pizza $.50/inch. Daily 11-11. **6** *to 28th St.*

Tavalon *Tea Bar*

Walls lined with test tubes invite customers to view and smell dozens of quality blends at this casual tea house, facilitating (or sometimes complicating) the difficult decision of what to buy. Grab a small cookie or pastry with your darjeeling before fighting to find a place to sit—space is limited, although a built-in stage and a live DJ help make the wait more enjoyable.

22 East 14th Street (at Union Square West). 212.807.7027. M-Sat 8am-10:30pm, Sun 10am-9:30pm. Tea and specialty drinks $2.50-5.75. **4 5 6 N Q R W L** *to Union Square.*

Zen Palate *Pan-Asian, Vegetarian*

This three-story Union Square vegetarian restaurant serves up tasty Asian and Asian-inspired dishes at student-friendly prices. Especially health-conscious patrons rave about the eggplant in garlic and the green iced tea, although many choose to stick to

BARNARD

THE LIBERAL ARTS COLLEGE
FOR WOMEN
IN NEW YORK CITY

WELCOME
CLASS OF 2011!

FOR ALL YOUR STUDENT NEEDS, PLEASE CONTACT
THE FOLLOWING OFFICES:

DEAN OF THE COLLEGE	(212) 854-3075
DEAN OF STUDIES	(212) 854-2024
CAREER DEVELOPMENT	(212) 854-2033
COLLEGE ACTIVITIES	(212) 854-2096
FINANCIAL AID	(212) 854-2154
HEALTH SERVICE	(212) 854-2091
FURMAN COUNSELING CENTER	(212) 854-2092
MULTICULTURAL AFFAIRS	(212) 854-9130
REGISTRAR	(212) 854-2011
RESIDENTIAL LIFE	(212) 854-5561

FAST FACTS

- Scenic Stroll: Irving Place, South of Gramercy Park

- Major Subway Stations: Union Square (4 5 6, N R Q W, L), 23rd St (6, R W), 28th St (6, R W), 33rd St (6)

- Kooky Corner: Museum of Sex

- Neighborhood Landmarks: Gramercy Park

- Neighborhood Foods: Indian Food on Curry Hill

- Famous Historical Moment: On October 27th, 1858, Theodore Roosevelt was born at 28 East 20th Street.

- Celebrity Hangouts: Gramercy Tavern

- Notable Residents: James Harper, Eugene O'Neill, Theodore Roosevelt, Edith Wharton

- Kid-Friendly Place: Books of Wonder, Cupcake Café

Asian staples like steamed vegetable dumplings, edamame, and wonton soup. Students looking for trendy and affordable food sit at café-style tables on the first floor, while adventurous families and first dates fill out the clientele in the feng shui-ed upstairs, ordering 3-course meals for $30. You might not enjoy the wait to get in, but the food and low prices are worth it.

34 Union Square East (at 16th). 212.614.9345. M-Th 5:30pm-10:30pm, F-Sun noon-10pm. Appetizers $2.75-7.50, Entrées $8-18. **4 5 6 N Q R W L** *to Union Square.*

Nightlife

Beauty Bar *Bar*

The owner's collection of '40s hairpins and pomade advertisements add to the deliciously kitschy mood at this beauty salon-turned-bar, where you can order a drink cutely named after a salon service. Come on Wednesday afternoons for a drink special and a manicure.

231 East 14th Street (at Second). 212.539.1389. M-F 5pm-4am, Sat-Sun 7pm-4am. **4 5 6 N Q R W L** *to Union Square.*

Believe Lounge *Lounge*

This inviting lounge, with warm red lights and velveteen chairs, is the brainchild of Chynna Soul, the music video director and artist who bought the space and renovated it herself. She's also responsible for the imaginative "magic potion cocktails"—try "Your Majesty," a cocktail made of wild berry vodka, champagne, and white cranberry juice. The lounge radiates positive energy, and the clever touches, like mini-flashlights that allow you to read the drink menu without using a candle or cell phone, make this place a must-visit.

1 East 36th Street. (at Fifth). 212.481.4955. M-Sat 5pm-2am, closed Sunday. Drinks $12. **N R Q W B D F V** *to Herald Square.*

Failte Irish Whiskey Bar *Bar*

Two floors of classic rock and thirsty people keep the intensity on high at this sports bar. Couches upstairs provide a respite from the energy of the lower level, where an active pool table and televisions contribute to the noise. With the radio blasting Guns N' Roses and Tom Petty, the bartenders serve up drafts of Guinness and Boddingtons, while wrought iron and a hearth add to the Gaelic atmosphere. Be warned—the bartender actually does have an Irish accent, and the regulars might take offense if someone toasts to the Queen.

531 Second Avenue (at 29th). 212.725.9440. Daily noon-4am. Drinks $4-7. **6** *to 28th St.*

Ginger Man *Bar*

Enjoy the sophistication of Fifth Avenue at this lounge and bar space, plus a large variety of beers from all around the world at surprisingly reasonable prices. Food runs the gamut—the Sloppy Joes and artisanal cheese plate are both delicious, especially when paired with the fantastically named Rogue Dead Guy beer. The lounge, done with modern, space age décor, has long ceilings and a lounge in the back for privacy. The atmosphere will appeal to both recent grads and folks in their 50s, and though the crowd consists mostly of groups, anyone can chug a beer and catch the game on their plasma tv.

11 East 36th Street (at Fifth). 212.532.3740. Drinks $6-8. M-W 11:30am-2am, Th- F 11:30am to 4am, Sat 12:30pm-4am, Sun 3pm-midnight. **6** *to 33rd St.*

Red Sky Bar *Bar*

With three very distinctive floors, this bar can accommodate a host of patrons from the sports bar enthusiasts on the first level to loungers and hipsters on the second upper level and roof. This flexibility has made Red Sky a popular spot for MTV shoots and celebrity parties, but the reasonably-priced drinks make it a destination for anyone.

47 East 29th Street (at Park). 212.447.1820. M-Sat noon-4am, closed Sunday. Drinks $4-7. **6** *to 28th St.*

Rocky Sullivan's *Music*

If you don't like the live music played by the Irish band Schanechia (Gaelic for storytelling), which plays here often, don't complain about it too loudly—the lead singer is the bar's owner. The Guinness crowd, with a hard-core constituency of Irish males who cluster in the simple, brick-walled beer hall downstairs, don't take kindly to naysayers, either.

129 Lexington Avenue (at 28th). 212.725.3871. M-Th 4pm-4am, F-Sat noon-4am, Sun 3pm-4am. **6** *to 28th St.*

Stone Creek *Bar*

If you've ever wondered where the frat boys go after graduation, look no further. While this East Side hotspot may look like a laid-back lounge, the chic décor is only a façade to make the clientele of 30-something lawyers and i-bankers feel comfortable—they're really here to let loose to cheesy '80s hits in their preppy button-downs. While the martini menu is top-notch, with yummy, fruity concoctions, the laid-back, party-seeking crowd prefers to knock back Bud Lights and rounds of Jaeger shots at the copper bar. If you're hungry, the kitchen stays open late into the night *140 East 27th Street (at Third). 212.532.1037. Sun noon-2am, M-W 4pm-2am, Th-Sat 4pm-4am. Drinks $7-9.* **6** *to 28th St.*

Arts

The Morgan Library and Museum

J. Pierpont Morgan, an intimidating railroad entrepreneur with more money than God and a grotesquely malformed nose, put much of his wealth into his art collection. After his death, those items stored in his three-room library on Madison Avenue became the founding donation to The Morgan Library and Museum, a publicly accessible institution since 1924. The Library itself is a McKim, Mead and White masterpiece; the collection includes Rembrandt portraits, original Beethoven manuscripts, and many of Dickens' early drafts. Go for the traveling

UNION SQUARE

Crowds rivaling those in Times Square make Union Square one of the best places in the city to people-watch—especially because the masses here aren't made up primarily of tourists. Commuters, demonstrators, hipsters, skateboarders, performers, NYU students, vendors, shoppers, couples in love, and solitary brooders all converge on this oasis on the edge of Gramercy, giving it an energy that epitomizes downtown New York.

In the wide treeless arena at the southern end of the park, scores of peddlers sell art, homemade T-shirts, jewelry, bumper stickers, and conspiracy theories: "The Bush regime engineered 9-11," reads a typical banner. Perhaps inspired by the statues of George Washington, Abraham Lincoln, and Mahatma Gandhi that grace the park's grounds, dissidents often choose Union Square for protests both large and small; stop by to watch and discover what issues are on New York's mind. All year round, foodies flock to the largest **GREENMARKET** in New York City (*17th Street at Broadway*) before checking out the sales at **WHOLE FOODS** (*40 East 14th Street at Union Square West*) and **TRADER JOE'S** (*142 East 14th Street at Irving Pl.*). It's during summer, though, that this paragon of urban planning truly blossoms; countless sunbathers and picnickers dot the lawns as businessmen nurse beers after work on the patio of **LUNA PARK** (*50 East 17th Street at Broadway*), the restaurant inside the square. In July and August, **SUMMER IN THE SQUARE** (*212-460-1208*), sponsored by the non-profit Union Square Partnership, hosts free yoga classes, children's concerts, dance performances, and musical acts every week. But in true New York form, the fun doesn't die out when the weather turns cold: each December, the **HOLIDAY MARKET** (*South End at West 14th*) sets up its red-and-white booths, offering ornaments, baked goods, hand-crafted jewelry, and other holiday gift items for those who want to feel the cheer of the season.

exhibitions, lectures, dramatic readings, forums, or musical performances, or just to bask in the opulence that once was one man's life.

225 Madison Avenue (at 36th). 212.685.0008. themorgan.org. T-Th 10:30am-5pm, F 10:30am-9pm, Sat 10am-6pm, Sun 11am-6pm, closed Monday. Adults $12, Students $8, Free Fridays 7-9. **6** *to 33rd St.*

Museum of Sex

A sign above the black leather divans in the lobby instructs visitors: "Please do not touch, lick, stroke, or mount the exhibits." The rest of the museum is less tongue-in-cheek and more tongue-on-nipple. If the gigantic phallus made of roses that looms

behind the ticket-takers makes you uncomfortable, it would behoove you to turn back now. With temporary exhibits on subjects like kink and sex in movies, the museum strives to make sex intellectually stimulating, but succeeds mostly at titillating the young couples who stroll through the exhibits grinning goofily. The permanent collection includes innovative homemade sex machines, explanations of "basic BDSM terminology," footage from early double-penetration porn movies, and old sex-ed teaching materials.

233 Fifth Avenue (at 27th). 212.689.6337. museumofsex. com. Sun-F 11am-6:30pm, Sat 11am-8pm. Adults (18 and older) $14.50, Students $13.50. **R W** *to 28th St.*

Repertorio Español (Gramercy Arts Theater)

The oldest off-Broadway theater in New York currently houses one of the few true repertories in the country, with a company of actors performing a constantly rotating selection of twenty plays. Spanish classics make up about half the works, in addition to contemporary plays by Hispanics born and raised in the U.S. If you don't speak Spanish, borrow a headset and listen to an English translation in real-time, or skip the drama and come watch Pilar Rioja, the so-called "Queen of Spanish Dance," who has been performing here bi-annually for 33 years.

138 East 27th Street (at Lexington). 212.889.2850. repertorio.org. Tickets $20–$60. 6 to 28th St.

Shopping

Calvary St. George's Vintage Furniture

This emporium of old furniture, located in a side arm and basement of the Calvary Church, is the anti-Ikea, specializing in well-made, distinctive vintage pieces. Tables, chairs, rugs, mirrors, and chandeliers are so tightly packed within the Gothic space, it's often difficult to maneuver, but prices are fairly reasonable. They also accept tax-deductible donations, in case you need to free rather than fill up space.

227 Park Avenue South (at East 19th). 212.475.6645. M-Sat 10:30am-5:30pm, closed Sunday. 6 to 23rd St.

Revolution Books

This homey countercultural bookshop sells everything from T-shirts reading *Danger: Police in Area* to books with titles like *10 Excellent Reasons Not to Join the Military*. The store is fairly quiet, but if you're lucky, you'll overhear a member of staff ranting about how Democrats are too conservative, or giving a similar passionate tirade.

9 West 19th Street (at Fifth). 212.691.3345. revolutionbooksnyc.org. M-Sat noon-7pm, Sun noon-5pm. R W F V to 23rd St.

Trixie + Peanut

Geared to a four-legged clientele (and credit card-wielding owners), this boutique purports to "celebrate the unique relationship between pets and the people who love them"—although the garish rhinestone-plated leashes ($55), designer carrying cases (up to $899), "Chewy Vuiton" pet beds ($149) and doggie T-shirts reading "Local Celebrity" ($29) might indicate obsession more than love. If the puppy in your life has been begging for Oreo-shaped carob cookies ($10 for four), you know where to take her. Cat people will find a relatively limited selection of feline toys, treats, and accessories, but everyone will find something to gawk at.

23 East 20th Street (at Broadway). 212.358.0881. trixieandpeanut.com. T-Sat 11am-8pm, Sun noon-5pm. R W to 23rd St.

MIDTOWN WEST

Take a look at Midtown late at night and it's easy to see why Frank Sinatra sang about waking up in "a city that doesn't sleep." The fluorescent buzz of Times Square, the crowds outside Madison Square Garden, and the 24-hour delis sprinkled throughout Midtown West keep both locals and the tourists up until dawn.

During the mid-nineteenth century, the Garment District flourished as Midtown West became a center of industry. North of the factories, filled with recent immigrants and sewing machines, Longacre Square fast developed a reputation as Manhattan's "red light district."

In 1904, when *The New York Times* moved their offices uptown to Longacre Square, they convinced the city to re-name the area in their honor. To celebrate, the paper hosted an extravagant fireworks-fueled bash on New Year's Eve, kicking off a tradition that has lasted for over 100 years. Later, around World War I, Times Square became one of the premier areas in the world for theater, rivaled only by London's West End; that reputation continues to this day

While Times Square was infested by flesh peddlers and drug pushers for most of the 20th century, the area was rid of its more unsavory parts in the 1990s when Mayor Rudolph Giuliani spearheaded a massive clean-up campaign. Thus, the turning of the millennium signaled the rebirth of Times Square as a buoyant, all-ages urban boardwalk, where the most common crimes are the inflated prices of kitschy souvenirs.

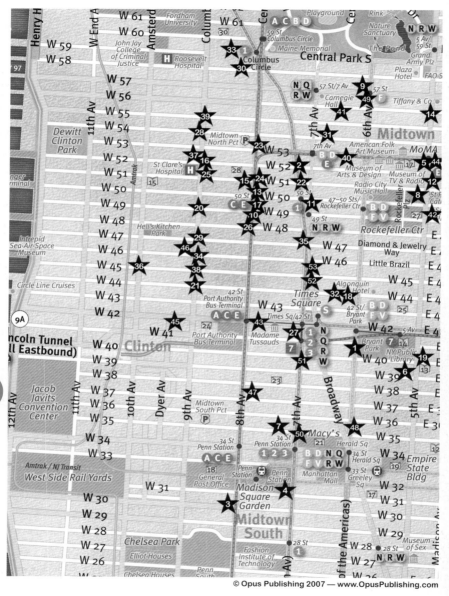

MIDTOWN WEST

SIGHTS
1 Bryant Park
2 Ed Sullivan Theatre
3 James A. Farley Post Office
4 Madison Square Garden
5 Museum of Modern Art
6 New York Public Library
7 Pennsylvania Station
8 Rockefeller Center
9 Sun Room Café
10 Worldwide Plaza

DINING
11 7Square
12 Anthos
13 Bann
14 Beacon
15 Blockheads
16 Casellula Cheese and Wine Café
17 Churrascaria Plataforma
18 DB Bistro Modern
19 Koi
20 Kyotofu
21 Marseille
22 Natsumi
23 Swizz
24 Thalia
25 Vynl
26 Zenith/Asahi

NIGHTLIFE
27 B.B. King Blues Club and Grill
28 Bar 9
29 Barrage
30 Dizzy's Club Coca Cola
31 Flute
32 Jimmy's Corner Bar
33 Lobby Lounge
34 Monday Night Magic
35 Supper Club
36 Tenth Avenue Lounge
37 Therapy
38 Zanzibar

ARTS
39 Alvin Ailey American Dance Theatre
40 American Folk Art Museum
41 Carnegie Hall
42 Christie's
43 Madame Tussauds New York
44 Museum of Television and Radio
45 Playwrights Horizons
46 St. Clements Church

SHOPPING
47 Arnold's Hatters
48 H&M
49 Joseph Patelson Music House
50 Macy's
51 Midtown Comics
52 Toys "R" Us
53 Virgin Megastore

Times Square

Sights/Attractions

Bryant Park

This grassy oasis, mere blocks from the lights and bustle of Times Square, serves as the unofficial backyard of the largest branch of the New York Public Library, and is home to New York Fashion Weeks in both the spring and fall. The free summer film festival, held each Monday at dusk, draws large crowds, and the free wireless keeps Midtown businessfolk connected on their lunch hours.

42ⁿᵈ Street at Fifth. bryantpark.org. **B D F V** *to 42ⁿᵈ St./Fifth Ave.*

James A. Farley Post Office

"Neither snow, nor rain, nor heat, nor gloom," is part of the American consciousness thanks to this building; the Herodotus quote that serves as the unofficial postal motto was first associated with the postal service when it was placed atop the long, columned façade. The McKim, Mead and White-designed Beaux-Arts giant gives you an idea of what they were going for with the original Penn Station—plus, its open 24/7 on non-holidays, for your mailing convenience.

Eighth Avenue at 30ᵗʰ Street. **1 2 3 A C E** *to Penn Station.*

Madison Square Garden

Sitting atop Penn Station, this "World's Most Famous Arena" has 20,000 seats and is home to the Knicks and Rangers. It hosts numerous, and diverse, high-profile events throughout the year, from blowout concerts to the Westminster Dog Show.

Seventh Avenue at 34ᵗʰ. 212.465.MSGI. thegarden. com. **1 2 3 A C E** *to Penn Station.*

Museum of Modern Art

A must-see for all modern art enthusiasts—and

Bryant Park

TIMES SQUARE

Like any manic-panic tourist destination, Times Square is shiny, gaudy, crowded, unpleasant—and unavoidable. The best way to see the glitz is while on your way to a Broadway show, but if you're going just for the experience, try to get there at night when the flashy signs are all lit up—a 1986 zoning ordinance, meant to preserve the cultural feel of the neighborhood, makes it illegal to develop a business in the area without them. Be prepared for crowds and plenty of pushing, shoving, and hustling. If you're just passing through and can't bear to go above ground, be sure to check out the famed subway performance area in front of the transfer to the Grand Central Shuttle. The MTA gives the space over to multi-talented musicians and performers who provide a great underground distraction—although, after a much-YouTubed incident in which a toddler wandered onto the performance space only to be inadvertently kicked by a breakdancer, you might want to keep tight hold of your kids while you watch.

just about everyone else, too—the recently-renovated MoMA has a sleekly beautiful new home just off Fifth Avenue. Six floors are filled with artists including Dali and Picasso, as well as enough innovative interior design, captivating photography, and thrilling inventions to keep you occupied all day long. Other attractions include the Rockefeller Sculpture Garden, an upscale restaurant, two cafés, daily film screenings that are free for museum members and college students, and two excellent design stores. Give yourself a few hours to peruse the artwork—even inevitable thoughts of, "My six year old could have drawn that," can't take away from the truly spectacular pieces that are part of the permanent collection.
11 West 53rd Street (at Fifth). 212.708.9400. moma. org. Sat-Th 10:30am-5:30pm, F 10:30am-8pm, Closed Tuesday. $20 Adults, $16 Students, Free Fridays 4-8. E V to 5th Ave/53rd St.

New York Public Library
The building may be one of the city's most recognizeable, but it's the knowledge inside that's the real draw. Along with the largest collection of books in the NYPL system, this library has a spacious and elegant main study room, a picturesque garden, and a staff who can help you find the answer to almost any question. If you can't make it down but are in search of a specific piece of information—the languages spoken in Uganda, for instance—call the telephone reference line *(212-340-0849)*. You'll be connected with a specially-trained staff of librarians at this branch whose sole job is to answer simple research questions over the phone.
455 Fifth Avenue (at 40th). 212.930.0800. nypl. org. T-W 11am-7:30pm, Th-Sat 10am-6pm, closed Sun-M. B D F V to Bryant Park.

Pennsylvania Station
These days, it's a crowded, underground tunnel of magazine kiosks, pizza stands, and low-end shopping; originally, it was a splendid Beaux-Arts masterpiece modeled on the Roman baths of Caracella, designed in 1910 by McKim, Mead, and White to upstage Grand Central. The 1964 demolition, ordered to pave the way for Madison Square Garden, was a wake-up call to New Yorkers to preserve their urban fabric.

KOREATOWN

Fill up on kimchee and Korean barbecue before showing off your karaoke skills in this cultural enclave just blocks from Times Square. K-Town, as it is affectionately known, may not be as large as Chinatown or Little Italy, but it's just as lively and fun—perfect for a day trip or an after-hours hangout. It's not a residential area, as most local business owners commute to the area from the Korean neighborhoods in Flushing, Queens. Instead, shopping and dining spots take centerstage, spilling over onto the upper levels of buildings. Korean art galleries and bookstores lie tucked between karaoke bars and 24-hour barbecue joints; when you get hungry, stop by **KOM TANG KOLBI HOUSE** (*32 West 32nd Street at Broadway*), one of the oldest and most delicious places of its kind, open 24-hours Monday-Saturday.

Fifth and Sixth Avenues between 31st and 36th. **B D F V** N R Q W *to Herald Square.*

34th Street at Seventh. **1 2 3 4 5 6 J M Z A C E** *to Penn Station.*

Rockefeller Center

With Radio City Music Hall, NBC studios, restaurants and shops, iconic art deco architecture, an observation deck for scenic views, plus world-famous sculptures, a skating rink, and the country's most famous Christmas tree, Rockefeller Center is a bona fide New York icon. Don't leave the city without stopping by at least once.

Fifth Avenue at 50th. **B D F V** *to 47th-50th Sts..*

Penn Station

The Sun Room Café

Part café, part reading room, and part art gallery, the most remarkable thing about this cozy space is that it operates by sheer goodwill—in other words, for free. Run by a Baptist Church group, this quiet oasis was created to provide an atmosphere of peace and community in a busy, disconnected, and often lonely city. Refreshingly, there's no religious sell; you're welcome to read the paper and eat some muffins no matter what your denomination (or lack thereof).

123 West 57th Street (at Sixth). 212.975.0170. T-Th, 11am-4pm, closed F-M. N R Q W F *to 57th St.*

Worldwide Plaza

The center courtyard of this mammoth complex, which takes up an entire city block, holds restaurants, a gym, and a quiet place to relax from the midtown bustle. Go to eat outside in the summer months and bask in the light of the Sidney Simon-designed fountain that depicts the four seasons.

309 West 49th Street (at Eighth). 212.765.0846. **1** *to 50th St.*

Dining
UPPER TIER

Anthos *Contemporary Greek*

The tasting menu at Anthos, which offers a culinary tour of the Greek islands guided by acclaimed chef Micheal Psilakis, might just be the best modern Greek meal in the city. Flavor combinations that sound unique—or just bizarre, depending on how you look at it—explode onto the tongue in unexpected ways; grapefruit and sea urchin, usually absent in Mediterranean cuisine, are somehow successful accents to dishes like sea bass and Tasmanian crab. The food is anything but traditional, but if you've got an adventurous side and a malleable idea of ethnic food, come for a truly modern treat.

36 West 52ⁿᵈ Street (at Fifth). 212.582.6900. Lunch M-F noon-2:45pm; Dinner M-Th 5pm-10:30pm, F-Sat 5pm-11pm. Appetizers $14-20, Entrées $28-46. **1** *to 50ᵗʰ St.*

Bann *Korean*

Don't let the hard-to-find entrance of this pre-theater dinner spot stop you from experiencing its deliciously "progressive" Korean cuisine. Adding unique seasonings and sauces to otherwise traditional Korean entrées, the restaurant offers a variety of dishes— from mouth-watering dumplings and soups to juicy barbecued short ribs—with unconventional flavors that will surprise even native Koreans. The impressive interior décor is lowly lit and chic, with a sleek, modern bar, intricate silk screens, and classy marble tables, each with its own innovative, smokeless grill for your cook-it-how-you-like-it dishes. The plethora of fruity cocktails and inventive desserts should not be missed.

350 West 50ᵗʰ Street (at Eighth). 212.582.4446. Lunch M-F 11:30am-2:30pm; Dinner M-F 5:30pm-10pm, Sat-Sun 5:50pm-10:30pm. Appetizers $8-15, Entrées $8-28, Barbecues $22-30. **C E** *to 50ᵗʰ St.*

Anthos

Beacon *New American*

They say it's pre-theater, but this classy Fifth Avenue restaurant is packed with business suits and Blackberrys instead of tourists—although the quiet intimacy of the setting makes it a great date spot, too. The open-fire cooking may seem like a gimmick at first, but it's validated by the delightfully smoky flavor of the roasted oysters. Try the soft shell crab with cornbread—crunchy, sweet, and original—or the flavorful garlic fries. End the meal with a heavy soufflé or homemade ice cream, better than anything you'll find in the grocer's freezer.

25 West 56th Street (at Fifth). 212.332.0500. Lunch M-F noon-2pm; Dinner M-Th 5:30pm-10pm, F-Sat 5:30pm-10:30pm, Sun 4pm-9pm. Appetizers $9-18, Entrées $18-41. **1** *to 59th St.*

Churrascaria Plataforma *Brazillian, Steakhouse*

With 15 different meats and an astonishing salad bar, don't attempt Churrascaria Plataforma on a full stomach—this all-you-can-eat steakhouse was built for gluttons. Upon being seated, each diner gets a two-sided disk; place the green side up if you want the food to keep coming, flip it to red when you've had your fill. Come with a big group of friends for an eating contest, or go it alone and gorge yourself on strips of meat, cut from the spit at each table.

316 West 49th Street (at Eighth). 212.245.0505. Daily noon-midnight. Prix Fixe dinner $52. **1** *to 50th St.*

DB Bistro Moderne

DB Bistro Moderne *French, Bistro*

This Daniel Boulud masterpiece, an attempt to blend the hustle and bustle of midtown with chic downtown dining, divides its unique menu into small families of food, each united by a single ingredient that changes regularly. It's not a bistro in the strict sense of the word—the dining room is too upscale for a quaint atmosphere, and the light, subtle dishes and simple ingredients seem completely estranged from typically hearty bistro fare—but while succumbing to the foie gras truffle burger or crispy duck confit, you won't care what they want to call it.

55 West 44th Street (at Sixth). 212.391.2400. Breakfast M-F 7am-10am, Sat-Sun 8am-11am; Lunch M-Sat noon-2:30pm; Dinner Sun-M 5pm-10pm, T-Sat 5pm-11:30pm. Appetizers $13-24, Entrées $28-36. **1 2 3** N R Q W **7** *to Times Square.*

Koi *Pan-Asian*

Bryant Park's hippest restaurant, located in a large open space beautifully designed with lattice sculptures, bamboo, and votive candles, is the quintessential New Age Asian experience. The menu blends one-of-a kind sushi creations with succulent meats in complex marinades. Be sure to order the restaurant's unique variation on the spicy tuna roll, in which white rice is mixed with butter, sautéed, and topped with fresh spicy tuna and jalapeños. The resulting sensation is near-paralyzing—the bite transitions from warm, sweet, sticky rice to cold, soft, zesty tuna in an instant—but the base thumping from the adjoining Cellar Bar will call you back to your senses. Stay after the exquisite meal to dance and drink in the chicly cavernous rooms of this trendy, upscale hotspot.

40 West 40th Street (at Fifth). 212.921.3330. Breakfast Daily 7am-11am; Lunch M-F noon-2:30pm; Dinner M-W 5:30pm-11pm, Th-Sat 5:30pm-midnight, Sun 6pm-10pm. **1 2 3** N R Q W **7** *to Times Square.*

LITTLE BRAZIL

For one small block of Midtown West, yellow and blue pushcarts with Brazilian flags and food line the sidewalk as the mellifluous sounds of Portuguese drifts through the crowd. Called "Rua 46" by the immigrants who set up shop here, this block and its surrounding area are home to Brazilian pharmacies and barber shops, the Brazilian Consulate, and the Banco do Brasil. The largest Brazilian business district outside of Astoria, this is the best place in the city to dine on native fare, although you can also find Japanese, Argentinean, Italian, and Mexican restaurants here. Try a sour capirinha, Brazil's signature drink, and fill up on good churrasco at **IPANEMA** (*13 West 46th Street at Fifth*), named after the famous neighborhood and beach in Rio de Janeiro.

West 46th Street between Fifth and Sixth. **B D F V** *to 47th-50th Sts.*

MID-RANGE

Casellula *New American*

Sophisticated but refreshingly unpretentious, this cheese and wine café seems perfectly designed for the drink and hors d'ouvre-seeking after-work crowd. It's easy to fill up on the tiny but rich culinary offerings; Casellula offers some of the most interesting cheese dishes in the city, with a menu that changes daily, ensuring freshness and variation. Although the focus is on the cheeses, the café's fromager brilliantly pairs each one with a unique side, such as crisp rice crackers or sweet pickles, that transforms the small plates from appetizers into mini-meals. Finish up with one of the restaurant's dairy-themed desserts; as the server pours thick, Meadow Brook Farm cream on a luscious chocolate cake right before your eyes, it looks and tastes so fresh you'll wonder where they're hiding the cow.

401 West 52nd Street (at Ninth). 212.247.8137. T-Sun 5pm-2am, closed Monday. Cheese and snacks $3-$15, Wine by the glass $7-$34. **1 C E** *to 50th St.*

Kyotofu *Modern Japanese*

Self-promoted as "mod-organic," this innovative hot spot—part bakery, part bar, part res-

Casellula

HELL'S KITCHEN

Once upon a time, Hell's Kitchen was one of the roughest neighborhoods in New York City, home to the mafia, gangs, and violent crime. As a result, you won't find any skyscrapers among the low-rise, five story apartment buildings that seem to be everywhere in the neighborhood; the area's gritty reputation, which dominated public perception over much of the last century, led to depressed rents and a lack of development. Only in the last two decades has gentrification started to take hold, as businesses move in and rents climb back up to market rate. Today, the trendy neighborhood is as safe as the rest of Midtown West, complete with delicious ethnic restaurants, Mom and Pop businesses, the **NINTH AVENUE INTERNATIONAL FOOD FESTIVAL** (*weekend after Mother's Day*), and more than one television studio.

Bordered by Eighth Avenue and the Hudson River from 34th to 59th. **A C E** *to Port Authority.*

taurant—defies easy definition. By day, it's an eat-in bakery serving appetizers, light lunch, and afternoon tea; by night, it's a dessert bar in the truest sense of the term, with drinks and desserts demanding equal focus. Don't expect to find sushi, or any sort of entrée, for that matter—the offerings are strictly small-scale modern, served in a warmly-lit space with a sleek design mirroring the culinary philosophy. Expand your palate with homemade tofu, sure to satisfy the health-conscious and indulgent alike, or the can't-miss warm raspberry mochi chocolate cake. The signature cocktails

Original Tofu at Kyotofu

verge on perfection, but don't overlook the impressive selection of specialty sakes and Japanese liquors. If you're feeling indulgent, the $15 dessert kaiseki prix fixe (with optional $12 sake pairing) is an especially good deal.

705 Ninth Avenue (at 49th). 212.974.6012. Lunch T-Sun noon-5:30pm; Bar T-W, Sun 6pm-1:30am, Th-Sat 6pm-12:30am, closed Monday. Appetizers $6-14, Dessert $7-10. **1 C E** *to 50th St.*

Marseille *French, Mediterranean*

It may be located just off Times Square, but with wide windows and well-spaced seating, Marseille provides a welcome respite from the busy crush of Midtown Manhattan. Arrive before seven to get a place at one of the comfortable red velvet booths, and enjoy your meal in art deco style. All the appointments—from the marble floor pattern to the bronzed light fixtures—highlight a Franco-Gotham fusion whose spirit is in the food as well, full of interesting twists on classic dishes. Start with a yellow heirloom tomato gazpacho and 2003 Bordeaux, then finish up with homemade square doughnuts drizzled with rich chocolate or refreshing raspberry sauces. With elegant service and a refined atmosphere, it's a nice spot for a casually classy affair.

630 Ninth Avenue (at 44th). 212.333.2323. Lunch M-F 11:30am-3pm, Sat-Sun 11am-3pm; Dinner T-Sat 5pm-midnight, Sun-M 5pm-11pm. Appetizers $8-15, Entrées $20-25. **1 2 3** N R Q W **7** *to Times Square.*

Natsumi *Japanese*

In this tight-but-comfortable dining room, expect to be surrounded by Japanese businessmen and pre-theatre couples—a mix of regulars who can't get enough and first-timers who wander in off the street. The extensive menu features both traditional and modern entrées, and although the cuisine is neither contemporary nor trendy, every dish features an unconventional twist, usually involving a fusion of traditional Japanese and Italian styles. To wash down your meal, try a few of the tangy, sake-infused house cocktails, or end with the cheesecake tempura, a crispy, creamy bite of pure bliss.

226 West 50th Street (at Broadway). 212.258.2988. M-F 11:30am-11pm, Sat-Sun 4:30pm-11pm. Appetizers $5-$15, Entrées $16-$58. **1** *to 50th St.*

Thalia *New American*

In a neighborhood full of pre-theatre dining options, Thalia distinguishes itself by attracting loyal patrons from all over Manhattan; after a meal in the lofty dining room or hors d'œuvres in the old-world lounge, you'll understand why. If you're lucky enough to be there in the right season, order the Escolar, a deep-sea white fish served on a bed of coconut-infused plantains. The indecisive diner may have trouble choosing between all the enticing options, but if you're lucky, Avi Camchi will be around to tell you his current favorites—the charismatic co-owner knows how to work a room, and will be happy to give you advice.

828 Eighth Avenue (at 50th). 212.399.4444. Lunch M-F noon-2:30pm, Dinner W-M 5:30pm-11:30pm, closed Tuesday. Appetizers $8-15, Entrées $17-29. **1** *to 50th St.*

Swizz *Swiss*

With warm lighting, red brick, and photography dispersed throughout, Swizz exudes a refreshingly unpretentious vibe. Designed for small gatherings and intimate dates alike, try to get a seat in the subterranean wine cave—by far the best in the house. Fabulous fondue and authentic Raclette cheese provide a so-called "unique Swiss alpine experience" that is simultaneously social and relaxed; make sure to embellish your fondue with several sides, ranging from sun dried tomatoes to tiger prawns. If sharing just isn't your thing, the veal in mushroom white wine sauce is a house favorite, especially when paired with one of the wine list's many $30 bottles. Expect to be full at the end of the meal—Swiss food is heavy by definition—but remember that with pumpkin cognac cheesecake and Toblerone fondue on the ready, saving room for dessert isn't an option; it's a requirement.

310 West 53rd Street (at Eighth). 212.810.4444. Daily 5:00pm-midnight. Appetizers $7-13, Entrées $14-32. **1** *to 59th St.*

Zenith/Asahi
Vegetarian/Japanese

The unique setup of this restaurant duo is perfect for couples who can never agree on a place to eat. Zenith, a vegan delight, and Asahi, a traditional Japanese restaurant, share a common dining area; the menu is divided into two sections, as is the kitchen. True vegetarians will flip over Zenith's faux chicken, beef, duck, ham, shrimp, and squid creations, while pescitarians can gobble up sushi from the kitchen in the next room. Of the soy *meats*, the *chicken* and *beef* have the most authentic flavor, and although some of the attempts at fusion cuisine make little sense (like a "burrito" stuffed with Asian-flavored vegetables and sliced like a sushi roll), the chefs have a knack for stir-fries. The service can be a little slow, and the loud country soundtrack clashes with the Eastern décor, but for the city's indecisive, it can't be beat.

311 West 48th Street (at Eighth). 212.262.8080. Daily 11am-11pm. Appetizers $4-6, Entrées $14-17. **1 C E** *to 50th St.*

CASUAL
Blockheads
Mexican

Arguably the best place around for vegan yuppies to partake in happy hour, Blockheads is a low key after-work spot for Mexican food and cheap drinks. The menu has all the usual suspects you'd expect to find at a burrito joint, with some unusual twists, like the highly-touted vegan options. The food is good, but it's also pretty standard; the restaurant's real strong points are its excellent margaritas and prime location, with outdoor seating in a hidden plaza complete with trees and fountain.

Worldwide Plaza (50th Street at Eighth) plus few other locations. 212.307.7029. Daily 11am-11pm. Appetizers $3-6, Entrées $4-12. **1 C E** *to 50th St.*

Vynl *Fusion*

Although the menu boasts an eclectic—perhaps even schizophrenic—blend of Thai, new American, and pan-Asian dishes, Vynl is all about the atmosphere. Inspired by album art and disco balls, a through-the-ages pop music theme allows you to enjoy the Hard Rock-esque kitsch we all secretly love, but without feeling like a tourist. The waitstaff is friendly and fun, serving up everything from fried wontons to all-day breakfast with panache. Brightly-colored drinks such as the White Album and Purple Rain are liquid remixes of perfect pop music, although like the genre that inspired them, they can err on the sweet side.

754 Ninth Avenue (at 51st). 212.974.2003. M 11-11, T-W 11am-midnight, Th-F 11am-1am, Sat 4pm-1am, Sun 4pm-11am. Appetizers $5-8, Entrées $10-18. **1** *to 50th St.*

Nightlife
Bar 9 *Bar*

Built back in the days when Hell's Kitchen was farmland, this bar was constructed on a curving cart road, explaining its unusual angle on the gridded streets of today. Though it sits in a centuries-old building, Bar 9 has only been serving businessmen and theater types for the last decade. Drinkers revel in a relaxed atmosphere, often complemented by the sounds of local Led Zeppelin cover band Led Blimpie—its lead guitarist is a bartender here.

807 Ninth Avenue (at 54th). 212.227.6463. Daily 5pm-3am. Drinks $4-9. **1** *to Columbus Circle.*

Barrage *LGBT*

This comfortable space plays hosts to some regulars and caters to the spillover from Therapy a few blocks north. A hotspot for the 25-30 crowd, this is not a meat-market, but rather a friendly place for casual flirting. The menu offers several beers (usually anathema to gay bars) on tap, and you can expect excellent service at the bar. Just don't put it last on the evening's agenda; the crowd begins to thin out around 2am.

401 West 47th Street (at Ninth). 212.586.9390. Daily 5pm-4am. Drinks $3-12. **1 C E** *to 50th St.*

B.B. King Blues Club & Grill *Music*

A prestigious place for New York musicians, this venue lodged between Broadway theaters serves as both a restaurant and a music hall, attracting both locals and tourists. Past performances have featured blues and jazz acts, by renowned artists like James Brown, Etta James, and—you guessed it—B.B. King. Contemporary hip-hop acts, however, like the Roots and pop bands like the Beach Boys have made appearances on the stage as well. Some 500 people pack this luxurious music hall nightly, relishing in classic American comfort food as they watch the live acts.

237 West 42nd Street (at Seventh). 212.997.4144. bbkingblues.com. Sun-Th 11am-midnight, F-Sat, 11am-2am. Drinks $8-11, Dinner $12-42. **1 2 3 A C E N R Q W 7 S** *to Times Square.*

FAST FACTS

⊘ Scenic Stroll: Times Square

⊘ Major Subway Stations: Penn Station (1 2 3), Times Square (1 2 3, N R Q W, 7, S), 8th Avenue (A C E)

⊘ Urban Oasis: Bryant Park, Worldwide Plaza Four Seasons Fountain

⊘ Kooky Corner: Madame Tussauds

⊘ Notable Buildings: Museum of Modern Art

⊘ Neighborhood Landmarks: Macy's, Madison Square Garden, New York Public Library, New York Times Building, Rockefeller Center

⊘ Neighborhood-specific foods: Brazilian and Portuguese cuisine in Little Brazil, Korean barbecue in K-town.

⊘ Quintessential Neighborhood Event: The ball drop on New Year's Eve

⊘ Celebrity Hangouts: MTV Studios in Times Square, Virgin Megastore

⊘ Kid-Friendly Place: The Museum of TV and Radio

Dizzy's Club Coca-Cola *Music*

Take a trip to Dizzy's for a fantastic introduction to Gotham's jazz universe. Located high up in the Time Warner building overlooking Central Park, this club offers three sets per night featuring both jazz legends and local emerging artists. Stick to the classic and reliable wine list, as the cocktails are a bit too ambitious. The club's southern-inspired menu doesn't compete with the music, but you can't go wrong with hearty dishes like gumbo and mac 'n' cheese.

10 Columbus Circle (at Eighth), 5th Fl. 212.258.9595. jalc.org. Sun-Th 6pm-1am, F-Sat 6pm-2:30am. Drinks $7-14. **1 A C B D** *to Columbus Circle.*

Flûte *Lounge*

Champagne aficionados, look no further—this romantic lounge is a bubbly heaven. Located

below ground in a former speakeasy, this art deco-inspired space offers 100 Champagnes and sparkling wines by the bottle, and 15 by the glass; try a sampling of three, called the Magic Flutes. Don't miss the refreshing champagne cocktails like the Hard Cider—apple Schnapps, Southern Comfort, pineapple juice, and champagne. Also noteworthy are the exotic spring rolls, such as the tasty Sateri, made of tuna, rice vermicelli, avocado, and fresh mint.

205 West 54th Street (at Seventh). 212.265.5169. flutebar.com. Sun-W 5pm-2am, Tu 5pm-2am, F-Sat 5pm-4am. Wines by the glass $12-22, Bottles $50-2000. **N Q R W** *to 57th St.*

Jimmy's Corner Bar *Bar*

If you're looking for a sanctuary from the pandemonium of Times Square, Jimmy's Corner is the place. The walls are plastered with boxing memorabilia, the jukebox is always pumping a steady stream of Motown, and Jimmy Glenn—the owner and a professional trainer—is in attendance most nights. A diverse assortment of suits, sports fans, and students pack the place to the brim every night, but don't expect any fancy specialties; Jimmy's is strictly an old-school beer and shot dive.

140 West 44th Street (at Sixth). 212.221.9510. M-Fri 11am-4am, Sat 11:30am-4am, Sun noon-4am. Drinks $4-7. **1 2 3** N R Q W **7** S *to Times Square.*

Monday Night Magic *Magic Show*
Maybe the greatest trick performed by the more than 350 magicians who've performed at St. Clement's Theater over the years is convincing jaded New Yorkers that they're not too cool for magic. Earning the perhaps-not-hard-to-attain title of "Longest Off-Broadway Magic Show" in New York, Monday Night Magic hosts a different performer every week, each bringing their own spin to the illusions. The act continues even during intermission, as audience members cluster to view the mini-stages set up throughout the auditorium. It's a good choice for a different kind of night out, especially on the day of the week that could most use to disappear.

St. Clement's Theater (423 West 46th Street at Ninth). 212.615.6432. M 8pm. Advance $32.50, Day of show $37.50. **1** C E *to 50th St.*

The Oak Room *Cabaret*
This intimate room nestled into the ritzy Algonquin Hotel hosts cabaret and jazz shows five nights a week for a seasoned and elegant audience. Polished oak walls and black leather booths surround a grand piano; renowned cabaret and jazz vocalists like Diana Krall and Jane Monheit have launched their careers here since 1939. Be sure to make a reservation—past spectators include Marian Anderson and Katherine Hepburn, and today the Oak Room still attracts stars like Tony Bennett. Save your money and eat before the show; the dinner isn't anything special, and you can always order drinks or dessert during the performance.

59 West 44th Street (at Sixth). 212.840.6800. algonquinhotel.com. T-Sat 9pm, closed Sun-M. Cover $60-70. Food and Drink Minimum $25. B D F V *to 42nd St-Bryant Park.*

The Supper Club *Music*
Dress up for a night of dinner and dancing in this art deco ballroom, one of New York's most elegant venues. The Supper Club has the best swing dance party in town every Friday and Saturday night; during the rest of the week, enjoy '40s lindyhop, and occasional private rock and pop concerrts under the sparkling chandelier and 25-foot painted gold starred ceiling.

240 West 47th Street (at Broadway). 212.921.1940. Daily 6pm-12:30am. N R W *to 49th St.*

Tenth Avenue Lounge *LGBT*
Off the beaten path for most, this is a classy and welcoming addition to the Hell's Kitchen LGBT scene. You won't find the typical gay bar "see-and-be-seen" clientele here—an unpretentious crowd lounges on the bar's velvet couches and leather armchairs, drinking classic (and affordable) cocktails and listening to progressive house music spun by guest DJs.

642 Tenth Avenue (at 45th). 212.245.9088. Daily 6pm-4am. Drinks $7-11. A C E *to Port Authority.*

Therapy *LGBT*
As its name implies, this bi-level gay bar aims to relieve the stresses of everyday life. And they just might succeed with a slew of potent $10 cocktails with names like *Coitus Interruptus*, *Freudian Slip*, *Oral Fixation*, and *Psychotic Episode*. The loud, packed upper-level offers performances with no cover, while the more tranquil, lower level is fitting for intimate conversations. Therapy also claims to have the

best fries in the city—a tasty treat for hungry drunks.

348 West 52nd Street (at Ninth). 212.397.1700. Sun-W 5pm-2am. Th-Sat 5pm-4am. Happy hour daily 5pm-8pm. **C E** *to 50th St.*

Arts

Alvin Ailey American Dance Theatre

Founded by the late Alvin Ailey and a group of African American dancers in 1958, this modern dance company has performed for 21 million people in 48 states, 71 countries, and six continents—but this is the theater the dancers call home. Ailey, a native Texan, created 79 ballets with inspirations as wide-ranging as the blues, spirituals, gospel, and his own childhood experience; works by more than 70 additional choreographers have graced the stage as well. Come to see breathtaking performances by powerful, athletic dancers, or just to check out what's new in the dance world.

405 West 55th Street (at Ninth). 212.405.9000. alvinailey.org. **1 A C B D** *to Columbus Circle.*

American Folk Art Museum

The expansive collection at this eight-story museum, dedicated to preserving and fostering an appreciation of early American folk art, will teach you everything you ever wanted to know about art you'd never find at the MoMA. Exhibits include painting, sculpture, textiles, and even antique trinkets like whirligigs and toys.

45 West 53rd Street (at Sixth). 212.265-1040. americanfolkartmuseum.org. T-Sun 10:30am-5:30pm, F 10:30am-7:30pm, closed Monday. Adults $9, Students $7, free Fridays 5:30pm-7:30pm. **E V** *to 53rd.*

Carnegie Hall

Known for its beautiful architecture and euphonious acoustics, this renowned institution is a symbol of musical appreciation—and a constant reminder of what it takes to get to the top. Often referred to as an instrument in itself, the hall makes the world's best musical artists sound even better. Go not just for the music, but for the experience.

881 Seventh Avenue (at 57th). 212.247.7800. carnegiehall.org. Tickets $15-$160. **N R Q W** *to 57th St/Seventh Ave.*

Christie's

No, you can't afford to buy anything from the New York branch of this London auction house legend, but you can scope out the goods up for sale at free public viewings, held five days prior to high-profile auctions.

20 Rockefeller Plaza (49th Street at Fifth). 212.636.2000. christies.com. M-F 10am-5pm, Sat 10am-5pm, Sun 1pm-5pm. **B D F V** *to 47th-50th Sts.*

Madame Tussauds New York

If you always thought Britney Spears seemed too plastic to be real, this so-called museum will almost prove you right. Billed as the "world's hottest interactive wax attraction," this Times Square tourist trap holds hundreds of wax representations of the world's famous and infamous, created—at least in the case of living subjects—by sculptors who base their work on more than 200 measurements taken of a celebrity's body. The painstaking attention to detail, right down to eye color and individually-inserted hairs, results in surprisingly life-like replications; come if you've ever wondered which stars are shorter in real life than they look in the movies.

234 West 42nd Street (at Seventh). 800.246.8872. nycwax.com. Sun-Th 10am-8pm, F-Sat 10am-10pm. Adults $29. **1 2 3 N R Q W 7 S** *to Times Square.*

Museum of Television and Radio

With multiple screening rooms and one of the largest TV and radio libraries in the country, this is the place to watch episodes of shows ranging from *I Love Lucy* to *Darkwing Duck*, from *Seinfeld* to *Wishbone*, at individual consoles.

25 West 52nd Street (at Fifth) 212.621.6800. mtr.org. T-W noon-6pm, Th noon-8pm, F-Sun noon-6pm, closed Sat-M. Adults $10. **E V** *to Fifth Avenue/53rd St.*

Playwrights Horizons

This self-proclaimed "writer's theatre" has been supporting new works by American playwrights, composers, and lyricists for 36 years. During that time, the theater has seen the premieres of works by over 350 playwrights, as well as four Pulitzer Prize-winning musicals.

416 West 42nd Street (at Dyer). 212.279.4000. playwrightshorizons.org . **1 2 3** N R Q W **7 S** *to Times Square.*

St. Clement's Church

After a meal on nearby Restaurant Row, catch a show at this local Episcopalian Church. In 1962, the circa 1830 building was redesigned with two performance spaces in order to facilitate the church's mission of providing a "theater ministry;" since then, the space has been home to many fantastic off-Broadway shows. Every Sunday, mass is held in the 151-seat theater upstairs, with a smaller, more intimate theater located on the first floor. As you might have imagined, the church is known for its liberal policies—it supports the ministry of women, and welcomes gay and lesbian parishioners.

423 West 46th Street (at Ninth). 212.246.7277. stclementcsnyc.org. **1 2 3** N R Q W **7 S** *to Times Square.*

Shopping

Arnold's Hatters

For over seventy-five years, this New York treasure has sold hats to celebrities, athletes, and regular Joes with cold heads. Products include fedoras, top hats, bowl caps, and whatever else you can think of—if it goes on your head, it's here.

535 Eighth Avenue (at 37th). 212.768.3781. ahat. com. **1 2 3** *to Penn Station.*

H&M

Although it can be crowded to the point of suffocation, the largest city branch of Euro-import H&M draws hordes of fashion-hungry New Yorkers looking for chic clothing at ludicrously cheap prices. The folks behind the brand are so quick at picking up the next season's trends that they often rip off designs that have yet to launch at more expensive stores; if you want to look like a million bucks and only pay wholesale, follow the Scandinavian lead.

1328 Broadway (at 35th). 646.473.1165. hm.com. M-Sat 10am-10pm, Sun 11am-9pm. N R Q W **B D F V** *to Herald Square.*

Joseph Patelson Music House

If you love music—or the smell of paper—make sure to check out this old, but still spry, shop that houses more than 47,000 pieces of sheet music for piano, strings, brass, woodwinds, and voice. Established in 1879, it's still considered to be one of the greatest musical libraries in the world.

160 West 56th Street (at Sixth). 212.582.5840. patelson.com. M-Sat 9am-6pm, Sun noon-7pm, closed Friday. N R Q W **F** *to 57th St.*

Macy's

Some consider this self-proclaimed "Largest Store in the World" as obnoxious as it is enormous, but this tourist-fueled madhouse is truly a New York City icon. With a wide array of mid-range and upscale clothing, large furniture galleries, multiple restaurants, and an excellent selection of cookware, this is where New York comes to shop. Prices are lower than at many other stores, although the service reflects that reduction. In December, the place truly comes to life (remember *Miracle on 34th Street?*); read David Sedaris' *Santaland Diaries*, a first-hand account of working as a store elf at Christmastime, then go see what all the fuss is about.

151 West 34th Street (at Broadway). 212.695.440. macys.com . M-Sat 10am-8:30pm, Sun 11am-7pm. N R W **B D F V** *to Herald Square.*

Midtown Comics

With over 500,000 back issues of mainstream and alternative strips to choose from, this shop is a dream come true for comic fanatics. You'll have no problem losing yourself in an old issue of *Batman* or *Shaolin Cowboy*, but if you have no time to browse, the attentive and knowledgeable staff will help you find what you need fast.

200 West 40th Street (at Seventh). 212.302.8192. midtowncomics.com. M-Sat 11am-9pm, Sun noon-7pm. **1 2 3** N R Q W **7 S** *to Times Square.*

Toys "R" Us

Now that you no longer have to get your parent's permission (and funds), come buy all those toys you always wanted but never got. The store, one of the city's great monuments to childhood indulgence through retail, has an indoor ferris wheel, a massive T-Rex, and bulk candy section that's both well-stocked and wide open.

1514 Broadway (at 44th). 646.366.8800. M-Th 10am-10pm, F-Sat 10am-11pm, Sun 11am-9pm. **1 2 3** N R Q W **7 S** *to Times Square.*

Virgin Megastore

As tempting as the pun is, you'll never find reason to refer to this place as a Virgin Megabore: Three bright, eye-catching levels offer a selection large enough to keep any shopper interested. With its very own movie theater, over 1,000 listening booths, and an overwhelming selection of books, video games, CDs, and DVDs, plan on spending an hour, or a few, browsing.

1540 Broadway (at 45th). 212.921.1020. **1 2 3** N R Q W **7 S** *to Times Square.*

Virgin Megastore

WINNER 8 TONY® AWARDS INCLUDING
BEST MUSICAL

SPRING AWAKENING

"Broadway may never be the same."
—The New York Times

Visit Telecharge.com or call 212-239-6200
♩ Eugene O'Neill Theatre, 230 West 49th Street
SPRINGAWAKENING.COM Original cast recording available on DECCA

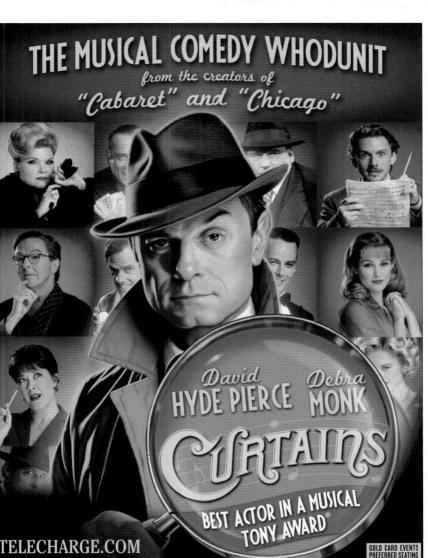

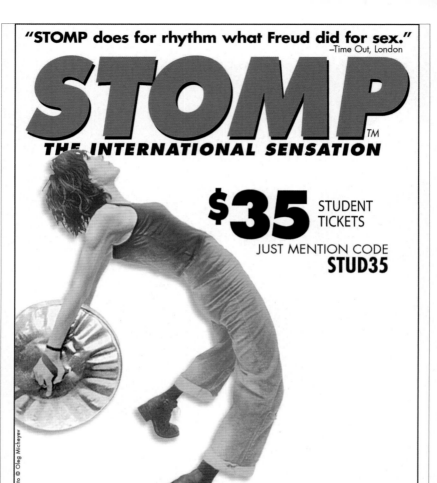

Amalia & **D'Or** named by **Conde Nast Traveler** as
*"one of the top 25 hottest new restaurants
and nightspots in the world"*

Restauranteur Greg Brier brings style and sophistication to new heights with the opening of Amalia adjacent to hotelier Vikram Chatwal's Dream Hotel. Executive chef Ivy Stark offers seasonal Mediterranean-American cuisine at this decadent 7,000-square-foot property, comprised of intimate and richly textured enclaves evocative of a Baroque-inspired European palace. Make your way downstairs for drinks in the ultra-chic, subterranean nightspot D'Or.

Amalia is open for lunch, dinner and Saturday brunch.
D'Or is open from 6:PM until late-night
For reservations, call 212.245.1234.
For special events, contact Kevin Crawford.

amalia

204 West 55th Street
New York New York 10019
P: 212.245.1234 F: 212.245.7715
www.amalia-nyc.com

MIDTOWN EAST

I f the rich and glamorous live on the Upper East Side, then Midtown East is where they work and play. With its old money clout and stately opulence, this neighborhood remains the place for designer diamonds and the latest upscale fashions. Here, Fortune 500 hundred companies have settled amid the dizzying heights of wall-to-wall "glass box" skyscrapers. By day, well-kept executives overrun the neighborhood, power lunching at some of the city's ritziest restaurants. At night, families and foreign dignitaries alike relax among the posh amenities of Park Avenue's Waldorf-Astoria Hotel, staying in suites that can go for well over 800 dollars a night.

In the 18th century, this land was known as Turtle Bay Farm, named after the turtle-heavy cove that lapped at its shores. It soon grew into a thriving wharf area, integral to the island's trading economy. Not long after the Civil War, Old Turtle Bay disappeared as slaughterhouses and breweries replaced the docks, and later, tenement buildings crowded out post-war brownstones. With the construction of the elevated trains that ran along Second and Third Avenues, the 40 acres that had been Turtle Bay Farm, now called Midtown East, joined the bustling world of a roaring metropolis.

During the 20th century, the neighborhood changed again. The area's ideal location spurred a growth in real estate value, and high prices replaced shabby tenements with luxury condominiums. In the wake of the Second World War, city officials razed the slaughterhouses and built the United Nations Headquarters in their place. Today, whether one feels exhilarated or daunted by Midtown East, it's hard to turn one's eyes—or wallets—away.

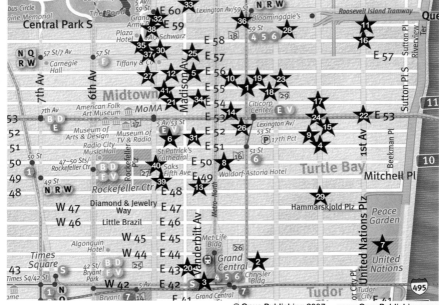

MIDTOWN EAST

SIGHTS/ATTRACTIONS

1. Central Synagogue
2. Chrysler Building
3. Grand Central Station
4. Greenacre
5. Sony Wonder Technology Lab
6. St. Patrick's Cathedral
7. United Nations Headquarters
8. Waldorf-Astoria Hotel

DINING

9. Ama
10. Aquavit
11. Casa La Femme North
12. Cosi
13. Inagiku

14. Lever House
15. Mantra 986
16. Nish
17. Taksim
18. Vong

NIGHTLIFE

19. Azza
20. Campbell Apartment
21. Monkey Bar and Grill
22. Parnell's Bar and Restaurant
23. Pig 'n Whistle
24. Sutton Place
25. The Four Seasons Bar
26. The Four Seasons Restaurant
27. Town

ARTS

28. ImaginAsian
29. Japan Society
30. Mary Boone Gallery
31. Urban Center Galleries

SHOPPING

32. Apple
33. Barney's New York
34. Bauman Rare Books
35. Bergdorf Goodman
36. Bloomingdale's
37. Chanel Boutique
38. FAO Schwartz
39. Kinokuniya Bookstore
40. Saks Fith Avenue
41. Takashimaya

Sights

Central Synagogue

The gold domes and geometric décor are just the two most recognizable features of this National Historic Landmark; go inside to check out the sanctuary, as stunning as it is sacred. As the oldest Jewish house of worship in continuous use in NYC, the Synagogue offers free tours every Wednesday at 12:45pm—no reservations required.

652 Lexington Avenue (at 55th). 212.838.5122. centralsynagogue.org. T-W noon-2pm; Shabbat services F 6pm, Sat 10pm and 10:30am. E V to Lexington Ave/53rd St.

Chrysler Building

This 77-floor, 1048-foot tall building was the tallest in the world for a few short months in 1930, helped skyward by a dramatic spire that awed architects and skyscraper enthusiasts alike. For all the glitz and glamour of its famed art deco exterior, however, it's primarily an office building—don't expect security to let you wander about. Still, if you find yourself passing through Grand Central Station, it's worth the two-block walk to see the triangular lobby, which has red Moroccan marble walls and ceiling murals celebrating the technological advances that were beginning to occur during the building's construction.

405 Lexington Avenue (at 42nd). 4 5 6 7 S to Grand Central.

Chrysler Building

Grand Central Station

With over 30 eateries, a fresh food market, and countless upscale chain stores, this is one hub worth hanging around—don't be one of the thousands of commuters who travel in and out without ever looking around. On Wednesday and Friday afternoons, learn about the history and architecture on a free guided tour, or check out the Transit Museum Annex on the first level. The Main Concourse, restored in '98 to resemble the 1913 original, has a truly spectacular celestial ceiling, and its whisper arches are true acoustic anomalies—ask a knowing native for the secret. The food court and restaurants below are fantastic, but be warned: you're paying their rent, and meals are priced accordingly.

42nd Street at Park Avenue. grandcentralterminal.com. 4 5 6 7 S to Grand Central.

Greenacre

Complete with a 25-foot waterfall, this urban sanctuary makes the most of its diminutive size with careful, tranquil landscaping smack in the middle of Manhattan. Built in 1971 by the Greenacre Foundation and designed by Hideo Sasaki, former chair of the Landscape Architecture Department at Harvard, this "pocket-park" is full of leafy trees and café tables that make it a soothing retreat for restless residents, businesspeople, and visitors alike. *East 51st Street at Second Avenue.* **6** *to 51st St.*

Sony Wonder Technology Lab

One of New York's best cost-free attractions, this virtual wonderland allows visitors to tinker with cutting-edge communications technology. On the main floors, explore exhibits that cover world-changing technologies new and old; skip to the bottom floor, and the latest PlayStation games are just waiting for your thumbs. Avoid the crowds of kids, and the Sony flagship stores that flank the facility, if at all possible.

Sony Plaza Public Arcade (56th Street at Madison Avenue). 212.833.5414. T-Sat 10am-5pm, Sun noon-5pm, closed Monday. **4 5 6 N R** *to 59th St.*

St. Patrick's Cathedral

Although Catholics gather here each week for one of the most popular Mass services in New York, anyone can appreciate the beautiful art and architecture of this true city landmark. The ornate Gothic edifice, awe-inspiring pietà, award-winning Stations of the Cross, and stained-glass rose window add to the majesty of the experience. Come to relax, worship, and reflect in this oasis from the oh-so-worldly bustle of Midtown, or just walk down the aisle and pretend you're a future Kennedy on your big day.

460 Madison Avenue (at 50th). 212.753.2261. Daily 6:30am-8:45pm. saintpatrickscathedral.org. **E V** *to Fifth Ave/53rd St.*

United Nations Headquarters

You won't need your passport to step onto international territory at this most ubiquitous of international icons, but you will need to join a guided tour—wandering around alone is decidedly prohibited. 192 member states

United Nations Headquarters

gather here to debate some of the most pressing issues of our time, and on good days, even hammer out agreements. Tours last about an hour, so be prepared for a long—and at times, drawn out—history lesson.

United Nations Plaza (First Avenue at 45th). 212.963.TOUR. un.org. M-F 9:30am-4:45pm, Sat-Sun 10am-4:30pm, closed weekends Jan-Feb. Adults $13, Students $8.50. 4 5 6 7 S to Grand Central.

Waldorf-Astoria Hotel

One of the most famous hotels in the world, this luxurious art deco masterpiece—now owned by Hilton—is no longer the society hotspot it once was, although the luster of its former glory hasn't completely disappeared. It's still the home of the annual International Debutante Ball, but with room rates that are reasonable, at least for New York, the hotel is surprisingly tourist friendly. Visit the stunning lobby to view exhibits detailing its long and illustrious past, but steer clear of the overpriced, underwhelming restaurants.

301 Park Avenue (at 49th). 212.355.3000. hilton. com. 6 to 51st St.

Dining
UPSCALE
Aquavit *Scandinavian*

If you have an adventurous spirit, a European palate, or a hankering for the best chocolate peanut butter cake in town, head to Aquavit. The restaurant distills its own vodkas and marinates them in glass jars that line the bar—flavors range from lychee to herring, a surprisingly tasty option. Be sure to try a few before your meal, served as shots in mini-martini glasses. For an authentic Scandanavian dish, try the *gravlax*: salmon, cured in salt, sugar, and dill, served over flatbread as an appetizer. The crowd is mostly after-workers and power-lunchers, and the place often clears out before nine, so arrive and leave early to get the full experience.

65 East 55th Street (at Park). 212.307.7311. Lunch Sun-F noon-2:30pm; Dinner Daily 5:30pm-10:30pm. Dinner Prix Fixe $82. E V to Lexington Ave/53rd St.

Lever House *New American, French*

This decadent dining room in Park Avenue's first skyscraper is shaped like a honeycomb with warm woods from floor to ceiling, the vision of designer Marc Newson. Enjoy the seasonal American cuisine from one of the comfortable back booths, which offer an incredible view of the restaurant and its well-dressed patrons. Try the tasting menu—oysters, crab cake, turbot, lamb and more—if your wallet is feeling a little heavy, or stick to the menu if you're only in it for a mini-splurge. Either way, everything is prepared to perfection, and the portions are generous enough to keep you happy well into the next morning.

390 Park Avenue (at 53rd). 212.888.2700. Lunch M-F 11:45am-2:30pm, Dinner M-Th 5:30pm-11pm, F-Sat 5:30pm-11:30pm. Appetizers $18-24, Entrées $24-42. V to Lexington Ave/53rd St.

Metrazur *New American*

This Charlie Palmer-owned establishment in the heart of Grand Central Station leaves no flavor un-accompanied. Although not always perfectly executed, the inspiration behind each dish is readily apparent; each has at least one tongue-numbingly-good component. The people-watching from the balcony at Grand Central is the perfect complement to the meal, but be prepared for the trade off; a cacophony of voices and train announcements makes it difficult to eat in peace. Save a special little place in your stomach for the Bittersweet Chocolate Torte; words can only fail to describe the decadence.

Grand Central Terminal (42nd at Park). 212.687.4600. Lunch M-F 11:30am-3pm; Dinner M-Sat 5pm-10:30pm. Appetizers $9-19, Entrées $21-33. 4 5 6 7 S to Grand Central.

Vong *Fusion (Asian/French)*

Located on the first floor of Phillip Johnson's famous Lipstick Building, this dining destination is one of chef Jean-Georges Vongerichten's eight New York eateries. The colorful interior, marked with stylized Thai flourishes, gives the restaurant its mystical atmosphere; the cuisine, a unique combination of Thai spice and French charm, is characterized by taste progressions alternating between sweet and spicy and then back again. The tasting menu truly pampers your palate, but if you're not up to the challenge, don't miss two gems: the black sea bass and the passion fruit sorbet-soufflé.

200 East 54th Street (at Third). 212.486.9592. Lunch M-F noon-3; Dinner M-Sat 5:30-11, Sun 5:30-10:30. Entrées $16-40, Appetizers $8-18. **E** **V** *to Lexington Ave/53rd.*

MID-RANGE

Amma *Indian*

If you're looking for a heaping plate of chicken *tikka masala* slopped over steamed basmati rice, you won't find it here. With its elegant plating, exquisite wine list, and innovative offerings—try the crispy spinach *chaat* with mung bean salad or the plantain dumplings in onion sauce with crackly okra—Amma defies what you've come to expect from an Indian restaurant in New York. The dishes come from the south, but the delicate spice combinations that pervade them are drawn from all over the subcontinent, and include some things you've never heard of—*mango dust* comes to mind. Though the décor isn't nearly as chic as the food, the Tandoor lamb chops and mango cheesecake are worth the $50 you'll drop on the tasting menu.

246 East 51st Street (at Second). 212.644.8330. Daily Lunch noon-2:30pm, Dinner 5pm-10:30pm. Appetizers $6-10, Entrées $12-28. **6** **E** **V** *to Lexington Ave/51st St.*

Casa La Femme North *Egyptian, Greek, Lounge*

Although the concept might seem like a far-fetched gimmick for out-of-towners with corporate accounts (and possibly mistresses), Casa La Femme somehow pulls off tented tables, belly dancing, and specialty martinis with understated class. The emphasis is on taking your time—sit at a table if you want, but recline on pillows under the tents for the full experience. A *meze* of assorted dips will turn you off supermarket hummus forever, and the starters and drinks alone—the fig martini is as sexy as the fruit it is derived from—are worth the trip. For the time-pressed, try the restaurant's tapas bar, located next door; the food and décor are just as good, but served without the belly dancing.

1076 First Avenue (at 59th). 212.505.0005. Sun-Th 5pm-midnight, F-Sat 5pm-3am. Appetizers $7-12, Entrées $18-25, Prix fixe $55. **6** *to 59th St.*

Inagiku *Japanese*

Waitresses dress in classical Japanese kimonos at this Waldorf-Astoria destination, and will eagerly explain to patrons the oft-confusing dishes that make up the menu; order a single entrée, or combine "classic little dishes" to sample various Japanese specialties. The shrimp and lobster tempura and eel *hagata*, imported from Japan, are both top-notch, as is the wide selection of sakes and unique array of bar beverages. Indulge at the *shabu shabu* station if you will, but make sure to leave room for the many creative desserts—the Ogura milk crepe is a must.

The Waldorf Astoria, 111 East 49th Street (at Park). 212.355.0440. Lunch M-F noon-2pm; Dinner daily 5:30pm-10pm. Appetizers $7-$16, Entrées $22-32. **6** *to 51st St.*

Mantra 986 *Contemporary Asian, American*

The fantastic creations served in the dining room at the back of this large bar have a complexity that goes far beyond mere bar food—the lobster guacamole is divine, especially when paired with the bar's delicious cocktails, and the substantive dinner soups are

FAST FACTS

⑦ **Scenic Stroll: Fifth Avenue**

⑦ **Major Subway Stations: Grand Central Station – 42ⁿᵈ St. (4 5 6, 7, S),**
47ᵗʰ-50ᵗʰ Rockefeller Center (B D F V), Lexington Ave-53ʳᵈ (E, V), Lexington
Ave-59ᵗʰ St (4 5 6, N R W)

⑦ **Urban Oasis: Greenacre Park**

⑦ **Kooky Corner: The Imaginasian (live cricket match screenings)**

⑦ **Notable Buildings: Chrysler Building, Empire State Building, Seagram**
Building, St. Patrick's Cathedral

⑦ **Neighborhood Landmarks: Bloomingdale's, Central Synagogue, Roosevelt**
Island Tramway, United Nations Headquarters, Waldorf-Astoria Hotel

⑦ **Best Deal: Food Court at Grand Central Station**

⑦ **Notable Residents: Dick Clark, Frank Sinatra, Sigourney Weaver, Kurt Von-**
negut

⑦ **Kid-Friendly Place: Sony Wonder Lab, FAO Schwartz**

one of the night's best deals. With a stated mission to bring a downtown vibe to Midtown East, the owners have struck the right chord: dominant flavors, a relaxing atmosphere, and an airy lounge upstairs all converge to make this a great place to kick off a night on the town.

986 Second Avenue (at 52ⁿᵈ). 212.813.1595. Lunch M-F 11am-3pm; Dinner M-Sat 5pm-11pm, closed Sunday. Appetizers $8-$10, Entrées $18-20. **E V** *to Lexington Ave/53ʳᵈ St.*

Nish *New American*
For one of the city's best upscale dates under $100, head to this American gem nestled in a cozy East Side townhouse. The cuisine, drawing its inspiration from several different cultures, features meats from Kobe beef to Scottish salmon, each presented as elegantly as the next. Eat the much-touted cheese plate, put together by the French company *fromages. com*, on the calming outdoor patio for the best experience possible.

405 East 58ᵗʰ Street (at First). 212.754.6272. Daily 5:30pm-11pm. Appetizers $12-22, Entrées $22-38. **N R W** *to Lexington Ave/59ᵗʰ St.*

CASUAL
Cosí *American, Sandwiches*
This chain of upscale sandwich shops is famous for salty homemade pressed breads and gourmet sandwiches, made to order at every location. Inspiration comes from a range of different cultures, from tandori chicken to black forrest

ham served with mustard so spicy it might actually knock your socks off. Come during the day for counter service and take-away, or after five for a casual sit-down. If you're not in a sandwich mood, grab a square bagel, pizza, or salad, then order the s'mores for dessert—they come to your table unprepared and in parts, with a do-it-yourself mini fire pit and skewers.

60 East 56thStreet (at Madison). 212.588.1225. Sun-Th 7am-11pm, F-Sat 7am-1am. N R W to Lexington Ave/ 59th St.

Taksim *Middle Eastern*

One of the best Turkish restaurants in the city, Taksim serves up great food without all the fuss. The laid-back atmosphere and reasonable prices put diners at ease, and the starters are so cheap it'd be a shame not to try a few—grab the falafel and hummus, along with whatever else strikes your fancy. After an entrée of classic lamb, finish up with baklava or kadayif, as economical as they are delicious.

1030 Second Avenue (at 54th). 212.421.3004. Daily noon-11:30pm. Appetizers $5-7, Entrées $10-16. 6 E V to 51st St.

Nightlife

Azza *Lounge*

This velvet roped French-Moroccan lounge is a destination spot for an elite and highly fashionable crowd in their late 20s and early 30s. Floor lanterns and flower petals line the hallway leading to the spacious lounge. Private rooms flank both sides of the dance floor and couches line the perimeter, but consider yourself forewarned: By 1am they'll be packed by those paying for bottle service and breathing room. The sounds change from more relaxed Middle Eastern beats to intense Euro-house as the night progresses. Azza serves hookah all night long, but the signature fruit and candy cocktails are quite the rave.

137 East 55th Street (at Lexington). 212.755.7055. M-Sat 10pm-6am, closed Sunday. Drinks $8-20. E V to Lexington Ave/53rd St.

The Bar (at the Four Seasons Hotel)
Bar

An airy and spacious room with elegant finishing touches houses this bar and lounge, designed for Manhattan's elite. The cocktail menu is creative and lengthy but also quite expensive: Prepare to pay $22 for a Martini. If money is no object, then the impeccable service and comprehensive comfort make this bar a desirable destination. Complementary snacks, like dried cranberries and spicy crackers, come with the drinks, a welcome departure from the standard bowl of peanuts. With heartier gourmet offerings available from the kitchen after 6pm, settle into a plush chair and be taken care of for the night.

57 East 57th Street (at Madison). Sunday 3pm-midnight, M-Sat 3pm-1am. Cocktails $20-22. N R W to Lexington Ave/59th St.

The Bar (at the Four Seasons Restaurant) *Food and Drink*

You may very well be the least-connected person sitting at the bar of this New York institution, but with a surprisingly friendly barstaff and even more astonishing low-key vibe, you're bound to get acquainted with that hedge fund manager sitting to your left. The bar is off the Grill Room, where Upper East Side movers and shakers gather for power lunches, and both are designed in 1960s height-of-chic minimalist décor. A four-sided bar lets you get a good look at the other patrons, and at the bottles which are clustered into a pyramid in lieu of a back wall; looking up you'll find a shower of thin bronze rods raining down over the bar in an art installation much more interesting than a chandelier. With classy drinks and classier bar snacks, it's the perfect place to make like Holly Golightly for a drink or two.

99 East 52nd Street (at Lexington). 212.754.9494. Daily 5pm-9:30pm. Drinks $5-15. 6 to 51st St.

Campbell Apartment *Bar and Lounge*

Once upon a time, this majestic room in Grand

Central Station was the private office of railroad tycoon John Campbell. Renovated and restored in 1999, it is now a high-end bar and lounge, complete with gorgeous furniture, a fireplace, and Tiffany stained-glass windows. On weekdays, the Campbell Apartment serves Midtown bankers and lawyers, and on weekends, it's often filled with tourists and private parties. The drinks are expensive, but the house specialties like the Prohibition Punch (passion fruit juice, Appleton Rum Estate VX, Grand Marniet, and champagne) are well worth it. While there's never a cover charge, Saturday nights the live jazz concerts require a two-drink minimum.Also beware of the strictly enforced business-casual dress code.

15 Vanderbilt Avenue (Grand Central Station, Lexington Avenue at 43rd). 212.953.0409. M-Sat 3pm-1am. Sun 3pm-11pm. Drinks $8-15. **4 5 6 7** S *to Grand Central.*

Monkey Bar & Grill *Bar*
Located in the Hotel Elysée, this chic art deco masterpiece attracts a glamorous older crowd sipping cocktails and flaunting Chanel. The bar and restaurant, which serves up sophisticated Asian fusion, is named after a '40s actress who once lived at the hotel and always brought her monkey down with her to the bar.

60 East 54th Street (at Madison). 212.838.2600. elyseehotel.com. M-Sat from 5pm, closed Sunday. Drinks $10-12. **E V** *to Fifth Ave/53rd St.*

Parnell's Bar and Restaurant *Food and Drink*
Rich oak paneling, hazy lighting, and an abundance of Guinness bottles adorning the bar counter may make you think that you just marched into Dublin, but this Irish pub and restaurant definitely has a New York spin. The menu features some traditional pub fare such as fish and chips, chicken pot pie, and bangers and mash, served alongside sirloin steak, shrimp linguini, and grilled calamari salad. The food is excellent, and the service prompt and attentive. Make sure to try the delicious Irish coffee.

350 East 53rd Street (at First). 212.753.1761. Daily 11am-4am. Drinks $6-10. **E V** *to Lexington Ave/53rd St.*

Pig 'n Whistle *Pub*
An excellent place to grab a drink after dining in Midtown, this classic Irish pub employs friendly bartenders who are happy to mix with the unpretentious clientele. The fine selection of whiskey and beer is an instant stand-out, and there is live music on Friday, Saturday, and Sunday nights.

922 Third Avenue (at 55th). Daily 11:30am-4am. 212.688.4646. pignwhistleon3.com. Drinks $5-15. **E V 6** *to 51st St.*

Sutton Place *Club*
There are four bars in this vibrant venue, which has two spacious levels and a large rooftop terrace. DJs spin current hits, and projection screens cover the walls behind the main bar downstairs, providing diverse coverage of sporting events. The typical crowd is of the after-work variety, but Saturday nights bring 20-somethings looking for a party.

1015 Second Avenue (at 53rd). 212.207.3777. M-W noon-1am, Th-F noon-4am, Sun noon-midnight. Drinks $5-16. **6** *to 51st St.*

Town *Food and Drink*
This stately bar offers expertly prepared cocktails with a posh twist. Try the signature Town Mojito, containing a fresh piece of lychee, or the Convent in Chile, uniquely flavored with muddled kumquat. The polished wood bar packs in droves of businessmen during happy hour, but those who wait until later in the evening can enjoy excellent service and exquisite appetizers – such as the tender serrano ham or the dreamy salmon lizette – at their own leisure. The spacious, modernized lodge next to the bar doubles as the Hotel Chambers' lobby.

15 West 56th Street (at Fifth). 212.582.4445. M-W 5:30pm-10:30pm; Th-F 5:30pm-11pm; Sat 5:30pm-11pm, Sun 5:30pm-9:30pm. Drinks $11-22. **F** *to 57th St.*

Arts
The ImaginAsian
In addition to showing Asian American films from

the U.S. and countries such as India, Japan, China, Korea, and Vietnam, this theater hosts live performances, film festivals, concerts, and satellite-fed cricket matches. All foreign language movies have English subtitles—enjoy them while snacking on wasabi peas, green tea cupcakes, and mushroom cookies from the cinema's concession stand.

239 East 59th Street (at Third). 212.371.6682. theimaginasian.com. Adults $10, Students $7. **4 5 6** *to 59th St/Lexington Ave.*

Japan Society

This booming cultural resource is worth a visit for the gallery alone—one of the foremost in America for the exhibition and research of Japanese art. In addition to presenting visual media, the Society hosts cultural events and lectures by prominent artists, writers, and leaders, and serves as an educational institute, offering Japanese classes at 12 different levels.

333 East 47th Street (at Second). 212.832.1155. japansociety.org. Institute M-F 9:30am-5:30pm; Gallery T-Th 11am-6pm, F 11am-9pm. **6** *to 51st.*

Mary Boone Gallery

This longtime SoHo staple for contemporary art recently moved to greener pastures up north, relocating to this elegant address on Fifth Avenue. The result, bringing downtown culture to an uptown audience, is a welcome addition to the neighborhood.

745 Fifth Avenue (at 57th), 4th floor. 212.752.2929. T-Sat 10am-6pm. N R W *to 5th Ave.*

Urban Center Galleries

As a subsidiary of the Municipal Art Society—a nonprofit group involved with urban planning and public art—this Gallery's main mission is to celebrate beautiful spaces. Exhibits, which change at 8-week intervals, canvas topics including city planning and design, preservation and development, and architectural excellence. The bookshop has an extensive collection of fascinating architectural texts, and the gallery hosts programs and lectures throughout the year on topics relating to architecture, urban design, and interior design.

457 Madison Avenue (at 51st). 212.935.3960. mas.org. M-W, F-Sat 11am-5pm, closed Th, Sun. Free. **6** *to 51st St.*

Shopping

The Apple Store

On Fifth Avenue, right across from the Plaza Hotel, the luminescent Apple logo that hovers within a 32-foot glass cube merely hints at the expansive store hidden below. Go inside for the familiar Mac products, but even if you're not planning to buy, the store is still worth a look—gray stone floors gently diffuse the light from the windows above, while an interior of pale wood and brushed aluminum focuses all attention on the sleek products on display.

767 Fifth Avenue (at 59th). 212.336.1440. apple. com. Open 24 hours. N R W *to 5th Ave.*

Barney's New York

Power dressers and chic shoppers put dents in their bank accounts at this airy, beautiful department store legend, whose fashion-forward, adventurous buyers pair classic styles with the latest trends. The men's department is solid, but shoe-aholics go crazy over the women's collection on the fourth floor. Be sure to check in every February and September, when New Yorkers wait in line for hours and fight like cats at the Barney's Warehouse Sales—stellar stuff sold for up to 70% off.

666 Madison Avenue (at 61st). 212.826.8900. M-F 10am-8pm, Sat 10am-7pm, Sun 11am-6pm. barneys.com. N R W *to 5th Ave.*

Bauman Rare Books

Boasting a vast selection of rare books from the 15th through 20th centuries, this 34-year-old store is the perfect resource for serious collectors. For hard-core book fans, it's worth a visit, but be prepared to shell out big money for immaculate first editions like Adam Smith's *The Wealth of Nations*.

535 Madison Avenue (at 54ᵗʰ). 212.751.0011. baumanrarebooks.com. M-Sat 10am-6pm, closed Sunday. **E V** *to 5ᵗʰ Ave/53ʳᵈ St.*

Bergdorf Goodman

Tour the museum-quality merchandise in this home of high fashion. Notorious for scorching price tags, mixing established designers with cool downtown brands, and the lush lavender salon-spa on the top floor, Bergdorf is as good as it gets when money is no object. To shield you from wincing as you swipe your AmEx, all cash and credit card transactions occur in a "back room" whose doors blend with the walls.

754 Fifth Avenue (at 58ᵗʰ). 800.558.1855. bergdorfgoodman.com. M-F 10am-8pm, Sat 10am-7pm, Sun noon-6pm. **N R W** *to Fifth Ave./59ᵗʰ St.*

Bloomingdale's

The so-called first department store, Bloomingdale's is a true New York icon, attracting the famous and fabulous alike—even Queen Elizabeth has stopped by—since it moved uptown in 1880. The massive store, which occupies an entire city block, launched the careers of luminaries like Ralph Lauren, Perry Ellis, and Norma Kamali, and created a sensation with trendy designer shopping bags in the 1960s. Today, you can find classic brands like Lilly Pulitzer and Diane von Furstenberg alongside hip favorites C & C California and 7 For All Mankind. Be prepared for crowds; claiming to be the third most-popular destination for tourists in New York, it has a Visitors Center on the first floor balcony which offers theater tickets, tour reservations, personal shopping assistance, even translators.

1000 Third Ave (at 59ᵗʰ). 212.705.2000. bloomingdales.com. M-F 10am-8:30pm, Sat 10am-7pm, Sun 11am-7pm. **4 5 6 N R W** *to Lexington Ave/59ᵗʰ St.*

FAO Schwartz

Whether you're looking for that one-of-a-kind toy or want to relive *Big* on the famous oversized piano, you've come to the right place. Prices are Manhattan-high, but don't let that stop you from visiting—there's no pressure to buy, and plenty for the kids to gawk at.

767 Fifth Avenue (at 58ᵗʰ). 212.644.9400. fao.com. Sun-W 10am-7pm, Th-Sat 10am-8pm. **N R W** *to 5ᵗʰ Ave.*

Saks Fifth Avenue

Browsing through this 10-story high-end retail destination will leave you both amazed and dizzy. As one of New York's most famous department stores, Saks has something for everyone—at least everyone rich. Expect to find furniture, housewares, books, and everything in between. The fashion focus seems to be on the older shopper, with an extensive classically-focused collection, although it attracts well-dressed 20-somethings as well.

611 Fifth Avenue (at 49ᵗʰ). 212.753.4000. saksfifthavenue.com. M-F 10am-8pm, Sat 10am-7pm, Sun noon-7pm. **B D F V** *to 47ᵗʰ-50ᵗʰ Sts.*

Takashimaya

Shopping at this Japanese import, synonymous with elegance and ambiance, is an experience in itself. A kind of Barney's-from-the-East, selling everything from clothing to giftware, there's no better place to find a rare gift or splurge item—the Asian tea and delicacies department is to die for, and the fresh flower department is a favorite of greenery-craving urbanites.

693 Fifth Avenue (at 54ᵗʰ). 212.350.0100. M-Sat 10am-7pm, Sun noon-5pm. **F** *to 57ᵗʰ St.*

NEW YORK EVENT PLANNING

EMRG MEDIA, is a Manhattan- based event planning marketing and publishing company specializing in corporate and executive event services.

Our specialities include:
Department Outings
Corporate Events
Fashion Events
Special Events
Private Parties
Photo Exhibits
Fundraisers

www.emrgmedia.com | 212.254.3700

UPTOWN

UPPER WEST SIDE

T hough it doesn't have the moneyed prestige of its twin neighborhood across the island, the Upper West Side does have something that the Upper East Side doesn't: accessibility. Three major subway lines cut through the area, making it a popular choice for tourists daunted by cross-town buses and residents who like having easy access to the rest of the city.

The Westside vibe is distinctly laid-back, and its proximity to some of the most pleasent parts of Central Park make this neighborhood an obvious destination for adventurous visitors or smart New Yorkers who want to benefit from a small town feeling in this otherwise crowded metropolis.

Though it may be difficult to imagine now, the Upper West Side was once viewed as a distant suburb of downtown Manhattan. Before the completion of the Ninth Avenue elevated train in 1879, the area known as Bloomingdale was a largely undeveloped pastoral refuge from the crowded city. The Dakota, once the backdrop for *Rosemary's Baby* and the site of John Lennon's assassination, was so christened because residents felt it was such a distance from the city's hub, it might as well have been in the Dakotas.

Since then, this neighborhood has grown rapidly into one of Manhattan's busiest cultural hubs, boasting internationally-acclaimed museums and cultural venues as well as demographic diversity. Its residents include aspiring artists and performers who grace the stage of the famed Lincoln Center, locals whose families go back several generations in the same apartment, students attending the city's most prestigious universities, and businesspeople who appreciate a quiet night home after a frantic day downtown.

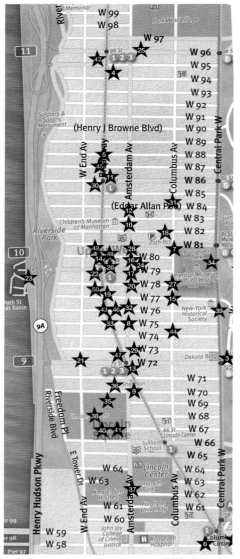

THE UPPER WEST SIDE

SIGHTS/ATTRACTIONS
1. Columbus Circle
2. Belvedere Castle
3. Dakota
4. Pomander Walk

DINING
5. Aix
6. Asiate
7. Calle Ocho
8. Citrus
9. Compass
10. Fred's
11. French Roast
12. Good Enough to Eat
13. Gray's Papaya
14. H&H Bagels
15. Jacque IMO's
16. Kefi
17. Nice Matin
18. Rain
19. Ruby Foo's

NIGHTLIFE
20. 420 Bar and Lounge
21. The All State Café
22. Blondie's
23. The Boat Basin Café
24. Bourbon Street
25. Dive Bar
26. Dublin House
27. Evelyn Lounge
28. Jake's Dilemma
29. The P&G
30. The Parlour
31. Prohibition
32. Time Out
33. Yogi's

ARTS
34. The American Museum of Natural History
35. Avery Fisher Hall
36. Julliard
37. Lincoln Plaza Cinemas
38. Metropolitan Opera House
39. New York Historical Society
40. New York City Opera
41. New York City Ballet
42. Symphony Space

SHOPPING
43. Barney's Co-Op
44. Housing Works Thrift Shop
45. Liberty House
46. Lush
47. Olive & Bette's
48. Westsider Rare and Used Books
49. Zabar's
50. West Side Market

© Opus Publishing 2007 — www.OpusPublishing.com

Sights/Attractions

Columbus Circle

This traffic circle and its surrounding area underwent a major renovation in 2003-2005 to become one of the most energetic and bustling intersections in the city, and a classy shopping and sightseeing destination. Enter the imposing Time Warner Building for upscale national chain stores like Coach and Armani Exchange, as well as Per Se, one of the city's most expensive restaurants (with a two-month waiting list for reservations). If malls aren't your thing, catch a carriage ride at the southwest corner of Central Park for a unique view of the greenery, or hang out by the huge central fountain and watch the world go by.

Intersection of Broadway, Central Park West, Central Park South, and Eighth Avenue. **A C B D 1** *to Columbus Circle.*

Belvedere Castle

Perched atop Vista Rock, Belvedere Castle is located on the second-highest natural elevation in Central Park, overlooking the Great Lawn. An unexpected visual treat, the miniature medieval castle, constructed in 1869, is home to the Henry Luce Nature Observatory, where amateur scientists of all ages converge to learn about the park's natural wonders. Borrow a Discovery Kit (containing binoculars, reference materials, and maps of the park) and let your inner child go exploring.

Mid-Park at 79th Street 212.772.0210. www.centralparknyc. org. Tu-Sun 10-5. **B C** *to 81st St.*

The Dakota

This classic Upper West Side residence was named for its northern location, considered when it was built in 1884 to be as remote from the rest of the city as the Dakota Territory. The imposing Renaissance masterpiece is a US National Historic Landmark, designed by the same architectural firm as the Plaza hotel. As famous for the residents as for the architecture, a myriad of celebrities have

Belvedere Castle, Central Park

owned apartments here, including Lauren Bacall, Leonard Bernstein, Bono, and John Lennon, who was famously killed in front of the entrance.

1 West 72nd Street. 212.362.1448. **B C** *to 72nd St.*

Pomander Walk

There's a reason why this enchanted English pocket of Manhattan feels more like the set of a play than a city neighborhood: the narrow, peaceful street was designed in 1920 to resemble the scenery from the British play of the same name. With quaint Tudor-style homes and perfectly maintained English country gardens, it's no surprise that rents aren't cheap. Though technically closed to non-residents—that alone should tell you it's desirable—if you hang around and look non-threatening, a resident might graciously let you in. If not, peek down the street through the gates; even through bars, the scene is adorable.

260-266 West 95th Street (at Broadway). **1 2 3** *to 96th St.*

Dining
UPSCALE

Asiate *French, Pan-Asian*

Perched 35 stories over Columbus Circle in the Mandarin Oriental Hotel, this sleekly-designed hotspot has windows that span wall-to-wall and floor-to-ceiling, boasting exceptional views of Midtown Manhattan and southern Central Park. With a delicious and creative blend of French and Asian cuisine, expect a truly fantastic dining experience that you can actually afford. The $24 Prix Fixe lunch is a year-round holdover from Restaurant Week; students, professionals, and millionaires alike can partake without breaking the bank. If you're willing to spend a bit more, order the bento box for some exquisitely delicate flavor pairings.

80 Columbus Circle (Broadway at 59th). 212.805.8881. Breakfast M-F 7am-10:30am, Sat-Sun 8am-3pm; Lunch M-F noon-3pm, Sat-Sun 8am-3pm; Dinner M-Sat 5:30pm-11pm, Sun 5:30pm-9pm. Appetizers $7-21, Entrées $28-35. **1 A C B D** *to Columbus Circle.*

Asiate

Compass *New American*

A behemoth by city standards, Compass' dark stone columns and white linen with oversized floral arrangements to accentuate the uncommonly spacious dining room. Though pricey, the portions are substantial; from the wide selection of breads to eclectic offerings like a foie gras Creamsicle, one look at the menu makes it clear that Chef John Fraser doesn't conform to the culinary status quo. Don't miss the bigeye tuna accented with pine nuts and garlic; for dessert, get adventurous with the peanut butter bon bons paired with smoked paprika potato chips. For those on a budget, the $35 prix fixe is a steal, sampling Compass' best.

208 West 70th Street (at Amsterdam). 212.875.8600. M-Th 5pm-11pm, F-Sat 5pm-midnight, Sun 11:30pm-2-:30pm and 5pm-10pm. Appetizers $12-18, Entrées $22-45. **1** *to 72nd St.*

MID-RANGE

Aix *French*

Offering elegantly crafted French cuisine with a touch of New York style, the seductive dining room at Aix is a warm refuge for fine dining. When open, the upstairs and outdoor seating areas offer great people-watching, but once the food arrives your interest in anything else will quickly evaporate. The *daurade*—a type of red snapper—is beautifully presented; if you're prone to addiction, be wary of the scallops, which melt on your tongue with a tang. For those who enjoy crafting their own dishes, Aix provides a selection of meat and fish from the grill, which can be prepared with any of several housemade sauces. Pair it all with a wine from the ample cellar, or an inventive cocktail from the bar.

2398 Broadway (at 88th). 212.874.7400. Lunch Sun 11:30am-2:30pm; Dinner Sun-Th 5:30pm-10:30pm, F-Sat 5:30pm-11pm; Bar Sun-Th 5:30pm-midnight, F-Sat 5:30pm-1pm. Appetizers $9-16, Entrées $17-36. **1** *to 86th St.*

Calle Ocho *Caribbean, Latin American*

A hip and lively crowd gathers at Calle Ocho every day at five, summoned by the delicious and unique happy hour drinks. The back room, almost invisible from the bar area, serves up traditional Latin fare in a quieter environment; grab a drink from the bar and start with any of the flavorful appetizers, including enticing ceviches. The often-disappointing entrées and desserts are not quite worth the prices, so fill up on small plates before heading back up front to rejoin the crowd.

446 Columbus Avenue (at 81st). 212.873.5025. Appetizers $9-23, Entrées $19-28. **1** *to 79th St.*

Citrus *Latin American/Japanese*

Wash down your sushi with a margarita at this delightful fusion restaurant, perfect for a celebratory dinner with friends. The spacious (and very orange) dining room is packed on weekday nights with diners seeking new pairings of classic flavors—the inspirations may sound strangely dissimilar, but somehow, it all comes together nicely. The inventive sushi rolls are always a hit, and while the standard Mexican fare can be disappointingly ordinary, the crunchy and tender textures of the pan-seared jumbo softshell crabs—served with tortillas and vegetables julienne—mix together in orgasmic perfection. The restaurant attracts mostly an after-work crowd in their 30s and 40s, but the tequila bar lures a younger, hipper clientele at night; the impressive selection of margaritas, specialty drinks and plentiful vegetarian and organic menu items keeps them coming back.

320 Amsterdam Avenue (at 75th). 212.595.3947. M-Th 5:30pm-11pm, F-Sat 5:30pm-1am. Appetizers $9-15, Entrées $16-$24. **1 2 3** *to 72nd St.*

Fred's *American (Traditional)*

It truly is a dog's life at Fred's; this canine-themed, subterranean restaurant has pooch photos on every wall and serves up specialty drinks with names like "Paw Punch" and "Hair of the Dog." While the highballs, many featuring Fred's homemade lemonade, are simple and tasty, the highlight of the drink menu is the sang-arita, a delicious half-sangria, half-margarita blend. Though the portions are large and the food hearty, preparation of the traditional American fare tends towards the prosaic here, with the exception of the mac 'n' cheese, a medley of aged cheddar and Parmesan (also offered with a variety of toppings, from black forest ham to beefsteak tomatoes) that's always worth ordering.

476 Amsterdam Avenue (at 83rd). 212.579.3076. M 5pm-11pm, T-Th 11am-11pm, F 11am-midnight, Sat 10am-midnight, Sun 10am-11pm. Appetizers $7-10, Entrées $13-18. **1** *to 86th St.*

French Roast *French*

The owners of this Parisian-kitsch café broke new restaurant ground when they opened a series of 24-hour French diners. With tasty, but decidedly American, food, some menu staples may underwhelm aficionados of French cooking, but a strong breakfast menu, attentive service, and decent prices more than compensate. Don't go expecting delicate European cuisine, but rather a hearty Manhattan meal at any hour of the day. When in doubt, ask the friendly staff for recommendations, or stick with the relatively lighter fare and baked specialties.

2340 Broadway (at 85th). 212.799.1533. Daily 24 hours. Appetizers $7-12, Entrées $12-24. **1** *to 86th St.*

Good Enough To Eat *American*

This cozy, candlelit little gem should satisfy your hankering for good home-style cooking; the brunches are especially fantastic, as the line around the block will attest. Try the Southern-style griddle corn bread, or the soft, subtle, and juicy organic-roast chicken. Steak fans should try the charcoal-grilled rib eye, served with a chimichurri sauce that adds a tangy depth. Even though you'll be full after eating the generous portions, try to stick it out for the excellent desserts; baked on-site, this restaurant's treats are scrumptious, especially when served with homemade ice cream—the flavor called "Kitchen Sink" tastes much better than it sounds.

483 Amsterdam Avenue (at 83rd). 212.496.0163. M-F 8am-10:30pm, Sat 9am-11pm, Sun 9am-10pm. Appetizers $5-9, Entrées $14-23. **1** *to 86th St.*

Jacques Imo's *Southern/Creole*

This casual restaurant serves up real New Orleans comfort cuisine in a relaxed environment devoid of tourists. Situated far from the gimmicky eateries of

Good Enough To Eat

Midtown, its large murals, jovial jester statues, and Mardi Gras beads complement colorful plastic table cloths and an equally vibrant clientele. A bustling bar scene begins in the early evening and continues long after the diners leave. While you'll probably get your hands dirty enjoying the famous fried chicken, olive oil dipped corn bread, and shrimp and alligator sausage cheesecake, you'll just end up licking your fingers clean. Some skeptics says it's no match for the original, but the combination of Cajun-Creole cooking and friendly service are sure to delight.

366 Columbus Avenue (at 77th). 212.799.0150. Dinner Sun-Th 5pm-10pm, F-Sat 5pm-11pm; Brunch Sat-Sun 11:30am-3pm. Appetizers $8-10, Entrees $15-24. **1** *to 79th St.*

Kefi *Greek*

Don't be intimidated by the plush interior—the grandeur of Kefi's décor is a holdover from the restaurant's previous life as Onera, esteemed chef Michael Psilakis' now-closed upscale Greek eatery. These days, Psilakis uses the space to serve up home-style, affordable Greek specialties with a friendly, knowledgeable waitstaff and a casual atmosphere. Traditional Greek dishes are worked over with subtle, elegant precision; be sure to try the perfectly grilled octopus and the flat pasta with pulled braised rabbit, as complex as it is hearty. Also deserving of special mention are the sheep's milk dumplings with spicy lamb sausage, and the extensive selection of Ouzo, a Greek anise liquor. It's cash only and doesn't accept reservations, but for the price, you'll get some of the best Greek food around.

222 West 79th Street (at Amsterdam). 212.873.0200. Sun-Th 5pm-10pm, F-Sat 5pm-1pm. Appetizers $5-10, Entrées $10-16, cash only. **1** *to 79th St.*

Mike's Bistro *Gourmet Kosher*

Some find the laws of kashrut gastronomically limiting, but you would never guess it after a look

at the menu at this gourmet kosher bistro. Dishes are original and innovative, full of fresh ingredients, and nicely presented, with main influences drawn from the New American culinary movement. With a friendly waitstaff and a spacious dining room, this upscale restaurant is one of the premiere kosher dining establishments in the city.

228 West 72nd Street (at Amsterdam). 212.799.3911. Sun-Th 5:30pm-10pm, Sat 7:30pm-11pm. Appetizers $7-17, Entrées $25-42. **1 2 3** *to 72nd St.*

Nice Matin *French*

Inspired by the tastes of the Côte d'Azur, this delightful French bistro—named for a prominent daily newspaper in Nice—nails the upscale-casual atmosphere that is fast becoming the Upper West Side's trademark. For the most part, the food is simple, with bold accents to awaken subtle flavors. Start with the *panisess*—deep fried chickpeas—served with a seriously addictive aioli garlic dipping paste. For a main course, try the melt-

in-your-mouth-buttery *daube* (stew) of beef short ribs or the *moules frites* (fried muscles), artfully arranged and decorated with tomatoes, garlic, and celery. Follow it up with the warm chocolate tart with passion fruit ice cream or a crisp apple tart, two of the outstanding desserts. In warm weather, ask to sit outside; a nice Bordeaux is the perfect complement to the summer air.

201 West 79th Street (at Amsterdam). 212.873.0049. M-Sat 7am-midnight, Sun 7am-11pm. Appetizers $4-13, Entrées $15-$26. **1** *to 79th St.*

Rain *Pan-Asian*

One of the Upper West Side's best-kept secrets, this treasure's colorful décor is echoed by its even more colorful food. The atmosphere has entertained locals for 12 years, and appeals to a diverse crowd—expect to find the large dining room and the comfortable lounge filled with trendy 20-somethings, parties of 20, and guests who still remember the 1920s. Executive chef Gypsy Gifford pairs pan-Asian flavors with classic French training; the blend produces such favorites as duck confit salad with duck prosciutto and bamboo roasted cod. The tuna three ways is a good place to start your meal, and the grilled baby octopus replaces the seafood's typical chewy texture with a crunchy char-grill. Don't miss the chocolate fondue for a decadent end to the meal.

100 West 82nd Street (at Columbus). 212.501.0776. M-Th 6am-11pm, F 6pm-midnight, Sat 5pm-midnight, Sun 5pm-10pm. Appetizers $7-24, Entrées $12-28. **1** *to 79th St.*

Ruby Foo's *Pan-Asian*
This pan-Asian mini-chain successfully combines Chinese and Japanese flavors and styles throughout its menu, which includes specialty sushi rolls, Peking duck, and so-called seven-flavor beef. The staff is friendly, happy to guide you through the menu, and adept at keeping your glass full of the fruity house drinks. A perfect place to bring a large group, Ruby Foo's is a fun and delicious experience—but beware of the chocolate layer cake, a colossal dessert that mocks any attempt to finish it off.

2182 Broadway (at 77th). 212.724.6700. Lunch daily 11:30am-5pm; Dinner Sun-W 5pm-11:30pm, Th-Sat 5pm-12:30am. Appetizers $6-13, Entrées $17-24. **1** *to 79th St.*

CASUAL
Gray's Papaya *Hot Dogs*
Low-brow Gray's and its cousin Papaya King both offer plenty of cheap hot dogs, papaya juice, and other heartburn-inducing fare. A hit with everyone from bankers slumming it during lunch hour to penniless students and out-of-work types, Gray's is a New York institution. Don't expect anything fancy, but you'll be surprised by the flavor that $1.25 can get you. If you need a quick bite, look no further.

2090 Broadway (at 72nd). 212.799.0243. Daily 24 hours. Menu items $1-7, cash only. **1 2 3** *to 72nd St.*

H&H Bagel *Bagels*
H&H's are *the* iconic, world-famous New York bagels; some swear by them, while others have moved on, although the multiple stores throughout Manhattan still command lines on weekend mornings.

The poppy and everything flavors go quickly, but the basic plain sourdough is also something special. It's not the most customer-driven experience; owners know they've got a captive audience, so folks have to buy in bulk, fix their own toppings, and put up with harried employees. If that's not your bag, call 1-800-NY-BAGEL to have mail orders delivered anywhere in the world.

2239 Broadway (at 80th). 212.595.8003. Menu items $1-5, Cash only. **1** *to 79th St.*

Nightlife
420 Bar and Lounge *College*
This swank member of the scene on Amsterdam Avenue, populated with the requisite professionals and well-heeled single malt sippers, could teach

Nice Matin

SoHo lounges a thing or two. The local scenesters who come here to save on cab fare won't mind throwing down the extra cash required for the pricey cocktails.

420 Amsterdam Avenue (at 79th). 212.579.8450. Sat-Sun 6pm-4am, M-F 5pm-4am. Drinks $4-10. **1** *to 79th St.*

The All State Cafe *Bar*

Once the Upper West Side's best singles bar, the All State is still a great place to grab a steak or a beer. The menu features hearty American offerings, the draughts run cool with several good ales, and the regular crowd is a mixed bag of young professionals and old-timers.

250 West 72nd Street (at West End). 212.874.1883. M-F 11:30am-4am, Sat-Sun 11am-4am. Drinks $6-11. **1 2 3** *to 72nd St.*

Blondies *Sports Bar*

Sports play continuously on mounted televisions above the heads of the bartenders, whose striking blonde coifs explain this boisterous sports bar's name. Try the "world-famous atomic wings," which we've never heard of, either.

212 West 79th Street (at Broadway). 212.362.4360. T-Th 11:30am-1am, Fri-Sat 11:30am-3am, Sun-M 11:30am-12am. Drinks $4-9. **1** *to 79th St.*

The Boat Basin Café *Food & Drink*

This open-air drink scene (with food thrown in) feels like a medieval courtyard; the sweet smell of barbecue drifts through the air as a clean-cut crowd in their 30s lounges on three separate levels under a Romanesque ceiling and thick stone pillars. Look out over the Hudson and the lights of New Jersey and enjoy tasty choices like smoked chicken and spinach salad with apples and toasted walnuts. Above all, dress to kill—this place is for groups looking for fun and singles looking for some action.

West 79th Street (at Riverside). 212.496.5542. M-F noon-11pm, Sat-Sun 11am-10pm. Drinks $6-8. **1** *to 79th St.*

Bourbon Street *Mardi Gras Bar*

Something for everyone: show up here to find athletic women dancing on the bar on Friday and Saturday nights, 50-cent beers on Thursdays, and a chill place to kick back early in the week. Neighbor-

hood sport teams love to frequent this dive bar and take in a few brews; make sure to try a potent frozen Hurricane or two.

407 Amsterdam Avenue (at 79th). 212.721.1332. Daily 12pm-4am. **1** *to 79th St.*

Dive Bar *Neighborhood*

Sure, it's got dive written all over it, but this SCUBA-themed haunt, owned by a local dive instructor, is actually quite tame. Even the resident pool sharks won't intimidate as you chug till 4am every day of the week.

732 Amsterdam Avenue (at 96th). 212.749-4358. Daily 11:30am-4am. Drinks $4-12. **1 2 3 B C** *to 96th St.*

Dublin House *Irish*

The straight-up Irish bar at Dublin House is a blessing to the Upper West Side nightlife scene. Its unpretentious atmosphere attracts the authentic old-timer and college student alike—even expat Irish come here for a whiskey or three on weekday nights.

225 West 79th Street (at Broadway). 212.874.9528. Cash Only. M-Sat 8am-4am, closed Sun. Drinks $3-4. **1** *to 79th St.*

The Gin Mill *Neighborhood*

Tasty shots with silly names abound at this casual hangout where there's never a shortage of Jaegermeister. It may not be a sports bar per se, but rest assured that you can always catch the Sunday game here and know you have a great place to chill, grab a bite, and drink.

442 Amsterdam Avenue (at 81st). 212.580.9080. Daily 11:30am-4am. Drinks $5-8. **1** *to 79th St.*

Jake's Dilemma *Dive Bar*

This bar steals attention from its competition along the Amsterdam bar strip in the West 80s—with three levels, a young, hip crowd, pool tables, and good looking bartenders, Jake's only dilemma is what drink to order next. Ladies' Night on Thursday features $1 margaritas for female patrons, and happy hour lasts until 8pm.

430 Amsterdam Avenue (at 80th). 212.580.0556. M-T 4pm-4am, F 3pm-4am, Sat-Sun midnight-4am, closed W-Th. Drinks $5-7. **1** *to 79th St.*

Lobby Lounge *Lounge*

Housed in the Mandarin Oriental Hotel, Lobby Lounge is not as stuffy as most Midtown hotel bars. But expect to pay top dollar for their signature cocktails, which include old classics and more creative offerings like a drink called "The Last Stand" which contains Red Bull, sake, Beefeater, and Smirnoff. However, its location is what sets this place apart—located 35 stories above street level, enclosed by glass walls, Lobby Lounge offers outstanding views of Central Park and Columbus Circle.

80 Columbus Circle (at 62ⁿᵈ). 212.805.8880. mandarinoriental.com. Daily 11am-12:30am. Cocktails $14-20. **1 A C B D** *to Columbus Circle.*

The P&G *Neighborhood*

You may know this old-school neighborhood bar from its cameo roles in Taxi Driver, Seinfeld, or Donnie Brasco, but it hasn't let fame go to its head. Around since the 1940s, the P&G is the real deal, filled with locals and old-timers drinking to tunes from the classic rock jukebox.

279 West 73ʳᵈ Street (at Amsterdam). 212.874.8568. **1 2 3** *to 72ⁿᵈ St.*

Prohibition *Neighborhood*

With live bands playing a blend of jazz and rock every night of the week, there's always something to see here from 10pm on. The upstairs section is great for private parties (with its own bar, a pool table, sofas, and tables), and the mini-cheeseburgers are some of the best pub-grub in town.

503 Columbus Avenue (at 84ᵗʰ). 212.579.3100. Daily 5pm-4am. Drinks $6-11. **1 B C** *to 86ᵗʰ St.*

Time Out *Sports*

This is the best bar on the UWS for true sports fanatics; know your stats and be ready to talk some serious trivia if you want to fit in. The crowd of cheering, jeering, 30-something men ignores the pool table in favor of the 23 televisions that will always be showing "the game." It's also the New York home base of the Celtic's soccer supporter club—be sure to know what you mean when asking about *football*.

349 Amsterdam Avenue (at 76ᵗʰ). 212.362.5400. **1** *to 79ᵗʰ St.*

Yogi's *Western*

This old-fashioned country saloon offers a stark contrast to the New Age eateries and standard pubs that line Broadway and Amsterdam in the 70s. Bras dangle behind the bar and the jukebox is stacked with hits by Creedence, Willie Nelson, Johnny Cash, and Dolly Parton. Enjoy $8 pitchers of Bud alongside shouting sports fans under a big American flag and a bear's head.

2156 Broadway (at 75ᵗʰ). 212.873.9852. Cash only.Daily 11:30am-4am. Drinks $2-6. **1 2 3** *to 72ⁿᵈ St.*

Arts

American Museum of Natural History

Following the classic American philosophy of "bigger is better," this is the world's largest museum of natural history; you could spend eons visiting the 45 exhibition halls, containing over 32 million artifacts and specimens. The most popular attractions include the famous dinosaur skeletons and the giant "Clash of the Titans" diorama (also known as "The Squid and the Whale," a partial inspiration for the 2005 movie of the same name), although the museum also offers less well-known displays on everything from human biology and evolution to African mammals. On Friday and Saturday nights, head over to the Rose Center for Earth and Space to see SonicVision, a digitally animated alternative music show co-produced by MTV2.

Central Park West at 79ᵗʰ. 212.769-5100. amnh.org. Open daily 10-5:45. Suggested donation $14 adults, $10.50 students. SonicVision: F-Sat 7:30 and 8:30, $15. **B C** *to 81ˢᵗ St.*

Avery Fisher Hall

Home to the famous New York Philharmonic, this is one of the city's two premier symphony halls (do you know how to get to the other one?), featuring a variety of performances each season. Almost all of the 2,738 seats feature plush upholstery and good sight lines—but with the best seats running an average of just under $100 per show, be prepared to pay for the most luxurious. Before you go inside, take a moment to marvel at the building itself and the fountain that sits in the plaza out front: lit up at night, the glass and concrete structure is a sight to see.

10 Lincoln Center Plaza (Broadway at 65th Street). 212.875.5900. lincolncenter.org **1** *to 66th St.*

Julliard

As one of the nation's premiere schools of music and performing arts, there's always something going on at Julliard; students and faculty give performances, many of which are free and open to the public, almost every day of the academic year. There's also an impressive library, home to over 70,000 scores—including the 138 autographed manuscripts and first editions of the Julliard Manuscript Collection—where the public can view materials by appointment. In springtime, the school's plaza erupts in flowering cherry and apple blossoms, perfect for a peaceful

American Museum of Natural History

respite from the city.

60 Lincoln Center Plaza (Broadway at 65th). 212.799-5000. juilliard.edu. **1** *to 66th.*

Lincoln Plaza Cinemas

Though the tiny screening rooms can be overcrowded with cinema snobs and film majors, and the screens aren't as big as at the nearby AMC, this charming theater presents a great selection of foreign and independent films. Buy some popcorn, a gourmet sandwich, or a coffee at the in-house café and settle in for something with subtitles.

1888 Broadway (at 62nd). 212.757.2280. Movies $10.50. **A C B D 1** *to Columbus Circle.*

Metropolitan Opera House

One of the world's premiere opera stages, this Lincoln Center theater is home to both the Metropolitan Opera and the American Ballet Theater. Initially built for millionaires, the opera house still retains plenty of old-money glitz—both performances and ticket prices are more traditional than at the nearby City Opera, but that's not necessarily a bad thing, and you'll get a thrill out of watching the Austrian crystal chandeliers rise to the ceiling before the curtain opens on each performance.

Lincoln Center (Broadway at 65th). 212.362.6000. metoperafamily.org **1** *to 66th.*

New York City Opera

Founded in 1944 with the mission of making opera financially accessible for New Yorkers (tickets start at $16, with discounts for those under 40) the New York City Opera is unique in its dedication to hosting innovative, contemporary repertory pieces. A cutting-edge aesthetic, designed to reinvigorate the public about this art form often relegated to an older audience, aims to convince young people that opera is indeed sexy (look out for their prominent advertising campaigns). As part of its mission to introduce the average person to this high-class performing art, the City Opera also hosts multiple series of lectures, panels, and talkbacks, intended to rid opera of its intimidation factor.

New York State Theater at Lincoln Center (Broadway at 65th St). 212.870.5570. nycopera.com. **1** *to 66th St.*

New York City Ballet

With over sixty ballets staged in the winter and spring seasons, and the largest repertoire of any American ballet company, the New York City Ballet is perfect for those who crave variety in dance. Most tickets cost about $80, but with some of the most talented names in ballet history behind the company, it's worth the price tag for the cultural bragging rights. Try to catch a performance of the famed *The Nutcracker*, choreographed by the eminent George Balanchine, performed each winter season.

New York State Theater (Lincoln Center, Broadway at 65th Street). 212.870.5570. nycopera.com. **1** *to 66th St.*

Symphony Space *Music*

Initially created as a small community theater dedicated to hosting local talent, this quirky venue that's often mentioned on NPR has come to host a variety of artistic programs from local and national artists alike. Events include film (the Repertory Film Series), literature (Selected Shorts, a series of short story readings), and music (Wall to Wall, an exploration of genre in music). Ticket prices vary, but they're generally reasonable, and student discounts are available.

2537 Broadway (at 95th). 212.864.5400. **1 2 3** *to 96th St.*

Shopping

Barney's CO-OP

The wayward offspring of upscale department store Barney's New York offers a trendy selection of clothing and accessories for a young, fashion-forward clientele—as the website says, "It's always downtown even when it's uptown." Students and yuppies can find hip clothing from up-and-coming brands like Nice or A.P.C., but don't let the store's lesser status fool you; prices are still comparable to the original store, and sometimes even more expensive.

2151 Broadway (at 76th). 646.335.0978. barneyscoop. com. M-F 10am-8pm, Th 10am-9pm, Sat 10am-7pm, Sun 11-6. **1** *to 79th St.*

Housing Works Thrift Shop

This sunny and clean thrift store, one of seven Housing Works locations in the city, sells clothing, electronics, and household goods to benefit the largest minority-controlled AIDS service organization in the nation. Get there early and be prepared to wait for dressing rooms—throngs of shoppers and donors know that this place is one of the best thrift stores in New York. The prices are higher than at the Salvation Army, but the quality of merchandise is, too, and designer finds are not uncommon.

306 Columbus Ave (at 74th). 212.579.7566. housingworks. org M-F 11am-7pm, Sat 10am-6pm, Sun noon-5pm. **1 2 3 B C** *to 72nd St.*

Lush

With its earthy, upscale-hippie vibe, this body-care shop specializes in handmade, organic, and non-animal tested bath and body products. There's an emphasis on whole, fresh ingredients free of chemicals, and product quality is high. The store is small but fun, with friendly employees making sure you find what you need, and offering free treatments as you shop.

2165 Broadway (at 76th). 212.787-5874. lush.com. M-Sat 10am-8pm, Sun 11am-7pm. **1** *to 79th.*

Olive and Bette's

With merchandise that is almost always dead-on the latest trend, this shop adheres closely to the fashion pack. Brands like Diesel, Seven, and Juicy attract a following of native New Yorkers who don't mind dropping extra bucks for casual quality.

252 Columbus (at 72nd). 212.579.2178. oliveandbettes. com. M-Sat 11am-8pm, Sun noon-6pm. Other locations: 1070 Madison Ave., 158 Spring St., 384 Bleecker St.

Westside Market *Gourmet Supermarket*

Hidden behind a somewhat unassuming storefront, Westside Market beckons patrons with an entrance full of fresh produce. As usual, extensive cheese and pre-made dinner selections make for a convenient meal, and while the desserts are less abundant than at some of Westside's other markets, the back of the store opens up to provide an incredible array of everyday grocery staples unique to the Upper West Side location. Providing an impressive menu of lunch and dinner options on its catering menu, Westside offers the best deal for any party.

2171 Broadway (at 77th). 212.595.2536. Daily 24 hours. 1 to 79th St.

Westsider Rare & Used Books

It's not the best place to find new releases—for that, go to the Barnes and Noble two blocks north—but if you're into old books and vinyl, Westsider is the place for you. For many customers, it's less about the books than the experience: a little, musty bookstore with that half intellectual/half arcane feel to it—small, disorganized, but full of charm.

2246 Broadway (at 80th). 212.362.0706. westsiderbooks.com. Open daily 10am-midnight. 1 to 79th.

Zabar's

This legendary "gourmet epicurean emporium" is a New York institution—as well as one of the best-smelling places in the city. The crowds coupled with the sheer amount of food and kitchen supplies in stock can make it difficult to navigate, but don't be deterred. Those who brave the bustle will be rewarded with a myriad of excellent fresh and freshly-prepared food, not to mention free samples. The second floor is filled with kitchen supplies and gadgets, the lox is purported to be the best in the city, and the prepared sandwiches get cheaper as the day goes on—stop by near closing for the best deal.

2245 Broadway (at 80th). 212.787.2000. zabars.com. M-F 8am-7:30pm, Sat 8am-8pm, Sun 9am-6pm. 1 to 79th St.

UPPER EAST SIDE

Woody Allen immortalized it, Tom Wolfe parodied it, *Sex and the City* reveled in it, and the tell-all book *The Nanny Diaries* scandalized it. The Upper East Side is the first and last word in old money, style and aristocracy.

Of course, an area as large as the Upper East Side could not be so homogenous; sprawling over nine avenues and almost 40 blocks, the neighborhood includes both palatial luxury apartments and cramped studios. A few blocks from Fifth Avenue lie the bars, burrito-joints, and high-rises that line Second, Third, and Lexington Avenues.

As with most of upper Manhattan, there wasn't much to see here until Central Park opened to the public in the 1860s. The eastern section of the region developed quickly as the Second and Third Avenue elevated lines, completed in 1879, eased transportation between the urban center and the outlying regions. The development that would earn the Upper East Side its elite reputation, however, was construction to the west along what would become the luxurious Fifth, Madison, and Park Avenues. From Astor to Tiffany, New York's wealthiest barons erected mansion after mansion facing the new park.

The Upper East Side today is a top cultural destination. Museum Mile, a section of Fifth Avenue home to nine museums, is here, in addition to the prestigious Frick Collection and Whitney Museum of American Art. The neighborhood's galleries are among the city's most esteemed, offering Picassos, Braques, and Chagalls to a public that can actually afford them. But don't let the gated community feeling intimidate you; the only thing you need to appreciate the artistic splendor of the Upper East Side is a pair of eyes.

THE UPPER EAST SIDE

SIGHTS/ATTRACTIONS
1. Carl Schurz Park
2. The Carlyle
3. Conservatory Water
4. Temple Emanu-El
5. Ukranian Institute

DINING
6. Café Boulud
7. Café D'Alsace
8. Candle 79
9. Daniel
10. DT UT
11. Gobo
12. Hacienda de Argentina
13. Ithaka
14. Kai
15. Park East
16. Sandro's
17. Saucy

NIGHTLIFE
18. Brother Jimmy's
19. Lexington Bar & Books
20. Loeb Boathouse
21. Mo's Caribbean Bar and Grill
22. Ship of Fools
23. Subway Inn

ARTS
24. Asia Society
25. Cooper Hewitt National Design Museum
26. The Jewish Museum
27. The Metropolitan Museum of Art
28. Mount Vernon Hotel Museum and Garden
29. Neue Galerie
30. The Guggenheim Museum
31. The Whitney

SHOPPING
32. Dylan's Candy Bar
33. Intermix
34. La Maison du Chocolat
35. Miu Miu
36. NV Perricone
37. Roger Vivier

Sights/Attractions

Carl Schurz Park

The oldest volunteer-run park in the city used to be the private garden for Gracie Mansion, located at the park's north end. Today, it is open to the public and has become a favored spot for locals to take a stroll. Brimming with lush vegetation and overflowing with families, joggers, tanners, and people watchers, the picturesque grounds are home to a playground and two dog runs. Relax on a park bench and enjoy the splendid view of the East River, Queens, and the Triborough and Queensboro bridges.

East 86th Street (at East End). 212.459.4455. carlschurzparknyc.org. Closes 1am. **4 5 6** *to 86th St.*

The Carlyle

With a regular clientele full of notables past and present, including several presidents who have resided in the exclusive suites, this Manhattan legend is a longtime landmark of New York glamour. Check out the entertainment calendar to see what celebrity is coming by to entertain tonight—the nightclub downstairs, Café Carlyle, has featured celebrated artists and performers from Bobby Short to Woody Allen. If you can't afford a ticket, stop by to poke around the elegant lobby.

35 East 76th Street (at Madison). 212.744.1600. thecarlyle.com. **6** *to 77th St.*

Conservatory Water

Radio-power boat racing takes place at the aptly named Model Boat Pond, a large ornamental pond modeled after those found in Paris. Come to sled down Pilgrim Hill in the winter, or enjoy the swells of Yoshino Cherries in the spring. Lucky bird watchers might spot the red-tailed hawks that reside in the area—a startling reminder that nature hasn't completely abandoned the urban landscape.

Central Park (east side from 72nd to 75th). centralparknyc.org. 6am-1am. **6** *to 68th St.*

Temple Emanu-El

With a membership of 10,000, this temple stands as the largest place of Jewish worship in the world. It was also the first Reform congregation in the city, established in 1845. Stop by to admire the huge limestone walls, adorned with beautiful Romanesque details, and the distinctive bronze doors displaying the symbols of the 12 tribes of Israel. Seating 2,500 in a high-ceilinged room, the expansiveness of the main sanctuary is humbling to believers and non-believers alike, with clerestory windows that filter the light and give the room an inspiring, spiritual glow. Go for a service, to learn about the temple's educational and volunteer programs, or to see the 500-piece Judaica collection.

1 East 65th Street (at Fifth). 212.744.1400. emanuelnyc.org. Daily 10am-5pm, services Sun-Th at 5:30pm, F at 5:15pm, Sat at 10:30am. N R W *to 5th Ave.*

Ukranian Institute of America

Housed in a resplendent turn-of-the-century French Renaissance-style mansion, this cultural center supports American awareness and appreciation of traditional and contemporary Ukrainian art. With the goal of strengthening the Ukrainian community's identity in America, the institute also hosts educational events, concerts, and exhibits.

2 East 79th Street (at Fifth). 212.288.8660. ukrainianinstitute.org. T-Sun noon-5pm, closed Monday. $5 (suggested). **6** *to 77th St.*

Dining
UPSCALE
Café Boulud *French*

The self-proclaimed "no-rules" menu at this French standout is divided into four sections, each of which reflect one of chef Daniel Boulud's diverse inspirations—World, Tradition, the Season, and the Market. Below each category is a list of dishes that draw their

❓ Scenic Stroll: Park Avenue, Carl Shurz Park

❓ Major Subway Stations: Lexington Ave-63rd St (F), 68th St – Hunter College (6), 86th St (4 5 6)

❓ Urban Oasis: Conservatory Water

❓ Kooky Corner: Dylan's Candy Bar

❓ Best View: The Metropolitan Museum of Art Roof Garden

❓ Neighborhood Landmarks: Gracie Mansion, Temple Emanu-El

❓ Notable Residents: Woody Allen, Richard Avedon, Naomi Campbell, Carrie Bradshaw, Jacqueline Kennedy, Ralph Lauren, Gwyneth Paltrow

❓ Neighborhood Trivia: During the 2004 Presidential campaigns, this area generated more money for both George W. Bush and John Kerry than any other neighborhood in the country.

❓ Schools: The Brearley School, The Chapin School, The Spence School

inspiration from the key word; a Tunisian lamb shank, for instance, falls under "World," while the raspberry napoleon goes under "Tradition." The gimmick might seem a little trying, but in the end, the quality of food makes up for it; order anything from foie gras *torchon* to a Macedonian shish kebab, and you're in for an excellent meal. The desserts, too, are enchanting; the clientele of Upper East Side regulars always remembers to save room.

20 East 76th Street (at Madison). 212.772.2600. Lunch T-Sat noon-2:30pm, Dinner M-Sat 5:45pm-11:00pm, Sun 5:45pm-10:00pm. Entrées $32-60, Appetizers $17-26. **6** *to 77th St.*

Daniel *French*

One of New York's finest and most exclusive restaurants, Daniel is the flagship location of acclaimed chef Daniel Boulud's trio of New York eateries (see Café Boulud, above). The haute French cuisine is served up in a beautiful setting—with prices to match. To up the chic factor, this restaurant is prix-fixe only, so be prepared to spend: one appetizer, one entrée, and one dessert for $96. The items on the menu rotate regularly, featuring seasonal ingredients prominently; if you need help deciding what to get for each course, the knowledgeable staff can help you navigate the often-intimidating menu. If you're not up for the splurge, you can order à la carte, but only in the lounge—the dining room is not for plebeians. For those who'd like to feel entitled for a day, though, the money is well worth it—a dining experience to remember forever.

60 East 65th Street (at Park). 212.288.0033. danielnyc.com. M-Th 5:45pm-11pm, F-Sat 5:30pm-

11pm, closed Sun. Prix Fixe $96, Appetizers $20-35, Entrées $35-48. **6** *to 68th St.*

Ithaka *Greek*

White walls and white columns, complemented by high ceilings and a cool red-stoned floor, make diners at this Greek restaurant feel more like they're on a remote isle than the Upper East Side. Only a soft murmur fills the space as elegant patrons sip *maleatis*, a dry white wine from Sparta, and enjoy traditional cuisine. The delectable *thalasino youvetsi*—shrimp, scallops, calamari, and mussels slow-cooked in a traditional clay pot, and served over orzo pasta, tomato sauce, and feta—covers a lot of Grecian ground in one dish. For a satisfying ending to any meal, sip on a cup of the full-flavored Greek coffee with a plate of *loukoumades*, deep-fried dough balls doused in cinnamon and honey.

308 East 86th Street (at Second). 212.628.9100. Lunch Sat-Sun 12:30-3; Dinner M-Sun 4:30-11. Appetizers $6-13, Entrées $17-32. **4 5 6** *to Spring St.*

Kai *Japanese*

Critics are right to place Kai alongside MASA and Nobu as one of New York's premier Japanese eateries. Perched above Madison Avenue's hottest teashop, dark woods and rustic stones radiate a sleek Zen vibe throughout the tiny dining room. True beauty, however, lies in the quality and presentation of each dish; from the magnificent sashimi, flown in fresh from Japan, to the tender and masterfully cooked Mishima Rib-Eye, it is clear that the chef here deals only in quality. If you join the dinner crowd, the 8-course prix fixe dinner ($85) is a relative bargain. For those on a modest budget, come at lunch for house specialties and the same attentive service.

822 Madison Avenue (at 68th). 212.988.7277. Lunch daily noon-2:30pm; Dinner daily 5:30pm-10:30pm. Closed M-Sun. Appetizers $10-15, Entrées $25-50. **6** *to 68th St.*

Park East *Kosher*

Yarmakules are par for the course at this kosher eatery, but that doesn't dissuade the goyim from hanging out at the bar or going early for the $20 prix fixe brunch with unlimited breakfast cocktails. Although the interior can be a little dull, the delicious steaks and fish are as tasty as their non-Kosher rivals. Try not to fill up on the irresistible hummus and pita chips, because the generously-portioned entrées of steak and fish are worth saving room for.

1564 Second Avenue (at 81st). 212.717.8400. Lunch M-Th noon-4pm, Dinner Sun-Th 4pm-10pm, F pre-paid Shabbat dinner, Brunch Sun 11am -3:30pm. Appetizers $8-13 Entrées $9-45. **6** *to 77th St.*

Sushi of Gari *Japanese/Sushi*

One of the top sushi restaurants in the city, this small hidden gem, tucked away on a side street, attracts everyone from Japanese businessmen in the know to celebrities looking for an outstanding, but still unpretentious meal. The simple, square pinewood tables that you'll sit at inside aren't very big, but they're able to hold the restaurant's trademark *omakase*—an assortment of 12 unique dishes, each exquisitely presented—an excellent way to sample what the chefs have to offer. Try the red snapper, with its unique, smoky flavor, or the chopped tuna and avocado appetizer, which, while not inventive, is superbly executed

402 East 78th Street (at York). 212.517.5340. T-Sat 5pm-10:45pm, Sun 5pm-9:45pm, closed Monday. Appetizers $4-$13, Entrées: $14-$45. **6** *to 77th St.*

Sandro's *Italian*

Simple equals elegant at this newly reopened Italian restaurant: Nothing hangs on the spotless white walls and there's no music playing in the background, so the food, from breadsticks to apple cake, receiving the whole of your attention. Unlike at many restaurants, the staff exhibits a genuine passion for the food; every dish is described vaguely but proudly as "à la Sandro." The delicate style they're referring to

YORKVILLE

Formerly known as the "German Broadway," this heavily German, Hungarian, and Ukrainian area, bounded by 72nd Street, 96th Street, Lexington Avenue, and the East River, is less consolidated—and less intense—than neighborhoods like Chinatown, although the ethnic influence is still a defining aspect of the community. For most of the 19th and 20th centuries, middle and working class people of European descent made their homes here; in the 1930s, pro and anti-Nazi Germany fights exploded on the streets. In recent years, gentrification has erased, or at least toned down, some of the distinct local flavor, although there are still some old-time haunts around today.

THE NEW YORK PSYCHOANALYTIC INSTITUTE (*247 East 82nd Street at Third*), the first psychoanalytic training institute in the United States, was founded in Yorkville by Freud enthusiasts in 1911. **THE FIRST HUNGARIAN REFORMED CHURCH** (*344 East 69th Street at Second*), built in 1916, is one of the oldest and most popular churches in the area, designed by the prominent Hungarian-born New York architect Emery Roth. At **YORKVILLE MEAT EMPORIUM** (*1560 Second Avenue at 81st*), the red-and-white checkered tablecloth, handmade sausages, and imported products from Eastern Europe make you feel as if you've stepped into a traditional Hungarian butcher shop.

For more boisterous displays of Germanic pride, go to the annual **VON STEUBEN DAY PARADE**, which marches through the area every September, or try out barn-dancing at the **HUNGARIAN HOUSE** (*213 East 82nd Street at Third*), which sponsors a number of Hungarian- and English-language events.

comes out in zesty spaghettini al limone worth returning for, and in meat dishes that live up to the enticing aromas that precede them. Don't expect a hip crowd—the small space is frequented by an older clientele who devotedly waited for Sandro's much anticipated return.

306 East 81st Street (at Second). 212.288.7374. M-Sat 4:30pm-2am, closed Sunday. Appetizers $12-15, Entrées $15-35. **6** *to 77th St.*

MID-RANGE

Angels Restaurant *Italian*

Don't let the location deceive you; this cozy restaurant is nothing like the *other* 60 Italian places you can find in a two-block radius. Small angels statues are perched in every nook, creating an intimate vibe without any stereotypical

romanticism. The warm homemade bread is outstanding, tempting you to fill up before you even order. An accommodating staff, generous portions, and affordable prices will ensure that you have an impressive meal without an impressive bill.

1135 First Avenue (at 63rd). 212.980.3131. M-Sat 10:30am-10pm, Sun 4-10pm. Appetizers $6-12, Entrees $7-20. **F** *to Lexington Ave/63rd St.*

Café D'Alsace *French (Alsace Region)*

Tucked into an unpretentious enclave in the upper reaches of the Upper East Side, Café D'Alsace merges the French and German flavors of authentic Alastian cuisine with more traditional brunch and dinner fare. A homemade pastry basket at the Sunday brunch features a myriad of French flavors, including croissants and chocolate pastries; snag a table on the patio for a classic brunch experience. The *choucroute garnie*, a sausage sampler laid atop a mountain of fresh sauerkraut, completes the other half of Alsatian dining. The restaurant is warmly lit to highlight a color scheme of champagnes and reds, and the main room contrasts nicely with an ornately decorated bar where regulars gush over the expansive beer list—with over 100 selections, the bar is sure to please even those with first-hand experience of Alsace-Lorraine.

1695 Second Avenue (at 88th). 212.722.5133. Lunch M-F 11am-4pm; Dinner M-Th 5pm-11pm, F-Sat 5pm-midnight; Brunch Sat-Sun 9am-4pm. Appetizers $7-12, Entrées $14-25. **4 5 6** *to 86th St.*

Candle 79 *Vegetarian*
A must-visit for every health-nut, Candle 79 is far and away one of the best vegan restaurants in the city. The restaurant works exclusively with natural, organic ingredients, but goes one step further than your average veggie joint by offering a sizeable gluten-free menu. If you're a vegan virgin, try the porcini-crusted seitan with garlic herb mashed potatoes or the ginger-miso stir-fry—both let you take baby steps into the cuisine, and crystal rolls with sesame miso dressing are guaranteed to please. The restaurant maintains its popularity by consistently serving up incredibly fresh produce at unusually affordable prices, especially given its normally-pricey location.

154 East 79th Street (at Lexington). 212.537.7179. Lunch M-Sat noon-3:30pm, Dinner M-Sat 5:30pm-10:30pm, Sun 5pm-10pm, Brunch Sun noon-4pm. Appetizers $3-9 Entrees $9-20. **6** *to 77th St.*

DT UT *Coffeehouse*
Those who've dreamed of hanging out at the Central Perk have their chance at this cozy and eclectic coffeehouse. With deep couches, low tables, internet, and delicious coffee and desserts, you can spend hours chatting with your airhead, beautiful, neurotic, nerdy, promiscuous, or awkward pals at this Upper East Side cafe. Widely considered the coolest coffee shop on the Upper East Side, it's also a low-key spot with features like do-it-yourself s'mores, and the "famous fondues" ordered at the bar. Stop by for happy hour from five to eight every week night—in addition to coffee and snacks, there's a limited selection of upscale wine and beer.

1626 Second Avenue (at 84th). 212.327.1327. Sun-Th 8am-midnight, F-Sat 8am-2am. Baked Goods $2-11, Sandwiches $5-8. **4 5 6** *to 86th St.*

Gobo *Eclectic Vegetarian*
There is vegetarian dining, and then there is Gobo. This organic, Pan-Asian restaurant rooted in what its owners call "Zen compassion" really does live up to its claim of offering "food for the five senses." This off-shoot of Zen Palate (another fabulous veggie joint) is has with aesthetically appealing wooden designs, an open kitchen, and a well-placed organic juice bar serving delicious smoothies. Chakra rolls are a must order, and smoked Beijing-style seitan with Chinese vegetables—just as flavorful as its duck counterpart—is as tasty as any meat dish out there. The expansive menu, although all veggie, has enough options that even non-vegetarians will be able to find something to delight.

1426 Third Avenue (at 80th), 212.288.5099. Daily noon-11pm. Appetizers $5-10 Entrées $9-18. **6** *to 77th St.*

Hacienda de Argentina *Argentinean*
The décor at this Argentinean spot approximates what you'd imagine to find in the dining room of a medieval lord: fireplaces, long wooden tables, even a suit of armor. The old-world accents don't cross over to the food, though; Hacienda offers a new take on some classic Argentinean themes. The warm homemade bread that starts the meal is worth indulging in, but portions are generous and the main dishes—such as the delicious empanada sampler with spicy mayo dipping sauce—are worth leaving room for. Two

types of filet, grass-fed Argentinean and USDA prime, are good choices, and they're well-complemented by Hacienda's fancier version of a mojito, the Limonata.

339 East 75th Street (at First). 212.472.5300. Sun-T 5pm-midnight, W-Sat 5pm-3am. Appetizers $8-10, Entrées $16-22. 6 to 77th St.

Saucy *New American*

This chic restaurant is ideal for the pickiest of eaters; nearly 50 different sauces make up the bulk of the menu, ranging from traditional choices like Italian pesto, to French apple brandy. After choosing your sauce, select among chicken breast, filet mignon, or various types of pasta to pair with it. Eating here can feel a bit like like a *Choose Your Adventure* situation—the most exciting and creative combinations on the page have the potential to overwhelm your palate. Fortunately, sauce and dish pairings are recommended on the menu, and it's wise to stick to these. The one-size-fits-all options and the intensely modern décor—designed to the ceiling with mirrors and spice bags—make this a great place to bring and impress trendy friends.

1409 York Avenue (at 75th). 212.249.3700. Daily noon-11pm. Appetizers $5-12, Entrées $16-24. 6 to 77th St.

Nightlife

Brother Jimmy's *Southern*

Anyone born south of the Mason-Dixon line will feel right at home at this laid-back bar, inspired by the glory that is down-home Southern culture. This original location of the New York mini-chain, one of five in Manhattan, is unapologetic in its admiration of all things country; their oft-quoted tagline that instructs patrons to "Put some South in yo' mouth" clearly indicates as much. Come for some home-style cooking in the early evening, but remember that sweet tea is always better when it's spiked—half the fun is kicking back with a drink or six as the diners file out and the drinkers file in. On Monday nights, hang out with the post-collegiate, pre-corporate crowd that flocks here for the weekly special: all-you-can-eat ribs and all-you-can-drink beer for $14.95.

1485 Second Avenue (at 77th). 212.288.0999. Noon-4am. Drinks $6-8. **6** *to 77th St.*

Lexington Bar and Books *Blue Blood*

With a clientele comprised mostly of "typical" Upper East Siders, this upscale bar and smoking room—cigars only, please—can sometimes feel like a secret society. To get in, customers have to ring the bell, wait to be approved for entry, and follow the strict dress code. Once inside, relax with a fine brandy and a good friend in stately, high-society elegance. Busboys wear tuxedos, waitresses wear red dresses and pearls, and the whole thing stinks so strongly of James Bond, they show his films behind the bar on a regular basis. The drink menu, which displays a rare affinity for bitters, is extraordinary, but the real draw are the cigars. As one of the few places in the city where smoking is still legal, this bar encourages you to indulge, preferably in a cigar purchased from their own selection—if you want to smoke anything that you've brought from home, be prepared to pay a nominal fee.

1020 Lexington Avenue (at 73rd). 212.717.3902. Cocktails $15. Sun-Th 5pm–3am, F-Sat 5pm–4am. **6** *to 68th St.*

Loeb Boathouse *Boathouse*

The only place to get a cocktail in Central Park is also one of the Upper East Side's most beautiful attractions. The outdoor tables at this Victorian-style landmark overlook the water of The Lake; pass an afternoon sipping a Manhattan as you watch paddleboats and gondolas float around the docks. Just don't expect to make a night of it—the dignified bar and restaurant close when the sun sets.

Central Park Lake (at 74th). 212.517.2233. M-Th 5:30pm-9:30pm, F-Sat 6pm-9:30pm. **B C** *to 72nd St.*

Mo's Caribbean Bar and Grill *Bar*

With twelve beers on tap and a monster fifty-ounce margarita on the drinks menu, it's clear that Mo's is no place for lightweights. The tropical décor outside lights up Second Avenue, and the inside is equally vibrant; large-screen televisions and video games keep the kids-at-heart happy, while neon-colored drinks look like they came straight out of a Jimmy Buffett song. Don't miss the pseudo-spring break parties, thrown all throughout the year.

1454 Second Avenue (at 76th). 212.650.0561. M-F 4pm-4am, Sat-Sun 11:30am-4am. Drinks $7-16. **6** *to 77th St.*

Ship of Fools *Bar and Grill*

With a large and boisterous local fan base, this laid-back bar offers neighborhood sports fans of all legal ages a safe haven from Upper East Side pretension. Forty-three TVs and thirteen big-screens (plus five different sound systems hidden in the wooden walls) create a blissful haven for the athletically-minded to grab a beer and watch the game. The bar broadcasts events and games from football to cricket, and the food is quite tasty to boot—go for wings and traditional bar fare, served up in an easy, relaxing environment.

1590 Second Avenue (at 82nd). 212.570.2651. M-W 3pm-4am, Fri-Sun noon-4am. Appetizers $6-10, Entrées $9-15. **4 5 6** *to 86th St.*

Arts

Asia Society Museum

Visit the museum at the headquarters of this global nonprofit educational organization, which aims to strengthen relationships and promote understanding between Asia and the U.S., to view its collection of art from over 30 Asian-Pacific countries. The pieces, most of which were donated by John D. Rockefeller III and date from 2000 B.C. to the 19th century, are clearly displayed amid the thin, minimalist screens of white silk that are used to separate and organize them.

725 Park Avenue (at 70th). 212.288.6400. asiasociety. org. T-Sun 11am-6pm, F 11am-9pm, closed Monday. Adults $10, Students $5. **6** *to 68th St.*

Cooper-Hewitt National Design Museum

As the home of over 250,000 objects, this branch of the Smithsonian has the largest design collection in the country. With its many exhibits and collections, the aim is to illuminate the indelible effects of design on our everyday lives—look for exhibits on wall coverings, textiles, drawings, graphic design, and even "staircase masterpieces." The cheerful outdoor terrace, which holds a rotating art exhibit, is always pleasant, and the funky (but expensive) gift shop sells untraditional objects like a fruit bowl made of mini fruit sculptures and a computer memory stick shaped like a log.

2 East 91st Street (at Fifth). 212.849.8400. cooperhewitt.org. M-Th 10am-5pm, F 10am-9pm, Sat 10am-6pm, Sun noon-6pm. Adults $12, Students $9. **4 5 6** *to 86th St.*

The Jewish Museum

One of the most distinguished Jewish museums in the U.S., this cultural institution displays video installations, ceremonial art, photography, sculpture, and even comics. Permanent exhibits of ancient artifacts illustrate the rich history of the Jewish people, while contemporary collections contain art that aims to explore the meaning of Jewish identity in today's global age.

1109 Fifth Ave (at 92nd). 212.423.3200. jewishmuseum.org. Sat-W 11am-5:45pm, Th 11am-8pm, closed Friday. Adults $12, Students $7.50, Free Saturday. **4 5 6** *to 86th St.*

The Metropolitan Museum of Art

Whether you're in New York City for a day or forever, you almost have no choice but to visit the Met at some point during your stay. This huge, stone, neoclassical building, holding one of the most important collections of any institution in

The Metropolitan Museum of Art

the world, is the most visited spot on Museum Mile—a museum so big and exciting, you could spend a whole week wandering its galleries. Works displayed run the entire range of human civilization, from drawings by Paleolithic humans made in 15,000 B.C., to photographs of post-Katrina New Orleans taken in 2006. The list of standout works is as long as it is storied, but make sure you find the Temple of Dendur (ca. 15 B.C.), given to the U.S. by the Egyptian government in 1965, and rebuilt on the edge of a peaceful body of water to replicate its original position on the Nile.

1000 Fifth Avenue (at 82nd). 212.535.7710. metmuseum.org. Sun-Th 9:30am-5:30pm, F-Sat 9:30am-9pm, closed Monday. Adults $20, Students $10 (suggested). **6** *to 77th St.*

Mount Vernon Hotel Museum and Garden

Take a step back in time at this one-time carriage house and the former home of the Mount Vernon Hotel, now a publicly accessible museum. This tiny stone building, often mistaken for a private home, was a country resort for the genteel and respectable in the 1820s and '30s—a wilderness destination in a time when 14th Street was the city's northern border. Today, eight rooms of the house are furnished to replica what the hotel looked like during its heyday. Enter through the quaint porch and garden, and then walk through the doors—the smell, music, and interior design will certainly take you back.

421 East 61st Street (at First). 212.838.6878. mvhm.org. T-Sun 11am-4pm, closed Monday. Adults $8, Students $7. N R W *to Lexington Ave/59th St.*

Neue Galerie

Inspired by its Viennese namesake, this stately Fifth Avenue landmark is the home of turn of the century German and Austrian fine and decorative arts from Bauhaus to Brücke. Just don't make it a family outing: no one under 12 is admitted, and those under 16 must be accompanied by an adult. The space itself can make you feel like you've trespassed on an old-

money family's fancy apartment: There's a small winding staircase and narrow, wooden halls. The hushed voices, strict museum rules, and the plethora of paintings, however, remind you that you're actually someplace much fancier. If you get hungry, head downstairs to Café Sabarsky, a Viennese café that offers strudel and Linzertorte at extravagant prices.

1048 Fifth Avenue (at 86th). 212.628.6200. neuegalerie.org. Sat-Th 11am-6pm, F 11am-9pm. Adults $15, Students $10. **4 5 6** *to 86th St.*

Solomon R. Guggenheim Museum

The infamous Frank Lloyd Wright spiral that houses the collection of this contemporary modern art museum sometimes overwhelms—and overshadows—the art that it displays. The core of the building consists of a continuing ramp, akin to the interior of a conch shell, that spirals upwards six times, forming six so-called "rotundas." Annexes on the side of the rotundas hold the permanent collections, consisting of 19th and 20th century paintings, while the walls of the spiral itself are home to special exhibitions. Come on the first Friday of each month to see the first level transform into a bar, complete with a DJ and dance floor, that brings 20- and 30-somethings together for "Art After Dark."

1071 Fifth Avenue (at 89th). 212.423.3500. guggenheim.org. Sat-W 10am-5:45pm, F 10am-7:45pm, closed Thursday. Adults $18, Students $15. **4 5 6** *to 86th St.*

The Whitney Museum of American Art

After the relatively mainstream art of the Metropolitan Museum, the vibrancy and eccentricity of the Whitney's art will shock you. Exhibits that launch full-scale assaults on your senses—some quite literally, with abrasive beeping noises or loud rock songs that blare from walls—fit right in at the esteemed, forward-thinking institution that has supported some of the most revolutionary artists of our time. A full seven floors are dedicated to 20th-century American art in a variety of mediums, including paintings, multimedia installations, and photographs, as well as the entire artistic estate of Edward Hopper. Don't miss the famous Whitney Biennial, a showcase of recently-created artwork that takes over the museum for three months every other year, often considered the best indication of what's hot in the art world at the current moment.

945 Madison Avenue (at 75th). 212.570.3676. whitney. org. W-Th 11am-6pm, F 1am-9pm, Sat-Sun 11am-6pm, closed M-T. Adults $15, Students $10. **6** *to 77th St.*

Shopping
Dylan's Candy Bar

Visiting this bright and colorful candy store is like fulfilling your childhood fantasy—it's just sweeter and more expensive than you imagined. No matter your age, you'll find something to satisfy your craving: giant lollipops, gummi bears divided into 10 individual flavor bins, and an indulgent ice cream shop entice all types of customers and palettes. It doesn't come cheap—sundaes are $10, and packaged candies are twice as expensive as they are at Duane Reade—but the selection is unparalled. As you descend into the basement level, which holds an expansive bulk section and dozens of specialty sweets, a warm message is written out in candies, placed in the illuminated glass of the stairs: "May each step you take be sweet."

1011 Third Avenue (at 60th). 646.735.0078. dylanscandybar.com. M-Th 10am-9pm, F-Sat 10am-11pm, Sun 11am-8pm. **N R W** *to 59th St./Lexington Ave.*

Intermix

This über-trendy boutique caters to a young, rich crowd and features a wide variety of American and European high fashion women's clothing. From up-and-coming brands like LaRok and Mint to well-established designers like Chloe or Michael Kors, Intermix truly mixes it up. Be prepared to brave loud, blasting music while dodging skinny women in designer jeans fighting for that last Diane Von Furstenberg dress—and

don't be surprised when you find out that cotton tee you've been eyeing is $200.

1003 Madison Avenue (at 77th). 212.249.7858. intermixonline.com. M-Sat 10am-7pm, Sun noon-6pm. **6** *to 77th St.*

La Maison du Chocolat

This small chocolatier has been handcrafting Parisian confections since 1977. Its French chefs—all chocolates are made at the headquarters in Paris—adhere to a strict standard of quality, and use only the best raw materials. In addition to standard milk and dark, the shop is known for its carefully crafted and unusual flavors; try mint or wild strawberry. The taste—and the price—will blow you away: expect to pay $5.50 for a square of delicious dark chocolate ganache.

1018 Madison Avenue (at 79th). 212.744.7117. lamaisonduchocolat.com. M-Sat 10am-7pm, Sun noon-6pm. **6** *to 77th St.*

Miu Miu

This Prada offspring is slightly more experimental than its parent, selling pieces that are funky but still distinguished. Shop here if you can afford designer names but crave something just a bit more eccentric—despite the occasionally unorthodox splotches of color, there is nothing juvenile about the designs. For a slightly more classic look, check out Prada, just two stores away.

831 Madison Avenue (at 70th). 212.249.9660, M-W and F-Sat 10am-6pm, Th 10am-7pm, closed Sunday. **6** *to 68th St.*

NV Perricone

It should come as no surprise that the only NV Perricone store in the entire world, complete with salesfolk in white lab coats, is located on the beauty-obsessed Upper East Side. Best-selling author Dr. Nicholas Perricone's skin-care line, otherwise available only through special order, is geared towards anti-aging; you can find the vitamins, diet, and skincare products required for his well-known "three-tiered system" here.

791 Madison Avenue (at 67th). 866.791.7911.

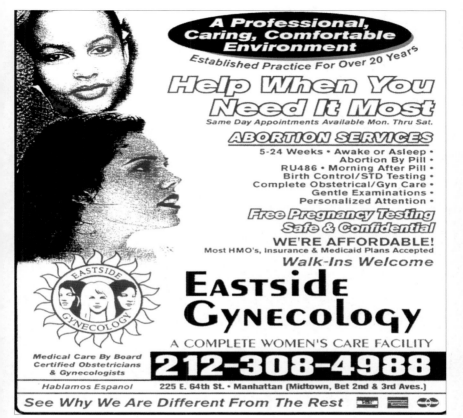
nvperriconemd.com. *M-W and F 10am-6pm, Th 10am-8pm, Sat 10am-5pm, closed Sunday.* **6** *to 68th St.*

Roger Vivier

This upscale boutique, the only outpost of Roger Vivier in the country, sells the designer's trademark line of patent leather shoes and handbags, plus a few more assorted items. The style of the goods—a glamorous, extravagant throwback to '60s French fashion—is as lavish as the store's interior: Modeled after the late Vivier's Parisian townhouse, the space is filled with African masks, authentic Picasso sketches, and a winding marble staircase. Although it's more exclusive than other up-market shoe companies, prices are comparable to Jimmy Choo or Manolo Blahnik; come here for a great pair of heels that you won't see on anyone else. *750 Madison Avenue (at 65th). 212.861.5371. rogervivier.com. M-Sat 10am-6pm, Sun noon-5pm.* **6** *to 68th St.*

MORNINGSIDE HEIGHTS

More than any other New York neighborhood, Morningside Heights is shaped by the academic institutions that call it home. While New York University manages to more or less blend in with its Village surroundings, the colleges that make their home in Morningside have an undeniable influence on the neighborhood, which stretches from 96th Street to 123th Street, bounded on the east and west by Morningside and Riverside Parks.

Throughout the school year, throngs of students from Columbia University, Barnard College, the Jewish Theological Seminary, Union Theological Seminary, Bank Street College of Education, and the Manhattan School of Music crowd the local bars and restaurants in between study sessions. With the summer comes a change of pace, although recently, more and more students have stuck around throughout the year.

The area remained a backwater through the turn of the 17th century, but the paving of area roads and the promise of subway accessibility encouraged development. In 1892, the Anglican Church began construction of the world's largest gothic cathedral, St. John the Divine, which remains unfinished to this day. After outgrowing Lower Manhattan, Columbia University moved into the neighborhood in 1897; their new campus, designed by famed architects McKim, Mead, and White, remains one of the area's most distinctive attractions to this day.

Morningside Heights is constantly in the throes of change. Currently, Columbia's proposed expansion into nearby Manhattanville, threatening to surpass the northern boundaries of Morningside Heights, is polarizing both sides of the school's walls, casting a spotlight on this otherwise quiet neighborhood.

FAST FACTS

⊘ **Scenic Stroll: Columbia University College Walk**

⊘ **Major Subway Stations: 96ᵗʰ St (1 2 3), 116ᵗʰ St-Columbia University (1)**

⊘ **Urban Oasis: Riverside Park, St. John the Divine Garden**

⊘ **Kooky Corner: Swing a Ring**

⊘ **Best View: Morningside Park, overlooking Harlem**

⊘ **Notable Buildings: Cathedral of St. John the Divine, Riverside Church**

⊘ **Neighborhood Landmarks: Grant's Tomb, Tom's Diner**

⊘ **Famous Historical Moment: Battle of Harlem Heights, September 16th, 1776**

⊘ **Community Issues: The expansion of Columbia University into Manhattanville**

⊘ **Schools: Bank Street College of Education, Barnard College, Columbia University, Jewish Theological Seminary, Manhattan School of Music, Union Theological Seminary**

Sights/Attractions

Cathedral Church of St. John the Divine

This largest Gothic cathedral in the world can accommodate a whopping 5,000 worshippers, and is so colossal, the Statue of Liberty could fit within its dark, thick walls. Work on the impressive building began in 1892, but "St. John the Unfinished" has been perpetually under construction ever since. The desperate lack of funding leads to some curious events—Elton John threw his 60ᵗʰ birthday party here last year. Make sure to check out the Great Rose Window above the main doors, which is the largest in the country, constructed with more than 10,000 pieces of glass. Afterwards, grab a sandwich on Amsterdam and sit in the adjacent garden; on a nice day, you might see one of the neighborhood peacocks roaming the grounds.

1047 Amsterdam Avenue (at 112ᵗʰ). 212.316.7490. stjohndivine.org. M-Sat 7-6, Sun 7-7. July and August: M-Sat 7-6, Sun 7-6. Public Tours: Tu-Sat 11, Sun 1. **1** *to 110ᵗʰ St.*

Columbia University

Stepping through the gates at 116th Street and Broadway onto Columbia University's Beaux-Arts campus feels like stepping into another world; domed buildings, sweeping columns and wide-open fields characterize this safeguarded academic haven, sitting aloof in the midst of gridlocked fenders. Although the school's origins date back to the mid-18th century, Columbia didn't move into its Morningside Heights campus—designed by famed architects McKim, Mead and White—until 1897. Come to sit on the steps of Low Memorial Library in warm weather, a favorite student pastime, or to enjoy the multitude of public sculpture, including a bronze casting of Rodin's The Thinker, located in front of Philosophy Hall.

2960 Broadway (at 116th). 212.854.1754. columbia. edu. **1** *to 116th St.*

Grant's Tomb

The largest mausoleum in America actually does contain the bodies of Ulysses S. Grant and his wife Julia, who are famously *entombed*, not buried, in the structure. Recent renovations for the site's centennial have made the structure and its surrounding park more impressive than ever; after years of neglect, the finally clean granite and marble mausoleum give a welcome historical luster to the area. The impressive architecture, modeled after the tomb of Mausolus at Halicarnassus, towers over the Hudson in Riverside Park; go on a Sunday to hang out on the grass and listen to the bells at Riverside Church.

Riverside Drive and West 122nd Street. 212.666.1640. grantstomb.org. Daily 9-5. Free. **1** *to 125th St.*

Morningside Park

You can thank Manhattan's natural geography for this 30-acre green space; in the 1860s, the naturally hilly land was deemed too steep for the roads that were initially planned for the area. The decision was probably a good one; sharp cliffs and dozens of staircases characterize the park today, whose land is generally thought to separate Morningside Heights from nearby Harlem. Wander along the winding and often secluded paths to find basketball courts, softball diamonds, picnic areas, and even a waterfall; just don't do it at night: The park and surrounding areas are notoriously dangerous after dark, although increased security has cause crime levels to drop in recent years.

West 116th at Morningside. 212.937.3883. morningsidepark.org. **B C** *to 110th St.*

Swing-A-Ring

Modeled after apparatuses used by California's strongmen in the 1930s, the swing-a-ring station in Riverside Park is a popular destination for kids, athletes, and those who wish they were kids or athletes. Consisting of a long line of hanging rings supported by beams, swinging around like a monkey from ring to ring is easy—as long as you know how to do it. Go on a nice day to watch experienced practitioners grab, swing, and flip through the air, or try it yourself—it's a great way to relieve stress, as long as you've got a good grip.

Riverside Park's Lower Level at 105th. **1** *to 103rd St. Free.*

Riverside Church

This church, built in the 13th century Gothic style, houses a carillon of 74 bronze bells—once

St. Paul's Chapel at Columbia University

the largest in the world—donated by John D. Rockefeller Jr. Hear them play every Sunday at 10:30am, 12:30pm, and 3pm, or climb the tower, which is often open, for spectacular views. If you're interested in attending a service, the interdenominational and interracial church is known for its long support of progressive causes and acceptance of all economic classes, cultures, ages, and sexual orientations.

91 Claremont Avenue (at 121st). 212.870.6700. theriversidechurchny.org. Daily 7am-10pm. Free. Feature Tours M-F 9-4. Adults $10. Free tours on Sundays, 12:15. 1 to 125th St.

Dining
UPSCALE
Terrace In The Sky *New American*
A plush dining room and panoramic city views set the scene at this lofty establishment, long recognized as the pinnacle of Morningside Heights cuisine. A harp player strums quietly in the background as the candle lights glow, creating an absurdly romantic setting. The food is packed with tumultuous flavors, kept in check by meticulously crafted presentation, that far outstrips any local competition. In the summer months, enjoy the open-air terrace for a Manhattan meal that is beautiful in every way.

400 West 119th Street (at Amsterdam). 212.666.9490. Brunch Sun 11am-3; Lunch T-F noon-2:30; Dinner T-Th 5:30-10, F-Sat 5:30-10:30; closed Monday. Appetizers $17-24, Entrées $30-42. 1 to 116th St.

MID-RANGE
Crepes on Columbus *French*
Exposed brick walls and ten small mahogany tables create an intimate atmosphere at this oft-overlooked neighborhood gem. The wide selection of delectable dinner and dessert crepes range from roasted chicken with mango red pepper sauce to nutella with mandarin orange; stop in early for a laid-back French brunch, or drop by in the afternoon for reasonably priced soups, salads, and sandwiches. Perhaps one of the

most underrated restaurants in Morningside, the friendly service, albeit slow, and unique cuisine certainly warrant a taste.

990 Columbus Avenue (at 109th). 212.222.0259. Daily 8am-10pm. Crepes $7.50-11, Salads and Sandwiches $5-10. 1 B C to 110th St.

Kitchenette *American*
Though it serves lunch and dinner daily, this uptown outpost of the Tribeca institution has the best brunch in town; expect to wait in line at least half an hour on weekends. From herbed omelettes overflowing with creamy goat cheese, to fluffy and eggy French toast, the offerings here are well worth a trek to 123rd. The homey, rustic atmosphere, with checkered tablecloths and soft drinks served in mason jars, only adds to the appeal.

1272 Amsterdam Avenue (at 123rd). 212.531.7600. M-F 8am-11pm, Sat-Sun 9am-11pm. Appetizers $3-$8, Entrées $8-$18. 1 to 125th St.

Max Soha *Italian*
This small, charming Southern-Italian joint attracts gaggles of broke Columbia students hungry for great food at reasonable prices. Though constantly crowded, the dull roar of over-educated blather adds to the cozy feel of the restaurant, complementing the exposed brick walls and sexily shabby décor. Large bowls of perfectly cooked, hand-made pastas slathered in any of their delicious sauces and toppings are sure to satisfy, and the specials, though always pricey, are usually a hit. Sit outside during the summer for a lovely view of Amsterdam.

1274 Amsterdam Avenue (at 123rd). 212.531.2221. Daily noon-midnight. Appetizers $4-9, Entrées $10-17. Cash only. 1 to 125th St.

Pisticci *Italian*
One of the area's best-kept culinary secrets, this rustic Italian eatery serves large dishes of hearty, delicious pasta at student-friendly prices. The food is simple but well prepared; everything, from the fresh, flavorful ingredients to the warm crusty bread baked in-house, makes every meal a treat.

Low lighting, a charming basement location, and tasteful, subdued décor make this the perfect restaurant for a first date that will impress—without breaking the bank.

125 La Salle Street (at Broadway). 212.932.3500. Daily 11am-11pm. Appetizers $5-10, Entrées $7-15. **1** *to 125th St.*

CASUAL

Artopolis *Dessert*

With flat-screened televisions silently broadcasting footage of the Aegean sea, this dessert café brings a Hellenic touch to Amsterdam Avenue. The dessert menu includes gelatos, crepes, espressos, and a gorgeous array of mouthwatering homemade pastries, all laid out in a glittering display case. The stracciatella gelato, a white chocolate cream base with crunchy bits of dark chocolate, is a standout, and the fruit tarts are divine.

1090 Amsterdam Avenue (at 114th). 212.666.3744. M-F 8am-11pm, Sat-Sun 10am-11pm. Desserts $2-8.50, Drinks $1.40-$5.50. **1** *to 116th St.*

Columbia Cottage *Chinese*

Typically crowded with groups of Columbia students who come here more for the free wine than the food (one carafe with every entrée), this drinker's paradise is still probably the best bet for Chinese food in the neighborhood. Though the cuisine here may not be the most authentic, there are a few gems if you know where to look. Try the Shanghai dumpling, bursting with broth and flavor, or the hearty Mandarin noodle soups.

1034 Amsterdam Avenue (at 111th). 212.662.1800. Sun-Th 11:30am-11:15pm, F-Sa 11:30am-11:30pm. Appetizers $2-8, Entrées $8-20. **1** *to 110th St.*

The Hungarian Pastry Shop *Dessert*

This pastry shop's cameo in Woody Allen's 1992 film Husbands and Wives cemented its status as a Morningside Heights institution. Now, the Hungarian attracts an intense crowd of precocious undergrads, grad students, and film majors, talking Baudrillard and Faulkner over cup after cup of strong, unlimited black coffee. The service lacks in friendliness, but no one comes here for the service; any place that lets you sit for hours at a cramped table in a poorly lit interior to read a book, talk to a friend, or just soak up the intellectual vibe is sure to become a Columbia mainstay.

1030 Amsterdam Avenue (at 111th). 212.866.4230. M-F 8am-11:30pm, Sat 8:30am-11:30pm, Sun 8:30am-10:30pm. **1** *to 110th St.*

Local Flavor *Mexican*

With the exception of the flavorful steak-filled offerings, the burritos aren't the best at this tiny, walk-up grab-and-go—but the mission beats Chipotle's hands down. Operated out of the Broadway Presbyterian Church, this Morningside newcomer employs exclusively local homeless people—plus a few supervising volunteers—who gain much-needed income and valuable work experience as they serve up the most heartwarming food in town. Skip the ill-advised barbecue chicken in favor of a bean and cheese for the unheard of price of $3—then tell your friends. The servers are upbeat and friendly, the portions are hearty, and the gratification of supporting the community is an ingredient you won't find on any other menu.

601 West 114th Street (at Broadway). 212.864.6100 ext. 129. T, Th, and Sat 11-7, closed M, W, F, and Sun. Burritos $3-$6. **1** *to 116th St.*

Nussbaum & Wu *Deli*

Watch out for crowds during breakfast, as fresh bagels and spreads make this deli/pastry shop combo one of the most popular early morning eateries in the neighborhood. The make-your-own salad is a featured attraction, and the Asian Sesame ginger dressing alone is worth the wait in line.

2897 Broadway (at 113th). 212.2805344. Breakfast $2-8 Sandwiches $5-9. **1** *to 110th St.*

Silver Moon Bakery *Bakery*

Every bread, cake, and cookie at this

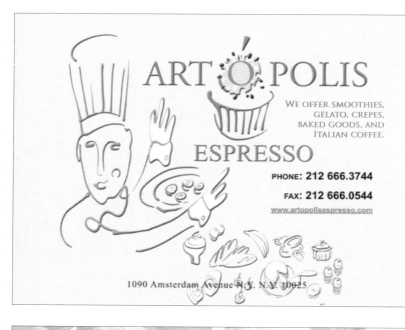

Columbia Ophthalmology Consultants, Inc.

The full-time faculty practice of the Department of Ophthalmology at Columbia University Medical Center. We are a group of consulting ophthalmologists trained and board certified in all subspecialties including:

General Ophthalmology, LASIK, Adult & Pediatric Glaucoma, Vitreoretinal and Macular Diseases, Cataract Surgery, and Pediatric Ophthalmology.

All are dedicated to offering outstanding clinical care.

We participate in many insurance plans and have several practice locations for your convenience.

212-305-9535
www.columbiaeye.org

COLUMBIA UNIVERSITY CATERING

WE CATER BREAKFAST, LUNCH, DINNER, & BARBEQUE. SPECIAL STUDENT MENUS AVAILABLE

212.854.4630
catering@columbia.edu
www.columbia.edu/cu/catering

COME DINE AT
COLUMBIA UNIVERSITY FACULTY HOUSE

ALSO AVAILABLE FOR MEETINGS, CONFERENCES, WEDDINGS, AND OTHER EVENTS.

212.854.7102 FOR INFORMATION, BOOKING, & MENUS
400 WEST 117TH STREET
MAIL CODE 2301
NEW YORK, NY 10027

CU IT

COLUMBIA UNIVERSITY
INFORMATION TECHNOLOGY

http://askcuit.columbia.edu

» email
askcuit@columbia.edu

» by phone
212.854.1919

» in person
102 Philosphy Hall

PRINT SERVICES

THE SERVICES YOU NEED... **FAST!**

DESIGN
Graphic design
Consultation
Scanning
Typesetting

OFFSET PRINTING
Prepress expertise
1 and full color printing

PRODUCTION
Full and self-service copying
Color and black & white copies
Poster and banner printing
Sheet-fed scanning

BINDERY
Binding
Foam-core mounting
Laminating

BULK MAIL
Addressing
Postage metering
Fulfillment

OFFICE COPIERS
Copier leasing and purchasing
Maintenance contracts

Ask About Our Wide Format Posters and Banners

Morningside Locations
SCHOOL OF JOURNALISM BUILDING
2950 Broadway, Room 106
Tel: 212-854-3233
Fax: 212-854-4421

INTERNATIONAL AFFAIRS BUILDING
420 West 118th Street, Room 401
Tel: 212-854-4300
Fax: 212-864-2728

Medical Center Location
PHYSICIANS & SURGEONS BUILDING
630 West 168th Street, Room 2-466
Tel: 212-305-3614
Fax: 212-342-2925

COLUMBIA UNIVERSITY

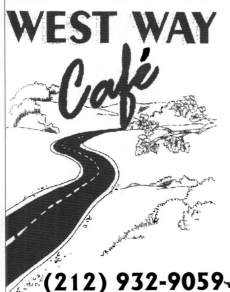

neighborhood favorite is baked right on the premises; in the mornings, locals devotedly line-up for delicious croissants, warm and just out of the oven. A carb-lovers paradise, display cases overflow with everything from Gruyere Cheese bread to Ethiopian bread, all as tasty as they look. Sadly, the bustle and minimal seating mean that it's not possible to linger; grab your bread and go, except for in the summer months, when several outdoor tables are added.

2740 Broadway (at 105th). 212.866.4717. M-F 7:30am-8pm, Sat-Sun 8:30am-7pm. 1 to 103rd St.

Tom's *Diner*

Seinfeld fans regularly stop to take pictures in front of this local legend, featured in the show as the exterior of Monk's, the gang's perennial hangout. Area residents simply know it as one of Morningside's only 24-hour diners—at least on weekends. Serving large, frosty shakes and steaming piles of cheese fries, Tom's is a frequent late-night pit stop for those returning from a night on the town, and a favored breakfast spot to take visiting relatives. It's not the best food around, but if you live in the area, you can't avoid going at least once.

2880 Broadway (at 112th). 212.864.6137. Appetizers $2-5, Entrées $6-12, cash only. 1 to 110th St.

Nightlife

1020 *Bar*

During the week, you can come to 1020 with a good friend to throw a few back in peace, but expect a bustling atmosphere on Thursday through Saturday, when you're likely to run into a collegiate crowd trying their luck at dating, darts, and pool. Come early if you want to play—the pool table in the back can get crowded quickly, and there are always locals who love to hog the dart board. The drinks are weak, but if you live in the area, odds are good that all your friends are here; a few rounds in, you're bound not to mind.

1020 Amsterdam Avenue (at 110th). 212.531.3468. Daily 4pm-4am. Drinks $2-6. **1** *to 110th St.*

The Abbey *Pub*

Both the food and the atmosphere are designed to comfort at this ideal neighborhood bar where older locals can co-exist—and even mingle—with a collegiate (and younger) crowd. It's a perfect spot to meet for beers and a shared basket of fish 'n chips, and a good place to bring a pack of friends on game day.

237 West 105th Street (at Broadway). 212.222.8713. Daily 4pm-4am. Drinks $5-12. **1** *to 103rd St.*

Havana Central at the West End *Cuban*

Floods of nostalgia hit Columbia's upperclassmen as they pass the orange awning of this new Cuban restaurant and bar, a sad reminder of what once was. During the good ol' days, first years and seniors alike piled in for cheap refreshment and a little history—the tradition of Beat poetry ran deep at the original West End, which once counted Jack Kerouac and Alan Ginsburg among frequent drinkers. Today, overpriced drinks and lame attempts at collegiate traditions like beer pong have turned a thriving establishment into a ghost town. Nonetheless, it's worth a visit, if only to pay homage to the last remaining relics of the former West End. Order some tapas and drown your sorrows with a massive mojito; as you wait for them to come, pray for the resurrection.

2911 Broadway (at 113th). 212.662.8830. Restaurant M-Sat 11am-11pm, Sun 11am-10pm; Bar W-Sat 11am-4am. Appetizers $2.50-7, Entrées $6-16, Drinks $6-16. **1** *to 116th St.*

The Heights Bar and Grill *Food and Drink*

During the day and the early part of the evening, this is a decent spot to head for a laid-back dinner; ask to sit on the popular upstairs deck, complete with retractable roof

cover. It's greatest use, though, is as a nighttime drinking spot for the local college scene. The margaritas are famous in the area for being good, strong, and cheap—$3 durng one of the evening's two Happy Hours (5pm-7pm and 11pm-1am). There's also an ample selection of microbrews on tap, and mixed drinks are of consistently high quality, but be careful coming here if you're underage—as a popular spot for Columbia sports teams and their new recruits, it's reputed to be the most raided bar in Morningside.

2867 Broadway (at 111th). 212.866.7035. Daily 11am-2:30am. Drinks $4-10. **1** *to 110th St.*

Koronet's *Pizza*

There is an age-old debate about the importance of size, with some arguing that it matters, and others focusing on compensating attributes. Dr. Emilius Koronet's opinions on the subject are clear: The huge slices served here will fill you up for hours, and at just $3, it's a tough deal to beat. When 3:30am rolls around and your stomach starts complaining, don't bother asking it what it wants; just stuff it into submission with a jumbo slice.

2848 Broadway (at 110th). 212.222.1566. M-W 10am-2am, Th-Sun 10am-4am. Jumbo Slice $3. **1** *to 110th St.*

Tap-a-Keg *Beer hall*

This neighborhood joint offers cheap beer and a low-key atmosphere; come with friends on any night of the week that you're not looking beer, not excitement. With a pool table, video games, a dartboard, a friendly and engaging staff, and most importantly, an extensive selection of quality beers, this could easily become your new favorite place to hang out uptown.

2731 Broadway (at 104th). 212.749.1734. Daily noon-4am. Drinks $5-6. **1** *to 103rd St.*

Smoke *Jazz, Lounge*

Sleek and simple—no bells or whistles here—

this well-regarded jazz club doesn't look like much more than a dive bar from the street. Get inside, though, and you'll find red velvet couches, black chairs, small tables, and jazz enthusiasts from all over the city. The lackluster cocktail list is fortunately eclipsed by the ample selection of wines by the glass, and the decent food is better than what you'd find at most similar lounges. The main attraction, though, remains the music; the singers are hot, the band is cool, and the combination of perfect acoustics and a small performance space provides both intimacy and symphony.

2751 Broadway (at 106th). 212.864.6662. Daily 5pm-2am. Appetizers $8-16, Entrees $16-39. **1** *to 103rd St.*

Arts

Manhattan School of Music

Founded in 1917 and located here since 1969, this elite conservatory has nearly 275 faculty members and 800 talented students, with notable alumni including Herbie Hancock, Harry Connick, Jr., and Regina Spektor. Promising youngsters who aren't afraid of a little competition can try out for the exclusive Precollege Division, while the less musically gifted can enjoy the usually free events in the John C. Borden Auditorium throughout the school year.

120 Claremont Avenue (at 122nd). 212.870.4100. msmnyc.edu. **1** *to 116th St.*

Miller Theater

This performance space on the campus of Columbia University hosts a variety of jazz, dance, opera, and gala events. Don't miss composer spotlight concerts, which highlight a range of international masters from the old (Edgard Varese) to the new (Frank Zappa). While ticket prices can be steep, those under 25 can get 40% discounts, while Columbia students can reserve their seats for a mere $7.

2960 Broadway (at 116th). 212.854.7799. *millertheater.com. Ticket prices and hours vary.* **1** *to 116th.*

Nicholas Roerich Museum

When Manhattan's griminess and materialism get you down, come to this small, cool museum, filled with exotic visions of faraway lands. The works, done by the museum's namesake, meditate on the difficulties of searching for peace and learning to develop spiritually. Roerich traveled extensively through India and Tibet looking for spiritual guidance, and left behind a legacy of exquisitely detailed paintings inspired by his travels. His strangely compelling pieces have an impressive technical range, from realistic to impressionistic to surreal, and are worth soaking in.

319 West 107th Street (at West End). 212.864.7752. T-Sun 2-5PM. Suggested donation. **1** *to 110th St.*

Shopping

Jas Mart

This Japanese convenience store has a plainer, more utilitarian front than nearby Asian food mart M2M, but its range of products, from snack foods to household goods to Japanese-print newspapers, is simply remarkable. Cheap prices enable hungry students to stock up on colorful, boldly designed packages of ramen, rice crackers, and candy; those with a more refined palate will appreciate the selection of reasonably priced delicacies. There's also a wide variety of unique Japanese kitchen goods; pick up a sushi-making kit and forget about that leftover pasta you have in the fridge.

2847 Broadway (at 110th). 212.866.4780. Daily, 10-10. **1** *to 110th St.*

Labyrinth Books

This community-based independent bookstore specializes in academic and high-brow humanities literature, providing local university professors with an alternative to the over-commercialized Columbia University

Bookstore. If you venture upstairs, don't hesitate to ask an employee for help—the layout is constantly changing, and the signage often doesn't match up with the books on the shelves. The store is also well known for its selection of inexpensive, boldly colored canvas totes; color schemes change each season, so you can always tell the freshmen from the color of their bags.

536 West 112th Street (at Broadway). 212.865.1588. labyrinthbooks.com. M-F 9-10, Sat 10-8, Sun 11-7. 1 to 110th St.

Morningside Bookshop

This small space on Broadway has housed a community bookshop for more than fifty years. The current incarnation stocks both new and used books, hosts monthly events, and has a friendly atmosphere, where locals and students converge.

2915 Broadway (at 114th). 212.222.3350. M-F 10-10, Sat-Sun 11-9. 1 to 116th St.

West Side Market *Gourmet Supermarket*

An oasis of wonderfully fresh and organic produce at affordable prices, this gourmet paradise is pleasantly modern and uncommonly spacious for a market in New York City. Whether you're hungry, bored, or unsure what to prepare for dinner, Westside Market offers a veritable cornucopia of delicious possibilities. Even if you don't have anything specific in mind to buy, the quality food and extensive variety ensure that you'll never leave empty handed. The market also offers innovative catering service, delivering delicious meals to whatever occasion you might be hosting.

2840 Broadway (at 110th). 212.222.3367. Daily 24 hours. 1 to 110th St.

Yarntopia

This newly-opened shop sells imported yarns of all colors and textures, as well as glow in the dark needles and how-to books. Downstairs, a 70s-themed room with bright purple walls and a neon orange couch serves as a knitting "lounge" for knitting and crocheting classes. Also available is custom-made clothing, hand-knit by the owner—though it may cost you upwards of $300 per piece.

974 Amsterdam Avenue (at 108th). 212.316.YARN. yarntopianyc.com. Tu, Th 12-9, W, F-Sun 12-7, closed Monday. 1 to 110th St.

Broadway in Morningside Heights

HARLEM

Harlem's famous 1920s Renaissance may have faded into the romance of history and cultural memory, but the last decade has seen a revitalization of the area's housing, business, and cultural capital. Long regarded as the top city destination for authentic soul food, now Harlem is popular for high-fashion clothing boutiques and innovative arts venues as well.

Since the Dutch settled the area in the mid-17th century, Harlem's borders and population have shifted more than once. Racial strife and a handful of race riots drove many African Americans from lower Manhattan up to Harlem in the early 20th century, while more transplants came from the American South, fostering a rich artistic, musical, and literary environment that nourished greats such as Langston Hughes, Zora Neale Hurston, Duke Ellington, Bessie Smith, and Jean Toomer.

At the same time, the area east of Fifth Avenue was becoming a destination point for Puerto Rican immigrants, calling themselves "Nuyoricans," who coined the name "el Barrio" for East Harlem. Though many Puerto Ricans and Dominicans began migrating to the Bronx when the neighborhood became too crowded, El Barrio remains the epicenter of Latino culture in the city today.

Safer streets, new restaurants, and the restoration of many buildings have proven positive byproducts of a recent boom, but the impact of further gentrification has yet to be seen. Some fear that rising rents and an influx of chain stores may force long-time residents and their businesses out of West and Central Harlem. East Harlem is still largely an inner-city neighborhood, but developers have been eyeing this area as well; on blocks anchored by housing projects, new galleries and condos are emerging at a slow, but steady pace.

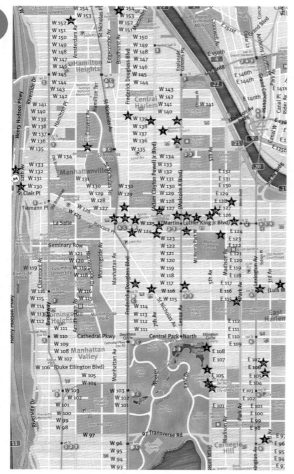

© Opus Publishing 2007 — www.OpusPublishing.com

HARLEM

SIGHTS/ATTRACTIONS
1. Abyssinian Baptist Church
2. The Apollo Theatre
3. Conservatory Garden
4. Harlem Meer
5. Islamic Cltural Center of New York
6. The Langston Hughs House
7. Little Mexico
8. Marcus Garvey Memorial Park
9. Rucker Park
10. Schomburg Center for Research in Black Culture
11. Striver's Row

DINING
12. Dinosaur BBQ
13. Londel's
14. Make My Cake
15. Mannais
16. Miss Maude's Spoonbread Too
17. MoBay
18. Revival
19. Sylvia's
20. Tribal Spears Gallery and Café

NIGHTLIFE
21. Cotton Club
22. Harlem Lanes
23. Lenox Lounge

ARTS
24. Showman's
25. ColaLex Gallery
26. Dance Theatre of Harlem
27. El Museo del Barrio
28. Harlem Stage at the Gatehouse
29. Julia de Burgos Latino Cultural Center
30. Museum of the City of New York
31. The National Black Theatre
32. The Studio Museum in Harlem

SHOPPING
33. 125th Street
34. Atmos
35. Brownstone
36. Casa Latina
37. Hue-Man Bookstore & Café
38. Kaarta Imports, African Fabrics
39. La Marqueta
40. Malcolm Shabazz Harlem Market

Sights/Attractions

Abyssinian Baptist Church

One of the most famous African American churches in the country, this long-time community leader is truly the soul of Harlem. Two key figures in the civil rights movement, Adam Clayton Powell, Sr. and his son, Powell, Jr., were pastors here, helping to place the church at the forefront of the fight for black rights and racial equality. Come to a Sunday morning service to hear the Sanctuary Choir accompanied by music from the five-manual 67 rank organ; when the congregation, filled with women in graceful church hats and men in pressed suits, joins them in song, the music is so rousing you can't help but feel the spirit.

132 West 138th Street (at Malcolm X). 212.862.7474. abyssinian.org. Service Sunday 9am-11am. **2 3** *to 135th St.*

The Apollo Theater

Originally founded in 1914 as a burlesque club that excluded African Americans, in the 1930s this legendary theater turned into a prized black cultural venue and symbol of the Harlem Renaissance, with Ralph Cooper, Sr. hosting a live version of his radio show, *Amateur Night at the Apollo*. Stars like Ella Fitzgerald, Billie Holiday, and Luther Vandross were discovered during this series, which still runs on Wednesday nights.

253 West 125th Street (at Frederick Douglass). 212.531.5300. apollotheater.org. Amateur Night W 7:30pm. Tickets $18-39. **A C B D** *to 125th St.*

Conservatory Garden

Central Park's only formal, landscaped garden—a six-acre gem, offering quiet nooks for reading and relaxing—contains a series of individual plots designed in English, French, and Italian styles. For a setting that feels straight out of a fairy tale, follow one of the winding paths to the "secret garden" in the South English section; in the center sits a trickling bronze sculpture fountain dedicated to

the children's writer Frances Hodgson Burnett, depicting characters Dickon and Mary from her most famous work.

Fifth Avenue (at 105th). 8am-dusk. centralparknyc.org. **2 3** *to Central Park North/110th St.*

Harlem Meer

The grassy area surrounding the lovely man-made pond in Central Park's far northeast corner is an important community space for the residents of East Harlem. Amid fishing men and children chasing ducks, it's easy to feel like you're in the countryside; closer to the street, you can watch pedestrians and cars streaming down bustling 110th Street. Don't miss nearby Central Park attractions like the Conservatory Garden, Lasker Ice Skating Rink and Pool, and the Dana Discovery Center, all located along the edge of the meer.

East Side, 106th-110th Street. centralparknyc.org. **2 3** *to Central Park North/110th St.*

Islamic Cultural Center of New York

The largest in New York City, this mosque and its courtyard occupies a whole city block, built at an angle off Third Avenue. As required by Islamic law, the altar inside the niche faces Mecca; as such, it doesn't fit into Manhattan's grid system—misbelieved to be directly north-south—but is built at an angle from the street.

1711 Third Avenue (at 96th). 212.722.5234. muslimsonline.com. Daily 9-5. **6** *to 96th St.*

The Langston Hughes House

Now a National Historic Landmark, this 138-year-old brownstone, whose third-floor back room was once occupied by the famous poet, aims to keep the spirit of the Harlem Renaissance alive by hosting open-mic nights, performances by Def Jam poet La Bruja, jazz shows and festivals, and speakers in the renovated downstairs parlor. In addition to being an evening destination for art-lovers from all over the city, the house is also establishing itself as a community center, supporting a teenage jazz ensemble that performs every

Sunday and an arts summer camp for Harlem youth.

20 East 127th Street (at Madison). 212.927.3413. langstonhugheshouse.com. Visit website for events calendar. 6 to 125th St.

Little Mexico

Although Puerto Rican immigrants have historically been the greatest ethnic presence in East Harlem, Mexican flags hang from the telephone poles and Mexican pride surges from every storefront on this block of East 116th Street. Pick up a taco or a quesadilla from one of the many vendors lining the street, then go check out the eccentric Casa el Rodeo, which only sells soccer uniforms and cowboy boots. A Mexican food stand occupies the front part of the store; sit on a stool by the counter to soak in the sights and sounds of the neighborhood.

116th Street between Second and Third. 6 to 116th St.

Marcus Garvey Memorial Park

In a bit of dubious public planning that has never been fully explained, this park was originally built on "Snake Hill," so named for its large population of...you know...snakes. Fortunately, the reptiles are now extinct, and have been replaced by a lively local population who comes to enjoy the pool, baseball field, playgrounds, and plenty of green space perfect for picnics. Take one of the winding paths to the top, and look out onto expansive views of Harlem and the West Side, but recruit a friend to accompany you—while the quiet paths and grassy nooks are charming, it's not the safest park in the city.

124th Street between Fifth Avenue and Mt. Morris Park West. nycgov.parks. 4 5 6 to 125th St.

Rucker Park

The playground of this park, named for a high school English teacher who ran a local streetball league here in the '50s and early '60s, is one of the most famous streetball courts in the country—many NBA legends honed their skills here, including Kareem Abdul-Jabbar and Julius Erving. A recent documentary, *The Real: Rucker Park Legends*,

examined the history of the park and its role as an inner-city superstar training ground. If you visit during the summer, you may even catch some current NBA players in action—Kobe Bryant and Allen Iverson are just two of the players who have participated in summer streetball tournaments at the park.

155th Street and Frederick Douglass Boulevard. B D to 155th St.

Schomburg Center for Research in Black Culture

This newly-renovated research facility, originally a branch of the New York Public Library, contains thousands of black periodicals, rare books, sheet music, video, recordings, and manuscripts, including the original manuscript of Richard Wright's *Native Son*. The center also displays many of its more than 20,000 paintings, sculpture, and textiles from Africa and the African Diaspora, and hosts frequent seminars, film screenings, and performances in the Langston Hughes Auditorium.

515 Malcolm X Boulevard (at 136th). 212.491.2200. nypl.org/research/sc. Library T-Sat 10am-6pm, closed Sun-M; Gallery T-Sat 10am-6pm, Sun 1pm-5pm, closed Monday. 2 3 to 135th St.

Striver's Row

When the white inhabitants of these elegant 1890s rowhouses started to abandon Harlem in the 1920s and '30s, upwardly mobile African-American professionals—strivers as they were called then—moved in. The gawk-worthy spaces were developed by David King, who is also responsible for Madison Square Garden.

138th and 139th Streets between Adam Clayton Powell Jr. and Frederick Douglass Boulevards. B C to 135th St.

Dining
UPSCALE
Londel's *Southern*

Owner Londel Davis greets customers at the door of his sophisticated new Strivers Row supper club, a restaurant that serves

FAST FACTS

⚑ Scenic Stroll: Mural Row, 125th Street

⚑ Major Subway Stations: 110th St (6), 125th St (A C, B D, 1 2 3, 4 5 6)

⚑ Urban Oasis: Conservatory Garden

⚑ Kooky Corner: Botanicas in el Barrio

⚑ Best View: Marcus Garvey Park

⚑ Neighborhood Landmarks: The Apollo Theater, El Museo del Barrio

⚑ Best Deal: Malcolm Shabazz Harlem Market

⚑ Celebrity Hangouts: Rucker Park, Sylvia's Restaurant

⚑ Notable Residents: Kareem Abdul-Jabbar, Marian Anderson, Marc Anthony, W.E.B. Du Bois, Julia de Burgos, Alexander Hamilton, Thurgood Marshall, Tito Puente, Paul Robeson, Sugar Ray Robinson, Cicely Tyson

as a harbinger of gentrification in this quickly changing neighborhood. Undeniably Harlem's hottest restaurant, it serves delicious, painstakingly prepared Southern food, such as smothered pork chops and pan-seared red snapper, to a slew of famous guests in an upscale setting. The flavors are traditional but bold, and the simple presentation allows you to enjoy without distraction.

2620 Frederick Douglass Boulevard (at 139th). 212.234.6114. T-Sat 11:30am-midnight, Sunday 11am-5pm, closed Monday. Appetizers $4-12, Entrées $14-22. **B C 2 3** *to 135th St.*

Revival *Soul, American*
Creole, Caribbean, and Soul influences converge at this low-key and elegant restaurant, producing flavorful combinations to revive the spirits of any weary diner. With a self-professed mission to breathe new life and culture into its

Harlem locale, this unique destination adds a little pizzazz to a sometimes monotonous dinner scene. Some of the best creations are the spicy butter shrimp, sizzler lobster tail with scallops, and LA lamb rack, each combining international accents with the large portions and aggressive flavors of traditional soul food. If you're going with a date, make sure to sample something from the full-page, well-priced martini menu—it becomes an even better deal during happy hour.

2367 Frederick Douglass Boulevard. 212.222.8338. Brunch Sat-Sun 11am-4pm; Dinner M-Th 5pm-10pm, F-Sat 5pm-11:30pm. Appetizers $6-9, Entrées $15.50-$26. **1** *to 125th St.*

MID-RANGE
Dinosaur BBQ *Barbecue*
From the chicken steak to the beef brisket to the classic barbecue pork, every meat served

here has been barbecued to perfection and monstrously portioned. The lively atmosphere , complete with energetic live music on Fridays and Saturdays and an impressive selection of 23 beers on tap, makes this the ideal place to bring a big group of friends to relax. But a word to the wise: this is not the place to bring first dates or vegetarians—neither will be particularly pleased with the oozing juice that is bound to end up all over your fingers.

646 West 131st Street (at Twelfth). 212.694.1777. T-Th 11:30am-11pm, F-Sat 11:30am-midnight, Sun noon-10pm, closed Monday. Appetizers $5-9, Entrées $13-24. **1** *to 125th St.*

Miss Maude's Spoonbread Too *Southern*

Opened by the owners of the famed Miss Mamie's on West 110th Street, Miss Maude's is the bigger and better of the two restaurants: you can't find higher quality soul food for a lower price. The interior is cute and carefree, casual enough to stop by for a piece of pie in lieu of a meal; come summertime, it's the perfect place to sip freshly squeezed lemonade at a window-side table. Owner Norma Jean Darden also runs a thriving catering service, offering you the chance to bring a little bit of soul to any meeting or event.

547 Lenox Avenue (at 137th). 212.690.3100. Sun 11am-9:30pm, M-Th noon-9:30pm, F-Sat noon-10:30pm. Entrées $6-15. **2 3** *to 135th St.*

MoBay *Caribbean, Soul*

The West Indies meets the Deep South in a hurricane of flavor at this casually elegant eatery, where local musicians regularly perform

during the evening hours, and a mahogany, purple, and saffron-colored interior adds a heavy dose of Harlem cool. Health food this is not: Heavily-seasoned slabs of meat, smoked until it falls off the bone, accompany hearty side dishes like the fabulous macaroni and cheese and the cinnamon-scented candied yams. Given most of the food, it's surprising to learn that this is also one of the few in Harlem to cater to vegetarians, offering soy-based meat substitutes seasoned much like its signature meat dishes. Sip on one of the bar's many tropical cocktails, enjoy the complimentary cornbread—a true treat baked with pineapple and served hot with a fruity sauce—and don't miss the rum cake, which mixes spicy flavor into its moist crumb.

17 West 125th Street (at Fifth). 212.876.9300. Daily 11am-midnight. Appetizers $5-13, Entrées $11-22. **2 3** *to 125th St.*

Sylvia's *Southern*

Although it's one of the most venerable soul food restaurants in New York, this much-hyped destination succeeds on more than its reputation. The self-proclaimed "Queen of Soul Food" serves delightfully crispy and flavorful fried chicken, though some of the sides could use reviving. Come Sunday for the after-church gospel brunch, and don't forget to leave room for the scrumptious sweet potato pie. And if you enjoy the flavors, you can even buy bottles of Sylvia's trademark sauces to take home.

328 Lenox Avenue (at 126th). 212.996.0660. M-Sat 8am-10:30pm, Sun 11-8. Appetizers $5-8, Entrées $9-19. **2 3** *to 125th St.*

CASUAL

Make My Cake *Dessert*

Even though it's tiny—there are only two tables in the entire place—this cupcake, cake, and pie shop is simply superb. The staff is super-friendly and the cake designer will draw almost anything you can imagine on one of Make My Cake's special-order creations. Try a red velvet slice—you'll want to return so often, they'll get

to know you by name.

121 St. Nicholas Avenue (at 116th). 212.932.0833. Sun 9-7; Mon-Thu 7am-8:30pm; Fri 7am-9pm, Sat 9am-9pm. Cake slices $3-5. **2 3** *to 110th St.*

Manna's *Soul*

Mrs. Betty Park and her family founded this homey, welcoming dining hall back in 1984, and garnered so much attention and acclaim that outposts can now be found throughout Harlem and Brooklyn. Painted yellow tulips and butterflies on the glass window hide crowds of people enjoying crispy fried chicken, BBQ pork ribs, collard greens, and other soul food favorites in the relaxed upstairs seating area. While not the most elegant place to dine, Manna's is an inexpensive buffet joint that doesn't sacrific quality, offering classic and tasty soul food in a welcoming atmosphere.

2331 Eighth Avenue (at 125th). 212.749.9084. Daily 7:30am-10pm. Buffet items $5/lb. **1 A C B D** *to 125th St.*

Tribal Spears *Café*

Enjoy organic teas and indigenous coffee while lounging on comfy leather couches at this spacious café with an artistic spin; the downstairs area often functions as an exhibition space for fine art, while the café walls serve as a gallery for tribal creations. Call in advance to ask about live music events, when the usually quiet café transforms into a lively social space. With beautiful bamboo tables and a stylish interior, it's a great place to bring friends to relax, listen to music, or soak in some art.

2167 Frederick Douglass Boulevard (at 117th). 212.666.6550. M-F 6:30am-6pm, Sat 7am-6pm, Sun 8am-6pm. **2 3 B C** *to 116th St.*

Nightlife

Harlem Lanes *Bowling*

Bowling is no longer just a kids' pastime at this 24-lane entertainment complex, which features a fully-equipped sports bar and a lounge with plush sofas and flat screen TVs. The grown-up atmosphere thankfully hasn't wiped out kiddie-sized prices: At $5.50-7.50 per person per game, and an additional $4.50 for shoe rental, Harlem Lanes is an inexpensive alternative to the Friday night club scene. Expect a few technical snafus—bowling balls can get caught in the machines—but on Mondays, you can forgo the game for karaoke if luck is not on your side. Likewise, Tuesday is Poetry Night, Wednesday is Open Mic Night, and Thursday is Singles Night.

*2110-2118 Adam Clayton Powell Boulevard (at 126th), 3rd and 4th floor. 212.678.2695. harlemlanes.com. Sun 11am-9pm, M-W 11am-11pm, Th 11am-1am, Fri-Sat 11am-2am. $5.50-$7.50 per person per game, $4.50 shoe rental. **2 3 A C B D** to 125th Street.*

Cotton Club *Music*

Every Monday is dance night at this legendary jazz club; come to enjoy a 13-piece swing and jazz band for a mere $15. Show times vary widely and you must call for reservations, but don't miss the $25 gospel brunches served every weekend. Or, stop by to sample the full Southern menu and bar every other day of the week.

*656 West 125th Street (at Twelfth). 212.663.7980. cottonclub-newyork.com. **1** to 125th St.*

Lenox Lounge *Music*

Since the 1930s, celebs like Billie Holiday and Miles Davis have frequented this music hotspot, as writers including James Baldwin and Langston Hughes used the acclaimed

Homage to Picasso by James de la Vega, 111th and Lexington

Zebra Room to gather their thoughts. With live jazz every night except for Tuesday, and recent renovations that make it look as good as it sounds, there's no excuse not to follow in the footsteps of the famous former patrons.

288 Lenox Avenue (at 124th). 212.427.0253. Daily noon-4am. Drinks $5-7. Cover W-Th $5, F-Sat $20, Sun-M $10. **2 3** *to 125th St.*

Showman's *Music*

Traditional jazz makes a comeback at Showman's, one of Harlem's longest running jazz houses. Offering live music to its patrons since 1942, the cozy alcove features a long and elegant bar, old-school jazz music, tap dance on Thursdays, unexpected karaoke nights, and large mirrors to create the illusion of a space much larger than it actually is. At night, the club overflows with a loyal clientele who chat loudly over the music as they down the third half of their two-drink minimum.

375 West 125th Street (at St. Nicholas). 212.864.8941. Daily 1pm, closing times vary. **1** *to 125th St.*

Arts

Boys' Choir of Harlem

Founded in 1968, this legendary choir has evolved from a small church group to an internationally acclaimed phenomenon—the choir has performed for Nelson Mandela and Pope John Paul III, among other notables. Hear them sing at year-round performances in venues all over the city, including Carnegie Hall, Lincoln Center, Radio City Music Hall, and the Schomburg Center in Harlem.

212.289.1815. boyschoirofharlem.org.

ColaLex Gallery

Opened in May 2007 by Haitian-born painter Pierre Colas, this tiny square space near Mural Row is dedicated to showcasing Hispanic and Caribbean art. The self-taught Colas claims to be living his own American dream as a gallery owner, and it seems that he is; the first

exhibition here was of his own large, brightly colored conceptual paintings.

1695 Lexington Avenue (at 106th). 212.348.2899. colalexgallery.com. M-F 10am-6pm, Sat-Sun 10am-3pm. **6** *to 103rd St.*

Dance Theatre of Harlem

This world-renowned neoclassical ballet company was founded by Arthur Mitchell, the first African American dancer to become a permanent member of a major ballet company. The school at the Theatre now offers classes in tap, modern, and jazz, in addition to ballet. Come to its monthly open house series (the second Sunday of each month), which features performances by the Company, students in the school, and guest artists.

466 West 152nd Street (at Amsterdam). 212.690.2800. dancetheatreofharlem.org. Adults $18 (open house). **B D C** *to 155th St.*

El Museo del Barrio

Located in the Heckscher Building—also the home of Boys and Girls Harbor, a renowned performing arts charter school—this Latin American and Caribbean art museum was founded by a group of Puerto Rican artists, educators, and community activists in 1969. With unique exhibits that aim to celebrate the cultural history and identity of East Harlem residents, and signage and employees that are exclusively bilingual, el Museo is one of East Harlem's premier attractions.

1230 Fifth Ave (at 104th St.). 212.831.7272. elmuseo.org.

Harlem Stage at the Gatehouse

Dedicated to nurturing artists of color, the Harlem Stage has hosted Bill Cosby, Maya Angelou, and Tito Puente, along with many other renowned artists, during its 38 year history. Throughout the year, the Stage presents plays, movie screenings, and a reading series, in addition to annual events like the Harlem Film Festival and the dance showcase, which features two weekends of performances by emerging and established artists. Check the Harlem Stage out in its new space, "The Gatehouse," a former operations center for the Croton Aqueduct Water System and a designated New York City landmark building. *150 Convent Avenue (at 135th). 212.650.6900. harlemstage.org.* **1** *to 137th St.*

Julia de Burgos Latino Cultural Center

Housed in a former public school and named after a Puerto Rican-born poet and civil rights activist who later lived in East Harlem, this arts center has a bustling energy that perfectly complements its vibrant neighborhood. Most prominently, community arts organization Taller Boricua operates out of the center, running many of the programs and exhibitions located here. Stop by the art gallery on the first floor, catch a theater performance in the evening, or come for one of the Center's popular "Uptown Salsa" after-work parties. *1680 Lexington Avenue (at 105th). 212.831.4333. tallerboricua.org. T-Sat noon-6pm, Th 1pm-7pm.* **6** *to 103rd St.*

Museum of the City of New York

It's impossible not to feel a sense of city pride as you walk among the awed tourists at this museum, housed in a magnificent stone and brick building that is a work of art in itself. Dedicated to the thriving metropolis we all know and love, even native New Yorkers will learn something new here, with diverse collections ranging from visual arts to costume and dress. Exhibitions regularly cover material from all five boroughs, and include photography, painting, sculpture, text, and artifacts. *1220 Fifth Avenue (at 103rd). 212.534.1672. mcny. org. T-Sun 10am-5pm.* **6** *to 103rd St.*

The National Black Theatre

For nearly 40 years, this acclaimed theater, founded by Broadway star Barbara Ann Teer, has hosted African American comedians, plays, and drum shows on its third floor stage. As a tribute to the theater's cultural importance, the block of Fifth Avenue on which it stands was renamed *National Black Theatre Way* in August 1994. Come for a performance and to admire the building itself—every part of the interior, including the stairwell, is decorated with African statues, paintings, and sculpture. *2031-33 Fifth Avenue (at 126th). 212.722.3800. nationalblacktheatre.org. Call for events schedule.* **2 3** *to 125th St.*

The Studio Museum in Harlem

Featuring contemporary exhibits that focus on African American art and the surrounding neighborhood, this museum proves that you don't have to go downtown for innovative visual art. The hushed galleries of the modern, glass-enclosed space are filled with paintings, installations, and video projections that challenge societal conceptions of people of color, delve into issues of identity politics, and memorialize victims of racial oppression. *144 West 125th Street (at Adam Clayton Powell). 212.864.4500. studiomuseum.org. W-F noon-6pm, Sat 10am-6pm, Sun noon-6pm, closed M-T. Adults $7, Students $3 (suggested).* **2 3** *to 125th St.*

Shopping

125th Street

Aside new outposts of chain stores like H&M, Modell's, Old Navy, and MAC, this strip offers a host of African specialty stores that you'll only find in Harlem. Scores of vendors sell their wares on tables lining the streets; look for inexpensive books, bootleg DVDs, incense, oils, African shea butter, and perfumes with names like "strawberry" and "booty call." *125th Street between Amsterdam and Fifth Avenues.*

Atmos

Shoppers flock to this Tokyo-based specialty store for its huge selection of outlandishly-patterned sneakers—think leopard print Nikes featuring Chinese characters—and colorful T-shirts with attitude; look for the lime green "Go ♥ Your Own City." Just be prepared:

The outrageous kicks can set you back around $275.

203 West 125th Street (at Adam Clayton Powell Jr). 212.666.2242. atmosnyc.com. M-Sat 10am-8pm, Sun noon-7pm. **2 3 A C B D** *to 125th St.*

Brownstone

Walk through the dark, narrow hallway of this residential brownstone and you'll find yourself in a high fashion clothing shop, described by the owners as "Harlem's greatest wonder." The claim might be a bit of a stretch, but the boutique is truly one-of-a-kind: most items in the shop, including hand-crafted jewelry and unusual fashion pieces, are culled from approximately 40 independent local designers.

2032 Fifth Avenue (at 126th). 212.996.7980. W-Sat 11am-7pm, Sun 1am-5pm, closed M-T. **2 3** *to 125th St.*

Casa Latina

If the booming salsa music inside Casa Latina doesn't lure you in, the store's extensive music selection will. Come for the best in reggaeton, bomba, merengue, and more; the store, family-owned and operated for more than 30 years, stocks CDs ($13.99) and old-fashioned cassettes ($7.95) by artists from all Latin musical genres, along with guitars, percussion instruments, sheet music, books, and DVDs.

151 East 116th Street (at Lexington). 212.427.6062. casalatinamusic.com M-Th 10am-6:30pm. F-Sat 10am-7pm, closed Sunday. **6** *to 116th St.*

Hue-Man Bookstore & Café

Energize youself for a lengthy browsing session with a guava protein smoothie from the café at Hue-Man, one of the most well-known African American bookstores in the country. Sit at the round tables near the window to read from the wide selection of books that center around African American issues, and those that don't; in the front, equally-sized sections are devoted to bestsellers from both *The New York Times* and *Essence*.

2319 Frederick Douglass Boulevard (at 124th).
212.665.7400. huemanbookstore.com. M-Sat 10-8, Sun 11-7. **A C B D** *to 125th St.*

Kaarta Imports, African Fabrics

This tiny shop sells hand-sewn fabrics imported from West Africa; go to learn the difference between Kente, a Ghanaian textile, and Mudcloth, a cotton fabric from Mali. There's also a large selection of colorful earrings, bracelets, and bags, along with authentic African hair products.

121 West 125th Street (at Malcolm X). 212.866.5190. M-F 10-8:30, Sun noon-8:30. **2 3** *to 125th St.*

La Marqueta

Constructed in 1936, La Marqueta ("the market") was once a thriving neighborhood icon, with stalls of Polish, Jewish, African, and Latino goods lining Park Avenue between 111th and 116th. Over the past 15 years, rising prices and competition from new area supermarkets have forced out nearly all of the vendors, but locals still flock here to get authentic Latin American foods from stalls that persist after more than 50 years—not to mention the best *bacalao* in the city.

115th and Park Avenue. M-Sat 8am-5pm, closed Sunday. **6** *to 116th St.*

Malcolm Shabazz Harlem Market

This large outdoor market, accessed via a gate on 116th Street, contains dozens of tables and stalls with beaded necklaces, hoop earrings, and wooden sandals. Bargain with the vendors, easy to recognize in their colorful full-length African dresses and headwraps, to get the best deals.

52 West 116th Street (at Malcolm X). 212.987.8131. Daily 10am-8pm. **2 3** *to 116th St.*

WASHINGTON HEIGHTS/INWOOD

Contrary to popular belief, life does indeed exist near Manhattan's extreme upper boundaries, where demographics change as rapidly as the weather. The story of Washington Heights and Inwood began with the extension uptown of the old IRT and BMT subway lines in the early 20th century. The first residents of the Heights were Jewish and Irish immigrants, but ethnic tensions caused both groups to abandon the area by the 1960s.

Soon after, the neighborhood housed a predominantly African American, Puerto Rican, and Cuban population. In 1965, the assassination of Malcolm X in the Audubon Ballroom was simultaneously a reminder of earlier conflict and a harbinger of the crime wave that would hit the area in the '80s and '90s—accompanied by an upswing in drugs, poverty, and overcrowding.

Dominicans came to outnumber other residents during this period; by 1990, there were more Dominicans in Washington Heights than in any other community in the United States. On hot weekends and afternoons, the streets pulse with salsa and merengue rhythms as the area's Dominican residents flock to the many grassy parks.

With gentrification on the rise, this neighborhood is anything but static. Lured by airy and affordable apartments and lush parks, students, artists, musicians, and families are moving here in droves. Residents love the area's generally easygoing vibe, comfortably removed from the aggressive urban grit many associate with Manhattan.

FAST FACTS

- Scenic Stroll: Broadway, North of 155th Street

- Major Subway Stations: 157th St (**1**), 168th St-Washington Heights (**A C**), 175th St (**A**)

- Urban Oasis: The Cloisters

- Kooky Corner: The Little Red Lighthouse

- Best View: Inwood Hill Park

- Notable Buildings: Dyckman House, Morris-Jumel Mansion

- Notable Residents: Alan Greenspan, Henry Kissinger, Stan Lee, Alex Rodriguez

- Kid-Friendly Place: The Little Red Lighthouse

Sights/Attractions

George Washington Bridge

This bridge, the only one connecting New Jersey and Manhattan, is practical, necessary, and one of the most recognizable urban structures in the world, thanks in large part to the famously exposed steel bracing of its main suspension towers. Originally, engineer Othmar Ammann and architect Cass Gilbert planned to encase the towers with granite sheathing, although those plans had to change when the Great Depression hit and money ran dry. The resulting design is what famed architect Le Corbusier referred to as the most beautiful bridge in the world.

175th at the Hudson River. **A** *to 175th St.*

Inwood Hill Park

Once inhabited by the Lenape Indians, this 196-acre park is home to the last surviving forest and saltwater marsh in the city. It was here that the supposed $24-for-Manhattan exchange occurred between the Lenapes and Dutch explorer Peter

Minuit, although the details are much less clear than local legend would have you believe. At the park, learn about the history of life on Manhattan before the first settlers arrived, or simply go for a hike on the beautiful nature trails—one of the only places in New York where you can find wild, uninhibited nature in all its glory.

Entrance at West 218th Street (at Indian). **1** *to 215th St.*

The Little Red Lighthouse

The last surviving lighthouse on Manhattan Island, immortalized in Hildegard Swift's 1942 children's book *The Little Red Lighthouse and the Great Gray Bridge*, is located 28 feet above the river and directly underneath the George Washington Bridge. The lighthouse, after 70 years of off-and-on service, was finally decommissioned in 1948 after the bright lights on the GW Bridge rendered it obsolete. In 1951, plans to sell the lighthouse were thwarted by a public outcry from dedicated fans of the Swift book; since then, it has been restored to its original color with a coat of red paint and bestowed with a protective gate. Entrance to the interior is granted during bi-monthly tours.

Fort Washington Park (at 179th). 212.304.2365. **A** **1** *to 181st St.*

Dining
UPSCALE
809 *Latin*

In a traditionally working-class neighborhood with few fine dining options, this upscale eatery steps in to fill the void. Offering gourmet twists on Dominican classics, chef Ricardo Cardona attempts to bring some downtown cuisine uptown…way uptown. While the chic interior is perhaps better suited for a lounge than a restaurant, that is precisely what the refined eatery transforms into late at night, complete with music and a dance floor Thursday through Sunday. While there is better food for the price to be had elsewhere in Manhattan, 809 is a welcome addition to the neighborhood for residents who want to stay local for an upscale meal.

112 Dyckman Street (at Nagle). 212.304.3800. M-W 5pm-11pm, Th-Sat 5pm-1am, Sun 5pm-11pm. Appetizers $6-15, Entrées $18-32. **1** *to Dyckman.*

MID-RANGE
107 West *Southwestern*

A successful blend of authentic, Americanized, and gourmet, this rare find delivers delicious Southwestern classics with all the trimmings, earning return visits by locals for years. The food is prepared with consistently high quality; the quesadillas in particular are cheese- and meat-filled slabs of flavor, and the accompanying guacamole is made with just the right amount of lime. Take advantage of the speedy delivery service on nights when you feel like staying in.

811 West 187th Street (at Fort Washington). 212.923.3311. M-Sat 11am-10:30pm, Sun 11am-10pm. Appetizers $5-8, Entrées $9-15. **1** *to 191st.*

Bleu Evolution *Italian*

Food at this funky neighborhood trattoria wanders in and out of the Italian genre, sometimes, as with the décor, hitting just the right spot. Plush, high-backed

seats, rich upholsteries, and velvet curtains are kept lively with bright stabs of color from carefully folded blue napkins on each table. With a cozy outdoor garden for summer dining and a lounge that stays open long after the kitchen closes, this mainstay is also undeniably hip, despite its out-of-the-way location.

808 West 187th Street (at Fort Washington). 212.9286006. Brunch Sat-Sun 10am-4:30pm; Lunch M-F 11am-4:30pm; Dinner Sun-Th 5pm-11:30pm, F-Sat 5pm-12:30am. Appetizers $7-10, Entrées $17-23. **A** *to 181st St.*

El Ranchito *Latin American*

If you're in the mood for Salvadoran food but not in the mood to break the bank, try this inexpensive restaurant rich in Latin flavors. The *pupusa* is similar to a quesadilla, but thicker and packing even more delicious corn flavor; the chicken is tasty and moist. Whatever you choose, you'll leave with plenty left in your wallet—and a new appreciation for a cuisine you may never have tried before. The eatery also offers cheap Salvadoran breakfasts for a fraction of what you'd pay for a slice of toast in Midtown.

4129 Broadway (at 174th). 212.928.0866. T-Th 10am-11pm, F-M 10am-1am. Entrées $3-15. **1** *to 168th St.*

Nightlife
Coogan's *Food and Drink*

This upscale Irish-influenced pub, in a setting strikingly reminiscent of the bar in *Cheers*, serves a multicultural clientele of neighborhood regulars and Columbia-Presbyterian Medical Center workers. A festive atmosphere and enjoyable bar food—the shell steak, shrimp scampi, onion soup, and roast beef au jus are highly recommended—make the trek uptown worth it, but the karaoke nights (Tuesday, Thursday, and Saturday) will make you wish the drunken doctors and locals sang here seven nights a week.

4015 Broadway (at 168th). 212.928.1234. Daily 11am-3am. Drinks $3-8. **A C 1** *to 168th St.*

Irish Brigade Pub *Pub*

A young female bartender serves an older crowd that wants to let loose at this traditional pub full of "silly and cool people." Go on a night when a guest DJ is playing if you really want to enjoy yourself.

4716 Broadway (at Arden). 212.567.8714. Daily 11am–4am. Drinks $4–6. **A** *to Dyckman.*

Arts

The American Academy of Arts and Letters

Tours of the offices and collection of this award-bestowing organization are available by appointment only—in some cases, only to "accredited scholars." It's worth it, though, if only to see the bizarre Membership Room, where the private leather chairs of each of the Academy's 250 members are engraved with the names of the previous (read: deceased) members who occupied them before. Aspiring artists should stop by to see where they might end up if they ever make it big; the membership roster includes names like Richard Serra, I.M. Pei, and Toni Morrison, each of whom had to wait for a literary or artistic icon to die before getting in. The Academy, which gives out a series of awards and prizes to support individual artists, also uses its facilities to show art exhibitions and host performances.

633 West 155th Street (at Riverside). 212.368.590. artsandletters.org. Free by appointment. **1** *to 157th St.*

The Cloisters

This subsidiary of the Metropolitan Museum of Art, housed in a unique medieval-style structure that combines design and structural elements from five different French cloisters, boasts the world's premier collection of art and architecture from Medieval Europe. Located in Fort Tryon Park overlooking the Hudson, the collection of 6,000 Gothic and Romanesque pieces includes stained glass panels, various sculpted tombs, and a roomful of the famed Unicorn Tapestries. In the summer months, go for a medieval music concert in the outdoor garden and café.

799 Fort Washington Avenue (in Fort Tryon Park). 212.923.3700. metmuseum.org. Daily 9:30-5, closed Mondays, hours vary slightly by season. Adults $20, Students $10 (suggested). **A** *to 190th St.*

The Cloisters

Dyckman Farmhouse Museum

Manhattan's last Dutch colonial farmhouse sits unexpectedly on a bustling neighborhood corner, nestled between an apartment building and a tattoo parlor. Follow the stone path up to the white cottage, pass the garden that holds only veggies grown in the 1800s, use the knocker to rap gently on the blue-green front door, and imagine rural farm life when Broadway was still called Kingsbridge Road. The rooms inside are complete with period chairs, tables, books, and even blankets, while the comfortable back porch overlooks a replica smokehouse and reconstructed Revolutionary War military hut.

*4881 Broadway (at 204th). 212.304.9422. dyckmanfarmhouse.org, W-Sat 11-4, Sun noon-4pm, closed M-T. Adults $1. **A** to Inwood.*

The Hispanic Society of America

The last remaining museum in the Audubon Terrace Museum Complex, which originally housed the Museum of the American Indian and the American Numismatic Society as well, has a collection that includes pieces of iron-age pottery, mosaic tiles, and portraits of snooty-looking Spanish nobles. In 2006, the Society announced the intention to join its former neighbors downtown, citing a lack of uptown visitors and the need for a more modern facility. Museum buffs should visit the original location before a move date is set (or the Society finds a facility) to see collection highlights like Francisco Goya's well-known Portrait of the Duchess of Alba, and the Sorolla Room, where a multi-paneled painting of Spain's provinces by Joaquín Sorolla y Bastida covers every wall.

*Audubon Terrace (Broadway at 155th). 212.926.2234. hispanicsociety.org T-Sat 10am-4:30pm, Sun 1am-4pm, closed Monday. $5 (suggested). **1** to 157th St.*

Morris-Jumel Mansion

This oldest remaining house in Manhattan, built in 1765, served as George Washington's Revolutionary War headquarters during September and October of 1776. Discover life before indoor plumbing on a Saturday tour, or visit for one of the many special events, including everything from colonial hat-making workshops to a free summer jazz series.

*65 Jumel Terrace (at 160th). 212.923.8008. morrisjumel.org W-Sun 10am-4pm, M-T by appointment, tours Saturday noon. Adults $4, Students $3. **C** to Amsterdam Ave.*

Shopping

Anna House

Baseball hats from every major league team and in every possible size and color line the walls of this small store—although the classic Yankees style dominates the racks. Unless a special promotion lowers the price of hats to $15, expect them to cost at least $27 each.

*1469 Juan Pablo Duarte Boulevard (at West 177th). M-Sat 9:30am-8pm, Sun 10-6. **1** to 181st St.*

Karrot

Natural food fiends buy their whole-wheat pasta, organic fruit, and shots of wheatgrass at this friendly, community-oriented grocery store, which claims to have the finest organic coffee in a 20-block radius.

*854 West 181st Street (at Cabrini). 212.740.4417. Daily 9am-8pm. **A** to 181st St.*

Moscow on the Hudson

This family-run Russian grocery carries traditional sweets and sausages, flavored kefir yogurt, exotic fruit juices (including a delicious cherry), and a wide assortment of homemade baked goods, made right on the premises. Look behind the counter for an array of Russian movies, stuffed animals, and souvenirs.

*801 West 181st Street (at Fort Washington). 212.740.7397. M-Sat 9am-10pm, Sun 9am-9pm. **A** to 181st St.*

Probus

Clothing by well-known brands like Diesel, G-Star, and Vans hangs next to apparel by niche local designers at this uptown version of a downtown boutique. The store features tops, footwear, accessories, and a large selection of men's attire, but a one-of-a-kind printed tee will set you back at least 50 bucks.

*714 West 181st Street (at Bennett). 212.923.9153. probusnyc.com. M-Sat 11am-8pm, Sun noon-7pm. **A 1** to 181st St.*

THE OUTER BOROUGHS

BROOKLYN

Home to the city's leafiest streets, best pizza, and oldest bridge, no other borough inspires as much pride among its residents as Brooklyn. Throughout its history, Brooklyn's enclaves have been defined by the dominant ethnic and immigrant groups residing here: Bensonhurst is largely Italian-American; Borough Park, Orthodox Jewish; Brighton Beach, Russian; Flatbush, Caribbean; Fort Greene, African American; Greenpoint, Polish. The resulting insular communities have distinct flavors whose eccentricities are still detectable today.

Like Manhattan, Brooklyn was originally settled by Dutch explorers. The name "Brooklyn" likely comes from "Brueckelen," the Dutch word for "broken land," though the settlers in effect consolidated several villages after "buying" land from the Canarsie Native Americans in 1642.

In 1833, Brooklyn was asked to join Manhattan in forming a city, but refused and instead incorporated itself as a separate city the following year. It remained independent even after the opening of the Brooklyn Bridge in 1883, and didn't become part of NYC until 1898, a decision that writer Pete Hamill once termed "The Great Mistake."

As is the case with the rest of the city, Brooklyn is changing—fast. Chinese restaurants are replacing Italian bakeries, luxury condos have opened up near housing projects, and rents are skyrocketing, along with the number of espresso bars. The previously gritty and dangerous area around Atlantic Avenue has been graced with a new mall and a slew of development deals; Fairway Market recently opened in the soon-to-be-chic Red Hook; and there's no stopping Williamsburg's hipster scene from spreading farther eastward.

Nevertheless, this most populous borough in New York continues to remain largely residential, maintaining its own spirit and symbolic autonomy.

BROOKLYN

SIGHTS/ATTRACTIONS
1. Brooklyn Botanic Garden
2. Brooklyn Brewery
3. Brooklyn Bridge Park and
   Empire-Fulton Ferry State Park
4. Brooklyn Historical Society
6. Front Greene Park
7. Historic Weeksville
8. McCarren Park
10. Prospect Park

DINING
11. Beast
12. Blue Ribbon Brooklyn
13. Brooklyn Ice Cream Factory
14. Lunetta
15. Madiba
16. Pete's Downtown
17. Relish
18. Stone Park Café

19. Toro

NIGHTLIFE
20. Black Betty
21. Boat
22. Brownstone Billiards
23. Floyd NY
24. Frank's Lounge
25. Galapagos Art Space
26. Last Exit
27. Mugs Ale House
28. Pete's Candy Store
29. Teddy's Bar and Grill
30. Union Hall
31. Warsaw Club

ARTS
32. BAM (Brooklyn Academy of Music)
33. Billie Holiday Theater
34. Brooklyn Museum of Contemporary

African Diaspora Arts (MoCADA)
35. Pierogi 2000
36. Skylight Gallery
37. St. Ann's Warehouse

SHOPPING
38. About Glamour
39. Beacon's Closet
40. Brooklyn Industries
41. Brooklyn Superhero Supply
   Company/826NYC
42. Brownstone Books
43. Buffalo Exchange
44. Future Perfect
45. Jay East Direct Import Warehouse
46. Mini Minimarket
47. Olive's Very Vintage
48. PowerHouse Arena

Brooklyn Neighborhoods
BROOKLYN HEIGHTS

In the immediate vicinity of the Brooklyn Bridge lies Brooklyn Heights, a charming, tree-lined neighborhood with distinguished townhouses and grand gardens so peaceful you might forget that Manhattan is minutes away. A stroll along the shoreline **Promenade**, however, built above the Brooklyn-Queens Expressway, brings the Big Apple back into sharp focus; gaze out at unimpeded views of the Manhattan skyline, the Statue of Liberty, and Ellis Island while you walk.

As the city's first declared historical district (since 1965), the Heights has maintained many of the original brownstones and buildings owned by the affluent families that populated it for decades. Some of the oldest, like the **Church of St. Ann's** (*157 Montague Street at Clinton*), are located next to upscale chain stores like Aerosoles and M.A.C. on Montague Street (*between Court and the Promenade*). After checking out the stores, wander out of your way to ooh and ahh at the cobblestone stretch of **Joralemon Street** (*between Hicks and Furman*) that just might be the loveliest road in the area; neat brick townhouses, covered with rose bushes, will no doubt make you long for a spouse, kids, and a few million dollars to buy up one of the remaining few.

M **R** *to Court Street.*

Brownstone in Brooklyn Heights

CARROLL GARDENS AND COBBLE HILL

Longtime Italian immigrant enclave Carroll Gardens is known primarily as a quiet residential neighborhood, boasting gorgeous brownstones set off from the street by 30-40 feet of front yard space filled with gardens and playing children. From the Smith Street subway station, walk north along Court Street and turn left onto almost any side street to marvel at the quaint urban plan.

Cafés, coffee shops, and boutiques on **Court Street** appeal to a crowd of mostly young, hip, well-to-do white families; stop in at the charming **Le Petit Café** (*502 Court Street at Nelson*) for brunch—you'll need your fuel for a day of shopping. Start by walking three blocks north to **Olive's Very Vintage** (*434 Court Street at 2nd Place*), the best vintage clothing store south of Williamsburg, then cross lively **Carroll Park** (*Court Street at Carroll Street*), named for the only Roman Catholic to sign the Declaration of Independence. Land on **Smith Street**, where a weekend **Indie Market** (*Smith Street at Union*) offers inexpensive T-shirts and jewelry by emerging designers, and where tiny, hip food spots like **Cubana Café** (*272 Smith Street at Sackett*) abound.

To the north lies **Cobble Hill**, which, in addition to its share of landmark buildings, is home to a vibrant Middle-Eastern community, especially along Atlantic Avenue.

F *to Bergen, Carroll, or Smith St.*

CONEY ISLAND AND BRIGHTON BEACH

In the years following the Civil War, this storied stretch of beach in Brooklyn became a wildly popular resort destination, due in large part to the sudden proliferation of commuter railways and streetcars that effortlessly whisked people to and from its shores. An ideal spot for escaping summer heat in the city, Coney Island—which is not, in fact, an island, but rather the southeastern-most edge of the borough—attracted a multitude of visitors each season with its amusement parks, horse racing, gambling, and plentiful hotel space.

Today, little remains of Coney Island's former glory as a playground for the city's well-to-do, but it still occupies a special place in the hearts of many New Yorkers who appreciate it as a fun (and only slightly seedy) summertime hangout. Many of those loyal fans are outraged by the proposed makeover of **Astroland Amusement Park** along the boardwalk (*1000 Surf Avenue*)—home to the Cyclone, a formidable wooden rollercoaster that has been threatening to fall apart since it was built in 1927.

After Astroland's last hurrah in the summer of '07, developers are planning to make Coney Island into a year-round Las Vegas-style destination, by building a glass-enclosed water park, hotels, shops, movie theaters, and arcades. Much to the chagrin of local preservationists, developers predict that the new Coney Island will be ready for business by the summer of 2011.

If you can't bear to look at the old haunts on the brink of demolition, go just west of the Boardwalk to **Brighton Beach**, sometimes called "Little Odessa" for its large Russian community. A recently revived area, the beach here is slightly cleaner and less chaotic than that of Coney Island, and the restaurants on Brighton Beach Avenue are worth a try for lavish Russian cuisine and revelry.

Coney Island: N Q D F *to Stillwell Ave/Coney Island. Brighton Beach:* Q B *to Brighton Beach.*

Boardwalk at Brighton Beach

DUMBO

Marketed by real estate agents as "the new TriBeCa," DUMBO—the curious acronym stands for Down Under the Manhattan Bridge Overpass—is home to a thriving arts scene, as well as some of the most luxurious (and expensive) condos and lofts in the city. Its beautiful waterfront parks, cobblestone streets, and cutting-edge art venues make it a worthy day-trip destination; rediscover your inner child on the pirate ship-themed playground of **Brooklyn Bridge Park** (*Main Street at the Waterfront*), or lounge on the rocky steps connecting **Empire-Fulton Ferry State Park** (*26 New Dock Street at the Waterfront*) and watch people skip stones into the East River. For dessert, head south to the Fulton Ferry Landing for delicious, homemade ice cream at the famous **Brooklyn Ice Cream Factory** (*Water Street at Old Fulton Street*); or, if you can't stand the crowds, pick up a rich hazelnut ice cream sandwich at **Jacques Torres Chocolate** (*66 Water Street at Main*). Venture a couple of blocks south to the corner of Water Street and Main while you eat: **the powerHouse Arena** (*37 Main Street at Water*), a gallery and bookstore, will thrill pop culture addicts and art history majors alike. As the sun sets, wait in line for sit-down pizza at the legendary **Grimaldi's** (*19 Old Fulton Street at Elizabeth*), or catch a theatrical performance at the eclectic **St. Ann's Warehouse** (*38 Water Street at Dock*).
A C *to High St.*

FORT GREENE

Just four stops from Manhattan on the C train, Fort Greene is one of Brooklyn's most dynamic neighborhoods. Although the area has historically been known as an enclave of upper middle-class African Americans, in the past decade it has absorbed a new wave of radically diverse hipsters, musicians, writers, and academics who've fled Manhattan in search of that ever-elusive bargain apartment or brownstone.

To get a feel for the neighborhood, stroll down one of the beautiful tree-lined streets of the **Fort Greene Historic District**, complete with Civil War-era brick houses and brownstones—Cumberland Street between Lafayette and DeKalb is a good place to start. Later, follow DeKalb Avenue along the border of the lush and lively **Fort Greene Park**, or enter its grounds to check out the Prison Ship Martyrs Monument, the park's main attraction.

East of the park, check out the thought-provoking works at the **Museum of Contemporary African Diasporan Arts** (*80 Hanson Place at Portland*) before heading over to Fulton Street for a warm, greasy slice at local landmark **Not Ray's Pizza** (*690 Fulton Street at South Portland*), rumored to be the model for the pizza place in Spike Lee's *Do The Right Thing*.
C *to Lafayette.*

GREENPOINT

Sometimes referred to as Little Poland because of the influx of Polish immigrants during the past 40 years, Greenpoint, on the northern tip of Brooklyn near the waterfront, is dominated by cheap rents and underground hangouts. Manhattan Avenue offers a wealth of hidden gastronomic gems; pick up a cheese danish at **Bakery Rzeszowska** (*948 Manhattan Avenue at Java*) or enjoy inexpensive borschts and blintzes at the acclaimed **Lomzynianka** (*646 Manhattan Avenue at Nassau*). As artists have moved into the area, the Polish and hipster communities have come together at the **Warsaw Club**, a concert and arts venue in the Polish National Home (*261 Driggs Avenue at Eckford*). If you're visiting, don't eat before you come; you can get a plate of authentic kielbasa and pierogies from the club's bistro for only $5. If you're in the mood to shop, visit **Franklin Street**, Greenpoint's main drag, for chic (and sometimes pricey) boutiques. The neighborhood also has its very own subway line: the G train, a Brooklyn/Queens Crosstown Local, is the only line that never enters Manhattan.

PARK SLOPE

In this long-established area just west of Prospect Park, baby strollers outnumber cars, Starbucks and Ozzie's Coffee shops co-exist in peaceful latte-chugging harmony, and Victorian row houses frame verdant **Prospect Park** (*Flatbush Avenue and Prospect Park West*). If you've ever been south of Times Square, you've probably heard the rumors about Park Slopers—vegan until proven otherwise, those not pregnant probably on paternity leave. Is Park Slope a great place to raise a family? Maybe, but for the rest of us, the streets of this idyllic "community" can feel oppressively sweet—anyplace where good Samaritans position lost pacifiers on cast-iron gateposts just in case the hapless owners return is probably a little too nice for its own good.

Gentrification in the Slope happened a couple of decades ago, but real estate agents still dub the lower edge of the neighborhood "South Slope," hoping to attract recent liberal arts grads to what they hope will be the next hot place to live—never mind the fact that just a few years ago the section was a well-established Mexican community. In center Slope, corporate-by-day, hipster-by-night types dwell alongside do-good freelance artists, giving this neighborhood its liberal-elite reputation.

Thanks in no small part to this gentrification, nightlife in Park Slope rivals that of Greenwich Village in both quality and cost. Though you can still find a damn good slice of pizza for under two bucks at **Pino's Pizzeria** (*181 Seventh Avenue at 2nd*), don't expect those kinds of prices at most of the hot spots on Fifth or Seventh Avenues, the neighborhood's most commerce-centric thoroughfares. Watching parents

Row of brownstones in Park Slope

tote their kids to yoga with Odwalla juice in hand, however, is always free, and inexpensive landmarks like the **Brooklyn Museum of Art** (*200 Eastern Parkway at Washington*) and the **Brooklyn Botanic Garden** (*1000 Washington Avenue at Montgomery*) are easily accessible by mass transit.
F M R *to 9th St/4th Ave.*

WILLIAMSBURG

What Haight-Ashbury was to the hippies of the 1960s, Williamsburg is to the hipsters of the new millennium. The 'burg is a mecca for indie music and fashion, a virtual sea of iPod earbuds tucked under shaggy haircuts and beautiful people in impossibly tight jeans. Get a taste for the scene by eavesdropping on the locals as they hop from one hot bar to the next, discussing bands still scuttling under the radar of mass taste.

The biggest draw for Manhattanites might be the multitude of high-quality vintage clothing shops that seem to be everywhere; you shouldn't get back on the L before going to **Beacon's Closet** (*88 North 11th Street at Wythe*), the most famous of them all. There's also a thriving art scene, visible at galleries such as **Pierogi 2000** (*177 North 9th at Bedford*), among a myriad of others. Just make sure you visit before all the best underground spots are priced out—leader of the pack **Galapagos Art Space** (*70 North 6th Street at Wythe*) is moving to DUMBO in mid-2008 due to the unbearable rent prices, and it surely won't be the last one to leave.

Despite skyrocketing rent and the too-cool-for-school hipsters, however, parts of the neighborhood still have a down-home feel. Grab a cold one at the **Brooklyn Brewery** (*79 North 11th Street at Wythe*), then head to Bedford Avenue, the neighborhood's main drag. Mom-and-Pop grocery shops line the streets, locals sell homemade pies on the sidewalk, and sausages dangle from the windows of local delis—a tribute to the area's Polish roots.

Sights/Attractions

Brooklyn Botanic Garden

The most popular botanic garden in New York is also the most beautiful; spend an afternoon strolling around the lovely 52 acres for less than $5. Be sure not to miss the Cherry Blossom Festival in May, which features more than 200 cherry blossoms in full bloom, or the 1,200 species of blooming roses in June.

1000 Washington Avenue (at Montgomery), Eastern Parkway. 718.623.7200. bbg.org. Hours vary by season. $8 Adults, $4 Students, free Tuesday all day and Saturday 10-noon. B Q S *to Prospect Park.*

Brooklyn Brewery

New York's hometown beer is brewed right here, and on weekends they open the place up—come for free brewery tours, beer tastings, and merchandise for sale. In the spring, the indulgent flock to the brewery for the Brooklyn Pigfest, where cold suds, tangy barbecue, and live music converge for the

ultimate down-home pig-out.

79 North 11th Street (at Wythe), Williamsburg. 718.486.7422. brooklynbrewery.com. Sat 12-5; tours at 1, 2, 3, and 4. L *to Bedford Ave.*

Brooklyn Bridge Park and Empire-Fulton Ferry State Park

Join families, couples, and dogs on this gorgeous stretch of unbroken nature—the two adjacent parks blend into each other somewhere between the Manhattan and Brooklyn Bridges. On a nice day, watch the sun bounce off the sparkling bridges as the muddy East River glistens below. Bring a friend and a bottle of wine, grab some ice cream to eat on a grassy knoll, or come by on Thursdays in July and August for Brooklyn Bridge Park's amazing Summer Film Series.

Brooklyn Bridge Park: Main Street at the Waterfront; EFF Park: 26 New Dock Street (at the Waterfront), DUMBO. 718.858.4708. bbpc.net. A C *to High St.*

Brooklyn Heights Promenade

Bring your camera to record the contrast between the iconic Manhattan skyline and the historic Brooklyn waterfront that flanks this shoreline promenade, running from Remsen to Cranberry Street.

Brooklyn Heights. **2 3** *to Clark St.*

Brooklyn Historical Society

According to this society's website, one in seven Americans can trace his or her family roots back to Brooklyn. If you're one of them—or just wish you were—pay a visit to this museum and library. Housed in a beautiful four-story National Historic Landmark building that was built with locally produced terra cotta, this site is the perfect rainy day alternative to a walk on the Promenade.

128 Pierrepont Street (at Clinton), Brooklyn Heights. 718.222.4111. brooklynhistory.org. W-Sun noon-5, closed M-T. Adults $6, Students $4. **2 3** *to Clark St.*

Fort Greene Park

The focal point of this 30-acre park is the 145-foot high Doric column that is the Prison Ship Martyrs Monument, dedicated to the 11,000 men who died on British prison ships in Wallabout Bay during the Revolutionary War. Although at one time Fort Greene Park was dangerous even during the day, it's now a safe and lovely place to relax, participate in a game of pick-up soccer, or just go for a stroll. Look out for views of this beauty in *She's Gotta Have It*, the film by director and long-time Fort Greene resident Spike Lee.

DeKalb Avenue at Washington Park, Fort Greene. 718.222.1461. www.fortgreenepark.org **R Q B M** *to DeKalb Ave.*

Historic Weeksville

From 1838 until the 1930s, this small plot of land in Crown Heights was one of the most prominent black communities in the country. During that time, Weeksville was home to over 500 politically active African American families, with an independent school system, multiple churches, an orphanage, a newspaper, teachers, tradesmen, and doctors. Although many of the town's homes and buildings were destroyed in the 1950s when the surrounding

Japanese garden at Brooklyn Botanic Garden

area was developed, today tour guides lead interested parties through the interiors of the three white-and-gray shingled wooden houses that still stand. Marvel at the copper boiler, used for doing laundry in the Johnsons' house and the original copies of W.E.B. Du Bois' *The Crisis* in the Williams family home.

1698 Bergen Street (at Rochester), Crown Heights. 718.756.5250. Tours T-F 1-3, Sat 11-3. $4. **A C** *to Utica Ave.*

McCarren Park

Pet owners flock to this 36-acre park for its social-spot dog run and the Annual Animal Show and Parade; the pet-less can enjoy the running track, handball courts, and baseball fields, and continue to wish the giant swimming pool (capacity 6,500) were reopened for more than just concerts. For a decidedly quainter alternative, go to nearby Monsignor McGolrick Park (*Driggs Street at Russell*), a beautiful European-esque square with a giant Greek-style temple at its center.

Nassau Avenue at Bayard, Greenpoint. L *to Bedford Ave.*

The New York Aquarium

Located just off the boardwalk, this aquarium is a great stop between riding the Cyclone and grabbing a hot dog at Nathan's (*1310 Surf Avenue at Schweikerts*), the ubiquitous Coney Island snack joint. Gawk at the huge tanks that replicate reef and wetland ecosystems (complete with endangered species), watch a sea lion show, or peer into the shark tanks and try not to think about Jaws. Don't miss the jellyfish: requiring unique care, they swim in lit cylinders that extend from floor to ceiling, providing light in an otherwise dark exhibit.

602 Surf Avenue (at West 8th), Coney Island. 718.265.FISH. Opens 10am daily; call for seasonal closing times. Adults $12. **D F** N Q *to Stillwell Ave/ Coney Island.*

Prospect Park

Designed by Frederick Law Olmstead, famed architect of Central Park, this 526-acre green space is home to an Audubon Center, the

Carousel at Prospect Park

Prospect Park Zoo, the Lefferts Historic House, a beautiful antique carousel, a trolley system for easy transportation (stops posted throughout park), and ice skating during the winter. Don't forget to take an electric boat tour of the park's 60-acre lake, and stay late on summer nights for the Celebrate Brooklyn! Performing Arts Festival at the Bandshell, where acts run the gamut from indie rock to modern dance.

Between Prospect Park West, Prospect Park Southwest, Parkside Avenue, Flatbush Avenue, and Ocean Avenue, Park Slope. 718.965.8951. prospectpark.org **2 3** *to Grand Army Plaza.*

Dining
UPSCALE
Blue Ribbon Brooklyn *Contemporary American*

At first, Blue Ribbon Brooklyn looks like your typical local family restaurant—the interior is cozy, filled with solitary couples and young parents with noisy Park Slope kids. But once you see what people are eating, you'll realize that this is no ordinary meal. Tables are covered with trays holding oysters on ice, smoked trout salad, Paella Magdalena (with accompanying lobster), chicken sausage, and utterly tender organic beefsteak. For dessert, chocolate cake and bread pudding ought to grace every table. The waitstaff nails a delicate balance of friendly and professional as they cater to early birds and late-nighters alike—the long hours are one of the restaurant's biggest draws. *280 Fifth Avenue (at Garfield), Park Slope. 718.840.0404. M-Th 6pm-2am, F-Sat 4pm-4am, Sun 4-midnight. Appetizers $8-19, Entrées $15-32.* **F** *to 9th St.*

MID-RANGE

Beast *Mediterranean/Tapas*

Winged gargoyles, dangling chandeliers, and heavy velvet curtains give Beast an almost dungeon-like vibe, but this culinary star in Prospect Heights will, in fact, unchain your appetite. Careful accents like wine served in quartino carafes and bewitchingly good charred flatbread set the stage for tapas as eclectic as the customers, and as big as some other restaurants' entrées. Lighter dishes, like a ricotta-and-onion tart served with spiced pears, whet the appetite for the heartier meals such as seared scallops served with squash puree and fried leeks. For dessert, the homemade pistachio ice cream atop grilled baby bananas or the specialty sticky toffee cake will leave your smile as wide as the pot-bellied stone monsters across the room. *638 Bergen Street (at Vanderbilt), Prospect Heights. 718.399.6855. Lunch M-F 11:30-4; Dinner Sun-W 6-10:30, F-Sat 6-10:30. Tapas $4-13.* **2 3** *to Bergen St.*

Lunetta *Tapas/Italian*

Simplicity is the name of the game at this Boerum Hill eatery—and that's a good thing. From the décor, understated and elegant, to the food, well-prepared and tasty, there are no unnecessary bells and whistles here; instead, a reliance on quality ingredients and the interaction of contrasting flavors provides all the layering you could ask for. The tapas, beefed up a little for American tastes, are perfect for sharing, but skip the too-large cheese

plate if you're in it for the long haul. As a general rule, it's probably a good idea to share everything, from bruschetta and contorni to entrées that are delicious, but often limited in scope. If you're in the area, the gelato is worth the trip all by itself—try the Campari grapefruit flavor and you'll wonder why you don't live closer by. *116 Smith Street (at Pacific), Boerum Hill. 718.488.6269. T-Sun 5:30-11, Sunday brunch 11-3. Small plates $4-21, Entrées $8-17.* **F G** *to Bergen St.*

Madiba *South African*

The term Madiba, once an honorary title given to respected elders in Nelson Mandela's South African clan, is now associated almost exclusively with the famed anti-apartheid leader; the name of this eatery, owned by native South Africans and frequented by Brooklyn locals and South African transplants alike, honor him. The authentic cuisine explodes with a multitude of flavors; dishes are influenced by the cooking traditions of the country's native tribes, along with its Dutch, English, and Indian settlers. Try the Durban bunny chow (South African slang for "food on the run")—a quarter loaf of white bread filled with curried stew of vegetables, chicken, or mutton—for a tasty and satisfying twist on a traditional lunch. For a delightful post-dinner digestive, ask for a glass of amarula, a creamy concoction made solely from fermented wild fruit. *195 Dekalb Avenue (at Carlton), Fort Greene. 718.855.9190. Brunch Sat-Sun 10:30-4; Lunch M-F noon-4; Dinner Sun-Th 5-midnight, F-Sat 5pm-1am; Lounge M-F 5pm-1am, Sat-Sun 5pm-2:30am. Appetizers $10-16, Entrées $14-24.* **C** *to Lafayette.*

Pete's Downtown *Italian*

This self-described "landmark restaurant" first opened its doors back when Brooklyn was still its own city; it's been serving up casual Italian fare at the foot of the Brooklyn Bridge since 1894, the year after the opening of the bridge itself. Inside the historic building, diners devour favorites like veal parmesan and lemon-baked clams while savoring a spectacular view of the Manhattan skyline. Three roomy seating areas and a friendly waitstaff make Pete's especially great for groups and short-notice dining; reservations are only necessary on weekends.

*2 Water Street (at Old Fulton), Brooklyn Heights. 718.858.3510. T-Th noon-10, F-Sun noon-11. Appetizers $7-9, Entrées $14-26. **C** to High St.*

Relish *American*

Don't let the 50s-era diner ambiance—complete with hamburgers, mac and cheese, and banana splits—fool you; this is no greasy spoon. Located in a beautifully restored stainless steel dining car, the New American cuisine at this revived diner draws its influences from places as wide-ranging as North Africa and Long Island, as eclectic as its Williamsburg clientele. Enjoy glazed salmon with lentils and spinach in the dining car's booths, sip a Singapore Sling in the "Gold Room," or perch on a counter stool for scrambled eggs with coriander chutney. In the summer, you can dine among the roses in one of Williamsburg's most spacious and beautiful restaurant gardens, with a smoking section—a strip of lawn presided over by a stone Madonna—that's as inviting as it is well-used.

*225 Wythe Avenue (at North 3rd), Williamsburg. 718.963.4546. Sun-Th 11am-midnight, F-Sat 11am-1am. Appetizers $6-12, Entrées $6-21. **L** to Bedford Ave.*

Stone Park Café *New American*

Situated in a long line of fabulous Park Slope bars, lounges, and gourmet restaurants, Stone Park Café shows up the competition not only in Brooklyn, but on the isle as well. The New American fare might look a little fatty, but as soon as you taste it, you'll understand why—and won't care. Ample use of

Manhattan Bridge

succulent pork belly bacon, found in the tender quail schnitzel, and gourmet twists on American favorites, like chicken soup with ginger and dumplings, characterize a menu full of vivacious flavors. Eat outside if you can; the atmosphere is pleasant, and the air is cleaner here.

324 Fifth Avenue (at 3rd), Park Slope. 718.369.0082. Brunch Sat-Sun 11-3; Dinner T-Th 5:30-10, F-Sat 5:30-11, Sun 5:30-9, Closed Monday. Appetizers $8-14, Entrées $12-28. R *to Union St.*

Toro *Spanish-Japanese Fusion*

Fusion cuisine isn't just a gimmick at this creative eatery, where a team of multicultural chefs crafts innovative and exquisite twists on ethnic favorites. French and Italian-inspired plates, such as honey-sweet scallops over asparagus, blend in seamlessly alongside Japanese hand rolls and sashimi. The tapas, artistically presented, could stand alone as meals—buy a few and share if you need to save money. But be sure to save some cash for a house cocktail such as the Zentini (citrus vodka, green tea

liqueur, and lime), which might be worth the trip in and of itself.

1 Front Street (at Old Fulton), DUMBO. 718.625.0300. T-Sun 5-11pm, closed Monday. Tapas $7-12. A C *to High St.*

CASUAL
Brooklyn Ice Cream Factory

Waiting in line is part of the experience at this ice cream parlor situated on the pier beside the Brooklyn Bridge. It's wildly popular among both tourists and locals; by the time you get your butter pecan cone on hot summer days, you'll be dripping with sweat and ice cream will never have tasted better. All ice cream is made on the premises and contains "only the finest, purest, natural ingredients," so feel free to indulge without worrying about mass-produced preservatives. The menu offers eight classic flavors, crafted with techniques perfected over time, and each is truly an excellent treat. Don't miss the vanilla chocolate chunk; it's creamy but not too rich, with chunks that offer texture and flavor without

toshiparties.com

overwhelming the vanilla.

Water & Old Fulton Street (on the Fulton Ferry Landing), DUMBO. 718.246.3963. Sun-W noon-10, Th-Sat noon.-11. Closed on winter Mondays. Desserts $3.50-$8. Cash only. **A C** *to High St.*

Nightlife
BARS
Boat *Dive Bar*

This place has everything you could want from a neighborhood bar: good, cheap drinks, a great jukebox, laid-back bartenders, and a customer-friendly, spacious layout. Located just off the F train, this local hangout is usually buzzing with regulars early in the week, and attracts a nightcap crowd on the weekends.

175 Smith Street (at Wyckoff), South Brooklyn. 718.254.0607. Daily 5pm-3:30am. Drinks $3-6. **F G** *to Bergen St.*

Floyd NY *Sports Bar*

The regular crowd of seasoned locals is happy to converse with newcomers at this low-key sports bar. The owner is from Kentucky, and it shows; while the bar fits perfectly in New York, it also has a strong southern personality, and the Kentucky Derby is the busiest day of the year. Along with bar staples, look for unique fare like the "Crapucopia," an assortment of six "crappy beers" for 12 bucks, and the Kentucky beercheese, a dip, served with crackers, whose ingredients are self-evident. If you're up on your skills, go for a game of bocce ball on the 40-foot, red clay court that runs the length of the room; just be sure to sign up as soon as you arrive, since the wait can get long.

131 Atlantic Avenue (at Henry), Cobble Hill. 718.858.5810. Daily 5pm-4am. Drinks $2-11. **F G** *to Bergen St.*

Mugs Ale House *Pub*

There are so many good beers on tap at this Williamsburg pub that most people never even think about investigating the vast selection of bottled imports—but they should. With a colorful local

contingent, a decent jukebox, and meetings of the local homebrewer's club every second Wednesday of the month, it's easy to see why Manhattanites don't mind schlepping all the way out here for a drink.

125 Bedford Avenue (at North 10th), Williamsburg. 718.486.8232. M-F 2pm-4am, Sat-Sun 11am-4am. Drinks $4-6. **L** *to Bedford Ave.*

Pete's Candy Store *Neighborhood Bar*

A combination of city bar, music venue, and Brooklyn apartment, Pete's laid-back, homey character offers a welcome change of scenery from the over-hyped pretentious atmosphere and double-digit prices of Manhattan nightlife. The seating area in the front is decorated with candles and clippings of international newspapers, while the dimly lit back-room holds a small stage for live music. It's always packed with a small, but loyal clientele—young post-grad Williamsburg residents and off-duty firefighters from the nearby department office. The cocktail menu is somewhat limited, but there are a few more creative items, like the blueberry pomegranate margarita.

709 Lorimer Street (at Richardson). 718.302.3770. petescandystore.com. Sun-W 5pm-2am, Th-Sat 5pm-4am. Cocktails $8-9. **L** *to Lorimer St.*

Union Hall *Bocce and Bar*

Hip scenesters and bocce fanatics alike will adore this popular Brooklyn bar. The basement stage, featuring live music, is decorated like a Victorian living room, with silky floral wallpaper and aged oval portraits. Up-stairs there are two bocce courts, but good luck getting a turn on a Friday night. Natural, though sometimes odd décor—think a two-headed chick and a formal-dehyde-preserved lizard fetus—provides a off-beat but down-to-earth environment for the scruffy, flannel-wearing local boys. The cheap selection of local beers, decently priced (Chelsea Blonde: $4) and the friendly neighborhood vibe just might remind you that you've been in Manhattan too long.

702 Union Street (at Fifth). 718.638.4400. unionhallny. com. Drinks: $4. M-F 4pm-4am, Sat-Sun noon-4am. **M R** *to Union.*

CENSUS FACTS

? Total Population: 2,465,326

? Median Age of Residents: 34.6

? Median Household Income: $37,332

? Individuals Below Poverty Level: 25.1%

? Race/Ethnicity: White 42.1%, Black or African American 36%, Asian 9.1%, Hispanic or Latino (of any race) 19.8%, American Indian and Alaska Native 0.4%, Native Hawaiian and Other Pacific Islander 0.1%, Other 11.2%, Two or more races 1.3%

? Language Other than English Spoken at Home: 46.2%

? Education (Population 25 years and over): High School Graduate or Higher 77.6%, Bachelor's Degree or Higher 26.7%

Source: U.S. Census 2000

CLUBS

Black Betty *Lounge*

Dishing up cool live music and North African cuisine seven days a week, this lively bar is a haven for a hip crowd of young Brooklynites who think that gritty charm makes the place all the more comfortable. The jazz, world music, and trip-hop acts brought in by the club's booking agent, lovingly referred to as the "Professor," have helped to make this one of Williamsburg's most popular nightspots. Be sure to call ahead for reservations.

366 Metropolitan Avenue (at Havemeyer), Williamsburg 718.599.0243. Daily 6pm-4am. Drinks $4-8. **G** *to Metropolitan.*

OTHER

Brownstone Billiards *Pool Hall*

Although it plays frequent host to daytime birthday parties for the under-12 set, this large, dimly lit cavern of pool, ping-pong, bowling, and air hockey tables has a significantly older clientele in the evening. Shoot some pool for $5 an hour.

308 Flatbush Avenue (at Seventh), Park Slope. 718.857.5555. Daily noon-2am. **B** **Q** *to Seventh Ave.*

Galapagos Art Space *Performance*

This Williamsburg staple started as an art gallery proper, but is well known today as an event space; everything from burlesque shows to television premiers have made use of the space's modest facilities, with many events open to the public. To preserve an underground feel, visitors pass by a large, unexpected pool of shallow water upon entrance; getting to the back feels almost like you're traveling through New York's sewer system. Once you're there, the interior opens into a long, narrow room containing a bar and a stage, with an additional room off to the side. Art fans should come now to see this important venue in its original home—rising rents, a side effect of Williamsburg's recent gentrification, are forcing it to move to DUMBO in the summer of 2008.

70 North 6th Street (at Kent), Williamsburg. 718.782.5188. Sun–Th 6-2, F-Sat 6pm-4am. Cover $5 and up, plus drinks. L to Bedford Ave.

Toshi Parties

Pleasure seekers from all over the New York metropolitan area head to the quarterly parties thrown by the promoter-turned-cameo actor known only as Toshi. (Look for him, briefly, in The Departed). The watered-down raves, featuring heavy doses of bare flesh and booze—parties are open bar, with servers who notoriously prance about bare-chested, covered only in body paint—typically attract over 5,000 people. Recently, parties have faced myriad problems that have made them lose some of their luster: Crowds are frequently infused with creepy 30-somethings hoping to bag drunken college girls, ticket holders are often forced to wait outside over-crowded venues for entry, and legal woes over questionable liquor licenses have caused alcohol service to be interrupted on more than one occasion. The parties are nothing, however, if not a good deal—go for the open bar, the wall-to-wall flesh, and a night you'll never remember.

Various locations throughout Brooklyn. toshifilms.com. Tickets $10-60.

Warsaw Club *Music*

The building housing this important local music venue is an antiquated brick structure with elaborate wood paneling, true to the Polish heritage of Greenpoint—on the entrance doorway, "Polish National Home" is painted in red letters. Formerly a meeting hall and center for the Polish community, this space has been transformed into the hangout for the new Brooklyn immigrants: hipsters. Those on the fringes of modern art claim this joint as their own, listening to new-age music at the frequently-held shows, but maintain the Polish vibe by chowing down on pierogis and blintzes.

Many Polish locals even come to mingle with the hipster scene, playing pool and chatting amid the tight pants and PBR; indeed, the club's self-given tagline is "Where pierogies meet Punk."

261 Driggs (at Eckford), Greenpoint. 718.387.0505. T-Sun 6-midnight, closed Monday. Cash only. G to Nassau.

Arts

BAM (Brooklyn Academy of Music)

The Brooklyn Academy of Music, never content to be limited by the scope of its moniker, is the undisputed crown jewel of Fort Greene; everything from independent movie screenings to full-blown productions of world-renowned theatrical works take place at this community and cultural powerhouse. Since 1861, the internationally recognized academy has brought the arts to Brooklyn through varied programs and performances, centered in a glorious Beaux-Arts theater that has become a neighborhood landmark. Catch a film at the BAM Rose Cinemas—one of their three screens is perennially devoted to screening classic movies—or check out BAMcafe's Next Next series, which showcases fresh-faced performers of all musical persuasions.

30 Lafayette Avenue (at Ashland), Fort Greene. 718.636.4100. bam.org **2 3 4 5 Q B** *to Atlantic Ave.*

Billie Holiday Theatre

For more than thirty years, this theater has been an acclaimed training ground for talented African American actors and playwrights, helping to jump-start the careers of Samuel L. Jackson and other notables. Housed in the same building as the Skylight Gallery, it boasts cheap tickets ($12-20), an intimate 200-seat theater, and a 10-month season. In large part, the theater focuses on plays with social commentary and material that's relevant to the current political climate; recent works include "The Desire," about a Hurricane Katrina survivor.

1368 Fulton Street (at Marcy), Bedford-Stuyvesant. 718.636.0918. thebillieholiday.org. Tickets $12-20. Call for showtimes and to reserve tickets. **A C** *to Nostrand Ave.*

Brooklyn Museum of Art

If you need an excuse to visit the impressive collection at this world-renowned museum, come on the first Saturday of every month from 5-11pm—that's when Target sponsors free First Saturday parties, featuring live bands, cheap drinks, and extended museum hours. If you don't need a party to lure you in, then you probably already know that the Museum, the second-largest in the city, is actually one of the most important art institutes in the world. The diverse collection is especially strong in non-Western and feminist art.

200 Eastern Parkway (at Washington), Eastern Parkway. 718.638.5000. brooklynmuseum.org. W-F 10-5, Sat-Sun 11-6, closed M-T. Adults $8, Students $4 (suggested). **2 3** *to Eastern Parkway-Brooklyn Museum.*

New York Transit Museum

Housed in a historic 1936 IND subway station in Brooklyn Heights, and easily accessible by subway, the New York Transit Museum is the largest museum in the United States devoted to urban public transportation history, and one of the premier institutions of its kind in the world. The Museum explores the development of the greater New York metropolitan region through the presentation of exhibitions, tours, educational programs and workshops dealing with the cultural, social and technological history of public transportation. Go to www.mta.info for details of current exhibits and programs, or to shop the Museum 's online store.

Court Street Station (at Boerum Pl), Brooklyn Heights. 718.694.1600. Adults $5. **2 3 4 5** *to Borough Hall.*

Museum of Contemporary African Diasporan Arts (MoCADA)

This modestly-sized museum, founded in 1999, uses art to explore the social, political, and economic issues faced by the African Diaspora. As part of its effort to alter that historically negative portrayals of blacks, the museum presents exhibitions that are not afraid to shock viewers, illuminating the oppression of people of African descent all over the globe.

80 Hanson Place (at Portland), Fort Greene. 718.230.0492. mocada.org. W-Sun 11-6, closed M-T. Adults $4, Students $3. **2 3 4 5** Q **B** *to Atlantic Avenue.*

Pierogi 2000

Fusing old-school Polish and new-school hipster, this gallery is housed in an abandoned warehouse but has a chicly new-age interior. Visit for exhibitions of traditional paintings as well as more, um, unusual works—like pistachio shells painted brown.

177 North 9th Street (at Bedford), Williamsburg. 718.599.2144. pierogi2000.com. Th-M 11-6. L *to Bedford Ave.*

Skylight Gallery

Located on the third floor of the Bedford-Stuyvesant Restoration Corporation's Center for Arts and Culture, this gallery showcases a wide variety of multicultural works. With a central skylight and huge glass windows overlooking the tops of Bed-Stuy rowhouses on Fulton Street, this sun-filled room is a pleasant community space in an art-starved neighborhood.

1368 Fulton Street (at Marcy), 3rd floor, Bedford-Stuyvesant. 718.636.6949. W-F 11-6, Sat 1-6. Closed Sun-Tu. restorationarts.org. **A C** *to Nostrand Ave.*

St. Ann's Warehouse

This 27-year-old arts organization, a recent transplant to DUMBO from Brooklyn Heights, hosts edgy performing arts shows in a former spice-milling warehouse. Committed to encouraging musical and visual artists to try their hand at theatrics, St. Ann's is an alternative, ever-evolving hybrid performance space. Try to snag tickets to the annual avant-garde puppet show, Labapalooza, held in late May and early June.

38 Water Street (at Dock), DUMBO. 718.254.8779. stannswarehouse.org. F *to York St.*

Shopping

About Glamour

Aiming to provide a one-stop shop for glamorous urbanites, this 2,400-square-foot space houses an art gallery, a clothing boutique, and a hair salon. Browse the boutique for one-of-a-kind hand-sewn garments and designer clothing, old children's books, and British housewares, or grab some stationery and household gifts by acclaimed Japanese designer Muji.

103 North 3rd Street (at Wythe), Williamsburg. 718.599.3044. aboutglamour.net. M-Sat 12-10, Sun 12-8. L to Bedford Ave.

Beacon's Closet

If you've heard of Williamsburg, you've probably heard of Beacon's Closet. Opened in 1997, this 5,500-square-foot used clothing store is the spot for stylish thrift store fanatics on a budget. The eminently rummage-able racks are organized by color, not size or style, and they've got a great selection of almost everything, including shoes, boots, and vintage dresses. Bring your own clothes to exchange for cash or a discount, but be prepared for rejection—the staff often politely refuses to buy clothes that aren't up to their standards of quality.

88 North 11th Street (at Wythe), Williamsburg. 718.486.0816. beaconscloset.com. M-F noon-9, Sat-Sun 11-8. L to Bedford.

Brooklyn Industries

In 1998, the founders of this iconic Williamsburg boutique and clothing line started making messenger bags out of recycled billboards. Today, they have eight stores all over the city, and a new contemporary art center in their native neighborhood. Here at the original store, opened in 2001, the line continues to define Williamsburg style with inventive clothing and accessories that unite hipster and urban trends.

162 Bedford Avenue (at 8th), Williamsburg. 718.486.6464. brooklynindustries.com. M-Th 11-9, F-Sat 11-9:30, Sun 11-8:30. L to Bedford Ave.

Brooklyn Superhero Supply Company/826NYC

Of all the gimmicky novelty shops on Fifth Avenue, the gimmick at this place is by far the cutest. The front of the store, which sells everything a superhero could possibly need to fight crime, is actually just that—a front, meant to bait students from local middle and elementary schools inside. Once there, kids are drawn to the back of the store, which functions as a tutoring and writing center. It's the tutors themselves, however, that are the biggest surprise of all; some of Park Slope's most well-known contemporary writers, including Dave Eggers and Jonathan Safran Foer, regularly stop by to teach workshops. Consider coming here for some Titanium-Encased Knee Guards, or to apply for a volunteer position.

372 Fifth Avenue (at 5th), Park Slope. 718.499.9884. 826nyc.org. Daily 11:30-5:30. F M R to 4th Ave/9th St.

Brownstone Books

One of a number of stores on this section of Lewis Avenue that are leading the push to gentrify the famously inner-city Bedford-Stuyvesant, Brownstone Books is as upscale as bookshops around here get. Books are organized and displayed neatly in this small, wooden shop, making it easy to browse. Community events, including a monthly book club and frequent poetry readings, prove that this independent shop is putting in the effort to add something currently missing from the neighborhood.

409 Lewis Avenue (at Decatur), Bedford-Stuyvesant. 718.953.7328. brownstonebooks.com. M-Sat 10-7, Sun noon-5. A C to Utica Ave.

Buffalo Exchange

The only city location of this popular national chain—which aims to protect the environment by promoting recycling—buys clothes from its customers and resells them, although you wouldn't know it from their pristine condition. Mainstream brands abound, but you can often find unique treasures, too; the well-organized selection and friendly staff make it easier to shop here than at almost any other second-hand store around.

504 Driggs Avenue (at North 9th), Williamsburg. 718.384.6901. M-Sat 11-8, Sun 12-7. L to Bedford Ave.

Future Perfect

If you need to spice up your living room, it's time to visit this home décor shop that could be considered a piece of art on its own. In addition to the art space downstairs and the fish tank toilet in the bathroom, the store features home décor that fuses retro and futuristic styles, and that's almost too beautiful to buy. If you're in a quirky mood, pick up a bin made of recycled newspaper and a set of ceramic antler chandeliers.

115 North 6th Street (at Berry), Williamsburg. 718.599.6278. thefutureperfect.com. M-Sun 12-7. L to Bedford Ave.

Jay East Direct Import Warehouse

Find gold Buddha statues, ornate opium pipes, and kitschy clocks featuring pictures of Chairman Mao at this Chinese antique furniture and artifacts warehouse. Prices, which vary dramatically based on the individual item, soar into the thousands for high-quality sculptures, although there are also plenty of cool items under $100. Splurge on an artsy gift or grab some unique imported decorations for your new apartment.

67 Jay Street (at Front), DUMBO. 718.237.8430. Daily 11-6. jayeast.com. F to York St.

Mini Minimarket

Successfully combining a hole-in-the-wall market with an upscale boutique, this unique shop features funky, top-of-the-line clothing as well as sunglasses, postcards, bags, and jewelry, much of it designed by local artists. Eccentric knick-knacks and vibrant clothes give the store a fun atmosphere, and though its screen-printed tees and wooden disc earrings seem a bit overpriced at $40-100, you can find good bargains on sale if you look hard enough.

218 Bedford Avenue (at North 5th), Williamsburg. 718.302.9337. miniminimarket.com. Daily 12-9. L to Bedford Ave.

Olive's Very Vintage

Sexy '80s one-piece swimsuits and colorful '50s frocks fill the racks of this delightful shop on Court Street, surprisingly spacious and uncluttered for a vintage store. Prices can run a bit high—it's not uncommon to find pieces by designers like Marc Jacobs and Oscar de la Renta—but browse hard enough and fashion devotees and hipsters alike are sure to find good deals.

434 Court Street (at 2nd), Carroll Gardens. 718.243.9094. olivesveryvintage.com. M-Sat noon-8, Sun 10-6. F to Carroll St.

The powerHouse Arena

Don't leave Brooklyn without visiting this self-described "laboratory for creative thought," located in a 5,000-square-foot space with pristine white walls and lofty ceilings. Eccentric and eye-catching exhibits, set to a soundtrack of soft French pop, cover a wide array of topics—graffiti to male sexuality. The organization's wide selection of photography books, from hardcover glossies to children's lookbooks, is so large you could spend hours perusing it; the art book publisher powerHouse Books has its offices in the back. The arena also hosts events, like the Brooklyn Hip Hop Festival.

37 Main Street (at Water), DUMBO. 718.666.3049. powerhousearena.com. M-F 10-7, Sat-Sun 11-7. F to York St.

QUEENS

Queens, two-time home of the World's Fair, is appropriately one of the most ethnically diverse spots in the world; more than 100 ethnic groups and 120 languages share space in this borough including prominent Jewish, Italian, Irish, Greek, African American, Latin American, and South Asian communities.

When Queens was merged into New York in 1898, much of it was still fenced-off farmland. But by the 1930s the borough was beginning to develop tree-lined rows of modest brick and wood-framed houses. With them, its current character began to appear. The 1939 World's Fair solidified the borough's role as one of New York's primary locales for recreation, and preparation for the Fair converted Flushing Meadows Corona Park from a dumpsite into the current urban oasis that it is.

Despite its reputation as Brooklyn's awkward little sibling, Queens has plenty to brag about. Few areas can outdo its ethnic and cultural diversity, museums, parks, and amazing food.

Still, many people are content to simply pass through; perhaps it's because Queens is home to both of the city's major airports, or maybe people are just boggled by the confusing street address system. Queens' addresses contain two numbers separated by a dash; the first refers to the closest cross street, while the second names the actual address. The address 34-21 42nd Street, for example, is on 42nd Street, closest to 34th Avenue. Got it? Good. Now that you know how to get around, you'll find plenty of reasons to stay a while.

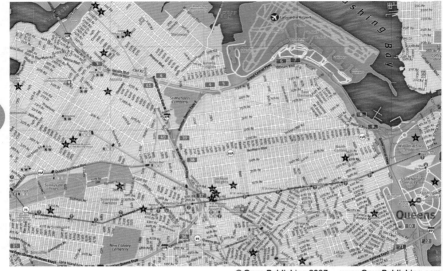

© Opus Publishing 2007 — www.OpusPublishing.com

QUEENS

SIGHTS
1. 5 Pointz
2. Flushing Meadows Corona Park
3. Louis Armstrong House Museum
5. Shea Stadium

DINING
6. Agnanti
8. Donovan's Pub
9. Freeze Peach
10. Lemon Ice King Corona
11. Pop Diner
12. Trattoria L'incontro

NIGHTLIFE
13. Bohemian Hall and Beer Garden
14. Café Bar
15. Irish Rover

ARTS
16. American Museum of the Moving Image
17. Eagle Theater
18. Isamu Noguchi Garden Museum
19. P.S. 1 Contemporary Art Center
20. Queens Museum of Art
21. Socrates Sculpture Park

SHOPPING
22. Butala Emporium
23. Flushing Mall
24. Patel Brothers
25. Queens Center Mall
26. Rudy Volcano

Queens Neighborhoods
ASTORIA

Long Island City's neighbor to the north is truly one of New York's great melting pots. Although the prominent Mediterranean population earns Astoria a reputation as "**Little Greece**," the neighborhood is also home to large numbers of Brazilian, Italian, Croatian, Colombian, and Egyptian immigrants, each group adding to the multi-national atmosphere. In recent years, Astoria has become popular with fresh college grads in search of affordable rent; trendy bars and cafés lie scattered in the vicinity of the **Museum of the Moving Image** (*35th Avenue at 36th*) to accommodate PBR-drinking hipsters. The family-owned restaurants that have been around for generations aren't going anywhere, either, however—enjoy a carafe of house wine and some tzatziki at one of the Greek restaurants on **Steinway Street**, named for Henry Steinway of the famed piano factory that still operates at the end of the street.

As a fun and relaxing evening destination, Astoria has a flavor that is all its own. Beer lovers should be sure to visit **Bohemian Hall** (*29-19 24th Avenue at 29th*). Built in 1910 by Czech and Slovak immigrants, it claims to be the city's oldest beer garden; choose from the extensive collection of Czech sausages if you're craving a slightly out-of-the-ordinary midnight snack. For a different but equally authentic experience, stop at one of the many cheap-as-dirt hookah bars in the area that are thankfully devoid of drink minimums. Sit under an elaborately decorated tent and drink freshly brewed mint tea as Lebanese men play backgammon at the next table. Just don't be shy around the belly dancers, because it only makes them work harder to get you to dance.

LONG ISLAND CITY

Located just one subway stop away from Manhattan on the 7 train, Long Island City is a factory town-turned art-paradise and yuppie haven. With luxury apartment buildings sprouting up along the East River—offering low rents and astounding views of the midtown Manhattan skyline—the area is booming in popularity. The resulting gentrification is still in its early stages; quaintly upscale French and Thai bistros look out of place next to run-down bodegas and liquor stores, and everything from television studios to coffee shops seems to be opening up in converted factories. Abandoned structures, grouped like phantoms of the 19th century's industrial boom, are oddly beautiful—although, like the area's relatively low rents, they may soon be a thing of the past.

Due to its gritty, industrial feel and up-and-coming status, Long Island City has attracted a diverse community of artists, making it a destination for art-lovers all over New York. Across from **P.S. 1** (*22-25 Jackson Avenue at 46th*), the lauded, alternative branch of MoMA, graffiti artists proudly and legally display their work at **5 Pointz** (*Jackson Avenue at Crane*). A few streets over, the **Isamu Noguchi Garden Museum** (*36-01 43rd Avenue*) features innovative and sophisticated sculpture.

If you're down to explore Long Island City, you might think about bringing along a date; this is one place in the city where you can have a romantic evening without emptying your wallet. Make a reservation at **Café Henri** (*10-10 50th Avenue at Vernon*) for crepes and live music, then stroll to the piers of **Gantry Plaza State Park** (*50-50 Second Street at 51st*), where award-winning designers paid homage to LIC's industrial history by integrating old train gantries into the park's architecture.

FLUSHING

With an East Asian population whose size rivals that of Manhattan's Chinatown, downtown Flushing provides one of the most intense and authentic cultural experiences in New York City. Take the 7 train all the way to the end, exiting at the corner of Main Street and Roosevelt, to get started—just don't be intimidated by the crowds on Main, the neighborhood's central artery. For the best bargains in the area, browse the small stores, which you've probably never heard of, in the **Flushing Mall** (*133-31 39th Avenue at College Point*). Once you work up an appetite, get some Chinese, Korean, Vietnamese, or Malaysian food from the mall's food court, or step outside and support one of the many independent East Asian eateries close by. If you've still got room for dessert, walk north along Main Street to **Fay Da Bakery** (*37-11 Main Street*), where you can gratify your sweet tooth with a wide variety of Chinese buns and cookies; and make sure to try your favorite flavor of bubble tea, the drink of choice in this vibrant neighborhood. Conclude your visit by heading southwest to the 1,255-acre **Flushing Meadows Corona Park** (*Roosevelt Avenue at Grand Central Parkway*); the largest park in Queens, it's home to the USTA Tennis Center, Shea Stadium, an ice skating rink, and even a science museum.
7 *to Flushing-Main Street.*

FOREST HILLS

Though it's a bit of a hike from Manhattan, this well-to-do neighborhood offers many attractions, and it's a great location for a day trip off the island. Just across from the 71st Avenue subway hub—the last stop on the G, R, and V trains—is the borough's best movie theater, **Midway Stadium 9** (*108-22 Queens Boulevard*). Just take caution when crossing Queens Boulevard, widely-known from the TV show *Entourage*; its many-faceted intersections are a challenge even to veteran New York pedestrians, earning it the fearsome nickname, "the Boulevard of Death." When the movie's over, go one block further to **Austin Street** (*at 71st Ave*) for a walk through the area's quaintest shopping and dining center. The neighborhood is heavy in national chain clothing stores, but don't miss local food favorites like the odiferous, one-of-a-kind **Cheese of the World** (*71-48 Austin*

Street), or one of the area's many resturants. After you've sated yourself, go back along the street to one of the local bars—try the loud and fun **5 Burro Café** (*72-05 Austin Street*) or the upscale **Billiard Company** (*70-49 Austin Street*). If romance is in the air, finish the evening with a stroll around the **Forest Hills Gardens**—cross under the LIRR archway and step onto the cobblestone roads and quiet, tree-lined streets of one of Queens' oldest and most exclusive neighborhoods. Well-kept Tudor homes and eclectic automobiles abound, as do chances to get lost under stone gateways, meandering roads, and peaceful cul-de-sacs.

E R F V G *to 71st-Continental Ave.*

JACKSON HEIGHTS

Visiting Jackson Heights is like traveling to a foreign country—or ten of them. In the early 20th century, the area was marketed as a "garden community" to lure upper middle class families out of Manhattan, but over the past 30 years, immigrants from all over the world have flocked here, resulting in a vibrant, thriving neighborhood with the best inexpensive ethnic food in the city. Near the 74th Street-Broadway transit hub lies **Little India**, a glittering stretch of sari shops, Indian jewelry stores, South Asian grocery stores, and Indian restaurants; stop at **Butala Emporium** (*37-46 74th Street*), for colorful bangles, framed portraits of Vishnu, or a Hindi-English dictionary. For a cheap and delicious Indian lunch buffet, go to the acclaimed **Jackson Diner** (*37-47 74th Street*), then head to the bakery counter at **Roti Boti** (*72-09 Broadway at 72nd*), where for just $3, you can get a colorful assortment of sticky, sweet desserts.

If you prefer plantain chips to Pakistani pastries, walk back to Roosevelt Avenue under the elevated tracks of the 7 train. You'll find Argentinean and Colombian restaurants, along with more than one food truck selling Ecuadorian snacks that you can take with you as you wander. There are plenty of bars and bailaderos as well, but if you don't speak Spanish, expect to be greeted by blank stares and puzzled looks. Before you leave, check out the stately garden apartments in the quiet, tree-lined **Jackson Heights Historic District**, some of which were designed by the planners of Central Park; the sophisticated **Greystones** (*80th Street at 37th and 35th*), constructed in 1917, were the first of these buildings.

As a general rule, most of the green space in Jackson Heights is private, located in the interior courtyards of apartment buildings. For public greenery, stop by **Travers Park** (*78th Street at 34th*)—a peaceful spot with fun people-watching, or ride the bike trails along 80th and 81st that link the neighborhood to Flushing Meadows Corona Park.

Sights/Attractions

5 Pointz

Graffiti artists from all five boroughs are invited to work on the outer walls of this converted warehouse, which is visible from the 7 train and takes up an entire city block. The building, covered with over 600 tags, is a showcase of graffiti masterpieces; check out the faux Rembrandt on the eastern wall. If you want to tag, show up Saturday afternoon to get permission from the building's private owner—space is limited, and respect of other artists' works is strictly enforced. *Jackson Avenue (at Crane), Long Island City.* **7** *to 45 Rd/ Courthouse Sq.*

Flushing Meadows Corona Park

There might be 1,255 acres of green space at this massive park, but the land that it occupies was once a landfill—only the prospect of a 1939 NYC World's Fair was enough to convince the city to plant some grass and build a park here. Remnants of that World's Fair, and of the 1964 Fair on the same spot, still characterize much of the land here; many of the park's most important buildings and most recognizable icons were Fair structures in their original incarnations, including the Unisphere and the Hall of Science. Today, the park is an asset to the Queens community in the same way that Central Park is to Manhattan; many important borough landmarks, including the Queens Museum of Art, the Queens Botanical Garden, Shea Stadium, Arthur Ashe Stadium (home of the US Open), and the Queens Wildlife Center are located on the park's grounds.

Flushing. **7** *to Shea Stadium/Willet's Point.*

Queens Botanical Garden

The quiet tranquility of the Queens Botanical Garden makes it an ideal retreat from the bustling streets of downtown Flushing. Indulge your senses with a stroll through Fragrance Walk, featuring an assortment of plants known for their strong scents, or simply sit and read on one of the many inviting benches. Don't miss the beautiful Perennial and Rose Gardens, two of several themed gardens that are worth checking out.

43-50 Main Street (at Dahlia), Flushing. 718.886.3800. queensbotanical.org. Hours vary by season. Free. **7** *to Flushing-Main St.*

Shea Stadium

Home to New York City's other baseball team, Shea Stadium attracts truly loyal, local fans—don't come wearing black and white stripes, or you might end up black and blue. Tickets are cheaper than at Yankee Stadium, and better seats are available on short notice; even though the Mets continue to have an impressive record season after season, this '60s expansion team lacks the long-time tradition of the Bronx Bombers, and has a harder time selling out seats. Be sure to make it to a game within the next year if you can; starting with the 2009 season, the Mets will be moving out of Shea for good, and into a larger, sleeker facility right next door.

Flushing Meadows Corona Park, Flushing. 718.507.TIXX. newyork.mets.mlb.com. **7** *to Shea Stadium/Willet's Point.*

Dining
UPSCALE

Trattoria L'incontro *Italian*

Excellent Italian prevails at chef Rocco Sacramone's spectacular upscale eatery in the heart of Astoria. High quality ingredients are paired with simple décor and a warm environment, effectively setting the mood for a special evening at a price unachievable in Manhattan. Though the wait staff is friendly and attentive, perhaps its biggest strength is the nightly recitation of a vast number of specials, which all but

Shea Stadium

render the menu secondary. With a wine list of over 200 bottles and rave reviews, Trattoria L'incontro is well worth the cost, and to some is reason enough to venture into to the borough. However, with such broad appeal, those willing to make the commute should be warned: reservations are an absolute must.

21-76 31st Street (at Ditmars), Astoria. 718.721.3532. T-Th noon-10pm, F-Sat noon-11pm, Sun 1pm-11pm, closed Monday. N W *to Ditmars Blvd-Astoria.*

MID-RANGE

Pop Diner *American*

This family-owned diner is an updated version of the traditional classic; comfortable booths and a sleek bar are vibrantly colored in an atmosphere that is simultaneously easy-going and stylish. The menu is as extensive as you'd expect from a well-run diner—grab anything from scrambled eggs to crab cakes—but it also includes an unexpected selection of Latin and Caribbean specialties, including items like Singaporean hakka noodles and mofongo, a Puerto Rican mash dish. Don't leave without trying

a home-baked dessert—heavy, indulgent, and definitely all-American.

80-26 Queens Boulevard (at 51st), Astoria. 718.426.2229. Sun-Th 7am-1am, F-Sat 24 hours. Entrées $10-20. N V G *to Grand Ave.*

CASUAL

Bon Chon Chicken *Korean Barbecue*

The focus at the first American outpost of this popular Korean fried chicken chain is definitely on the wings, which are flash fried (unlike the greasy deep frying techniques of Buffalo-style wings) and lightly tossed in either garlic sauce or hot sauce to ensure a light, crispy product that's unlike anything you've ever tasted. It's still up for debate whether or not they're better than the American kind, though it's certainly a close race; either way, it's a fascinating—and delicious—comparative study.

157-18 Northern Boulevard (at 157th), Flushing 718.321.3818. Daily 11am-10pm. Appetizers $6-9, Entrées $8-20. 7 *to Flushing/Main St.*

Donovan's Pub *Irish-American*

This neighborhood favorite has been in business for almost half a century, and once you taste the superb bar food, you'll quickly see why. Located in the heart of Woodside's Irish community, folks around here are fiercely loyal to Donovan's; many of the customers have been coming here week after week for years. Grab a pint and soak in the castle-like atmosphere if you're short on time, or indulge in everybody's favorite—the hearty $6.75 burgers, which are worth every penny, from the hot juicy beef and fresh toppings to the accompanying fat-roasted fries.

57-24 Roosevelt Avenue (at 58th), Woodside. 718.429.9339. Sun-Th 11:30am-11pm, F-Sat 11:30am-1am. Entrées $4-12, cash only. **7** *to 61st St/ Woodside.*

Eddie's Sweet Shop *Ice Cream and Candy*

This old-time candy shop feels and feeds like an authentic relic of the 1950s; sit on a high stool at the bar and order a real old-fashioned malted, or slide into a booth with some friends and order one of the ice cream sundaes served in stainless, stemmed cups and topped with rich, homemade whipped cream. On a nice evening, get some candy on your way out and walk back to the subway through the beautiful Forest Hills Gardens, one of Queens's oldest and most exclusive communities.

105-29 Metropolitan Avenue (at 72nd), Forest Hills. 718.520.8514. T-F 1pm-11:30pm, Sat-Sun noon-11:30pm. Ice cream $3-7. **E N Q R F V** *to 72nd.*

The Lemon Ice King of Corona *Italian Ices*

In the heart of Queens' Italian section, this Italian ices stand serves up dozens of homemade varieties. A staple of the local community, it's worth a visit on humid city nights to cool down; grab a paper cup of classic lemon, and head across the street, where the kids (and the adults) hang out and play bocce; games often get intense, and if you're lucky, you're in for some entertainment.

52-02 108th Street (at 52nd Avenue), Corona. 718.699.5133. 10am-midnight. Ices $1-3, cash only. **7** *to 111th St.*

Nightlife

BARS

Café Bar *Café, Bar*

As an honest-to-goodness neighborhood hangout, this café/bar hybrid attracts all kinds of Long Island City dwellers. During the day, a veritable cross-section of the local population comes for coffee, lunch, or dessert, hanging out for hours at a time over a book or a conversation. At night, the drink scene takes over, but remarkably, the crowd stays the same; it's not uncommon for Old Country locals to stick around past dark to hang out with new-school club kids.

32-90 36th Street (at 34th Avenue), Astoria. 718.204.5273. Sun-Th 9:30am-2am, F-Sat 9:30am-3am. Drinks $9-11. **R V** *to Steinway St.*

Bohemian Hall and Beer Garden *Beer Garden*

Once a haven for recent immigrants and neighborhood locals, this Czechoslovakian beer garden has recently morphed into a picnic-tabled destination for fresh college graduates. Use the money you save on cheap kielbasa and sauerkraut to pay for a quality beverage—order something from the garden's extensive selection of European beers, perfect for those looking to educate themselves about brews from around the world. On summer nights, make sure you show up early—by late evening, the line to get in can stretch around the block.

29-19 24th Avenue (at 29th Street), Astoria. 718.274.4925. M-Th 6pm-11pm, F 6pm-midnight, Sat noon-midnight, Sun noon-11pm, closed Tuesday. **N W** *to Astoria Blvd.*

Irish Rover *Pub*

This pub pours a mean pint of Guinness—and makes a pretty good shepherd's pie to boot. The clientele is mostly local, and the regulars are mostly Irish, but the crowd on any given night is a mixed bag of ages and types. Performances by local bands are scheduled occasionally to liven things up; call ahead for a schedule.

37-18 28th Avenue (at 37th Street), Astoria. 718.278.9372. Daily 10am-4am. Drinks $4-6. **G R V** *to Steinway St.*

Arts

American Museum of the Moving Image

Create your own cartoon, report on a storm in front of a green screen, or play an original Pac-Man game at this museum dedicated to the history of film and TV. Memorabilia appeal to all ages, from *The Empire Strikes Back* Yoda to a collection of Bill Cosby's sweaters from the *The Cosby Show*. Seek out the costume simulator booth, where you can see what you'd look like in Dorothy's prairie dress from *The Wizard of Oz*, or stop by on weekends to catch one of the free screenings that are the museum's bread and butter.

35th Avenue (at 36th Street), Astoria. 718.784.0077. movingimage. us. W-Th 11am-5pm, F 11am-7:30pm, Sat-Sun 11am-6pm. Adults $10, Students $7.50, free Fridays 4pm-8pm. R V G *to Steinway.*

Isamu Noguchi Garden Museum

A perfect place to escape the summer heat, this museum devoted to Isamu Noguchi, a sculptor and Columbia drop-out, showcases his art in cool gardens and dark interior spaces. Admire the stone, metal, wood, and clay sculptures in the tranquil outdoor area, or enter the surrounding galleries to see the models for public projects, gardens, and dance sets. The converted warehouse and garden architecture are notable spaces in themselves, and pay tribute to Noguchi's belief in the "sculpture of spaces."

36-01 43rd Avenue (at 36th Street), Long Island City. 718.784.2084. naguchi.org. W-F 10am-5pm, Sat-Sun 11am-6pm. Adults $10, Students $5. N W *to Broadway.*

P.S. 1 Contemporary Art Center

This affiliate of the Museum of Modern Art showcases some of the most experimental art in the city. Housed in what used to be an elementary school, enormous murals line the staircases and distinct exhibits occupy each of the classrooms. With no permanent collection, the gallery always features the newest and hottest art; it hosts over 30 exhibits a year along with a few long-term installations. During summer Saturday afternoons, check out Warm Up, a weekly series of dance parties in the courtyard featuring internationally renowned DJs.

22-25 Jackson Avenue (at 46th), Long Island City. 718.784.2084. www.ps1.org. Th-M noon-6pm. Adults $5, Students $2. 7 *to 46th Road-Courthouse Square.*

Queens Museum of Art

The New York City Building, which currently houses this modest museum's collection, was the original headquarters of the United Nation's General Assembly. Today, the collection's claim to fame is its awe-inspiring Panorama of the City of New York, a 9,335-square-foot scale model of the five boroughs. The permanent collection also includes the 1939 and 1964 World Fair Archives, and the Neudstat Collection of Tiffany Art.

NYC Building. Flushing Meadows Corona Park. 718.592.9700. queensmuseum.org. Hours vary by season. Adults $5. 7 *to Willets Point/Shea Stadium.*

Socrates Sculpture Park

In another life, this space was a waterfront dumpsite; now it's a quirky public art space and neighborhood park, offering one of the most breathtaking views of the Manhattan skyline. The sculptures scattered throughout are anything but ordinary; picnic or sunbathe under a shipwrecked boat or a displaced house from New Orleans.

32-01 Vernon Boulevard (at 32nd), Long Island City. 718.956.1819. socratessculpturepark.org. Daily 10-sunset. N W *to Broadway.*

SHOPPING

Flushing Mall

Don't expect to find large department stores or chains here. With its specialty Chinese shops and colorful, mismatched walls and floors, the Flushing Mall feels like a massive flea market. A great place to find bargains, this shopping center carries everything from jewelry to sushi snacks by the indoor fountain.

139-31 39th Avenue. 718.888.1234. 888Flushingmall.com. 7 *to Main St-Flushing*

Queens Center Mall

If street shopping isn't for you, come here for to find 70 stores all under one roof, including an Urban Outfitters, Gap, H&M, Macy's, and Forever 21. On weekdays, it transforms into a teen hotspot; students from all over Queens flock to the mall as soon as the last school bell rings. Stop at the food court for choices ranging from bubble tea to Bourbon Chicken.

90-15 Queens Blvd (at Woodhaven). M-Sat 10-9:30, Sun 11-8. R V G *to Woodhaven Blvd.*

THE BRONX

The 1950s Hollywood version of New York—the one where kids play stickball in the streets while their mothers sit on stoops and gossip while folding laundry—is alive and well, at least in some parts of the Bronx. While communities are often close-knit and child-centric, they're also incredibly diverse: In Riverdale, the wealthy locals spend their weekends in the gardens of Wave Hill, while in Mott Haven and City Island, the landscape best compares to a New England fishing village.

Officially declared a part of New York City in 1898, the Bronx, which is the only borough on the mainland, underwent rapid urbanization once it joined the city. As Jewish, Italian, and Irish immigrants arrived in large numbers, the buildings along the Grand Concourse were decorated with lavish architectural flourishes, and an entrepreneurial spirit prevailed throughout a growing middle class.

In the postwar era, many of the Bronx residents who could afford to leave did so, flocking to the northern suburbs. The Latino and African-American population who followed faced severe housing shortages, high crime rates, and indifference on the part of government and financial institutions. Drug trafficking, arson, and poverty took root in the South Bronx in particular.

Community organizations have worked relentlessly to revitalize the South Bronx and other crime-ridden areas, helping to turn the borough into a more sustainable and pleasant place to live. It's still not advisable to visit certain areas at night, such as Hunts Point, but those who visit in the afternoon will find vibrant pockets of arts and culture tucked between abandoned and decrepit storefronts—signs of the turmoil of past decades, and the effects of development and investment to come.

© Opus Publishing 2007 — www.OpusPublishing.com

SOUTH BRONX

SIGHTS
1. **Bronx Culture Trolley**
2. **Point**
3. **Rincón Criollo**
4. **Writer's Beach**

ARTS
5. **Bronx Museum of the Arts**
6. **Hostos Center for the Arts and Culture**
7. **Mud/Bone Studio 889**

SHOPPING
8. **Casa Amadeo**
9. **The Hub**

Sights/Attractions

Bronx Culture Trolley

On the first Wednesday evening of every month, you can take a ride through the South Bronx on this trolley sponsored by the Bronx Council on the Arts. The ride, and all of the stops and events along the way, including poetry readings, art exhibitions, and theater performances, are free—a great chance to explore this culturally rich neighborhood without having to brave the confusing bus routes.

450 Grand Concourse (at 149th; Hostos Community College). 718.401.9558. bronxarts.org First Wednesday of each month, 5:30pm, 6:30pm, 7:30pm. Free. **2 4 5** *to Grand Concourse.*

The Bronx Zoo

The sheer number of wildlife exhibits and activities at this most eminent of city zoos is enough to merit an entire day of exploration, at least. The summer crowds and the distance between exhibits can be trying, but nothing can detract from the overall beauty and educational value of a day among the wildlife at one of the country's best-run facilities. If you can only go once, pay the extra $11 for an expanded admissions pass; it'll get you access to numerous additional areas of the park, including the monorail, butterfly garden, and Congo gorilla exhibit, easily the best attraction in the park.

Fordham Road (at Bronx River Parkway). 718.367.1010. bronxzoo.com. Daily 10am-5pm; hours vary slightly by season. Adults $14 (suggested donation on Wednesday). **2 5** *to West Farms Square.*

Edgar Allen Poe Cottage

The area surrounding this tiny 1812 beige-shingled cottage, now a park next to the bustling Grand Concourse, was a rural refuge with a full apple orchard in the back when the original master of suspense spent the last years of his life here from 1846-1849. Step inside to enter the world as it was then as you wander through the room where Poe wrote his famous prose poem *Eureka* and the one where his wife died of consumption in 1847. Skip the lengthy movie upstairs and ask for a tour by one of the knowledgeable and passionate guides—just call before you visit, as the cottage will be closed for construction in early 2008.

Grand Concourse (at East 192nd), Fordham Heights. 718.881.8900. bronxhistoricalsociety.org Sat 10am-4pm, Sun 1pm-5pm. Adults $3, Students $2. **B D** *to East Kingsbridge Road.*

New York Botanical Garden

This garden's 250 serene acres, set amid the urban sprawl of Central Bronx, has long lived in the shadow of its famous neighbor, the Bronx Zoo. As one of the major players in worldwide botany research and a family-friendly tourist destination, it certainly deserves better. Visit often to stroll through all 50 gardens on the campus, filled with roses, crabapples, waterlillies, orchids and more, as well as to see frequently-changing exhibitions on everything from blown glass to holiday toy trains.

200th Street (at Kazimiroff), Central Bronx. 718.817.8700. nybg.org. Hours vary by season. Adults $6, Students $2. **4 B D** *to Bedford Park.*

New York Botanical Garden

FAST FACTS

⑦ **Scenic Stroll:** Arthur Avenue

⑦ **Major Subway Stations:** Hunts Point Ave (6), Pelham Bay (6), West Farms Square/East Tremont (2, 5), 149th St-Grand Concourse (2, 4 5), 161st St-Yankee Stadium (4, B D), 242nd St-Van Cortlandt Park (1)

⑦ **Urban Oasis:** New York Botanical Garden, Wave Hill, Van Cortlandt Park

⑦ **Kooky Corner:** Heinrich Heine Memorial Fountain in Joyce Kilmer Park

⑦ **Best Deal:** The Hub

⑦ **Famous Historical Moment:** On October 1, 1961, Roger Maris broke Babe Ruth's record of 60 home runs in a single season

⑦ **Notable Residents:** John Adams, E.L. Doctorow, Theodore Dreiser, Lou Gehrig, Fat Joe, John F. Kennedy, Calvin Klein, Ralph Lauren, Edgar Allen Poe, Colin Powell, Babe Ruth, Mark Twain

Orchard Beach

The 1.1-mile "Bronx Riviera," built in the 1930s as a public works project by Parks Commissioner Robert Moses, is a popular summertime destination for Bronx residents, site of the annual Tropical Music Festival (concerts every Sunday in July and August), and a marvel of modern engineering—the bedrock the sand sits on is actually made of three million cubic yards of sanitation landfill.
718.430.1825. **6** *to Pelham Bay Park.*

The Point

This vibrant community center, run by the Point Community Development Corporation, marks a significant step in the process of revitalizing the inner-city Hunts Point neighborhood of the Bronx; a mural by the entrance, dedicated to a slain young man from the area, serves as a poignant reminder of why the work is so crucial. The decade-old nonprofit focuses on youth education and economic

and cultural development in the neighborhood by organizing classes and neighborhood events. Most famously, the center hosts a year-long photography program for kids ages 9-18, run by the International Center for Photography and taught by downtown artists; graduates go on to schools such as SVA and Cooper Union. While you're there, also peek into the studio of acclaimed Tats Cru, a group of graffiti artists and muralists, housed in a space off the Point's courtyard.
940 Garrison Avenue (at Manida Street), Hunts Point. 718.542.4139. thepoint.org. Hours vary by season. **6** *to Hunts Point Ave.*

Rincón Criollo

This cultural center and community garden, also called La Casita de Chema after its founder José Chema Soto, is housed in one of the last remaining casitas in the Bronx. Built in the '70s and '80s by Puerto Rican immigrants, these structures were designed to resemble island buildings, helping recent transplants feel more at home in New York. Many were destroyed in the '90s in order to make way for condos and apartments, yet Rincón Criollo remains after more than 30 years. Today, the center keeps an admirable community-run herb and vegetable garden, as well as apple, pear, prune, peach, and fig trees; visit during the summer to see occasional performances by groups such as Grammy-nominated Yerba Buena, a Latin funk band that got its start here.

East 157th Street (at Brook), Melrose. myspace.com/ rinconcriollo. M-F noon-5pm. **2 5** *to 3rd Ave.*

Wave Hill

Today an official New York Public Garden and Cultural Center, this site overlooking the Hudson River was once home to some of the most distinguished people in America, including Mark Twain and Theodore Roosevelt. The Center, dedicated to promoting environmental awareness and examining the human relationship with nature, organizes cultural programs, hosts events, and maintains the 28-acre estate, which features several dazzling gardens and greenhouses with a variety of exotic plants. Pack a picnic—or pick up a cup of spiced chilled cucumber soup from the Wave Hill café—and enjoy one of the most scenic and relaxing outings in the city.

West 248th Street (at Independence), Riverdale. 718.549.3200. wavehill.org. Hours vary by season. Adults $4, Students $2, free Saturday 9am-noon, all day Tuesday, and December-February. **1** *to 231st St.*

Dining
UPSCALE
Le Refuge Inn *French*

When urban life has got you down, Le Refuge Inn provides an escape to old world leisure. A bite of the delicious French fodder served up by owner and chef Pierre Saint-Denis might make you want to extend your stay at this quaint bed and breakfast—a refined destination spot for a romantic evening, where the only tedious thing is getting there. The hideaway's prix fixe menu

specializes in fresh seafood, such as saffron lobster ravioli or the more extravagant bouillabaisse de crustacés, a broth of fish and shellfish. Those with an aversion to the sea should settle for the orange duck. Relaxed and amiable service ensures that nothing moves too fast, and reminds patrons that they are indeed outside Manhattan. Make sure to end the evening with a nightcap by the warm fireplace.

620 City Island Avenue (at Sutherland), City Island. 718.885.2478. T-Sun 6pm-10pm, closed Monday. Lunch $35, Dinner $45. Cash or check preferred. **6** *to Pelham Bay Park.*

Lobster Box *Seafood*

Though not what it used to be, this continental establishment still provides an amazing view of the Long Island Sound and some of the best lobster this side of Manhattan. That lobster is the top draw, with the Alaskan king crab a close second; for those in the mood for something other than seafood, the barbecue ribs are consistently saucy and come with a mountain of sweet, delicious corn bread. A relaxed vibe and comfortable seating make it a fun place to go for an evening with family or friends, and though prices are steep, large portions and a beautiful setting make sure that no one leaves on a disappointed—or an empty—stomach.

34 City Island Avenue (at Belden), City Island. 718.885.1952. Lunch Sun-Th 11:30am-11:30pm, F-Sat 11:30am-1:30am. Appetizers $8-16, Entrées $20-42. **6** *to Pelham Bay Park.*

MID-RANGE
Coals *Pizza*

This cozy joint is by no means an ordinary pizzeria: Its approach, for one, is unique, with all of the pizzas cooked on a grill instead of in an oven. The result is flaky, thin, and satisfyingly crunchy crusts, available in an assortment of robust flavors including white, whole-wheat, and cornmeal. Even the edges of the menu are purposefully burned into an irregular pattern, giving diners a hint of the forthcoming char-grilled dough. The "pure bliss" pizza—a concoction composed of colorful globs of fontinella, ricotta, tomato, pesto, and pecorino—is a great choice. For dessert, try the mouthwatering fluffernutter pizza. More reminiscent of a crepe than anything else, it melts Nutella and marzipan together in a folded-over crust sprinkled with powdered sugar.

1888 Eastchester Road (at Morris Park). 718.823.7002. M-Th 11:30am-10pm, F 11:30am-midnight, closed Sat-Sun. Appetizers $4.50-$8.50, Entrées $6.25-$14. **4 5** *to 138th St-Grand Concourse.*

Arts

Bronx Museum of the Arts

If not for the focus on community themes, you'd never know this Manhattan-caliber museum was out of range of the city's big-name museums. With the same concrete floors and sleek design as many of the trendy Chelsea spots, this two-room space feels part-gallery and part-museum, with a permanent collection that focuses on contemporary works by artists of African, Asian, and Latin American descent, and exhibitions that are designed to appeal to a local urban audience.

1040 Grand Concourse (at 165th), Mott Haven. 718.681.6000. bronxmuseum.org. W-Sun noon-6pm, F noon-8pm, closed M-T. Adults $5, Students $3, free Fridays. **B D** *to 167th St.*

Hostos Center for the Arts and Culture

The innovative Longwood Art Gallery is the main attraction at this center, built on the campus of Hostos Community College in 1994, which also contains a 367-seat repertory theater and a 907-seat concert hall. Many exhibits focus on the local population and the citizens' interaction with the art world. A prominent photo series, for instance, depicts a day in the life of an elderly, Latina Bronx woman who works as a cleaner, while a video, "Ask Chuleta," explores the difficulty of bridging the gap between the "white box" art community and people of color.

450 Grand Concourse (at 149th). 718.518.4455. hostos.cuny.edu/culturearts. M-Sat 10am-6pm, closed Sunday. **2 4 5** *to Grand Concourse.*

Mud/Bone Studio 889

This art gallery and theater aims to culturally revive Hunts Point, credited as the birthplace of hip hop, breakdancing, and salsa, by nurturing and supporting both urban artists of color and local neighborhood youth. The studio's print-making workshop gives artists free instruction, studio time, and exhibition space, theatrical performances employ only local artists, and displayed artwork usually involves themes promoting positive social change.

889 Hunts Point Avenue (at Garrison), Hunts Point. 718.620.2824. mudbone.org. Call for gallery hours, visit website for event listings. **6** *to Hunts Point Ave.*

Shopping

Casa Amadeo

This oldest Latin music store in New York was founded in 1927 by two siblings in East Harlem; they moved the shop to the Bronx in 1941 in order to participate in the uptown Latin music scene. Since the store was purchased in 1969 by Mike Amadeo, the son of a well-known Puerto Rican composer, it has remained a hotspot for musicians and aficionados of the Hispanic Caribbean.

786 Prospect Ave (at Macy Place), Longwood. 212.328.6896. casaamadeo.com. M-Sat 11am-7pm, closed Sunday. **2 5** *to Prospect Ave.*

The Hub

The commercial area surrounding the intersection of Third Avenue and East 149th Street in the South Bronx, affectionately referred to as the Hub, is a mainstay of urban fashion and a popular destination for bargain hunting. If you believe the rumors, clothing designers visit the shops here to discover the newest in urban street style, before marketing them to the suburbs.

Third Avenue (at East 149th), Mott Haven. **2 5** *to Third Ave.*

City Island

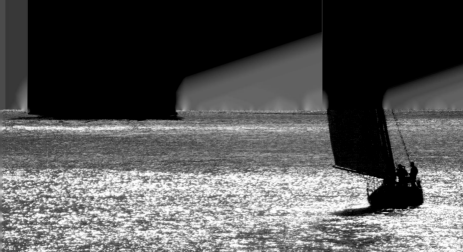

STATEN ISLAND

When asked what there is to do on Staten Island, most residents reply with a look of disbelief. "Do you really want to know?"

This self-deprecating attitude is characteristic of an area not always comfortable alongside its more-famous neighbors. Perpetually snubbed by the other boroughs for its telltale accent and legendarily big-haired residents, the most suburban of the five boroughs also has the smallest population and the least representation in the City Council. Adding insult to injury, for many years the rest of the city sent all its garbage to the island's Fresh Kills landfill, so big it's purportedly visible from space.

Largely known as a secluded spot for fishing and farming, for years, reachable only by boat, Staten Island remained isolated until 1713, when a public ferry began carrying passengers to and from New York. In 1898, the Island was incorporated into New York City, but even the 1898 construction of the Verrazano-Narrows Bridge, connecting the island to Brooklyn, did little to change its reputation as the borough most likely to be confused with New Jersey.

Today, Staten Island is largely residential and happy to stay that way. Communities are small and tight-knit, and although Indian and Latino populations are growing rapidly, Staten Island is still predominantly Italian.

The lack of neighborly feelings between Staten Island and the rest of the city goes both ways. Fed up with garbage dumps filled largely with trash from elsewhere, the citizens of Staten Island's Richmond County voted overwhelmingly in 1993 to secede from the city, although the vote was only symbolic. The Fresh Kills landfill was closed in 2001, but like the smell, Staten Islanders' ambivalence about being part of the city still lingers. For some residents, the lure of the Big City, just a ferry ride away, is too great to ignore.

STATEN ISLAND

SIGHTS/ATTRACTIONS
1. Historic Richmond Town
2. Staten Island Yankees
3. The Staten Island Zoo

DINING
4. Goodfellas
5. Lento's
6. Nurnberger Bierhaus
7. Ralph's Ices
8. Ruddy & Dean

NIGHTLIFE
9. Blu Lounge

ARTS
10. Jacques Marchais
    Museum of Tibetan Art
11. The Alice Austen House

Sights/Attractions

Historic Richmond Town

During the 18th and 19th centuries, Dutch, English, and French settlers gathered in the courthouse, church, and taverns of this town, which served at the time as the island's government center. When Staten Island was incorporated as a borough of New York in 1898, St. George, which is closer to Manhattan, became the main location for civic activity, and the once-bustling Richmond Town became a quiet, forgotten village. Fortunately, a local preservation movement saved the town in the 1950s; today, most of the 27 restored buildings on-site—including the oldest surviving one-room schoolhouse in America—are open for tours. Volunteers dress in 18th-century costumes to reenact everything from candlemaking to declarations of war. *441 Clarke Avenue (at St. Patrick's). 718.351.1611. historicrichmondtown.com. Hours vary by season. Adults $5. S74 to St. Patrick's Place.*

Sandy Grounds Historical Society

The first freed slave community in North America and a stop on the Underground Railroad, Sandy Grounds was founded in the early 19th century by a group of black men from New York. Today, a small library documents the life of these first residents, and a museum is devoted to letters, photographs, films, rare books, and artwork pertinent to the colony. The Historical Society also hosts quilt-making workshops and special events to celebrate historical African American culture. *1538 Woodrow Road (at Lynbrook). 718.317.5796. Hours vary by season. Adults $6. statenislandusa.com. S74 to Woodrow and Bloomingdale Rds.*

Staten Island Ferry

As the world's cheapest 25-minute boat ride (it's free!), the Staten Island Ferry is a great experience for commuters and tourists alike. Stand on the outer decks on warm days, feel the wind in your hair, and enjoy awesome views of the skyline: The Statue of Liberty, Ellis Island, Governor's Island, the Brooklyn Bridge, lower Manhattan skyscrapers, and the Verrazano-Narrows Bridge are all visible. The on-board snack bar serves coffee, sandwiches, and even beer and wine—finally, a form of public transportation where you can drink without fear of being ticketed and fined (we're looking at you, *the subway*). On a hot weekend

SNUG HARBOR CULTURAL CENTER

This former sailors' retirement home is a hotbed of arts and cultural activity on a serene beach at the north end of the Island. You'll find both traditional and contemporary visual art at the museums that make up the Center; the 20th century paintings of legendary marine artist John A. Noble at the **NOBLE MARITIME COLLECTION** (*718.447.6490*) provide a contrast to the photographs and works on display at the **NEWHOUSE CENTER FOR CONTEMPORARY ART** (*718.425.3560*).

At the other end of the Cultural Center, pagodas, ponds, and a peaceful atmosphere comprise the **STATEN ISLAND BOTANICAL GARDEN** (*718.273.8200*), determined to make you forget you're still in the city. The Garden's main attraction is a traditional Chinese Scholars' Garden; with eight pavilions and several covered walkways, this intricately designed space captures the spirit of the natural landscape.

Though Staten Island may feel like it's the middle of nowhere, the **STATEN ISLAND CHILDREN'S MUSEUM** (*718.273.2060*) takes you to the ends of the earth, literally, with its "extreme environments" simulation exhibit; drive a dogsled in the tundra and then dive to the ocean floor before you board the ferry back to Manhattan.

1000 Richmond Terrace (at Snug Harbor Rd). 718.273.8200. snug-harbor.org. S40 to Snug Harbor.

summer evening, it makes for a great inexpensive date, leaving from Manhattan.

1 Whitehall Street (at South). siferry.com. Check website for updated timetable. Free. R W to Whitehall St-South Ferry.

Staten Island Yankees

Just a few blocks from the ferry terminal gates stands the Richmond County Bank Ballpark, home to minor league baseball team the Staten Island Yankees. The setting is intimate, the players are approachable, and the hot dogs are just as juicy as they are at those other Yankee games. Tickets are only $5-11, and you'll get a wholesome baseball experience without all the commercialism.

75 Richmond Terrace (at Wall). 718.720.9265. siyanks. com. Late June-early September. SI Ferry to St. George.

The Staten Island Zoo

Although it's decidedly smaller than that *other* zoo in the outer boroughs, the Staten Island Zoo is a favorite destination for locals looking to walk with the animals. Come to see mammals, birds, amphibians, tropical fish, or the reptile collection, which has garnered the zoo the most amount of attention. The grounds are manageable (read: small), so come with the kids.

614 Broadway (at Harvest). 718.442.3100. statenislandzoo.org. Daily 10am-4:45pm. Adults $7, entry by donation Wednesday after 2pm. S48 to Forest Ave and Broadway.

Dining
UPSCALE

Carmen's *Spanish-Mexican*

The lights you're looking out on may be shining from industrial New Jersey, but while sipping sangria and eating truly huge portions of paella at this Mexican-Spanish hybrid on the Staten Island shoreline it's easy to convince yourself otherwise. The bustling energy makes this restaurant ideal for big parties, as do the dishes, whose sheer size almost demands they be shared. Although the waitstaff can at times get lost amid the crowd, they're consistently friendly and accomodating when they get to you. With an expansive menu—made even more extensive thanks to the option of selecting between sauces—this Spanish eatery far surpasses the standard fare typical in the city.

750 Barclay Avenue (at Hylan). 718.356.2725. M-Th noon-10pm, F-Sat noon-11pm, Sun noon-10pm. Appetizers $5-10, Entrées $14-38. SIR to Annadale.

Ruddy & Dean *Steakhouse*

Self-described as Staten Island's premiere steakhouse, Ruddy and Dean's hearty fare—which literally goes from meat to potatoes—ensures that no one will leave hungry. A convenient location near the ferry terminal makes this scenic spot a great pick for those seeking a temporary respite from Manhattan's crowded city streets. From the outside patio, patrons enjoy an impressive view of the downtown skyline.

44 Richmond Terrace (at Wall). 718.816.4400. Lunch M-Sun 11:30am-3pm, Dinner Sun-Th 5-10pm, F-Sat 5-11pm. Appetizers $10-14, Entrées $17-35, cash only. SIR to St. George.

MID-RANGE

Goodfellas *Pizzeria/Italian*

Watch out Grimaldi's: This award-winning brick-oven pizzeria has been voted the best slice in not just the country, but the world. The hype—its hard to take a bite here without some mention of the award-winning pies—would be grating if it weren't backed up by the fabulous taste. Specialty pies, like the "Vodka Pizza" (with vodka sauce, peas, mushroom, and prosciutto) and the "Goodfella" (cherry tomato sauce, sausage, roasted red peppers, and garlic) are excellent thanks to quality toppings, fresh mozzarella, and that holy grail of pizza—a perfect, not-too-thin-or-too-thick, crust. The menu also offers a long list of good, standard Italian fare. Décor is simple but well kept, and you get the sense that if you come back a few times, the friendly waitstaff will begin to remember your favorite order.

1718 Hylan Boulevard (at Garretson). 718.987.2422. M-Th 11:30am-11pm, F-Sat 11:30am-2am, Sun 2-11pm. Appetizers $6-14, Entrées $13-23. SIR to St. George.

The Statue of Liberty

Lento's *Italian*

The food at this quintessential neighborhood Italian joint is like the ideal Tuesday night home-cooked meal: dependable, filling, and tasty. The restaurant caters to locals who are looking for good food above anything else, with a menu of Italian staples that's uniformly satisfying, and avoids the all-too-common trap of equating "good" with "cheese and oil." Try the zucchini sticks and any of the pastas, or one of the thin crust pizzas if you're looking for something light. With two rooms and a bar in front, this is the sort of unpretentious, welcoming place you can return to again and again.

289 New Dorp Lane (at Clawson). 718.980.7709. Sun-Th noon-11, F-Sat noon-midnight. Appetizers $6-12, Entrées $8-22. SIR to New Dorp.

Nurnberger Bierhaus *German*

With servers clad in lederhosen, walls adorned with red, yellow, and black flags, and a drink list longer than the Rhine, this cheery brasserie brings a taste of Deutschland to the littlest borough. As one of the most interesting dining destinations in the area (especially when the biergarten opens in the summer), the restaurant draws all types, from working-class bachelors to yuppie families. Though German liquors, creative cocktails (including one made with gin and sauerkraut), and wines are available, you'd be crazy not to take advantage of the reasonably-priced draught and bottled beer list. After quenching your thirst, go straight to the sausage section of the menu, not just because "Bratwurstteller" is easier to pronounce than "Gebackene Kartoffelsuppe mit Lauch und Speck," especially when you're buzzed, but also because the wursts are the best. Don't shy away from the pleasantly gamey rabbit or boar sausages when they're available—the kitchen expertly seasons these challenging meats without masking their essence.

817 Castleton Avenue (at Davis). 718.816.7461. M-Sat 11am-11pm, Sun noon-9pm. Appetizers $4-$10, Entrées $10-$30. S46/S96 bus to Davis Ave.

CASUAL

Ralph's Ices *Dessert*

As close to iconic as they come in Staten Island, this flagship location has been serving Italian ice since 1928. From honeydew to strawberry margarita, innovative ices consistently delight. And if sherbet is more your style, the black cherry cheesecake and chocolate hazelnut are divine. Dieters fear not: hip to the health conscious times, Ralph's has adopted its menu to include a slew of fat-free, cholesterol-free, and now even low-carb options. In addition to a wide variety of sweet treats, the icery also features a plethora of refreshing blended drinks; the Vanilla Ralphie is a definite crowd pleaser.

501 Port Richmond Avenue. 718.273.3675. Daily 11:30am-10pm. Ices $1.50-4. Staten Island Ferry to S44.

Nightlife

Blu Lounge *Lounge*

With diso and pop playing loud enough to shake the neighboring buildings, this club is a magnet for young Staten Islanders. A multi-leveled space is flanked by roped-off areas for private parties, and a spacious dance floor is lit by, you guessed it, blue strobe lights. The drinks are straightforward, but for a little flair, try one of the fishbowls: the huge amount of fruity alcohol for only $25 could suit a group of 3-4 people for the whole night. On Saturdays, there's an open bar until 2 am for $25, fishbowls not included. The crowd is young—18 to get in, 21 to drink—making the Blu Lounge a nice oasis of young urban life in this most suburban of boroughs.

492 Bay Street (at Stapleton). 718.720.6818. W-Sun 8pm-4am. Drinks $4-7. Cover $15. S76 to Bay Street.

Hush *Club*

Nestled deep in the southernmost tip of Staten Island, this club plays host to young, fashionable, and up-and-coming Staten Island socialites. The Club's décor has a lot to offer patrons: two bars, a smoking terrace, and a huge dance floor lined with leather couches. As is typical in Staten Island clubs, the crowd is on the younger side, meaning you'll be surrounded by 18-year-olds bumping and grinding to beats ranging from techno to classic hip hop. If the kids get to be too much, know that while the drinks are slightly pricey for an outer borough, the cups are equally bigger.

20 Ellis Street (at Arthur Kill). 718.227.1500. T-Sat 8pm-3-am. Drinks $6-10. Cover $15. SIR to Nassau.

Arts

The Alice Austen House

The former home of Alice Austen, a prolific photographer, as well as the first woman in Staten Island to own a car, is is now a tiny, quaint museum overlooking the Verrazano-Narrows. A small room holds archives of Austen's own work, but the real draw are the rotating exhibits of contemporary photography, which are surprisingly high-quality and contemporary for such a small, out of the way museum; photographers like showing here so much, it's gained a reputation as one of the few attractions on Staten Island that it's worth riding the ferry for. Also be sure to check out the facilities themselves; the park surrounding the museum is a nighttime hang out for teenagers and college kids, and the historic house dates back to 1690.

2 Hylan Boulevard (at Edgewater). 718.816.4506. aliceausten. org. March-December Th-Sun noon-5pm. Closed Jan-Feb. Suggested $2. S51 to Hylan Boulevard.

Jacques Marchais Museum of Tibetan Art

Most of the exhibits in this 60-year-old museum come from the private collection of Jacques Marchais, an American woman and artist with a passion for studying the ancient cultures of the Tibetan and Himalayan regions. The permanent collection of the Museum contains sculptures, paintings, ritual artifacts, instruments, and old photographs of Tibet, and one of the buildings is designed to resemble a small Himalayan monastery, complete with tranquil meditation gardens. Every October, the museum hosts a two-day festival with mask-making, Mongolian children's games, and Tibetan crafts.

338 Lighthouse Avenue (at Richmond). 718.987.3500. W-Sun 1pm-5pm. tibetanmuseum.org. Adults $5. S74 to Lighthouse Ave.

INDEX

#

809 (Bar) 301
1020 (Bar) 282
107 West (Southwestern) 301
125th Street 22, 296
15 East (Sushi) 182
192 Books 171
401 Projects 130
420 Bar and Lounge 243
5 Burro Café 331
5 Pointz 330, 331
5th Avenue Shopping 22
92nd Street YMCA 17, 51

A

A1 Trails 45
Abbey 283
ABC No Rio 114
About Glamour 326
Abyssinian Baptist Church 289
Acting Studio, The 50
Address Organization 54
Aikido of Manhattan 50
Airports 13
Aix 239
Alice Austen House 351
Alife Rivington Club 116
All State Café 244
Alliance Francaise 50
Almond Flower Bistro 100
Alvin Ailey American Dance Theatre 207
Ama 90
Amato Opera House 143
AMC/Lowes 17
American Academy of Arts and Letters 302
American Apparel 132
American Ballet Theater 17
American Folk Art Museum 24, 207
American Museum of Natural History 16, 25, 29, 38, 245
Amma 224
AMNY 33
Amtrak 12
Angelika Film Center 93
Angels Restaurant 256
Anna House 303
Anna Sui 94
Annual Events 68
Anthology Film Archive 143
Anthos 199
Anthropologie 22
Apartment Hunting 14
Apex Art 157
Apollo Theater 289
Apple Store 22, 229
Aquavit 223
Architecture Guide 28
Area Codes 54
Arlene's Grocery Picture Show 17
Arnold's Hatters 208
Art Deco 30

Art Galleries 16
Artisanal Fromagerie 166
Artopolis 269
Arts Guide 16
Asia de Cuba 183
Asia Market 105
Asia Society Museum 259
Asian American Arts Centre 104
Asiate 238
Aspen 166
Astor Place Hair 145
Astoria 329
Astroland Amusement Park 310
AT&T Long Lines Building 151
Atlantic Yards 31
Atmos 296
ATMs 54, 63
Audre Lorde Project 36
Austin Street 330
Avery Fisher Hall 245
Azza 227

B

B Bar and Grill 141
B.B. King's Blues Club & Grill 204
Babeland 116
Bailey House 36
Bakery Rzeszowska 311
Balenciaga 172
Ballet Academy East 50
Bally Total Fitness 43
BAM 322
Banking 54
Bann 199
Bar (at the Four Seasons Hotel) 227
Bar (at the Four Seasons Restaurant) 227
Bar 13 127
Bar 9 204
Bar Carrera 139
Barnes and Noble 17
Barney's CO-OP 247
Barney's New York 22, 229
Barney's Warehouse Sale 39, 229
Barracuda 168
Barrage 204
Battery Park 80
Bauman Rare Books 229
Beaches 45, 49
Beacon 200
Beacon's Closet 23, 313, 324
Beast 316
Beauty Bar 188
Beaux Arts Clasicism 29
Believe Lounge 188
Belvedere Castle 237
Bergdorf Goodman 22, 230
Bethesda Terrace 48
Betsey Johnson 94
Big Apple Performing Arts Festival 71
Big Swim, The 70
Biking 45
Billabong 23
Billiard Company 331
Billie Holiday Theatre 322
Billie Jean King National

Tennis Center 42
Birdland 17
Bitter End 17
Bittersweets 23
Black Betty 321
Blades Over Broadway 69
Bleeker Bob's 133
Bleeker Street 123
Bleu Evolution 301
Blind Tiger Ale House 127
Blockheads 57, 204
Blondies 244
Bloomberg, Michael 57
Bloomingdale's 22, 230
BLT Fish 166
Blu Lounge 350
Blue Hill 123
Blue Note 17
Blue Ribbon Brooklyn 315
Blue Water Grill 183
Bluestockings 116
BLVD 112
Boat 320
Boat Basin Café 244
Bodanna 145
Bohemian Hall 329, 334
Bon Chon Chicken 333
Bond St. 138
Bone Lick Park 126
Borders 17
Botanica 92
Bourbon Street 244
Bowery Ballroom 16
Bowery Poetry Club 143
Bowlmor Lanes 127
Boys Choir of Harlem 295
Brandy Library 156
Bridge Café 84
Bridle Paths 45
Brighton Beach 310
Broadway on Broadway 72
Broadway United Church of Christ 36
Bronx 336
Bronx Culture Trolley 339
Bronx Museum of the Arts 38, 342
Bronx Zoo 339
Brooklyn 306
Brooklyn Academy of Music 17, 322
Brooklyn Botanic Garden 313
Brooklyn Brewery 313
Brooklyn Bridge Park 311, 313
Brooklyn Heights 309
Brooklyn Heights Promenade 309, 314
Brooklyn Historical Society 314
Brooklyn Ice Cream Factory 311, 318
Brooklyn Industries 324
Brooklyn Museum of Art 24, 38, 313, 323
Brooklyn Rail, The 33
Brooklyn Superhero Supply Company 324
Brother Jimmy's 258

Brownstone 297
Brownstone Billards 321
Brownstone Books 324
Bryant Park 196
Bubble Lounge 156
Buenos Aires 110
Buffalo Exchange 23, 324
Bumble and Bumble 38
Buses 11
Business Hours 54
Butala Emporium 331
Butter 138

C

Cable 66
Café Bar 334
Café Boulud 253
Café D'Alsace 256
Café Gitane 101
Café Henri 330
Café Wha? 127
Calle Ocho 239
Calvary St. George's Vintage Furniture 191
Campbell Apartment 227
Candle 79 257
Caracas Arepa Bar 141
Caravan of Dreams 139
Carl Schurz Park 253
Carlyle, The 253
Carmen's 348
Carnegie Hall 16, 207
Carroll Gardens 309
Carroll Park 309
Casa Amadeo 343
Casa La Femme North 224
Casa Latina 297
Casellula 201
Castle Clinton 80
Cathedral Church of St. John the Divine 29, 266
Cattyshack 35
Ceci-Cela 92
Celiac Disease 57
Cell Phones 65
Central Park 44, 48
Central Park Zoo 48
Central Synagogue 219
Century 21 23, 39, 85
Cercle Rouge 154
Charlton Street 89
Chatham Square 99
Cheese of the World 330
Chelsea 162
Chelsea Art Museum 170
Chelsea Market 172
Chelsea Piers 165
Cherry Lane 130
Chianese New Year Festival 68
Chicago School 29
China Institute in America 50
Chinatown 96
Chinatown buses 12
Chisholm Larsen Poster Gallery 172
Chocolate Show 73
Christie's 207

Christmas Tree Lighting at
  Rockefeller Center   73
Chrysler Building   30,
                               221
Chumley's   125
Church of St. Ann's   309
Churrascaria Platorma   200
Cinema Village   132
Circa Tabac   156
Citarella   59
Citrus   239
City Bakery   40
City Center   17
City Council   57
City Deals   38
City Island   45
City Opera   39
Classes and Workshops   50
Climate and Seasons   54
Cloisters, The   24, 38,
                               302
Club Groove   127
Club Rules   21
Club Sports Teams   43
Coals   341
Cobble Hill   309
ColaLex Gallery   295
Collective Unconcious   158
Collector's Toy Den   158
Colonial Architecture   28
Columbia Cottage   269
Columbia Presbyterian
  Medical Center   40
Columbia University   266
Columbus Circle   44,
                               237
Columbus Day Parade   72
Columbus Park   99
Comiissioner's Plan of 1811   58
Comme des Garçons   172
Community Gardens   137
Compass   239
Coney Island   46, 49,
                               310
Confucious Plaza   100
Congregation Beth
  Simchat Torah   36
Conservatory Garden   289
Conservatory Water   253
Coogan's   301
Cooper Union   123
Cooper-Hewitt
  National Design Museum   260
Cornelia Street Café   130
Corner Bistro   128
Cosi   226
Cotton Club   294
Counseling Services   56
Counter   139
Court Street   309
Coyote Ugly Saloon   141
Craigslist   33, 39
Crepes on Columbus   268
Crunch Fitness   43
C-Town   59
Cub Room   92
Cuba   126
Cubana Café   309
Cubbyhole   35,
                               128
Culture Club   92
Curry Hill   33
Curry In A Hurry   183
Curry Row   137
Cutting Room, The   168

D

Dachshund Spring Fiesta   70
D'Agostino   59
Daily News, The   33
Dakota, The   237
Dance Theater of Harlem   17,
                               295
Dance Theater Workshop   170
Daniel   254
Dave's Quality Meat   145
DB Bistro Moderne   200
Dean and Deluca   59
Deitch Projects   93
Delacorte Theater   48
Dining Guide   18
Dinosaur BBQ   291
Dive Bar   244
Diversity Staffing   36
Dixon Place   115
Dizzy's Club Coca-Cola   205
Donovan's Pub   334
Double Happiness   103
Down The Hatch   129
Downhill Skiing   46
Downtown Boathouse   45
DT UT   257
Duane Park   151
Dublin House   244
DUMBO   311
Duvet   166
Dyckman Farmhouse
  Museum   303
Dylan's Candy Bar   262
Dynasty Supermarket   105

E

East Village   134
Easter Day Parade   68
Eddie's Sweet Shop   334
Edgar Allen Poe Cottage   339
El Maguey Y La Tuna   110
El Museo del Barrio   24,
                               295
El Ranchito   301
Eldridge Street Synagogue   109
Ellis Island   29, 80
Emerald Nuts Midnight Run   73
Emergency Phone Numbers   57
Empire State Building   30,
                               181
Empire-Fulton Ferry
  State Park   311
Equinox Fitness   43
Esperanto   141
Esplanade   81
Ess-a-Bagel   185

F

Face Stockholm   94
Failte Irish Whisky Bar   189
Fairway   41, 59
Famous Joe's Pizza   126
FAO Shwartz   230
Fashion Weeks   68, 72
Fay Da Bakery   330
Federal Hall   28
Federal Reserve Bank
  of New York   81
Fiamma Osteria   89
Fifth Avenue Shopping   22
Film Forum   131

Financial District   76
Fishing   46
Fishs Eddy   172
Five Points   99
Flatiron Building   29,
                               165
Flatiron Lounge   168
Flea Theater   158
Fleet Week   70
Florent   131
Flower District   181
Floyd NY   320
Flushing   330
Flushing Mall   330,
                               335
Flushing Meadows
  Corona Park   330,
                               331
Flute   205
Food Emporium   59
Forbes Galleries   131
Forest Hills   330
Forest Hills Garden   331
Forever 21   22
Fort Greene   311
Fort Greene Historic District 311
Fort Greene Park   46,
                               311,
                               314
Frankie's Spuntino   111
Franklin Street   311
Fraunces Tavern   28
Fred's   239
Freecycle NYC   39
Freedom Tower   30
Freeganism   40
French Roast   239
Fresh   151
Fresh Fruit Festival   37
Frick Collection   24
Fung Wah   12,
                               100
FusionArts Museum   115
Future Perfect   325

G

g Lounge   35,
                               168
Gagosian Gallery   171
Galapagos Art Space   313,
                               321
Gallery   112
Gantry Plaza State Park   330
Gawker   33
Gay and Lesbian
  Affirmative Psychotherapy   36
Gay and Lesbian Life   34
Gay and Lesbian New
  York Gallery Tour   37
Gay Men's Health Crisis   36
Gay Pride Month   37
Gay Pride Parade   37
George Washington Bridge   300
Getting Around   10
Getting Settled   14
Gin Mill   244
Ginger Man   189
Girlshop   23
Giuliani, Rudy   58
Gobo   257
Golden Unicorn   101
Gold's Gym   43
Good Enough to Eat   240

Good World Bar   112
Goodfellas   349
Gotham Bar and Grill   123
Gotham Bikes   159
Gotham Writer's Workshop   51
Gothamist   33
Gothic Revivalism   28
Gowanus Dredgers
  Canoe Club   46
Gramercy   178
Gramercy Park   181
Grand Central Terminal   29,
                               221
Grand Sichuan   101
Grant's Tomb   267
Gray's Papaya   243
Great Five Boro Bike Tour   70
Great New York Noodletown   101
Greek Revivalism   28
Green Construction   31
Greenacre   221
Greenmarkets   57,
                               190
Greenpoint   311
Greenwich Village   120
Greenwich Village
  Halloween Parade   72
Greyhound   12
Greystones   331
Grid System   58
Grimaldi's   311
Gristedes   59
Grocery Stores   59
Ground Zero   81
Guggenheim Museum   16, 24,
                               38,
                               261
Gusto Ristorante   124
Gyms   43

H

H&H Bagel   243
H&M   22,
                               208
Hacienda de Argentina   257
Hallal Dining   56
Haloween Parade   72
Hamptons, The   49
Hangawi   184
Happy Ending Lounge   103
Harbour Lights   84
Harlem   286
Harlem Lanes   293
Harlem Meer   48,
                               289
Harlem Stage at the
  Gatehouse   295
Harlem Week   71
Harrison, The   151
Harry's at Hannover Square   84
Haughwout Building   89
Havana Central at
  the West End   283
Headhuntersdirectory.com   15
Hearst Magazine Building   30
Hedeh   139
Heights Bar and Grill   283
Helen's   35
Hell's Kitchen   202
Henri Bendel   22
Henrietta Hudson   35,
                               129
Herald Square   22

Hideaway, The	155
High Line, The	165
Hiking	45
Hispanic Society of America	303
Historic Richmond Town	347
Historic Weeksville	314
Historist Skyscrapers	29
Holiday Market	190
Holiday Mountain	47
Homelessness	61
HopStop	10
Horseback Riding	45
Hospitals	60
Hostels	52
Hostos Center for the Arts and Culture	342
Hotel Chelsea	166
Hotels	39, 52, 94
Housing Works	39, 94 245
Hub, The	343
Hudson Bar and Books	129
Hudson Street Paper	117
Hue-Man Bookstore & Café	297
Hung Chang Imports Inc.	105
Hungarian House	256
Hungarian Pastry Shop	271
Hungarian Reform Church	256
Hunter Mountain	47
Hush	350

I

Identity	112
IFC Center	131
Il Mattone	155
ImaginAsian	228
Inagiku	224
Incredi Fusion	184
Indie Market	309
Inoteca	112
InterActive Corp Building	31
Intermix	262
International Art Expo	68
International Center for Photography	24
International Dance Festival	71
International Vintage Poster Fair	73
Internet	60
Inwood Hill Park	45, 300
Ipanema	201
Iridium	17
Irish Brigade Pub	301
Irish Hunger Memorial	81
Irish Pub Ulysses	85
Irish Rover	334
Isamu Noguchi Garden Museum	330, 335
Islamic Cultural Center of New York	289
Issey Miyake	159
Ithaka	255
Ivy's Bistro	155
Izakaya Ten	167

J

J&R Music and Computer World	85
Jackson Diner	331

Jackson Heights	331
Jackson Heights Historic District	331
Jacqueline Kennedy Onassis Reservoir	44, 48
Jacques Imo's	240
Jacques Marchais Museum of Tibetan Art	351
Jacques Torres Chocolate	311
Jake's Dilemma	244
James A Farley Post Office	196
Japan Society	229
Jas Mart	284
Jay East Direct Import Warehouse	325
Jeffery New York	23
Jeremy's Ale House	85
Jewish Museum	25, 260
JFK Airport	13
JFK AirTrain	10, 13
JFK Runway Run	69
Jim Kempner Fine Art	171
Jimmy Jazz	22
Jimmy's Corner Bar	205
Jivamukti Yoga Center	51
Job Hunting	15
Joe's Pub	16
Joe's Shanghai	101
Jones Beach	49
Joralemon Street	309
Joseph Patelson Music House	208
Josie's	57
Joyce SoHo Theater	17, 93
Joyce Theater	17
Julia Burgos Latino Cultural Center	296
Julliard	246
Just Scandinavian	159

K

Kaarta Imports	297
Kai	255
Kalustyans	183
Karrot	303
Kefi	241
Kensington Stables	45
Kimono Lounge	157
Kitchen Center	170
Kitchenette	268
Knitting Factory	17
Koi	200
Koreatown	198
Koronet's	283
Kosher Dining	56
Kuma Inn	111
Kush	112
Kyotofu	201

L

L Magazine, The	33
La Maison du Chocolat	260
La Mama	143
La Marqueta	297
La Paella	139
Labryinth Books	284
Lactose Intolerant Dining	57
LaGuardia Airport	13
Landmark Sunshine Cinema	115
Langston Hughes House	289
Le Petit Café	309

Le Refuge Inn	341
Le Souk	140
L'École	91
Leela Lounge	126
Lemon Ice King of Corona	334
Lenox Lounge	17, 294
Lento's	350
Les Halles Downtown	84
Lesbian Herstory Archives	36
Leslie/Lohman Gay Arts Foundation	36
Lever House	223
Lexington Bar and Books	259
LGBT Community Center	35, 40
LGBT Guide	34
LGBT March	70
Libation	113
Life Café	140
Life in Motion Yoga	51
Lighting by Gregory	117
Lincoln Center	17
Lincoln Center Festival	71
Lincoln Center Out of Doors	71
Lincoln Plaza Cinemas	17, 246
Liquor Laws	60
Literary Pub Crawl	125
Little Brazil	201
Little Giant	109
Little Greece	329
Little India	331
Little Italy	96
Little Mexico	290
Little Red Lighthouse	300
Little Singer Building	89
Little Ukraine	137
Lobby Lounge	245
Lobster Box	341
Local Flavor	269
Loeb Boathouse	46, 48, 259
Loehmann's	39
Lolita	113
Lombardi's Pizza	102
Lomzynianka	311
Londel's	290
Long Island City	330
Long Island Railroad	12
Louis 649	142
Lounge	22
Lower East Side	106
Lower East Side Bargain District	109
Lower East Side Tenement Museum	25, 109
Lucky Star	12
Luna Park	190
Lunch Deals	19
Lunetta	314
Lush	245

M

MacMenamin's Pub	85
Macy's	29, 208
Macy's Thanksgiving Day Parade	73
Madame Tussaud's	25, 207
Madame X	92
Madiba	316

Madison Avenue	22
Madison Square Garden	42, 196
Mahayana Buddhist Temple	100
Mai House	152
Make My Cake	293
Malcolm Shabazz Harlem Market	297
Mangia	84
Manhattan Bridge	100, 317
Manhattan Motion Dance Studios	50
Manhattan School of Music	284
Manna's	293
Manor, The	129
Mantra 986	224
Marc by Marc Jacobs	133
Marc Jacobs	22
Marcus Garvey Memorial Park	290
Markt	167
Marquee	169
Marseille	202
Marshall's	39
Martin Luthur King Jr. Day	68
Mary Boone Gallery	229
Mas (farmhouse)	125
Matsuri	167
Matthew Marks Gallery	171
Max Soha	268
Mayle	23
McCarren Park	315
McSorley's Ale House	137
Meadowlands	42
Meatpacking District	23
Mental Health	56
Mercedes Benz Fashion Week	69
Mercer Kitchen	89
Merchant's House Museum	143
Mercury Lounge	113
Metrazur	223
Metro	33
Metro North	12
Metrocard	10
Metropolitan Community Church of New York	36
Metropolitan Museum of Art	16, 25, 38, 260
Metropolitan Opera House	17, 246
Midtown Comics	208
Midtown East	218
Midtown West	192
Midway Stadium 9	330
Mike's Bistro	241
Miller Theater	284
Mini Minimarket	325
Miss Maude's Spoonbread Too	292
Miu Miu	262
Mo Pitkin's House of Satisfaction	35
MoBay	292
Monday Night Magic	206
Monkey Bar & Grill	228
Moomia Bar & Lounge	103
Mooshoes	117
Morgan Library and Museum	189
Morningside Bookshop	284
Morningside Heights	264
Morningside Park	267
Morris-Jumel Mansion	303

Morton Williams 59
Mo's Caribbean Bar and Grill 259
Moscow on the Hudson 303
Mount Vernon Hotel
Museum 261
Mr. Black 35, 129
Mr. Chow's Tribeca 152
MTA, The 58
MTV Experience Store 23
Mud/Bone Studio 889 343
Mugs Ale House 320
Mulberry Street Bar 103
Murray Hill 178
Museum at the Fashion
Institute of Technology 38, 170
Museum Guide 24
Museum Mile Festival 70
Museum of Arts and Design 25
Museum of Contemporary
African Diasporan Arts 311, 323
Museum of Jewish Heritage 81
Museum of Modern Art 16, 17, 25, 38, 196
Museum of Sex 16, 25, 37, 190
Museum of Television
and Radio 26, 207
Museum of the City
of New York 38, 296
Museum of the Moving Image 329, 335
Music 16
MXYPLYZYK 133

N
Ñ 92
Nassau Veterans Memorial
Coliseum 42
National Arts Club 182
National Black Theatre 296
National Museum of
LGBT History 132
National Museum of
the American Indian 26, 38, 82
Natsumi 203
Natural Gourmet Institute 51
Neera Saree Palace 183
Neighborhoodies 85
Nelson Blue 111
Neue Galerie 261
New Directors/New
Films Festival 17
New School 123
New Year's Eve 73
New York Airport
Service Express 13
New York Aquarium 315
New York Botanical Garden 339
New York City Ballet 17, 247
New York City Fire Museum 94
New York City Marathon 73
New York City Opera 246
New York City Sports Club 43
New York City

Supreme Court Building 28
New York Comedy Festival 73
New York Earth Room 94
New York Fast Pitch
Softball League 43
New York Film Festival 17, 72
New York Headache Center 40
New York Historical Society 26
New York Institute
of Photography 50
New York International
Beauty School 38
New York International
Fringe Festival 71
New York Magazine 33
New York Natonal Boat Show 68
New York Post, The 32
New York Press 33
New York Psychoanalytic
Institute 256
New York Public Library 197
New York Times Arts
and Leisure Weekend 68
New York Times Building 29
New York Times, The 32
New York Transit Museum 27, 323
New York Zendo Shobo-ji 51
New Yorker, The 33
Newark Airport 13
Newark Airport Liberty
Express 13
NewFest 37
Newhouse Center for
Contemporary Art 348
Newspapers 32
Nice Matin 242
Nicholas Roerich Museum 284
Night of a Thousand Gowns 70
Nightlife Guide 20
Ninth Avenue International
Film Festival 70
Nish 226
NJ Transit 12
Noble Maritime Collection 348
Nobu Next Door 153
NoLIta 22
Nonsense NYC 33
North Cove 81
Northsix 17
Not Ray's Pizza 311
Nurnberger Bierhaus 350
Nussbaum & Wu 269
Nutcracker, The 73
Nuyorican Poetry Slam 17
Nuyorican Poets Café 115
NV Perricone 262
NY Giants 42
NY Islanders 42
NY Jets 42
NY Knicks 42
NY Liberty 42
NY Mets 42
NY Rangers 42
NY Red Bulls 42
NY Titans 42
NY Underground
Film Festival 17
NY1 32
NYC Adventure Boot
Camp for Women 43
NYC Condoms 40
NYC Fitness 43
NYC Run 44
NYPD 57

NYU 123

O
Oak Room 206
Old Navy 22
Old Town Bar 169
Olive and Bette's 247
Olives NY 184
Olive's Very Vintage 309, 325
Olympus Fashion Week 72
Once Upon a Tart 92
One Times Square 30
Onieal's Grand Street 102
Orchard Beach 340
Organic Avenue 117
Oscar Wilde Bookshop 37
Out & Faithful 36
Out of Bounds 43
Outdoors Guide 44

P
P&G 245
P.S. 1 27, 330, 335
P.S. 122 17
Pacewildenstein 171
Panhandling 61
Paris Sandwich Shopw 102
Park East 255
Park Slope 312
Parks 44
Parnell's Bar and Restaurant 228
Participant, Inc. 116
Pasita 125
Passerby 169
PATH Trains 12
Patriot Saloon 85
Pay-What-You-Wish 38
Pearl Paint 105
Pearl River Mart 105
Pennsylvania Station 197
People Lounge 114
Performance Space 122 144
Pete's Candy Store 320
Pete's Downtown 316
Pets 62
Pier 17 Mall 23
Pierogi 2000 313, 323
Pig n' Whistle 228
Pilgrim Hill 46
Pillow Fight, Annual Urban 68
Pinch Pizza By the Inch 185
Pino's Pizzeria 312
Pisticci 268
Planned Parenthood 40
Playwrights Horizon 208
Plumm 160
Point, The 340
Polish General Consulate 182
Pomander Walk 238
Pond, The 46
Pongal 185
Pop Diner 333
Port Authority Bus Terminal 12
Port Authority, The 58
powerHouse Arena 311, 325
Prada 22, 95
Pravda 93

Probus 301
Prohibition 245
Prospect Park 312, 315
Public (Fusion) 90
Puerto Rican Day Parade 70
Puglia 102
Pyramid 142

Q
Queens 326
Queens Botanical Garden 332
Queens Center Mall 335
Queens Museum of Art 27, 335
Quicksilver 23

R
Radio City Christmas
Spectacular 73
Radio City Music Hall 30
Radio Stations 32
Rain (Pan-Asian) 242
Rain/Precipitation 56
Rainbow Roommates 36
Ralph's Ices 350
Ramble, The 48
Real Estate Brokers 14
Rebel 169
Recycle-a-Bicycle 145
Red Sky Bar 189
Relish 316
Repertorio Espanol
(Gramercy Arts Center) 191
Reservations 19
Restaurant Row 18
Restaurant Week 18, 68, 71
Resurrection 23
Revival 291
Revolution Books 191
Rewind 114
Rialto 91
Rincon Críollo 340
Riverside Church 267
Riverside Park 44
Rivington Arms 144
Road Runners 44
Rockaway Beach 49
Rockefeller Center 30, 46, 198
Rocky Sullivan's 189
Roger Vivier 263
Romanesque Revivalism 29
Roosevelt Island Cable Car 11
Rosanjin 153
Roti Boti 331
Rubin Museum of Art 171
Ruby Foo's 243
Rucker Park 290
Ruddy & Dean 349
Running 44

S
Safety 10, 21, 63
Saks Fifth Avenue 22, 230
Salam 126
Sales Tax 64
Salvation Army 39

Sandro's 255
Sandy Grounds Historical
  Society 347
Sandy Hook 49
Saucy 258
Schomburg Center for
  Research in Black Culture 290
Scoop 95
Screaming Mimi's 145
Seagram Building 30
Seaport Café 85
Sephora 38
Setback Skyscrapers 30
Shake Shack 168
Shakespeare in Central Park 71
Shape of Lies 145
Shea Stadium 42,
  330
Shebeen 103
Sheep Meadow 48
Sheep Meadow Café 48
Ship of Fools 259
Shopping Guide 22
Showman's 295
Silver Moon Bakery 269
Skating 46
Skiing 46
Skylight Gallery 323
Skype 66
Skyscraper Museum 27, 81
Slate 170
Sledding 46
Smith Street 309
Smith-Stewart 116
Smoke 17,
  283
Smoking 65
Smorgas Chef 84
Snapshot 35
Sniffen Court Carriage
  Houses 182
Snug Harbor Cultural Center 348
Socrates Sculpture Park 335
SoHo 86
SoHo Antiques Fair and
  Flea Market 95
SoHo Grand 93
Sony Wonder Technology
  Lab 222
South Beach 49
South Street Seaport 23, 82
South Street Seaport Museum 27
Spanish Institute 50
Spice Corner 183
Spice Market 125,
  131
Splash 34,
  170
Sports Guide 42
St. Ann's Warehouse 311,
  323
St. Clement's Church 208
St. George Church 137
St. John the Divine 29,
  266
St. Mark's Place 137
St. Nick's Pub 17
St. Patrick's Cathedral 28,
  222
St. Patrick's Day Parade 68
St. Paul's Chapel 28, 83
Stanton Social 110
Staten Island 344
Staten Island Botanical

Garden 348
Staten Island Children's
  Museum 348
Staten Island Ferry 11,
  347
Staten Island Yankees 348
Staten Island Zoo 348
Statue of Liberty 80
STD Clinic, Central Harlem 40
STD Clinic, Chelsea 40
Steinway Street 329
Stella McCartney 23
Steven Alan 159
Stone Creek 189
Stone Park Café 317
Stonewall Chorale 36
Stonewall Inn 35,
  123
Strand 133
Strand Annex 85
Strata 170
Striver's Row 290
Student Rush 16, 38
Studio Museum in Harlem 27,
  296
Stuyvesant Town 182
Subways 11
Suicide Prevention 56
Summer in the Square 190
Sun Room Café 198
Supper Club 206
Surma Store 137
Sushi of Gari 255
Sutra Lounge 142
Sutton Place 228
Sweet and Vicious 93
Swift Hibernian Lounge 143
Swing-a-Ring 267
Swizz 203
Sylvia's 293
Symphony Space 247

Tai Pan Bakery 102
Takashimaya 230
Taksim 227
Tap City 71
Tap-a-Keg 283
Tavalon 185
Tavern on the Green 29, 48
Taxis 11
TEANY 111
Teardrop Park 81
Telephones 65
Television 66
Television Stations 32
Tello's 167
Temple Bar 93
Temple Emanu-el 29,
  253
Ten Ren Tea and
  Gingseng Co. 105
Tenth Avenue Lounge 206
Terrace in the Sky 268
TG-170 117
Thalia 203
Theater 16, 38
Theodore Roosevelt Birthplace
  National Historic Site 182
Therapy 34,
  206
Thirty-Five 155
Three Lives & Co. 133

Tiffany's 30
Tiffin Wallah 185
Time Out (Bar) 245
Time Out New York 33
Times Square 23,
  197
Times Square New Year's
  Eve Bash 73
Time's Up Bike Repair 51
Tipping 67
TKTS 16
Tocqueville 184
Tom & Jerry's 143
Tompkins Square Park 138
Tom's Diner 282
Town 228
Toys "R" Us 23,
  209
Trader Joe's 59,
  190
Trapeze School of New York 89
Trattoria L'incontro 332
Travers Park 331
Tribal Spears 293
TriBeCa 148
Tribeca Cinemas 158
TriBeca Film Festival 17, 70
Tribeca Girls 159
Tribeca Performing
  Arts Center 158
Trinity Church 28
Trixie + Peanut 191
Tuts 114

U.S. Open 42, 71
Ukrainian Museum 137
Ukranian Institute of
  American 253
Underage Drinking 61
Union Hall 320
Uniqlo 22
Unitarian Universalism 36
United Nations Headquarters 222
Unterberg Poetry Series 17
Upper East Side 250
Upper West Side 234
Urban Center Galleries 229
Urban Outtings 36
Urban Park Rangers 45
Useful Information 54

Vacation Rentals 53
Van Cortland Park 45
Vegan Dining 57
Verlaine 114
VietCafe 155
Village Chess Shop 133
Village Vangaurd 17,
  130
Village Voice, The 33
Virgin Megastore 209
Vol de Nuit 130
Volunteer Ushering 38
Von Steuben Day Parade 256
Vong 224
Vynl 204

Waldorf-Astoria Hotel 223
Walker's 156
WalkNY.org 45
Wall Street Bull 83
Wall Street Journal 32
Walter Reade Theater 17
Warsaw Club 311,
  322
Washington Heights 298
Washington Market Park 151
Washington Square Arch 29
Washington Square
  Outdoor Arts Exhibit 70
Washington Square Park 44,
  123
Water Taxi Beach 49
Wave Hill 341
West Side Pistol and
  Rifle Range 51
Westminster Kennel
  Club Show 68
Westside Market 173,
  247,
  285
Westsider Rare & Used Books 248
Whiskey Ward 114
White Horse Tavern 125
Whitney Museum of
  American Art 16, 27,
  38, 261
Whole Foods 59,
  190
Williamsburg 313
Winnie's Karaoke 104
Wireless Internet 60
Wollman Rink 46, 48
Woo Lae Oak 91
Worldwide Plaza 198
Writer's Studio, The 51
Wyckoff House 28

Yaffa's Tea Room 156
Yankee Stadium 42
Yarntopia 285
Yoga Works 51
Yogi's 245
Yorkville 256
Yorkville Meat Emporium 256
Yuca Bar 141

Zabar's 40, 59,
  248
Zara 22
Zen Palate 185
Zenith/Asahi 203
Zip Codes 67
ZipCar 13
Zipper Tavern 167
Zoë 91
Zog Sports 43

DINING

American

Aspen	166
Beacon	200
Beast	316
Blue Hill	123
Blue Ribbon Brooklyn	315
Bone Lick Park	126
Bridge Café	84
Butter	138
Casellula	201
Compass	239
Cosi	226
Fred's	239
Fresh	151
Good Enough to Eat	240
Gotham Bar and Grill	123
Gusto Ristorante	124
Harbour Lights	84
Harrison, The	151
Hideaway, The	155
Kitchenette	268
Lever House	223
Life Café	140
Little Giant	109
Luna Park	190
Lunetta	316
Mercer Kitchen	89
Metrazur	223
Nish	226
Onieal's Grand Street	102
Pop Diner	333
Relish	316
Rialto	91
Ruddy & Dean	349
Saucy	258
Seaport Café	85
Stone Park Café	317
Terrace in the Sky	268
Thalia	203
Walker's	156
Zipper Tavern	167
Zoë	91

Asian

Asia de Cuba	183
Kuma Inn	111
Mantra 986	224

Bakery

Ceci-Cela	92
Ess-a-Bagel	185
Fay Da Bakery	330
Once Upon a Tart	92
Silver Moon Bakery	269

Café

DT UT	257
Le Petit Café	309
Tavalon	185
Tribal Spears	293
Yaffa's Tea Room	156

Chinese

Almond Flower Bistro	100
Columbia Cottage	269
Golden Unicorn	101
Grand Sichuan	101
Joe's Shanghai	101
Mr. Chow's Tribeca	152
Tai Pan Bakery	102

Dessert

Artopolis	269
Brooklyn Ice Cream Factory	311, 318
Eddie's Sweet Shop	334
Hungarian Pastry Shop	269
Jacques Torres Chocolate	311
Lemon Ice King of Corona	334
Make My Cake	293
Ralph's Ices	350

French

Aix	239
Artisanal Fromagerie	166
Asiate	238
Café Boulud	253
Café D'Alsace	256
Café Gitane	101
Café Henri	330
Cercle Rouge	154
Crepes on Columbus	268
Daniel	254
DB Bistro Moderne	200
Florent	131
French Roast	240
L'Ecole	91
Le Refuge Inn	341
Les Halles Downtown	84
Marseille	202
Mas (farmhouse)	125
Nice Matin	242
Tocqueville	184

Fusion

Mai House	152
Public	90
Vong	224
Vynl	204

Kosher

Mike's Bistro	241
Park East	255

Greek

Anthos	199
Ithaka	255
Kefi	241

Indian

Amma	224
Curry In A Hurry	183
Jackson Diner	331
Leela Lounge	126
Pongal	185
Roti Boti	331
Tiffin Wallah	185

International

Aquavit	223
Bakery Rzeszowska	311
Bar Carrera	139
Counter	139
Cuba	126
Hacienda de Argentina	257
La Paella	139
Le Souk	140
Lomzynianka	311
Madiba	316
Mangia	84
Markt	167
Nurnberger Bierhaus	350
Paris Sandwich Shopw	102

Salam

Salam	126
Smorgas Chef	84
Stanton Social	110
Swizz	203
Taksim	227
Thirty-Five	155
Woo Lae Oak	91

Italian

Ama	90
Angels Restaurant	256
Bleu Evolution	301
Coals	341
Fiamma Osteria	89
Frankie's Spuntino	111
Goodfellas	349
Grimaldi's	311
Il Mattone	155
Ivy's Bistro	155
Lento's	350
Max Soha	268
Not Ray's Pizza	311
Pete's Downtown	316
Pino's Pizzeria	312
Pisticci	268
Puglia	102
Sandro's	255
Tello's	167
Trattoria L'incontro	332

Japanese

15 East	182
Bond St.	138
Hedeh	139
Inagiku	224
Izakaya Ten	167
Kai	255
Kyotofu	201
Matsuri	167
Natsumi	203
Nobu Next Door	153
Rosanjin	153
Sushi of Gari	255
Zenith/Asahi	203

Korean

Bann	199
Bon Chon Chicken	333
Hangawi	184

Latin

Caracas Arepa Bar	141
Citrus	239
Cubana Café	309
El Ranchito	301
Yuca Bar	141

Mexican

5 Burro Café	331
Blockheads	204
Carmen's	348
El Maguey Y La Tuna	110
Local Flavor	269

Pan-Asian

Incredi Fusion	184
Koi	200
Rain	242
Ruby Foo's	243
Spice Market	125, 131
Verlaine	114

Zen Palate

Zen Palate	185

Pizza

Famous Joe's Pizza	126
Lombardi's Pizza	102
Pinch Pizza By the Inch	185

Seafood

Blue Water Grill	183
BLT Fish	166
Duvet	166
Lobster Box	341

Southern

107 West	301
Jacques Imo's	240
Londel's	290
Manna's	293
Miss Maude's Spoonbread Too	292
MoBay	292
Revival	291
Sylvia's	293

Steakhouse

Buenos Aires	110
Harry's at Hannover Square	84

Vegetarian

Candle 79	257
Caravan of Dreams	139
Counter	139
Gobo	257
Hangawi	184
Incredi Fusion	184
Pasita	125
Pongal	185
TEANY	111
Zenith/Asahi	203
Zen Palate	185

NIGHTLIFE

Bars

1020	282
Abbey	283
All State Café	244
B Bar and Grill	141
Bar (at the Four Seasons Hotel)	227
Bar (at the Four Seasons Restaurant)	227
Bar 9	204
Beauty Bar	188
Blondies	244
Boat	320
Bohemian Hall	329, 334
Botanica	92
Bourbon Street	244
Café Bar	334
Circa Tabac	156
Coogan's	301
Corner Bistro	128
Coyote Ugly Saloon	141
Dive Bar	244
Double Happiness	103
Down The Hatch	129
Dublin House	244
Failte Irish Whisky Bar	189

Floyd NY	320	Mo's Caribbean Bar		Swift Hibernian Lounge	143	Marquee	169
Gallery	112	and Grill	259	Tap-a-Keg	283	Moomia Bar & Lounge	103
Gin Mill	244	Mugs Ale House	320	Temple Bar	93	Plumm	160
Ginger Man	189	Mulberry Street Bar	103	Time Out	245	Rebel	169
Good World Bar	112	Ñ	92	Tom & Jerry's	143	Sutra Lounge	142
Havana Central at the		Old Town Bar	169	Town	228	Tuts	114
West End	283	P&G	245	Vol de Nuit	130		
Heights Bar and Grill	283	Parnell's Bar and		Whiskey Ward	114	**LGBT**	
Hudson Bar and Books	129	Restaurant	228	Winnie's Karaoke	104	Barracuda	168
Irish Brigade Pub	301	Passerby	169	Yogi's	245	Barrage	204
Irish Rover	334	Pete's Candy Store	320			Cubbyhole	35,
Jake's Dilemma	244	Pig n' Whistle	228	**Clubs**			128
Jimmy's Corner Bar	205	Pravda	93	Bar 13	127	G Lounge	35,
Lexington Bar and Books	259	Red Sky Bar	189	BLVD	112		168
Loeb Boathouse	46, 48,	Ship of Fools	259	Esperanto	141	Henrietta Hudson	35,
	259	SoHo Grand	93	Hush	350		129
Lolita	113	Stone Creek	189	Libation	113	Mr. Black	35,
Monkey Bar & Grill	228	Sweet and Victoria	93	Manor, The	129		129

Pyramid	142
Splash	34,
	170
Tenth Avenue Lounge	206
Therapy	34,
	206

Lounges

420 Bar and Lounge	243
Azza	227
Believe Lounge	188
Black Betty	321
Blind Tiger Ale House	127
Blu Lounge	350
Boat Basin Café	244
Brandy Library	156
Bubble Lounge	156
Campbell Apartment	227

Chumley's	125
Cub Room	92
Culture Club	92
Flatiron Lounge	168
Flute	205
Happy Ending Lounge	103
Identity	112
Inoteca	112
Kimono Lounge	157
Kush	112
Lobby Lounge	245
Madame X	92
People Lounge	114
Rewind	114
Shebeen	103
Slate	170
Strata	170
Sutton Place	228

White Horse Tavern	125

Music

Café Wha?	127
Club Groove	127
Cotton Club	294
Cutting Room, The	168
Dizzy's Club Coca-Cola	205
Lenox Lounge	294
Louis 649	142
Mercury Lounge	113
Prohibition	245
Rocky Sullivan's	189
Showman's	295
Smoke	283
Village Vangaurd	130
Warsaw Club	322

Other

Billiard Company	331
Bowlmor Lanes	127
Brother Jimmy's	258
Brownstone Billards	321
Harlem Lanes	293
Monday Night Magic	206
Oak Room	206
Supper Club	206
Union Hall	320

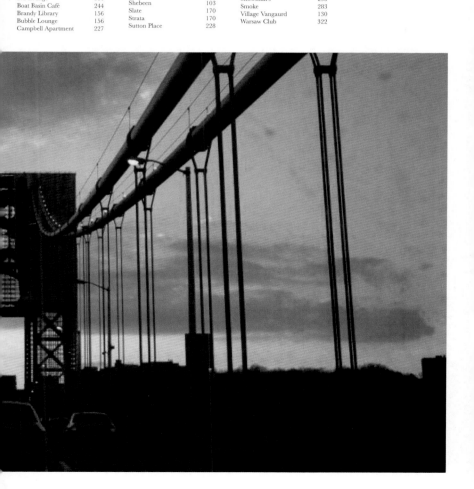